Gareth Williams

Biology for You

Revised National Curriculum Edition for GCSE

First published in 1996 by Stanley Thornes (Publishers) Ltd
Second edition published in 2002 by:
Nelson Thornes Ltd
Delta Place
27 Bath Road
CHELTENHAM
GL53 7TH
United Kingdom

08 / 10

A catalogue record for this book is available from the British Library

ISBN 978 0 7487 6232 3

Illustrations by Barking Dog, Mike Gordon and Jane Cope
Page make-up by Tech Set

Printed and bound in Spain by Graficas Estella

For Diana, Jill and Gail

Introduction

Biology For You is designed to introduce you to the basic ideas of Biology. These ideas will show you how living things are able to exist, from the smallest microbe to the largest whale, from the tiniest spore to the tallest tree. These ideas will also show you how plants and animals interact with each other and with their environment and how differences between living things are passed on to the next generation and how they can change with time.

Biology for You aims to be interesting and to help you pass your exams. It covers the work needed for Double Science, Single Science or Biology at GCSE.

The book is carefully laid out so that each new idea is introduced and developed on a single page or on two facing pages. Words have been kept as simple and straightforward as possible. Pages with an orange stripe in the top corner are the more difficult pages, which are needed to achieve grade B or above in the Higher Tier exam. Pages with a red triangle in the top corner cover the extra work that you may need if you are taking Science: Biology.

Throughout the book there are many simple experiments and investigations for you to do. A safety sign ⚠ means your teacher should give you further advice (for example to wear safety glasses). Plenty of guidance is given on the results of these experiments, in case you don't actually do the practical in school or you are studying at home.

Each new biological word is printed in **heavy type** and important points have a box drawn around them. There is a summary of important facts at the end of each chapter. Also near the end of many of the chapters are 'Biology at work' pages. These show you how Biology can be useful to us in everyday life.

There are questions at the end of each chapter. They always start with a simple fill-in-the-missing-words question which is useful for writing notes or for revision. Other questions check your understanding of the work covered and need more thought.

At the end of each of the five main sections you will find plenty of further questions taken from recent GCSE papers.

Extra sections at the back of the book give you advice on how to do your course work, revision and examination techniques, key skills and careers.

I would like to thank my family, Diana, Jill and Gail, for all their help and encouragement during the writing of this book.

I hope that reading the book will make Biology interesting and easier to understand. Above all I hope that using **Biology For You** will be fun!

Gareth Williams

Contents

Biologists work with living things –
from the very small
to the very large ...

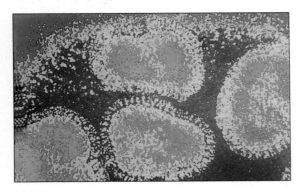

Influenza viruses

Humpback whale

Plants as organisms

Variation, inheritance, evolution and biotechnology

Living things and their environment

Extra sections

The following chapters may be required for a single science GCSE course.

Look at www.biologyforyou.co.uk to see exactly what you need for your specification.

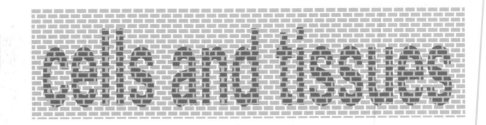

cells and tissues

Biology is the study of living things.
We call living things **organisms**.
Plants and animals are all living organisms.

But how do we decide if something is living
or non-living?
If something is alive it will carry out **all**
these seven **life processes**:

Feeding

Food is needed for energy and growth.

Plants make their own food.
They use sunlight to turn carbon dioxide
and water into sugars.
This is called **photosynthesis**.

Animals eat plants or other animals.

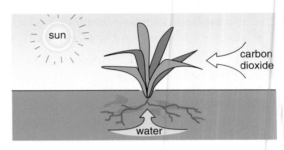

Respiration

Getting the energy out of the food you eat
is called **respiration**.
All living things **respire** because
they all need energy.
Oxygen is usually needed for respiration
to happen

Food + oxygen ⟶ carbon dioxide + water + **energy**

Living things use this energy for moving, growing and
repairing the body.

Movement

Plants move slowly when they grow.
Roots move down into the soil.
Stems move up towards the light.

Animals move their whole bodies.
They can move to get their food or
to avoid being caught.

Growth

All living organisms **grow**.

Growth is a permanent increase in body size.

Plants carry on growing all their lives.
Most growth occurs at the shoot and root tips of a plant, although stems can increase their girth.

Animals stop growing when they reach a certain size.
At what stages in a person's life is growth fast?

Excretion

All living things produce waste substances.
Excretion means getting rid of the waste substances that are made during chemical reactions in the cells.

Plants store waste substances in their leaves.
The waste is removed when the leaves fall off.

Animals breathe out waste carbon dioxide.
Other waste substances leave the body in the urine and in the sweat.

Sensitivity

Living organisms are **sensitive**.
They react to things happening around them.

Plants will move their leaves to face the light.
The flowers of some plants open in the morning and close at night when it is dark.

Animals have different **sense organs**.
What sense organs is this rabbit using?

Reproduction

All living things must make new individuals like themselves.
If a particular animal or plant did not **reproduce** it would die out.

Plants make seeds that grow into new plants.

Animals lay eggs or have babies.

▷ Cells

Houses are built up of bricks stuck together.
Plants and animals are built up of **cells**
stuck together.
Cells are the tiny building blocks that
make up all living things.

Very small living things like bacteria are
made of only one cell.
An insect like a fly has millions of cells in it.
A small animal like a mouse is made of hundreds
of millions of cells and a human being like you
is made up of billions and billions of cells.

How many types of cell can you name?

Different cells make up your blood, your
muscles, your brain and even your bones.
There are many different types of cell.

Look at the photograph of human cheek cells:
They are magnified 500 times.
Use a ruler to measure the length of one.
Now divide by 500 to find out how big
a cell really is.

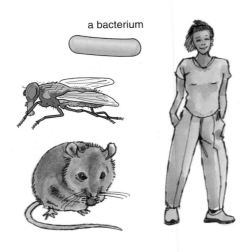

a bacterium

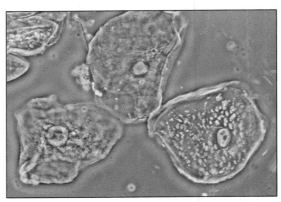

Human cheek cells (×500)

▷ Animal cells

All animal cells have the following parts:

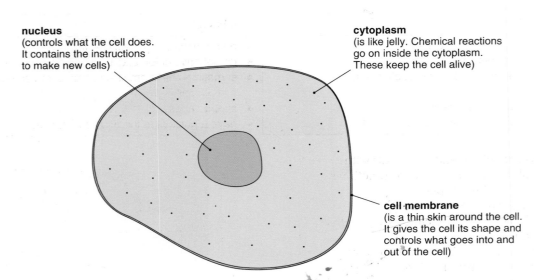

nucleus
(controls what the cell does.
It contains the instructions
to make new cells)

cytoplasm
(is like jelly. Chemical reactions
go on inside the cytoplasm.
These keep the cell alive)

cell membrane
(is a thin skin around the cell.
It gives the cell its shape and
controls what goes into and
out of the cell)

▶ Plant cells

Look at the plant cell below.
In what ways is it different from the animal cell?

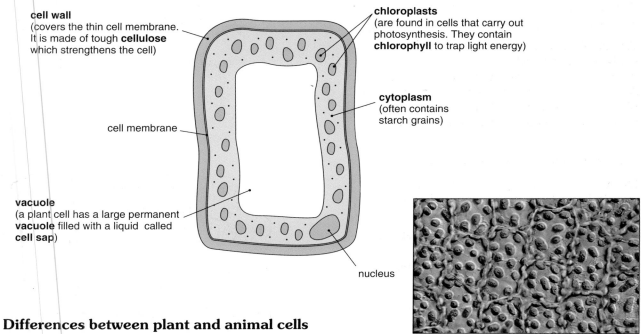

cell wall
(covers the thin cell membrane.
It is made of tough **cellulose**
which strengthens the cell)

chloroplasts
(are found in cells that carry out
photosynthesis. They contain
chlorophyll to trap light energy)

cell membrane

cytoplasm
(often contains
starch grains)

vacuole
(a plant cell has a large permanent
vacuole filled with a liquid called
cell sap)

nucleus

Differences between plant and animal cells

There are similarities and differences between plant
and animal cells.
In what ways are they similar?

Here are some differences between them:

Chloroplasts in moss cells

Plant cells	Animal cells
• have tough cellulose cell walls	• do not have cellulose cell walls
• have chloroplasts	• do not have chloroplasts
• have a large permanent vacuole containing cell sap	• sometimes have small vacuoles but they never contain cell sap
• many have a box-like shape	• shape varies
• have a nucleus to the side of the cell	• have a nucleus in the middle of the cell

If you look at animal and plant cells with
a powerful microscope you can sometimes
see tiny dots in the cytoplasm.
Many of these are **mitochondria**.
At a much higher magnification they look like
the diagram.
Respiration happens inside a mitochondrion
to release energy from food molecules.

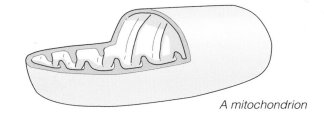

A mitochondrion

9

▶ Microscopes

As you know cells are too small to see
with the naked eye.
So we use a **microscope** to magnify them.

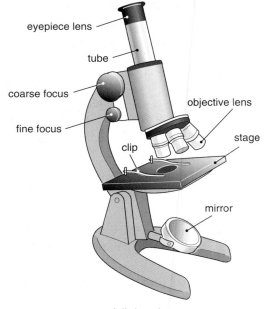

Light microscope

You have probably used a **light microscope**
like the one shown:

Can you remember what all the different
parts are for?

This type of microscope has *two* lenses,
the **eyepiece lens** and the **objective lens**.

How do you work out the total magnification?

You multiply the magnifying power of one
lens by the magnifying power of the other.

Total
magnification = magnifying power of eyepiece lens × magnifying power of objective lens

Light microscopes can magnify 1000 times.

A light microscope

Electron microscope

Some things are too small to be seen with
a light microscope.
Instead we use an **electron microscope**.

Electron microscopes use a beam of electrons
instead of light rays.
The image shows up on a fluorescent screen.
This can be photographed.
Electron microscopes can magnify
up to 500 000 times.

Electron microscopes help us to see the
structures *inside* cells in detail.
This photograph is taken with an
electron microscope:
It shows details of a chloroplast.

An electron microscope in use

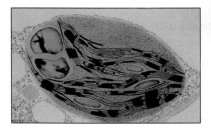

A chloroplast

▶ Looking at plant cells

You can look at onion cells under the microscope.
First you must peel off a very thin layer:

1 Cut out a small piece of onion

2 Use forceps or your finger nails to peel off the inner surface (this looks like tissue paper)

3 Put the piece of onion "skin" flat on a slide and add 2 drops of iodine solution

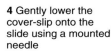

4 Gently lower the cover-slip onto the slide using a mounted needle

cover-slip

5 Place the slide onto the stage of the microscope

6 Focus carefully onto the onion skin using the lowest power objective lens in your microscope

7 Turn on the high power objective lens to see details of the onion cells

Onion cells do not have any chloroplasts. If you want to look at chloroplasts, find a moss plant.

Use tweezers to remove one of the smallest leaves from the tip of the plant.

Put it onto a slide with a drop of water and place a cover-slip over it.

Look at it under high power with your microscope.

▶ Looking at animal cells

To avoid any chance of infection carry out these instructions carefully: ⚠

1. Your teacher will give you a cotton bud from a freshly opened pack.

2. Gently wipe the lining of your cheek with one end of the cotton bud.

3. Smear the cotton bud over the centre of a slide.

4. Immediately dispose of the cotton bud into a beaker of disinfectant provided by your teacher.

5. Put a drop of methylene blue stain on top of the smear.

6. Place a cover-slip on top and look for cells under the microscope at high power.

7. At the end of the activity put the slide with its cover-slip into a beaker of disinfectant.

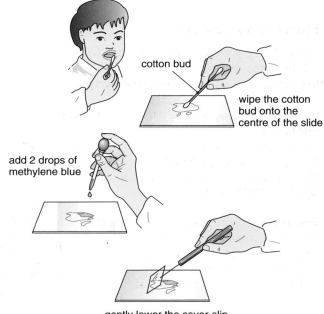

cotton bud

wipe the cotton bud onto the centre of the slide

add 2 drops of methylene blue

gently lower the cover-slip with a mounted needle

▶ Specialised cells

Many cells look different.
This is because they have their own special jobs to do.
Different cells do different jobs.
They share the work of the body.

xylem cells are small tubes that carry water up the stem

leaf palisade cells contain lots of chloroplasts for photosynthesis

root hair cells are long and thin to absorb water from the soil

nerve cells are like wires to carry messages around the body

red blood cells have a substance that carries oxygen

bone cells make bone to support the body

muscle cells can shorten to move bones

sperm cells have a tail to swim to the egg

egg cells have a store of food in the cytoplasm

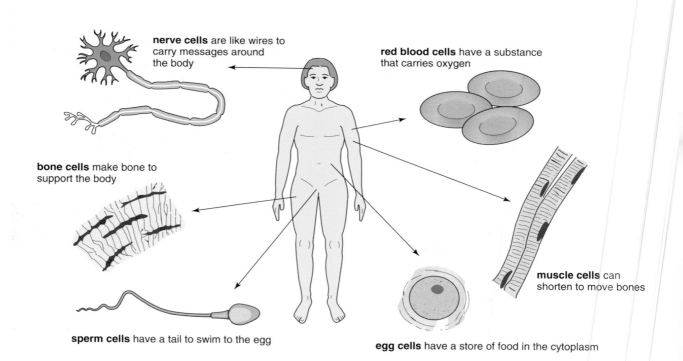

▶ Single cells

Some living organisms are made
up of just *one* cell.
We call them **unicellular**.

Amoeba is unicellular.
All 7 life processes take place
inside the one cell.

Amoeba lives in ponds and ditches.
It moves by changing its shape.
It pushes out **pseudopodia**
in the direction it wants to go.
The rest of the cell 'flows' after them.

Amoeba feeds on smaller things like bacteria.
Pseudopodia flow around the food.
The food is taken into the cytoplasm
in a **food vacuole**.

Chemicals called **enzymes** are added to the
food to break it down.

Oxygen is dissolved in the water around Amoeba.
It passes into Amoeba by **diffusion**.
Waste substances like carbon dioxide diffuse
out into the water.
You will find out more about diffusion in Chapter 2.

Amoeba reproduces by splitting into two.

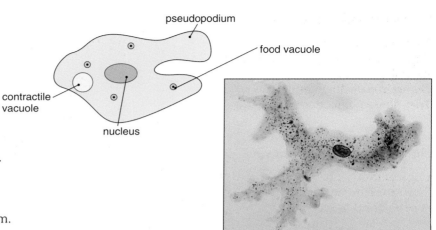

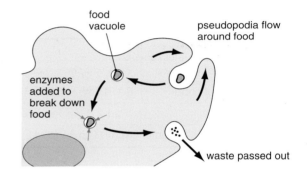

▶ Many cells

Spirogyra is a very small living thing too.
But it is made up of more than one cell.
We say that it is **multicellular**.

Spirogyra floats on the surface of ponds.
It is made up of cells that look alike.
All 7 life processes take place in each cell.
In Spirogyra the cells are joined end
to end to make **filaments**.

Spirogyra has a spiral, green chloroplast.
It makes its own food by photosynthesis.

Both Amoeba and Spirogyra belong to a
group of organisms called **Protists**.

You can find more about Protists on pages 268–9.

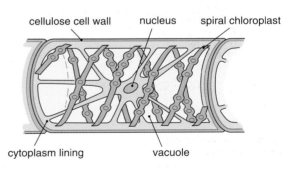

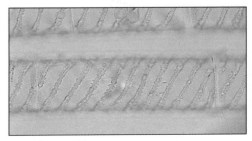

Spirogyra filaments

► Cell size

Cells are very small.
You need a microscope to see them.
As they grow they get bigger.
But eventually they divide into two.
Why do you think this is?

Surface area and volume

Look at the 3 cubes.
They are different sizes.
A cube has 6 faces.

  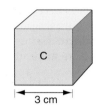

A
1 cm

B
2 cm

C
3 cm

Copy and complete
the table:

	Cube A	Cube B	Cube C
surface area of one face	1 cm × 1 cm = 1 cm²		
surface area of cube	6 × 1 cm² = 6 cm²		
volume of cube	1 cm × 1 cm × 1 cm = 1 cm³		
ratio : surface area / volume	6 cm²/1 cm³ = 6 : 1		

What happens to the surface area /volume
ratio as the cube increases in size?

As a cell grows its surface area /volume ratio
gets smaller.
This means that the volume of the cell is
increasing a lot faster than its surface area.

But as the cell gets bigger it needs more food
and oxygen and these have to be absorbed
through its surface.

Eventually the surface area becomes too small
for enough food and oxygen to get into the cell.
The cell must now divide or die.

Look at the different cells sizes in the diagram:
Bigger cells tend to use up food and oxygen
quicker than smaller cells.

Which cells here would use food and oxygen
quickest?

What sort of materials need to pass **out** of a
cell? (**Hint**: think back to respiration.)

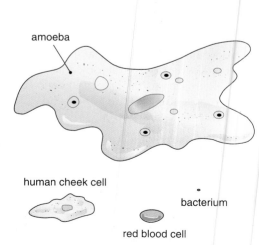

amoeba

human cheek cell

bacterium

red blood cell

These cells are drawn to the same scale

14

▶ Tissues and organs

A group of similar cells is called a **tissue**.
All the cells in a tissue look the same
and do the same job.
Your muscle tissue is made up of identical
muscle cells.

An **organ** is made up of different tissues.
These work together to do a particular job.
Your heart is an organ.
It is made up of different tissues that work
together to pump blood around your body.

Your stomach, lungs, brain and kidneys are
all organs.
Do you know what each of them does?

Different organs work together as part
of an **organ system**.
Your heart and blood vessels work together
as part of your circulatory system.

All of your organ systems make up a living
organism – that's you!

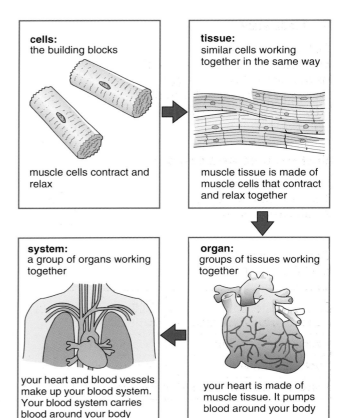

cells:
the building blocks

muscle cells contract and relax

tissue:
similar cells working together in the same way

muscle tissue is made of muscle cells that contract and relax together

organ:
groups of tissues working together

your heart is made of muscle tissue. It pumps blood around your body

system:
a group of organs working together

your heart and blood vessels make up your blood system. Your blood system carries blood around your body

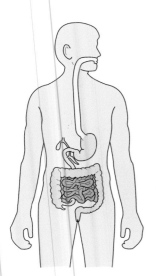

The digestive system is made up of your gullet, stomach and intestines

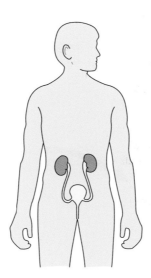

The excretory system is made up of your kidneys, ureters and bladder

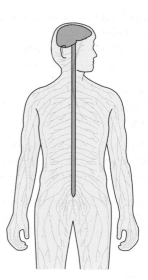

The nervous system is made up of your brain, spinal cord and nerves

▶ Plant organs

Try putting these words into the correct order, starting with the smallest and ending with the largest:

organ   system   tissue   organism   cell

Although plants do not have proper systems like we do, they do have tissues and organs. Let's look at an example:

The cells that carry out photosynthesis are called **palisade cells**.
They are rectangular and full of chloroplasts.

Lots of palisade cells make up the **palisade tissue**.
All the cells making up this tissue look alike and do the same job – they make food for the plant.

The palisade tissue is found in a **leaf**.
A leaf is made up of lots of other tissues as well as palisade tissue.
A leaf is an organ.

Can you think of any other plant organs? Roots, flowers, stems and fruits are all organs too.

All these different organs make up an organism – the buttercup plant.

cells: The building blocks.

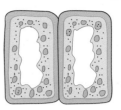

Leaf palisade cells absorb light.

tissue: Similar cells working together in the same way.

Photosynthesis takes place in the palisade tissue.

organ: groups of tissues working together.

organism: The buttercup plant is made up of many organs.

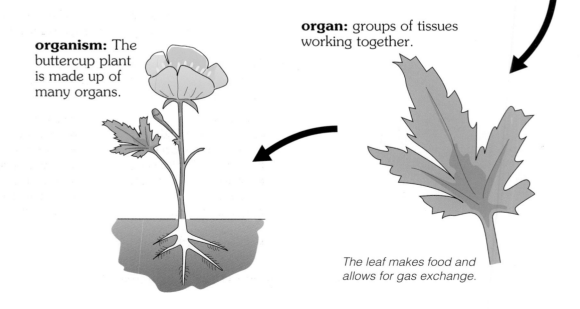

The leaf makes food and allows for gas exchange.

Summary

- The 7 life processes are feeding, respiration, movement, growth, excretion, sensitivity, and reproduction.

- Cells are the basic units of which all living organisms are made.

- There are differences in the structure of plant and animal cells.

- As a cell's size increases its surface area/volume ratio gets less. This limits the size of a cell.

- Some organisms are unicellular and some are multicellular.

- Cells are specialised to do a particular job.

- In a multicellular organism the jobs are shared by all the cells.

- Cells that do the same job are grouped together into tissues.

- Different tissues make up organs and different organs make up systems.

▶ Questions

1. Copy out the activities listed in the left-hand column, then match each with the correct example from the right-hand column :

growth	*escaping from danger*
respiration	*laying eggs*
excretion	*making new leaves*
feeding	*hearing a whistle*
sensitivity	*sweating*
movement	*using up energy in a race*
reproduction	*having a snack*

2. The 3 cells A, B and C are not drawn to scale.

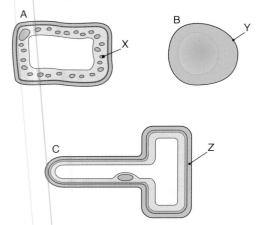

a) Name the parts X, Y and Z.
b) Give 2 reasons why cell A is a plant cell.
c) State one way in which the structure
   of each cell helps it to carry out its function.

3. a) What are the structures A, B and C in the diagram ?
b) What is the function (job) of C ?

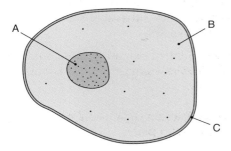

c) Draw and label 3 extra structures that would change this animal cell into a typical plant cell.

4. Copy out the organs listed on the left. Match each with the correct system from those listed on the right :

Organs	System
• lungs and windpipe	• digestive
• heart and blood vessels	• nervous
• brain and spinal cord	• respiratory
• ovaries, oviducts and uterus	• excretory
• gullet, stomach and intestines	• circulatory
• kidneys and bladder	• reproductive

Further questions on page 40.

chapter 2

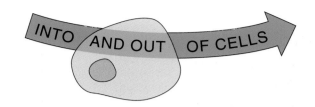
There are billions of tiny particles all around you.
These particles are called **molecules**.
They are so small that we can not even see them with
a very powerful microscope.

Each breath of air that you take contains billions of molecules
of oxygen, nitrogen and carbon dioxide.
In a glass of water there are billions of water molecules.
The chair that you are sitting on is made of billions of
molecules.
In fact everything around you is made of molecules.

Three states of matter

Every substance can exist in three states : **gas**, **liquid** and **solid**.
Water can be a solid (ice), a liquid and a gas (steam) :

solid water (ice)

liquid water

water droplets

invisible **gas**
(steam)

Ice, liquid water and steam are all made from exactly the
same type of water molecules. But the water molecules
behave differently in the 3 different states.

solid	liquid	gas
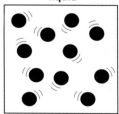		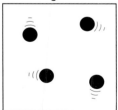

*In a **solid** the molecules can only vibrate – they can not move out of position.*
They are held together by strong forces between the molecules.
This gives a solid a definite shape.

*In a **liquid** the molecules are moving slowly.*
Forces between the molecules hold them together more closely than in a gas.

*In a **gas** the molecules are moving very quickly*

▶ Dissolving

Many substances dissolve in water.
How does this happen?

There are tiny spaces between the water molecules.
When something like sugar dissolves, each grain breaks up into thousands of tiny sugar particles.
These tiny particles spread out and fit into the spaces between the water molecules.

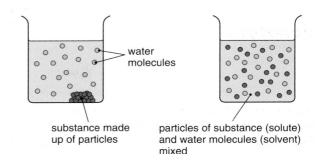

water molecules

  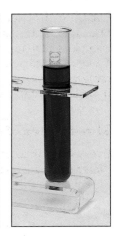

substance made up of particles

particles of substance (solute) and water molecules (solvent) mixed

Look at the photographs:

- A purple crystal was dropped into the test-tube of water.
  At first the molecules were concentrated in one place – in the crystal.

- After 30 minutes some of the purple molecules had left the crystal and spread out.

- After 24 hours all the purple molecules had spread evenly through the water.

The purple molecules spread out by **diffusion**.

When molecules diffuse they spread out from where there are lots of them (a high concentration) to where there aren't many of them (a low concentration).
They do this until they are spread out evenly.

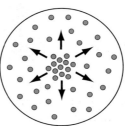 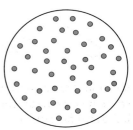

molecules of solute spread out in all directions

solute molecules spread out evenly

A **solution** is made up of two parts, the **solute** and the **solvent**.
The **solute** dissolves in the **solvent**.

If you dissolve sugar in water you make a sugar solution.
The sugar is the solute and the water is the solvent.

The solute is not always a solid like sugar.
Liquids and gases can be solutes as they can dissolve in solvents too.

A **concentrated solution** has a lot of solute dissolved in the solvent.

A **dilute solution** has a small amount of solute dissolved in the solvent.

► Diffusion

When food is cooking in the kitchen you can smell it in other rooms in the house.
This is because molecules are leaving the food as a gas and moving around at high speed, eventually reaching all parts of the house.
This is called **diffusion**.

> **Diffusion** is the movement of particles from a high concentration to a low concentration until they are spread out evenly.

Demonstration 2.1   Diffusion in a gas

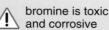 bromine is toxic and corrosive

Your teacher may be able to show you the diffusion of some bromine.
This brown gas is very poisonous.
What will happen when the gas jar of air is put on top of the gas jar of bromine?

Gases diffuse quicker than liquids.
Why do you think this is?

Demonstration 2.2   Rate of diffusion

⚠ ammonia is toxic and irritant

Your teacher may show you this experiment.
Eight pieces of red litmus paper are hung in a glass tube as shown in the diagram:
Some ammonium hydroxide solution is added to the cotton wool pad and placed into the hole in the bung.
As alkaline ammonia gas diffuses along the tube it turns the litmus paper blue.
Time how long it takes for each piece of litmus paper to turn blue.
The greater the difference in concentration, the greater the rate of diffusion.

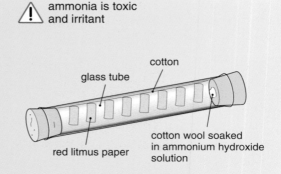

cotton

glass tube

cotton wool soaked in ammonium hydroxide solution

red litmus paper

Your body cells need food and oxygen.
These are carried to our cells in the blood.
What happens when the blood reaches the cells?
The molecules of food and oxygen diffuse out of the blood and into the cells.

As cells use up food and oxygen they make waste.
This waste is carbon dioxide and waste chemicals.
These will poison the cells if they build up.
Carbon dioxide and waste chemicals diffuse out of the cells and into the blood.

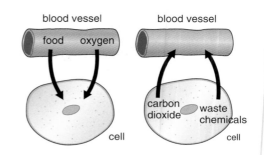

blood vessel

food   oxygen

blood vessel

carbon dioxide   waste chemicals

cell

cell

▶ Osmosis

Each cell is surrounded by a cell membrane.
It separates the contents of the cell from
the outside.
The cell membrane has tiny holes in it.
This allows small molecules to pass through
but not large ones.
The cell membrane is **partially permeable**.

Osmosis is a special kind of diffusion involving
water molecules.
It occurs when two solutions are separated by
a partially permeable membrane.

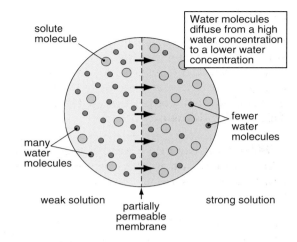

> **Osmosis is the passage of water molecules from
> a weaker solution into a stronger solution through
> a partially permeable membrane.**

The water is in fact diffusing from :
the weaker solution (high water concentration)
into the stronger solution (low water concentration).

The tiny holes in the membrane allow small
water molecules to pass through.
But the large solute molecules are too big to pass
through the partially permeable membrane.

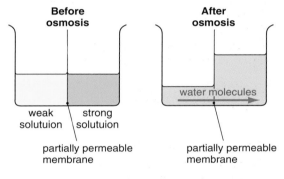

Experiment 2.3   A model cell
Visking tubing is partially permeable.

Cut 2 pieces of Visking tubing 12 cm long.

Tie one end of each with cotton.

Fill 'cell A' with sugar solution and
'cell B' with water.

Tie the other end and weigh each 'cell'.

Put 'cell A' into a beaker of water.

Put 'cell B' into a beaker of sugar solution.

After 30 minutes re-weigh each 'cell'.

Cell A increases in weight because water has
passed into the cell, into the strong solution
by osmosis.

Cell B decreases in weight because water has
passed out of the cell, into the strong solution
by osmosis.

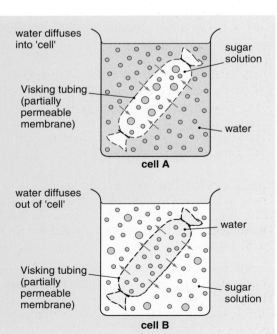

▶ Osmosis in plant cells

Osmosis is the way in which many living things take up water.

Experiment 2.4   An osmometer

You can see the effects of osmosis if you set up this apparatus:

Fill the partially permeable membrane with strong sugar solution.

Tie it to a capillary tube and stand it in a weak sugar solution.

Use your ideas about osmosis to explain why the liquid rises in the tube.

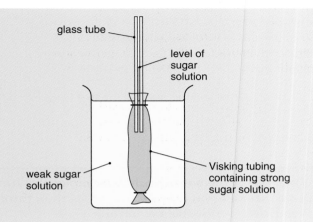

glass tube

level of sugar solution

weak sugar solution

Visking tubing containing strong sugar solution

Water will move into plant cells by osmosis.
- The cell membrane of the plant cell acts as a partially permeable membrane.
- The cell sap inside the vacuole is a strong solution.
- Water passes into the plant cell by osmosis.
- The concentration of the sap in the vacuole is now weaker.
- Water passes from the weak solution into the strong solution in the next cell by osmosis.

cell wall (fully permeable)

cytoplasm

weak solution

osmosis

strong solution

cell membrane (partially permeable membrane)

vacuole

Experiment 2.5   Osmosis in potato cells

Cut 3 potato chips to exactly the same size.

Measure their length and write it down.

Set up the following test-tubes:
test-tube A – distilled water
test-tube B – weak sugar solution
test-tube C – strong sugar solution.

Place one potato chip in each test-tube and leave it for 30 minutes.

Re-measure each chip.

- Which chip has increased in size?
  Is this because it has taken in water by osmosis?

- Which chip has got shorter?
  Is this because it has lost water by osmosis?

- Feel the chip that was in test-tube A.
  Why does it feel firm?

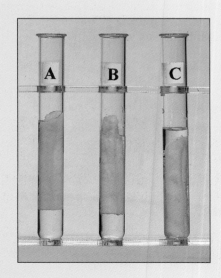

A   B   C

▶ Turgidity

When plant cells are placed in water, the water enters the cells.
This is because their cell sap contains a strong solution.
So water passes *into* the cells by osmosis.
The cell membrane is the partially permeable membrane.

As water enters it makes the cell swell up.
The water pushes against the cell wall.
Eventually the cell contains as much water as it can hold.
It's like a blown-up balloon.
The strong cell wall stops the cell bursting.
We say that the cell is **turgid**.

If you've cut chips and put them into water you will know that they soon go firm.
This is because they have taken in water by osmosis and are now turgid.

Can you think why turgid cells are useful to plants?

Turgid cells give the plant support.
They keep the stems of many plants upright.

But what happens when these cells lose water?
The cells are no longer firm and turgid.
Plant stems that have lost water **wilt**.

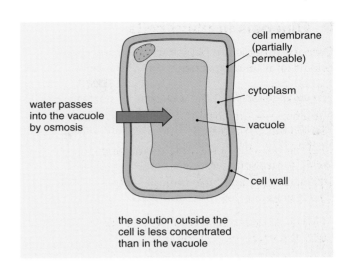

cell membrane
(partially
permeable)

cytoplasm

water passes
into the vacuole
by osmosis

vacuole

cell wall

the solution outside the
cell is less concentrated
than in the vacuole

Investigation 2.6   Plan an investigation into the effects of sugar solution on potato cells

You could find out how different concentrations affect the mass or the length of potato chips.

You could also measure the flexibility of the chips.

You could find out the effect of temperature on turgidity.

Before carrying out your plan, check with your teacher that it is safe to do so.

23

▶ Plasmolysis

When plant cells are placed into a strong sugar or salt solution water passes **out** of the cells by osmosis.
As water passes out, the sap vacuole starts to shrink.
These cells are no longer firm, they are limp. We say that they are **flaccid**.

As more water leaves the cells the cytoplasm starts to peel away from the cell wall.
These cells are now **plasmolysed**.

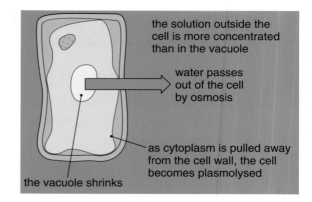

the solution outside the cell is more concentrated than in the vacuole

water passes out of the cell by osmosis

as cytoplasm is pulled away from the cell wall, the cell becomes plasmolysed

the vacuole shrinks

Experiment 2.7   Plasmolysis

Put some red onion skin onto a slide with a drop of water.

Put a cover-slip on the slide and focus it under the microscope.

Add a few drops of strong sugar solution to the edge of the cover-slip.

Describe what happens to the cells.

▶ Osmosis in animal cells

What do you think animal cells will do if placed in different strengths of solution ?

The cell membrane is the partially permeable membrane in animal cells.

The red blood cells in the picture have been placed in distilled water.
Their cytoplasm is a strong solution.
Water passes into the cells by osmosis.
But animal cells have no cell wall to stop them swelling too much – so they burst !
We call this **haemolysis**.

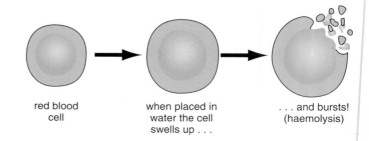

red blood cell

when placed in water the cell swells up . . .

. . . and bursts! (haemolysis)

▶ A constant blood concentration

What would happen if the liquid part of your blood was too watery and dilute?

What would happen if the liquid part of your blood was too strong and concentrated?

The red blood cells in this picture have been placed in a concentrated solution.
Water has moved out of their cytoplasm by osmosis.
The cells have shrunk.
Do you think these red blood cells would be able to do their job properly?

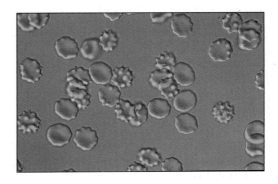

Can you see why it is so important to keep the concentration of our blood constant?
(We will find out more about keeping our water content constant in Chapter 7.)

The red blood cells in this picture are in a solution that is the same concentration as their cytoplasm.
Why have they kept their shape?

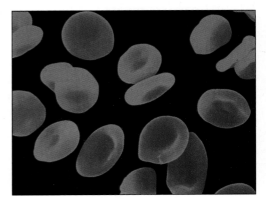

The solutions on each side of their cell membranes are the same concentration.
So the cells neither gain nor lose water.

Why doesn't Amoeba burst?
Water enters Amoeba by osmosis.
The water goes into a **contractile vacuole**.
Eventually the contractile vacuole becomes so full of water that it moves to the cell membrane and bursts.
The water has been removed from the cell.

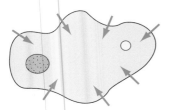

water enters *Amoeba*
by osmosis

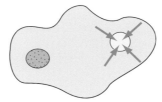

water taken into
contractile vacuole

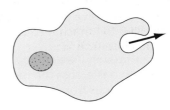

contractile vacuole bursts
removing water from the cell

▶ Active transport

Cells can take up some particles and keep them in high concentrations.

Look at the concentration of magnesium ions in the root hair cell:
Look at the concentration of magnesium ions in the soil solution:
Which way would you expect magnesium ions to move by diffusion?

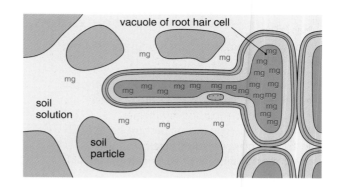

Sometimes cells can keep hold of particles and not let them diffuse out.
What's more they can even take in *more* particles against a concentration gradient.

Look at the histogram:
It shows the concentrations of some salts inside the cells of a water plant and outside in the water.

These salts cannot have been taken in by diffusion.
They are taken in against a concentration gradient.
They are taken in by **active transport**.
Active transport needs energy from respiration to make it happen.

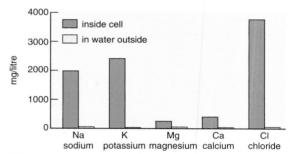

The concentrations of salts found inside and outside the cells of a freshwater plant

> **Active transport** is the uptake of particles by cells against a concentration gradient.

Sugars can be absorbed from the intestine and from the kidney tubules by active transport.

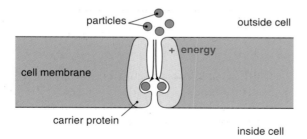

Carrier protein takes up particles on outside of membrane

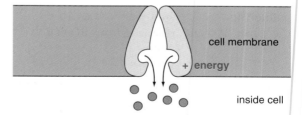

Carrier protein releases particles on inside of membrane

The carrier protein uses energy to transport molecules or ions across the membrane.
This energy comes from respiration inside the cell.
Poisons like cyanide can stop respiration.
Do you think that this would stop active transport too?

Summary

- Everything is made up of molecules that are always moving.

- Molecules move from a high concentration to a low concentration by diffusion.

- Food and oxygen diffuse into cells. Carbon dioxide and waste substances diffuse out.

- Osmosis is the movement of water molecules from a weak solution into a strong solution through a partially permeable membrane.

- Water passes into plant cells by osmosis. A plant cell that is full of water is turgid. If plant cells are placed in a strong solution, water passes out by osmosis. As the vacuole shrinks the cell membrane eventually peels away from the cell wall – the cell is plasmolysed.

- If animal cells are put into a weak solution they take in water and burst.

- Particles can be taken into a cell against a concentration gradient. This process needs energy so is called active transport.

▶ Questions

1. Copy and complete:
   Molecules move from a .... concentration to a .... concentration by .... .
   Osmosis is the movement of .... molecules from a .... solution into a .... solution across a .... permeable membrane. When plant cells take up water by osmosis they become ..... Turgid cells help support parts of a plant like the ..... If plant cells lose water the stem lacks support and ..... If plant cells lose a lot of water the cell .... peels away from the cell .... and the cell is said to be ..... .

2. a) Which diffuses faster, a liquid or a gas? Why is this?
   b) What would heating do to the rate of diffusion of a salt crystal in water?
   c) What things diffuse:
      i) into cells   ii) out of cells?

3. The test-tube containing agar jelly and blue dye was set up as shown in photo A.

   A   **B**

   Photo B shows its appearance after a week.
   a) Explain as fully as you can what has happened to the blue dye.
   b) Why did it take a week for this to happen?

4. a) Is a cell membrane permeable, impermeable or partially permeable?
   b) Is a cell wall permeable, impermeable or partially permeable?
   c) These two chips were cut from a potato. Each **was** 50 mm long. One was put into water and the other was put into strong sugar solution. Use your ruler to measure each chip.

   chip A

   chip B

   i) Which chip was put in water? Explain your answer.
   ii) Which chip was put into strong sugar solution? Explain your answer.

5. a) Explain why red blood cells burst if they are put into water.
   b) Explain why Amoeba does not burst when put into water.
   c) Some plant cells are put into a solution. They neither take up water nor lose water. What can you say about the strength of the cell sap and the external solution?

6. The experiment was set up as shown :

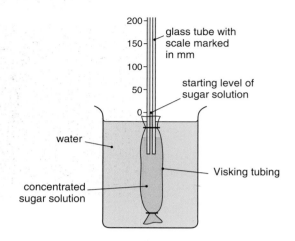

The level of the liquid in the tube was measured every minute.

The results are shown in the graph.

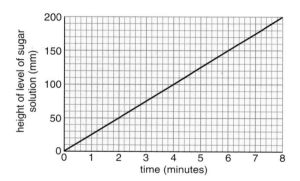

a) Explain why the liquid rose in the tube.
b) What was the level of the liquid after 4 minutes ?
c) How much longer did it take for the liquid to reach the top ?
d) Would the liquid take longer to reach the top if the sugar solution was weaker ? Explain your answer.

7. Two freshly cut potato chips were set up as shown.

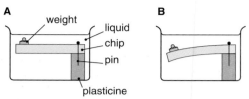

Each was covered with a colourless liquid.
a) What liquid was used in **A** ?
b) Explain why the chip in **A** was able to support the weight.
c) What sort of liquid was used in **B** ?
d) Explain why the chip in **B** bent under the weight.

8. Batches of 10 potato discs were weighed and then placed into one of 10 different concentrations of sugar solution. After 30 minutes the potato discs were removed and re-weighed. Their percentage change in mass was worked out. The results are shown in the graph :

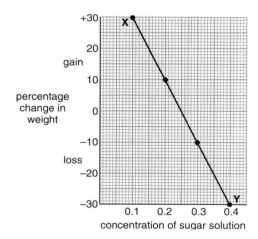

a) What process caused the change in mass of the potato discs ?
b) What would the potato discs be like at **X** ?
c) What other differences apart from weight would you be able to observe between the discs at **X** and **Y** ?
d) Use the graph to find the concentration of sugar solution that would cause no change in the weight of the potato discs.

Further questions on page 41.

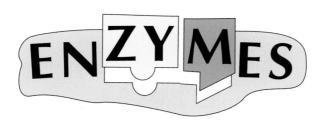

chapter 3

Thousands of chemical reactions take place in our cells.
We need these reactions to happen quickly to keep us alive.
Luckily for us there are chemicals called **enzymes**.
Enzymes make reactions happen at a much faster rate.

Chemicals that speed up reactions are called **catalysts**.
Since enzymes speed up chemical reactions in our cells,
they are often called **biological catalysts**.

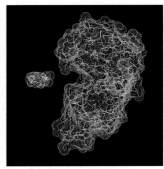

Computer model of an enzyme

Breakers and builders

Enzymes come in two main types:

Breakers
Sometimes we need to break down large molecules into
smaller ones. Breaker-enzymes speed up these reactions.
This is important in digestion when large food molecules
are broken down into small ones so that we can use them.

Builders
In other reactions small molecules are joined together to
make large ones. Builder-enzymes speed up these reactions.
These enzymes build important molecules inside our cells.

▶ How an enzyme works

Enzymes work on substances called **substrates**.
The reaction takes place on a part of the surface of
the enzyme called the **active site**.

This is how a breaker-enzyme works:

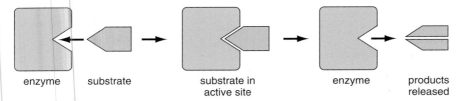

enzyme   substrate   substrate in   enzyme   products
                             active site   released

Use the diagram below to explain how a builder-enzyme works:

The fastest enzyme in the west !

Potato cells contain an enzyme called **catalase**.
It speeds up the breakdown of hydrogen peroxide
into water and oxygen.

Do you remember how to test for oxygen?
Add a small piece of potato to 5 cm^3 of
hydrogen peroxide in a test-tube.

 eye protection

CARE : hydrogen peroxide is corrosive and an irritant.

Test the gas which is given off with a glowing splint.

Experiment 3.1   Fast froth

Cut 2 pieces of potato to the same size.

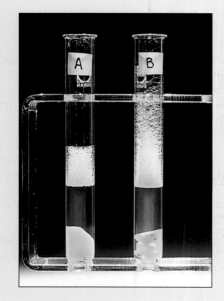

Put one piece into a boiling-tube containing   eye protection
5 cm^3 of hydrogen peroxide.

CARE : hydrogen peroxide is corrosive and an irritant.

Use a ruler to measure the **highest point** that the
froth gets to in the tube.

Now do the same with the second piece, but this time
chop the potato up into small pieces first.

- Which tube made the most froth?
  Why do you think this is?

- Where is the enzyme found in this reaction?

- Was the enzyme a breaker or a builder?

Catalase is found in many living cells.
It breaks down hydrogen peroxide to water and oxygen,
that's where the bubbles come from.

$$\text{Hydrogen peroxide} \xrightarrow{\text{catalase}} \text{water} + \text{oxygen}$$

Chopping up the potato releases *more* catalase from the cells.

Catalase is the fastest enzyme known.
Hydrogen peroxide is often formed as a product of reactions
in cells. It can be poisonous if it builds up.
Why do you think catalase has to work so quickly?

► Enzymes are particular . . .

All enzymes have five important properties:

> **1. They are all proteins.**
> **2. Each enzyme controls one particular reaction.**
> **3. They can be used again and again.**
> **4. They are affected by temperature.**
> **5. They are affected by pH.**

Look at the diagram:
Use it to explain why each enzyme will only work
on **one** particular substrate.
Does the shape of the active site decide this?

Why is only a **small** amount of enzyme needed
to control a reaction?

Enzymes can be used over and over again.
Once the products leave the active site,
more substrate can enter.
So the enzyme will keep on working until all
the substrate is used up.
Just a little enzyme goes a long, long way!

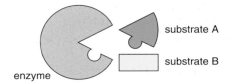

Which substrate fits the active site?

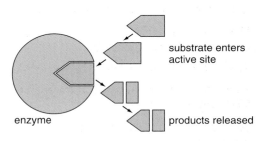

An enzyme can act on lots of substrate

Enzymes in digestion

Enzymes break down large food molecules into
smaller ones inside your gut.
This is called **digestion**.
Why do these food molecules have to be broken
down into smaller ones?

Look at the diagram:
The wall of the gut works a bit like a net.
What sort of molecules can get through?

Two large food molecules are shown below.
Copy and complete these sketches to show what they
would look like **after** enzymes have digested them.

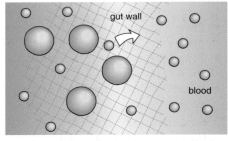

*Only small molecules can get through the
gut wall into the blood*

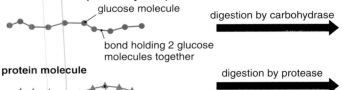

How quickly do enzymes work?

There is a **carbohydrase** enzyme in our saliva.
What type of food does it act upon?

The carbohydrase in our saliva is called **amylase**.
It breaks down starch to sugar:

starch $\xrightarrow{\text{amylase}}$ sugar

Experiment 3.2   The effect of amylase on starch

Starch turns iodine solution blue-black.
When starch is broken down it will not turn
iodine blue-black.

Put one drop of iodine into each well on a
spotting tile.

Add 1 cm³ of 1% amylase solution to 5 cm³ of
1% starch solution in a test-tube.

Start the stop-clock immediately.

At the times shown in the diagram take a drop
out of the test-tube and add it to the iodine on
the spotting tile.

Record your results in a table like this:

- How did you know when all the starch had gone?
- How long did it take before all the starch was broken down?
- What did the starch form when it was broken down?

add one drop of starch alone to this well

add one drop of starch/1% amylase to this well

add one drop of starch/1% amylase to this well after 30 seconds

0 min	30 secs	1 min
1 m 30 secs	2 min	2 m 30 secs	3 min
3 m 30 secs	4 min	4 m 30 secs	5 min

starch alone	mixture straight after mixing	mixture after 30 secs	mixture after 1 minute
Black (starch present)	Black (starch present)	_____	_____
after 1½ mins	after 2 mins	after 2½ mins	after 3 mins
_____	_____	_____	_____
after 3½ mins	after 4 mins	after 4½ mins	after 5 mins
_____	_____	_____	_____

Could a **protease** have broken down the starch?

Remember, an enzyme is **specific**.
It can only control *one* kind of reaction.

> **Carbohydrases can only break down carbohydrates.**
> **Proteases can only break down proteins.**
> **Lipases can only break down fats.**

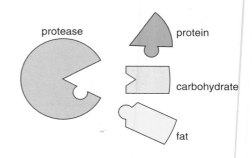

protease   protein

carbohydrate

fat

▶ Hotting up

Enzymes are affected a great deal by temperature.

This graph shows the effect of increased temperature on an enzyme-controlled reaction:

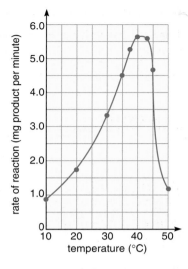

Look at the graph.

- How fast is the reaction going at 10 °C?
- How fast is the reaction going at 20 °C?
- How much faster is the reaction at 20 °C than at 10 °C?

- At what temperature is the reaction going fastest?
- Why do you think the reaction goes faster as the temperature increases?
  (**Hint:** what happens to molecules when they warm up?)

- How fast is the reaction going at 50 °C?
- What do you think is happening to the enzyme at high temperature?

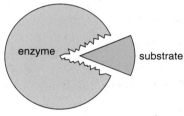

Enzyme denatured – substrate no longer fits the active site

As you know, all enzymes are proteins.
At high temperatures the protein breaks down.
The active site is changed, so the substrate no longer fits.
We say that the enzyme has been **denatured** and it no longer works.

Investigation 3.3   Effect of temperature on enzyme action

Plan an investigation into the effect of temperature on the action of an enzyme.
You could use either amylase or catalase.

- What temperatures will you use?

- How will you tell how fast the reaction is going?

- How will you know when the enzyme has finished working?

- How will you show your results?

- Check your plan with your teacher before you begin.

Enzymes are useful in industry.
They can make chemical reactions take place at lower temperatures.
Why do you think this saves money?

► Enzymes and pH

An enzyme is affected by how much acid or how much alkali is present.
Many enzymes work best in neutral conditions, but some prefer acid and some alkali.

Look at the graph showing the action of enzymes X and Y:

- At what pH does enzyme X work best?
- At what pH does enzyme Y work best?
- What happens to the action of enzyme X above pH 5.5?
- What happens to the action of enzyme Y below pH 5?

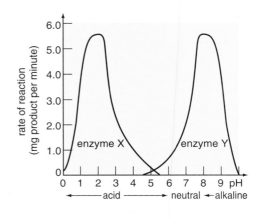

The active site of an enzyme can be changed by very acid or very alkaline conditions.
How do you think that this could reduce the rate of a reaction?

Experiment 3.4   The effect of pH on the action of a protease

Exposed photographic film contains black grains of silver.
These are stuck on by a layer of gelatin.
Gelatin is a protein.

You can investigate the effect of a protease on gelatin at different pHs.

Set up the experiment as shown in the diagram:

After 30 minutes, take out each strip with tweezers.

Gently rub the film, between your finger and thumb, under a cold tap.

If the gelatin has been digested, the film will turn colourless.

Record your results in a table.

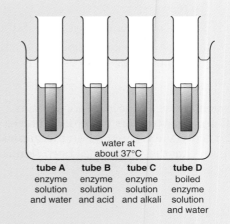

- In which test-tubes did the protease break down gelatin?

- What effect does boiling have on the action of the protease?

- In which conditions of pH does the protease work best?

- Why do you think that the test-tubes were kept at 37 °C?

This protease breaks down proteins to amino acids in the small intestine.
It works best at a pH of about 8.5 and at 37 °C.
Like other enzymes, it is denatured at high temperatures.

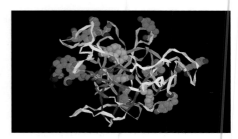

Computer model of a protease

▶ Enzymes as builders

Proteases break down the proteins into amino acids. The amino acids are small enough to get through the gut wall and into our blood.

These amino acids join our body's amino acid pool. When we grow we take amino acids out of this pool. Enzymes join these amino acids to make new proteins.

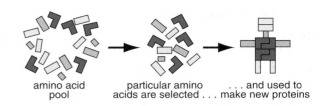

amino acid pool   particular amino acids are selected . . .   . . . and used to make new proteins

Experiment 3.5   Building starch from glucose

Green plants make glucose during photosynthesis.
Many plants store this glucose as starch.
Potato has an enzyme that changes glucose into starch.

glucose molecules   enzyme   starch molecule

First you have to make an extract of potato enzyme.

Grind a small piece of potato with $5\,cm^3$ of water.

Centrifuge the extract for 2 minutes.

Now test a drop of the extract with some iodine to make sure that the solution is starch-free.

You will use $1\,cm^3$ syringes to deliver drops of liquids.

Now get your iodine ready.

Make up row A and immediately add one drop of iodine to the first well on the spotting tile.

Repeat at the times shown.

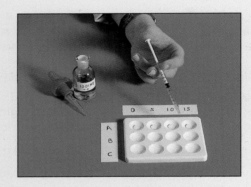

Copy the table and record your results in words or with crayons.

Starch forms when the iodine turns blue-black.
● How long did it take for starch to form in row A?

Now set up rows B and C using clean syringes.

Repeat the procedure.

● Will row B make starch without any enzyme?

● Will row C make starch without any glucose?

● Would there be any starch in potatoes without this builder-enzyme? Why not?

Row	To each well add :	Time (minutes)			
		0	5	10	15
A	2 drops glucose monophosphate, 2 drops potato extract				
B	2 drops glucose monophosphate, 2 drops water				
C	2 drops water, 2 drops potato extract				

► Immobilised enzymes

Breaker-enzymes break down complex chemicals into simple ones.
At the end of the reaction, the enzyme and these simple
chemicals are mixed together.
In industry, it can be very expensive to separate the enzyme
from these simple chemicals.

We solve this problem by *fixing* the enzyme to small resin beads.
In this form, we say that the enzyme is **immobilised** because
it can not move.

The resin beads are packed into a glass tube.
The complex chemical is poured in at the top.
As it trickles through the beads, the reaction takes place.
Simple chemicals run out of the bottom of the tube.

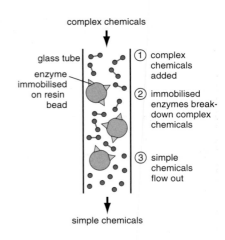

Lumpy ice cream

Sucrose forms crystals more easily than simple sugars like glucose.
This can cause sweet foods, like ice cream, to go hard and lumpy.
Manufacturers use yeast enzyme to break the sucrose down into
simple sugar molecules.

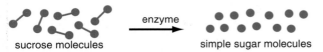

Experiment 3.6   *Changing sucrose into simple sugars*

1. First make your resin beads.
   Mix some yeast paste with some sodium alginate paste in a beaker.
   Add drops of the mixture into calcium chloride solution.

2. Wash the beads (coated with yeast enzyme) in a sieve.

3. Fill a glass tube with the beads, leaving a space at the top.
   Make sure that the tap on the glass tube is closed.

4. Test the sucrose solution with a glucose-detecting strip.
   No glucose should be present.
   Pour the sucrose solution into the glass tube and leave
   for 5 minutes.

5. Open the tap and run out the solution into a clean beaker.
   Test the solution with another glucose-detecting strip.

- Does the second glucose-detecting strip turn purple?
  Why does this happen?
- How do you think the sucrose has been changed to glucose?
- Where was the enzyme in this experiment?
- Why can this enzyme be used again?

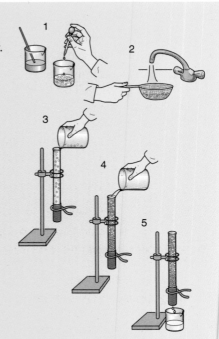

► Biology at work : Enzymes in industry

Enzymes are cheap to use in industry.
They do not need high temperatures to work.
This reduces the cost of fuels in industry.
Also enzymes can be re-used. This means that they
are only needed in small amounts.

Biological washing powders

Biological washing powders contain proteases.
This is because stains like grime and sweat contain protein.
These washing powders work at quite low temperatures.
What would happen to the enzymes if they were boiled?
What might happen to the material in the clothes if it was boiled?
What might happen to the dye in the material if it was boiled?
Why do you think that low temperatures make it more
economical for the user?

Investigation 3.7

Plan an investigation to either:
● compare the action of biological and non-biological washing powders, *or*
● see the effect of temperature on the action of a biological washing powder.
Check your plan with your teacher before you start.

Extracting fruit juice

Pectinases are enzymes that break down plant cell walls.
They can be used for extracting fruit juice and for softening vegetables.

Experiment 3.8   Getting the juice

Cut an apple in half.

Chop each half into small pieces and put them into
separate beakers.

Pour 4 cm³ of pectinase over the apple in beaker A and
4 cm³ of water over the apple in beaker B.

Place both beakers in a water bath at 40 °C for 20 mins.

Filter the juice from each of the beakers of apple pieces.

● Which of the apple pieces will make most juice?
● How does the pectinase release this juice from the apple cells?
● Why were 4 cm³ of water added to beaker B?

Some other uses of enzymes:
● Proteases are used to tenderise meat and to remove hair from skins.
● Enzymes from microbes are used in fermentation to make beer, wine and vinegar.
● Carbohydrases are used in the making of chocolates, syrups and other food products.

Summary

- Enzymes speed up chemical reactions in our bodies.

- Breaker-enzymes split up large molecules into smaller ones.

- Builder-enzymes join small molecules together to make large ones.

- Enzymes are specific. They will only act on one particular substrate. This is because the substrate has to fit the enzyme's active site.

- An enzyme is unchanged after the reaction, so can be used many times. This is why only a small amount of enzyme is needed.

- Enzymes work faster as the temperature increases up to 40°C, but eventually they are denatured at about 60°C.

- Each enzyme works best at a particular pH.

▶ **Questions**

1. Copy and complete:
   a) Enzymes .... up the rate of chemical ..... .
   b) Enzymes are .... because they only work on one substrate.
   c) The substrate fits into the .... site on the surface of the ..... .
   d) With an increase in .... , the rate of reaction ..... . But eventually a temperature is reached which .... the enzyme.
   e) Enzymes can be re-used, so only .... amounts are needed.

2. a) To which group of chemical compounds do enzymes belong?
   b) Which enzymes work on
      i) carbohydrates   ii) proteins   iii) fats?
   c) Name the products which are formed in each case.

3. An enzyme has an 'active site' on its surface on which the reaction takes place. Use the idea of an active site to explain:
   a) Why an enzyme is specific for a particular substrate.
   b) Why enzymes are denatured at high temperatures.
   c) Why an enzyme can be used again and again.

4. Lipase is an enzyme that breaks down fats. We can use an indicator to follow this reaction. The indicator is red to start with but turns yellow when all the fat has been broken down.

Test-tube	Temp. °C	Original colour	Final colour
1	0	red	red
2	10	red	orange
3	40	red	yellow
4	60	red	orange
5	100	red	red

Look at the results:
a) At what temperature does lipase work best?
b) Why do you think the colour did not change in test-tube 1?
c) Why do you think the colour did not change in test-tube 5?
d) Predict what you think would happen if you warmed test-tubes 1 and 5 up to 40 °C. Try to explain your prediction.

5. A number of things can alter the rate of an enzyme-controlled reaction. Say what each of the following would do to the rate of reaction, and give your reasons:
   a) An increase in enzyme concentration.
   b) A decrease in temperature.
   c) A lowering of pH.

6. The following experiment was set up to investigate the action of protease on egg-white. When enzymes break down the protein in egg-white, it changes from cloudy to clear.

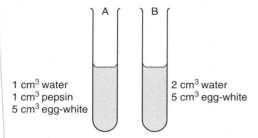

1 cm^3 water
1 cm^3 pepsin
5 cm^3 egg-white

2 cm^3 water
5 cm^3 egg-white

a) Explain why the contents of test-tube A went clear after 15 minutes.
b) Explain why the contents of test-tube B stayed cloudy after 15 minutes.
c) How could you increase the speed of the reaction in test-tube A?
d) What do you think the egg-white protein was broken down to form?

7. The graph shows how temperature affects an enzyme-controlled reaction.

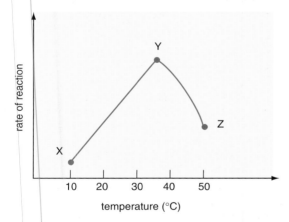

temperature (°C)

a) Explain what is happening:
   i) between X and Y
   ii) between Y and Z.
b) Suggest how increasing the temperature affects the rate of reaction of the enzyme.
c) What is happening to the active site of the enzyme at the higher temperatures?

This graph shows how pH affects the rates of two enzyme-controlled reactions.

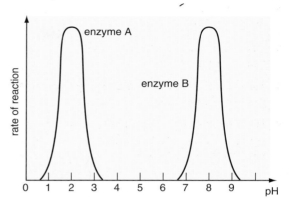

d) Which enzyme works best in acid conditions?
e) Which enzyme works best in alkali conditions?
f) What does the graph tell you about the **range** of pH over which each enzyme is active?

8. In 1989 a new fat-digesting enzyme was found in a fungus.
This enzyme works best at a pH of 7.5.
The enzyme can act at low temperatures and, after a few days, breaks down into carbon dioxide, nitrogen and water.

a) Give two reasons why this enzyme is now used in washing powders.
b) Why do you think that this enzyme is 'environmentally friendly'?
c) Why would a washing powder of high pH or low pH be difficult to handle?

Further questions on page 42.

Further questions on Life processes and cells

▶ Cells and tissues

1.

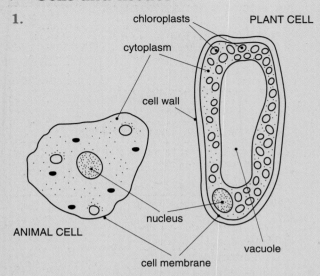

a) Use **only** the drawings above to copy and complete the table below to show **three** differences between plant and animal cells. [3]

	Plant cells	Animal cells
1		
2		
3		

b) What is the job of **each** of the following parts of a cell:
  i) nucleus;   ii) cellulose cell wall;
  iii) cytoplasm;   iv) cell membrane? [4]
c) i) What substance is contained in the chloroplasts?
  ii) Why is this substance important to **all** living things? [2]   (WJEC)

2. The diagrams below show five cells, some from animals and some from plants. Note that the diagrams are not all drawn to the same scale.

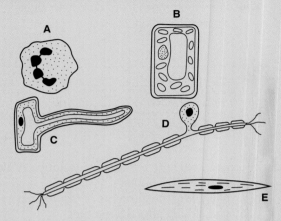

The cells are specialised to carry out certain functions. The list below gives the functions of these five cells.

1. absorbs salts and water from the soil
2. kills bacteria
3. makes food by photosynthesis
4. carries electrical impulses
5. shortens to bring about movement

a) i) Copy and complete the table below by matching the cells with the letters from the diagrams.
  ii) Complete the column ii) of your table by matching the cells with the correct number from the list of functions.

Name of the cell	i) Letter of diagram	ii) Number of function
Muscle cell	E	5
Palisade cell		
Root hair cell		
Sensory neurone		
White blood cell		

[4]

b) Choose **two** of the cells shown in the diagram and for each one describe how its structure allows it to perform its function efficiently. [2]   (EDEX)

3. Many of the cells in the body die and need to be replaced by new cells.
The table shows how long different types of cell live.

Type of cell	Life (in days)
liver cell	250
muscle cell	240
red blood cell	100
skin cell	18

a) Using the information in the table, draw a bar-chart on graph paper with type of cell on the horizontal axis and life (days) on the vertical axis. [5]

b) Read the following information about nerve cells.
   - All nerve cells develop when a person is very young.
   - Most people in Britain live for 70 years or more.
   - As people become older, they often find it more difficult to remember things.
   - The things we remember are stored in the nerve cells of our brains.
   - Nerve cells are never replaced.

   Explain, as fully as you can, what this information tells you about how long nerve cells live. [4]   (AQA)

4. The key below lists organs of the human body.

Letter	Organ
A	Brain
B	Heart
C	Lung
D	Diaphragm
E	Stomach
F	Large intestine
G	Kidney
H	Bladder
I	Uterus

The table which follows shows a function of each of these organs. Copy the table and match the correct function to each organ by writing the correct letter in each box.

The first one has been done for you.

Function	Letter
Stores waste fluid called urine	H
Breaks food down into smaller chemicals	
Can contain a developing fetus	
Controls other organs	
Filters the blood to help remove waste	
Helps oxygen to enter the blood and carbon dioxide to leave	
Helps to move air in and out of body	
Pumps blood through the body	
Takes water from food into the blood stream	

[8]   (EDEX)

▶ Into and out of cells

5. Lengths of visking tubing were set up as follows:

   A contained 1% starch and amylase;
   B contained 1% starch and boiled amylase.

   Both were left in water at 30°C for one hour. They were then placed in beakers of dilute iodine solution and left for five minutes as shown below. Iodine solution can pass through visking tubing.

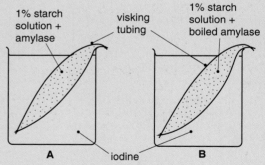

a) What colour would you expect to see inside
   i) A   ii) B? [2]
b) Explain what has happened inside **A**. [2]
c) i) Describe a test to prove your explanation. [2]
   ii) State the expected results. [1]
d) What appears to be the effect of boiling the amylase? [1]   (WJEC)

Further questions on Life processes and cells

6. A student carried out an investigation on the effects of various sugar solutions on rods of potato tuber. The student used a cork borer to remove the rods which were gently blotted and weighed.

Each rod was then placed in distilled water or in one of several sugar solutions of different concentrations. After 2 hours the rods were removed, gently blotted and reweighed. The results, expressed as a percentage change in mass, are shown in the table.

Concentration of sugar solution in arbitrary units	Percentage change in mass
0 (distilled water)	+8
0.25	+4
0.50	−1
1.00	−7
1.50	−10

a) i) Plot a line graph of the data on a sheet of graph paper.
Put concentration of sugar solution in arbitrary units on the horizontal axis and percentage change in mass on the vertical axis [3]

ii) From the graph, work out the concentration of sugar solution which would result in no change in mass of the potato tuber. [1]

b) Name the process which causes the mass of the potato to change in this experiment. [1]

c) What else might the student have measured to investigate the effect of the sugar solutions on the rods? [1]

d) Some people soak salad vegetables, especially lettuce, in salt water to remove animals such as slugs and greenfly. However, if the lettuce is left too long in the salt water the leaves become limp.

i) Explain why the lettuce leaves become limp. [1]

ii) Suggest how the lettuce leaves could be made crisp again [1] (EDEX)

7. A pupil set up the apparatus shown in the diagram.

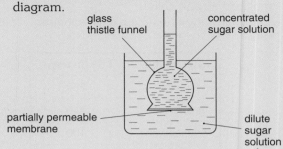

a) What happens to the height of the sugar solution in the funnel? [1]

b) Explain why this happens.
You may use the diagram below to help with your answer.

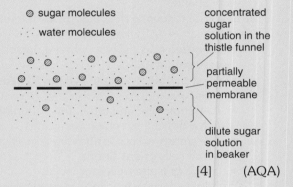

[4] (AQA)

▶ Enzymes

8. The graph below shows the effect of pH on the time taken for carbohydrase to break down starch.

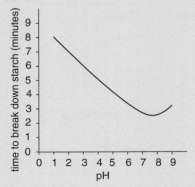

From the graph we can conclude that this enzyme works fastest …

A at pH1

B in acid conditions

C between pH 7 and 8

D at pH 9 [1] (AQA)

9. Dilute iodine solution forms a deep blue compound with starch. This colour disappears if the starch is broken down.

a) Three test tubes were set up as shown:

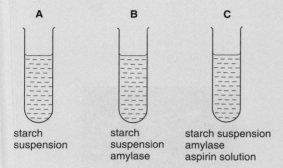

A — starch suspension

B — starch suspension amylase

C — starch suspension amylase aspirin solution

A few drops of iodine solution were added to each tube. After 10 minutes the contents of tube A were still deep blue, that of tube B were colourless, while that of tube C were pale blue.

  i) What do the results from tubes **A** and **B** indicate about the action of amylase on the starch? [1]

 ii) How does the presence of aspirin, in tube **C**, appear to affect the action of the amylase? [1]

iii) State **two** precautions which should have been taken to give the results greater validity. In each case explain the reason for the precaution. [4]

b) When fats are digested, fatty acids are formed. These can be detected by a blue indicator (bromothymol blue) which turns yellow in the presence of an acid. You are provided with a supply of the enzyme lipase, olive oil and bromothymol blue. Using any equipment normally present in a laboratory, design an experiment to investigate the effect of temperature on the activity of lipase. Give clear details of the way in which you would carry out the investigation. [8] (OCR)

10. Experiments were carried out to investigate the action of two enzymes at different pH values. The enzymes were pepsin (a protease) and amylase. All experiments were carried out at 37°C for 20 minutes. The results are shown on the graph below.

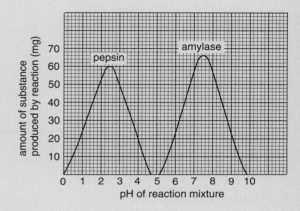

a) How much substance was produced in the pepsin-controlled reaction at pH 3? [1]

b) At which pH values were 60 mg of substance produced by:
   i) pepsin; ii) amylase? [2]

c) Which substance is produced when amylase acts on starch? [1]

d) Name the enzyme which works best in acid conditions. [1]

e) Scientists were searching for an enzyme to remove lipids (fats and oils) from clothes to make Zappo, a new biological washing powder.
   i) Name an enzyme which could be added to the washing powder to remove fat stains. [1]
   ii) Which two substances would be produced as the enzyme digests fat? [2]
   iii) Why should washing powder containing this enzyme **not** be used at high temperatures? [2] (EDEX)

chapter 4

Food AND digestion

Your body is made up of chemicals.
You get these chemicals from the food that you eat.
What do you think your body uses your food for ?

- **For energy**

You need food to work your muscles and other organs.
Your food is the fuel that keeps you going.
Just like a car won't start without petrol, your
body won't work without food.

- **For growth and repair**

As you grow, you make new cells.
You also need to replace old or damaged cells.
You make new cells from chemicals in your food.

- **To stay healthy**

Lots of reactions take place in the cells of your body.
Chemicals in your food are needed for these reactions.

What's in the food we eat ?

These are some of the things that are in our food :

*proteins   carbohydrates   fats   water
vitamins   minerals   fibre*

Some foods may have a lot of protein in them.
Other foods may not have much protein at all.
Some foods may have a lot of carbohydrate or fat.
Different foods have different vitamins and minerals.

If we are to stay healthy our bodies must have :

- enough food
- a variety of foods – so that our body gets all
the different things it needs.

We need a healthy, **balanced** diet.

Which is the better balanced meal ?

▶ Proteins

Your body is made up of billions of cells.
These cells are made mainly from protein.

When you grow your body needs protein to make new cells.
Your body may need to replace old or damaged cells.
You need enough protein in your food for this as well.

Proteins are made up of lots of **amino acids**.
There are about 20 different types of amino acids.

Here are 2 different proteins:
Can you see what makes them different?

There are thousands of different proteins in our bodies,
each with a different job to do.

Some protein-rich foods

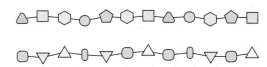

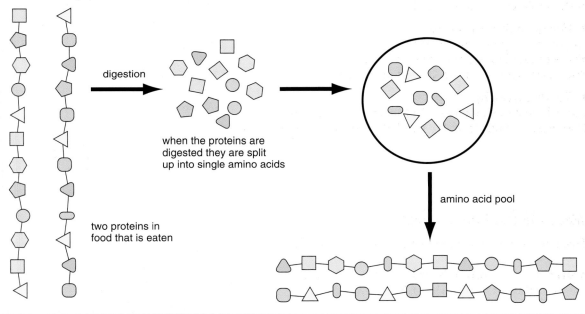

digestion

when the proteins are
digested they are split
up into single amino acids

amino acid pool

two proteins in
food that is eaten

Experiment 4.1   Testing for protein

Add a few drops of copper sulphate solution to
some protein solution in a test-tube.
Now *carefully* add a few drops of sodium hydroxide
solution.
Take great care as sodium hydroxide solution is **corrosive**.

Did the protein go purple?

⚠ eye
protection

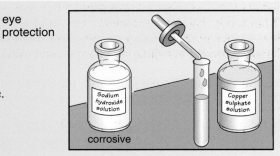

corrosive

► Carbohydrates

Sugars are carbohydrates.

Did you know that there are different kinds of sugars?
The kind of sugar you put in your tea is called **sucrose**.
The kind of sugar that is in milk is called **lactose**.
The sugar that our bodies use most is **glucose**.

We need carbohydrates to give us energy.
Sugars are the fuel that our bodies need.

Some foods rich in carbohydrates

Experiment 4.2   Testing for glucose

Pour some glucose solution into a test-tube.
Add a few drops of Benedict's solution.
(Be careful, this is harmful.)
Carefully heat the test-tube in a water bath.
Did the glucose turn orange?

 eye protection

Starch is also a carbohydrate.
You already know that starch is a large molecule.
It is made up of lots of smaller glucose molecules
joined together.

What do you make when you digest starch?

large starch molecule   **digestion**   small glucose molecules

Experiment 4.3   Testing for starch

Half fill a test-tube with starch solution.
Add 2 drops of iodine solution.
Does the starch turn blue-black?

 eye protection

Plants often turn their glucose into starch to store it.

Glycogen is a large carbohydrate molecule like starch.
Glycogen is also made up of glucose molecules joined
together.
We store glycogen in our liver and muscles.
Our bodies change glycogen to glucose when we need it.

Many cheaper foods contain a lot of carbohydrates.
Do you think foods containing a lot of protein would
be more or less expensive?

▶ Fats

There are many different kinds of fats.
Fats are made up of 3 **fatty acids** joined together.
There are different kinds of fatty acids.
Do you think that different fats have different
kinds of fatty acids in them?

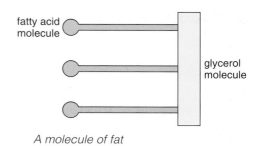

A molecule of fat

Fats also give us energy.
Fats actually contain more energy than carbohydrates.
Our bodies use fats as an energy store.
We store fats under the skin and around the heart and kidneys.
When we are short of energy our body uses the fat.
What do you think happens if we eat too much fat?

Experiment 4.4   Testing for fat

Put 4 drops of cooking oil into a test-tube.

⚠ ethanol is highly flammable

Add 2 cm³ of ethanol to the oil and shake the test-tube.

Add 2 cm³ of water to the test-tube and shake again.

Does the oil turn cloudy white?

Fats are good insulators. They cut down heat loss.
Which animals have a lot of fat under the skin?
Fats also give buoyancy.
Why do whales have a thick layer of blubber?

> **We need : proteins for growth and repair of cells**
> **carbohydrates for energy**
> **fats as a store of energy and for warmth**

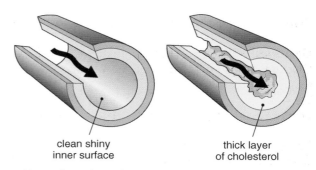

Some foods rich in fat

Why can fat be bad for us?

There are 2 main types of fat :
Saturated fat and **unsaturated fat**.
Fat that comes from animals is saturated.
Fat that comes from plants is unsaturated.

If we eat too much saturated fat it sticks to
the lining of our blood vessels and builds up.
This makes our blood vessels narrower.
Our heart has to work harder to push the
blood through narrow blood vessels.
This can increase the risk of a heart attack.

Many school children already have narrow
blood vessels.
Why do you think this is?

What would your advice be to reduce heart disease?

clean shiny
inner surface

thick layer
of cholesterol

How a fatty deposit can narrow an artery

► Food and energy

Our food gives us our energy.
We need energy for all the activities that we do.
Carbohydrates and fats are high-energy foods.

Energy in food is measured in **kilojoules (kJ)**,
where **1 kilojoule = 1000 joules**.

Look at these 2 meals:
Which meal has the highest energy content?
By how much?
Which meal is the most healthy?
How could you reduce the energy content in the first meal?

sausage 500 kJ
cup of tea with milk 150 kJ
bread and butter 600 kJ
fried egg 650 kJ
chips 1000 kJ

brown rice 200 kJ
fresh fruit juice 150 kJ
salad 20 kJ
yogurt 45 kJ
curried chicken 300 kJ

Measuring the energy in food

We can measure the amount of energy in some
food by burning it.
As the food burns, it gives out energy.
We can use this energy to heat up some water.
The hotter the water gets the more energy is in the food.

Experiment 4.5   Measuring the energy in a peanut

Copy the results table.
Use a measuring cylinder to pour out exactly 20 cm³
of water into a boiling-tube.
Take the temperature of the water and write it down
in your table.
Weigh a peanut and write down the weight in your table.
Put the peanut on the end of a mounted needle.
Set the peanut alight and hold it under the boiling-tube
of water.
When the peanut has burnt out, take the temperature
of the water again. Write your result in your table.

Weight of peanut (g)	Temp. of water at start (°C)	Temp. of water at end (°C)	Temp. rise of water (°C)

eye protection
peanut allergy

Work out how many joules of energy were given out
by your peanut using this equation:

Energy (joules) = 20 × 4.2 × temperature rise of water

Work out the energy content per gram (g) of peanut
using this equation:

$$\text{Energy content (joules/g)} = \frac{\text{energy given out by your peanut (J)}}{\text{weight of your peanut (g)}}$$

Rather than use such large numbers, you can change the
units from joules to kilojoules by dividing by 1000.

Try the experiment again using a pea instead of a peanut.

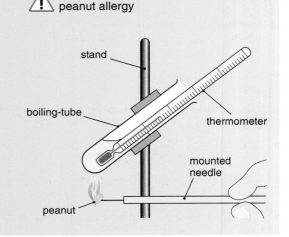

stand
boiling-tube
thermometer
mounted needle
peanut

▶ How much energy?

Most foods have their energy content on the label.
The amount of energy is given in kilojoules per 100 g of food.
How much energy is there in 100 g of these foods?

BRANFLAKES

Wheatflakes Enriched with Bran

INGREDIENTS

Wheat, Wheat Bran, Sugar, Malt Extract, Salt, Niacin, Iron Pantothenic Acid, Thiamin (Vitamin B₁), Vitamin B₆, Riboflaviv (Vitamin B₂), Folic Acid, Vitamin B₁₂, Vitamin D.

INGREDIENTS

Typical Values	Per 100g	Per (30g) serving
Energy	1411 kJ (333kcal)	422 kJ (100kcal)
Protein	10.1g	3.0g
Carbohydrate	67.7g	20.3g
of which sugars	16.9g	5.1g
starch	50.8g	15.2g
Fat	2.4g	0.7g
of which saturates	0.4g	0.1g
mono-unsaturates	0.4g	0.1g
polyunsaturates	1.6g	0.5g
Fibre	12.7g	3.8g
Sodium	0.7g	0.2g

WALKERS CRISPS

Prawn Cocktail Flavour

INGREDIENTS: potatoes, vegetable oil, prawn coctail flavour (flavouring, acidity regulator (sodium diacetate), flavour enhancer (monosodium glutamt–ate), citric acid, sweetner (saccharinl), salt.

Typical Nutrition Information	Per 100g	Per 28g pack
Energy	2300 kj	644 kj
	550 kcal	154 kcal
Protein	6.0g	1.7g
Carbohydrate	46.0g	12.9g
Fat	38.0g	10.6g

Dawn

Rice Pudding

NUTRITION INFORMATION

100 grams of this rice pudding typically provides:

Energy Value	363 kj
(calries)	(86 kcal)
Protein	3.4 grams
Carbohydrate	16.0 grams
Fat	0.9 grams

How much food do you need?

The amount of food that you need depends upon
how much energy you use up every day.
The amount of energy you need depends on:
- your body size
- how active you are
- how fast you are growing.

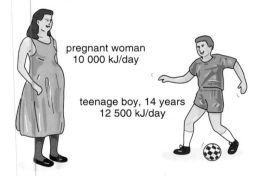

pregnant woman
10 000 kJ/day

teenage boy, 14 years
12 500 kJ/day

	Energy used in a day (kJ)	
	Male	**Female**
8-year-old	8 500	8 500
Teenager, aged 14	12 500	9 700
Adult office worker	11 000	9 800
Adult manual worker	15 000	12 500
Pregnant woman		10 000
Breast-feeding mother		11 500

- Why do you think that males usually need more
  energy than females?

- Why do manual workers need more energy than
  office workers?

- Why does the 14-year-old boy need more energy
  than the male office worker?

- Why does pregnancy increase the energy needs
  of a woman?

- Why does a breast-feeding mother need more energy
  than a pregnant mother?

male manual
worker
15 000 kJ/day

girl, 8 years
8 500 kJ/day

▶ Getting the balance right

The food you eat in a day should provide you with enough energy to get through that day. Even if you are lying in bed, completely inactive, you are still using energy to keep:

- your heart beating
- your lungs working
- your body temperature constant
- all the chemical reactions in your body going.

This 'ticking over' speed at which our bodies work is the **basal metabolic rate (BMR)**.
The BMR varies from person to person, but roughly it uses 7000 kJ per day. So even if you lie around doing nothing you still need this amount of energy.

A well-balanced meal is important at lunchtime

What happens if we eat too much?

If you eat more food than you need, your body stores the extra as fat.

Your **energy intake** is the amount of energy you get in your food in a day.

Your **energy output** is the amount of energy your body uses up in a day.

If our energy intake is greater than our energy output, then we put on weight.
We may run the risk of becoming fat **(obese)**.
People with a low BMR are more likely to get overweight.
Why do you think this is?
Fattening foods are those with most energy content.

So how could someone lose weight?
They could:

- eat less high-energy foods (lower their energy intake),
- take more exercise (increase their energy output).

A sensible approach to slimming should combine:

- a balanced lower-energy intake, and
- a gradual increase in exercise.

▶ Taking things to extremes

If you don't eat enough food you lose weight.
You feel weak and have no energy.

Some people eat so little that they suffer from **anorexia**.
Most anorexics are women, aged between 15 and 25.
Anorexia is more than just slimming and loss of appetite.
Sufferers have an 'attitude' to their bodies.
They want to stay as thin as possible.
Even when they weigh a lot less than they should,
they still 'see' themselves as being 'fat'.

▶ Vegetarians

Vegetarians do not eat meat.
But there is more to it than just leaving the meat
at the side of the plate.
It is important to replace the meat with other forms
of protein, like cereals, seeds and nuts.

There are different kinds of vegetarians.

Some people do not eat meat but eat fish.

Others eat no meat or fish but eat dairy products.

Vegans eat no animal products at all.
Vegans have to make sure that they have enough
vitamins and minerals (like iron and calcium).

In what ways might vegetarians be healthier than
other people?

Would they eat less saturated fats?

Would they have more fibre?

Why do you think people choose to become vegetarians?

THE BRAMBLES
Vegetarian Restaurant

25 The Avenue
Rusthall
Kent

(01536) 8954542

MENU

Mushroom Pizza
Three cheese Risotto
Nut Roast
Bean Salad
Stuffed Onions
Pease Pudding
Leek & Potato soup
Vegetable Lasagne
Golden Stuffed Peppers
Vegetarian Shepherds Pie
Chocolate Terrine

▶ Vitamins and minerals

You need small, regular amounts of vitamins and minerals.
Vitamins and minerals are essential for good health.
They must be present in our balanced diet.
If they are missing we can become very ill.

Name	Rich food sources	Use in body	Deficiency disease
A	carrots, milk, butter, liver	good eyesight, healthy skin	sore eyes, poor night vision, unhealthy skin
B_1	yeast, cereals, beans, egg yolk	healthy nerves, growth	a disease called beri-beri, retarded growth
C	oranges, lemons, other citrus fruits	tissue repair, resistance to disease	a disease called scurvy (bleeding gums)
D	fish oil, milk, butter, made by body in sunlight	strong bones and teeth	a disease called rickets (soft bones)
iron	liver, meat, cocoa	healthy red blood cells	anaemia
calcium	milk, green vegetables	strong bones and teeth	soft bones
iodine	fish, iodised salt tablets	thyroid gland	goitre (enlarged thyroid)

Deficiency diseases are caused when the body
doesn't have enough of a certain vitamin or mineral.
They are easily cured by eating the right kinds of food.

Look at the information in the table above and answer
these questions:

- Why does a pregnant woman need lots of calcium
  and iron in her diet?

- A 13-year-old girl starts her 'periods'.
  Why might she become a bit anaemic?

- In olden days sailors developed scurvy on long
  sea voyages. How do you think they cured it?

Experiment 4.7   Estimating the amount of vitamin C

DCPIP is a liquid that loses its colour when it
comes into contact with vitamin C.

Pour 1 cm³ of DCPIP solution into a test-tube.

Take a 1 cm³ syringe of vitamin C and see how
many drops it takes to decolourise the DCPIP.

Compare the amounts of vitamin C in different
fruit juices.

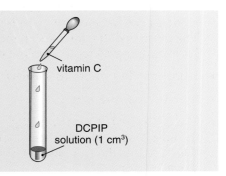

vitamin C

DCPIP
solution (1 cm³)

▶ Water

Water makes up two-thirds of your body weight.
You take in water when you drink or eat.
You could go without food for a number of weeks.
But you would die in a few days without water.

Why do we need water?

- In our cells, chemical reactions take place in water.
- Waste chemicals are passed out of our bodies in water.
- Our blood transports substances dissolved in water.
- Water in our sweat cools us down.

Water : our daily losses and gains

Gains (cm³/day)		Losses (cm³/day)	
drinks	1400	urine	1500
food	800	faeces	100
respiration	300	breath	350
		sweat	550
Total	2500	Total	2500

▶ Fibre

Dietary fibre or roughage comes from plants.
It is mainly cellulose from plant cell walls.
Although it can not be digested, it is an important
part of your diet.
High-fibre foods include bran cereals, potato skins,
sweetcorn and celery.

Why is fibre important?

- Fibre adds bulk to our food. Since it is not digested,
  it passes down the entire gullet from mouth to anus.
  The muscles of the gut need something to push against.
  It's like squeezing toothpaste out of a tube.

- Fibre absorbs poisonous wastes from digesting foods.

- It prevents constipation.

- Many doctors believe that a high-fibre diet lowers
  the level of cholesterol in the blood.
  Fibre reduces the risk of heart disease and
  bowel cancer.

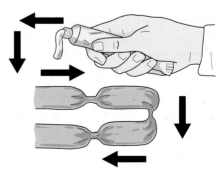

▶ Food additives

When some foods are manufactured, chemicals are put in them.
These chemicals are called food additives.
They are added for a number of reasons:

Preservatives *keep the food fresh*

Flavourings *replace the flavour of the food that is often lost when it is processed*

Colourings *make the food look more attractive and appetising*

All food additives must be tested before they can be used.
Over 300 additives are approved in Britain.
Most of these have 'E numbers'.
Additive E215 is a preservative called
sodium ethyl para-hydroxybenzoate!
Try fitting that on a food label!

Some people avoid eating food additives because they
think that they are harmful.
Some may cause asthma and headaches.
Others are blamed for over-activity in children.
There is evidence that some additives destroy vitamins.

Activity 4.8 Looking at food labels

Look at some of the food labels in your home.
Make a list of the additives and find out why they
are put into the food.

If the E number starts with 1, it is a **colouring**.

If it starts with a 2, it is a **preservative**.

If it starts with 3, it is an **antioxidant** which
helps to stop the food from going off.

If it starts with 4, it is to help with the **texture** of the food.

▶ Teeth

Your teeth don't just give you a nice smile.
They have an important role in digestion.

By chewing our food, we break it down into
smaller pieces. This:

- makes it easier to swallow,
- gives it a large surface area open to enzyme action.

A full set

Adults have 32 teeth (if they are all there).
But not all your teeth are the same.
Some have different shapes for different jobs.

Incisors are chisel-shaped for biting and cutting.

Canines are pointed for piercing and tearing.

Premolars have uneven 'cusps' for grinding and chewing.

Molars are like premolars and are for chewing up the food.

Look at the diagram of the mouth:
Count how many of each type of tooth there is.

You should find that there are:

8 incisors, 4 canines, 8 premolars, and 12 molars.

That makes 32 in all.

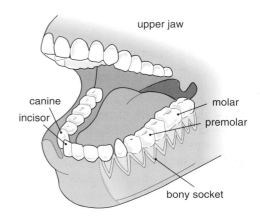

During our lives we have two sets of teeth.
As a child we had fewer **milk teeth** because
our jaw was smaller.
Between the ages of 6 and 12 these teeth gradually
fell out, to be replaced by our **permanent teeth**.
The last of our permanent teeth will come through when
we are at least 18, if at all!
These are our back molars or **wisdom teeth**.

Experiment 4.9   Examining your teeth
Look at the inside of your mouth with a small mirror.
Count how many teeth you have got altogether.

- How many have you got of each type?
- Have you lost any teeth?
- Which ones have not come through yet?

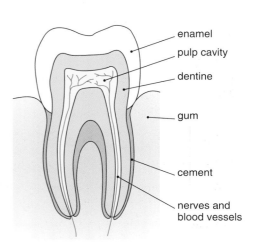

Healthy teeth and gums

Tooth decay is caused by bacteria in your mouth.
They mix with saliva to form **plaque**.
Plaque is an invisible layer that sticks to your
teeth and gums.

After a meal, sugary food may be left between your teeth.
Bacteria, in the plaque, change the sugar into **acid**.
The acid can attack the surface of your tooth.
This starts off tooth decay.
The acid can also make your gums red and swollen.

Periodontal disease can occur if bacteria get into
the space between the teeth.
They can make your gums unhealthy.
The bacteria can rot the fibres holding the
teeth in position and make them fall out.

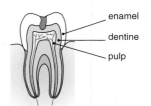

enamel
dentine
pulp

No pain
decay has started
in the enamel

Slight toothache
decay is eating
through the dentine

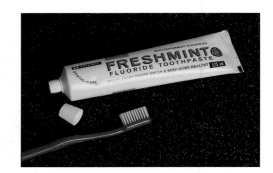

abscess

Severe toothache
decay eventually
reaches the pulp

Agony!
germs get to the
base of the tooth
forming an abscess

Looking after your teeth

Here is some good advice to help you keep your teeth :

- Avoid sugary food and drinks between meals.
- Clean your teeth at least twice a day.
- Replace your toothbrush when it wears out
  (every 4–6 months).
- Visit your dentist regularly (every 6 months).

Fluoride strengthens teeth by making the enamel
more resistant to acid.
In many places, like Birmingham, fluoride is put
in the drinking water. Here there has been a big
decrease in tooth decay.
Fluoride toothpaste can also help.

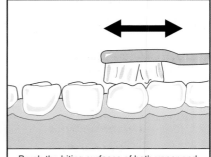

Give decay the brush off !

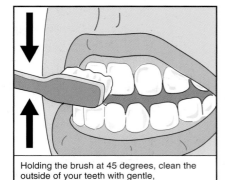

Holding the brush at 45 degrees, clean the
outside of your teeth with gentle,
short up-and-down movements.

Clean the inside surface of your teeth moving
your brush gently back and forwards. Be sure
not to forget the back teeth.

Brush the biting surfaces of both upper and
lower teeth with short, scrubbing strokes.

▶ Digestion

What happens to your food when you eat it?

Before your body can use the food you have eaten it must be broken down to very small molecules.

Large food molecules like proteins must be broken down into small amino acids.
Large carbohydrate molecules like starch must be broken down into small sugar molecules.
Large fat molecules must be broken down into small fatty acids.

The breakdown of large food molecules into small food molecules is called **digestion**.
It's a bit like pulling Lego bricks apart.

When the food has been digested, it is **absorbed** through the wall of the gut into the blood.
Before the food molecules can go through the gut wall they must be dissolved.

Large food molecules are insoluble, they will not dissolve.
Large food molecules can not get through the gut wall.
Small food molecules are soluble, they will dissolve.
Small food molecules can get through the gut wall.

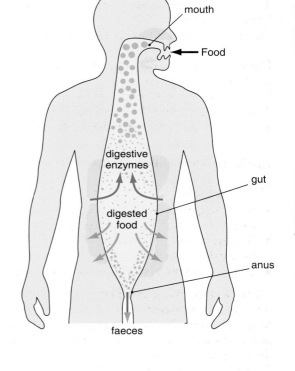

> **Digestion is the breakdown of large, insoluble food molecules into small, soluble food molecules so that they can be absorbed into the bloodstream.**

You know that enzymes are important chemicals.
They help digestion by breaking down large food molecules into small food molecules.
There are three main kinds of enzymes in your gut:

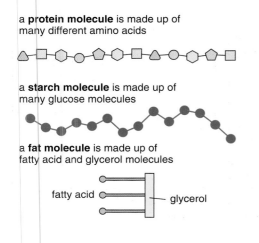

a **protein molecule** is made up of many different amino acids

a **starch molecule** is made up of many glucose molecules

a **fat molecule** is made up of fatty acid and glycerol molecules

fatty acid — glycerol

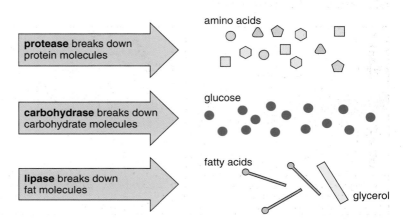

protease breaks down protein molecules

carbohydrase breaks down carbohydrate molecules

lipase breaks down fat molecules

amino acids

glucose

fatty acids

glycerol

▶ The gut – your inner tube

Your gut or digestive system is about 9 metres long.
It starts at your mouth and ends at your anus.
It bends and twists a lot to fit inside your body.
But your gut is not just a simple tube.
There are many different parts to it.

▶ In your mouth

Food enters your mouth in bite-sized chunks.
Chew your food well – it's important for digestion.

The chewed food is mixed with **saliva**.
Your **salivary glands** make saliva.

- Saliva contains a carbohydrase enzyme called **amylase**. This starts to digest starch to sugar.

- **Mucus** is a slimy substance in saliva.
  It helps the food slip down your throat!

Swallowing

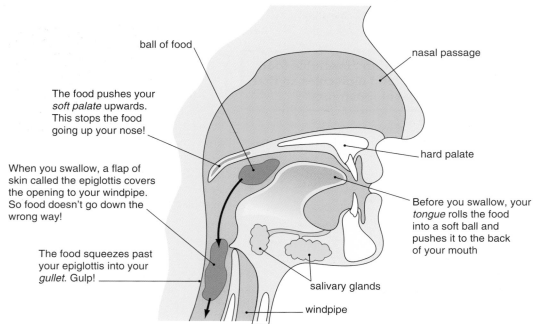

ball of food

nasal passage

The food pushes your *soft palate* upwards. This stops the food going up your nose!

hard palate

When you swallow, a flap of skin called the epiglottis covers the opening to your windpipe. So food doesn't go down the wrong way!

Before you swallow, your *tongue* rolls the food into a soft ball and pushes it to the back of your mouth

The food squeezes past your epiglottis into your *gullet*. Gulp!

salivary glands

windpipe

Swallowing is a reflex – it happens without you thinking about it.
Next time you swallow, think about all the things that are happening.

▶ Down the tube !

The gullet is also called the **oesophagus**.
Its job is to pass the food down to your **stomach**.

The gullet has circular muscles in its wall.
These muscles contract and squeeze in behind
the food to push it along.
It's a bit like squeezing toothpaste out of a tube.

In front of the food the muscles relax.

This way of moving food down your gut is
called **peristalsis**.

▶ In your stomach

Your stomach is a muscular bag that will hold
up to 2 litres of food.
When food reaches your stomach it really gets the
treatment !

- The stomach makes digestive juices.
  These contain proteases which start the digestion
  of proteins to amino acids.

- The juices also contain **hydrochloric acid**.
  This is because stomach protease works best in
  an acid pH.

- Babies make the enzyme **rennin**.
  It makes milk solid so it stays in the stomach
  longer. The milk can then be digested.

- The muscular walls churn up the food making sure
  that it is mixed up well with the juices.

The stomach acid also kills germs.

After 2–3 hours of churning, the food is a runny liquid.
A ring of muscle opens to let the food squirt out.
It passes into the **small intestine** a little at a time.

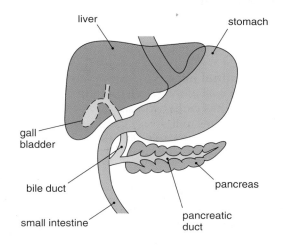

Investigation 4.10   What affects the clotting of milk ?

Plan an investigation into how quickly rennin clots milk.
What sort of factors will affect how quickly the rennin
works ?
Choose *one* factor and investigate its effect.

▶ In your small intestine

This is not really so small, it's about 6 metres long!
Everything is much calmer here.
The liquid food is squeezed gently along.

Three important liquids are added to the food:

- **Pancreatic juice** contains carbohydrases, proteases and lipases. These enzymes carry on digesting the food.

- **Bile** enters the small intestine from the **bile duct**.
  Bile is made in the **liver** and is stored in the **gall bladder**. It has 2 important jobs:

  i) Bile is alkaline and neutralises acid which was added to the food in the stomach. This gives the best pH for enzymes in the small intestine to work.

  ii) Bile **emulsifies** fats (breaks large drops of fats into small droplets). This increases the surface area of fats for lipase enzymes to act upon.

- **Intestinal juice** is made by glands in the wall of the small intestine. It also has carbohydrases, proteases and lipases in it. These enzymes complete the digestion of the food:

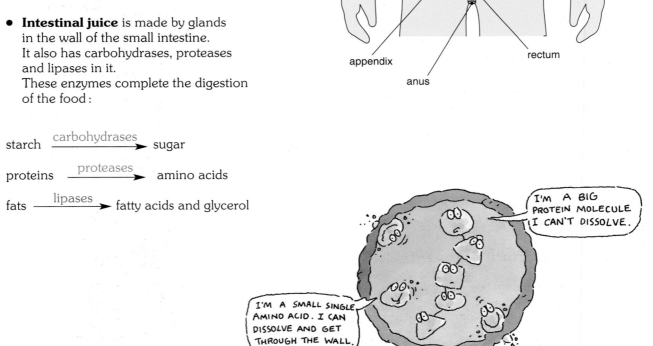

starch $\xrightarrow{\text{carbohydrases}}$ sugar

proteins $\xrightarrow{\text{proteases}}$ amino acids

fats $\xrightarrow{\text{lipases}}$ fatty acids and glycerol

I'M A BIG PROTEIN MOLECULE. I CAN'T DISSOLVE.

I'M A SMALL SINGLE AMINO ACID. I CAN DISSOLVE AND GET THROUGH THE WALL.

▶ Absorption

The small intestine has another important job apart from digestion.
Digested food has to pass through the wall into the blood.

The small intestine is well designed for absorption.
It has:
- a thin lining
- a good blood supply
- a very large surface area.

The surface area of the small intestine is about 9 square metres.
How is this large surface area fitted into such a small space?
- The small intestine is very long (at least 6 metres).
- It has a folded inner lining.
- It has millions of tiny, finger-like processes called **villi** (the singular of villi is **villus**).

All this means that the digested food can pass through easily into the blood vessels.

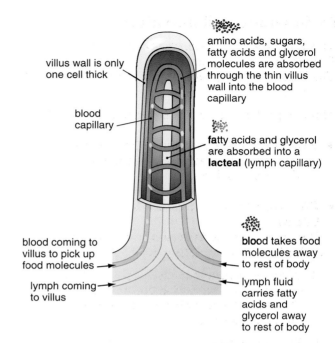

villus wall is only one cell thick

amino acids, sugars, fatty acids and glycerol molecules are absorbed through the thin villus wall into the blood capillary

blood capillary

fatty acids and glycerol are absorbed into a **lacteal** (lymph capillary)

blood coming to villus to pick up food molecules

lymph coming to villus

blood takes food molecules away to rest of body

lymph fluid carries fatty acids and glycerol away to rest of body

---

Experiment 4.11   Making a model gut

Try making a model gut out of Visking tubing.

Wash a 12 cm length of the tubing in warm water to soften it. Then tie a knot in one end.

Fill the tubing with 5 cm³ of starch solution and 2 cm³ of amylase solution. Put it into a boiling-tube of water (as shown).

After 10 minutes, test the water for starch and for sugar.
What do you find?

⚠ eye protection

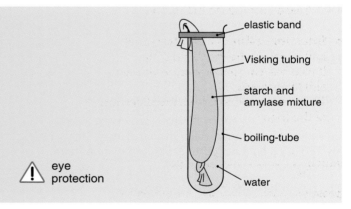

elastic band

Visking tubing

starch and amylase mixture

boiling-tube

water

Your large intestine

By the time your food gets here there's not much useful food left.
It's mainly fibre, dead cells, bacteria and water.
As it passes along the large intestine some of the water is absorbed into the blood.
The solid waste or **faeces** are stored in the **rectum**.
Eventually the faeces are egested through the anus.

Normally it takes between 24 and 48 hours for food to pass along the whole length of your digestive system.

▶ Feeding in other mammals

Unlike humans most mammals are either **carnivores** (meat eaters), or **herbivores** (plant eaters).

Carnivores

Carnivores, like lions, have teeth and jaws specifically designed to kill and eat their prey as quickly as possible.

They have sharp and pointed canines that can grasp their prey and tear the skin and muscle. The incisors though are much smaller but are sharp and can pull meat away from bone.

The molars and premolars include the **carnassial** teeth. These are large and sharp and when combined with the up and down action of the jaw, cut through flesh and bone in a scissor-like action.

Carnivores tend to swallow a lot of their food whole. This means that the molars are not used to grind food.

Herbivores

Herbivores, like sheep, have to cope with tough plant material that contains a lot of cellulose.

They have broad, sharp incisors, which are used to 'snip off' plant material. Often the upper incisors are replaced by a horny pad which the lower teeth bite against.

The premolars and molars are very well developed and covered with ridges. These ridges create a good grinding surface, and this grinding is aided by the side to side movement of the jaw.

A consequence of the grinding is that the teeth are being constantly worn away. However this is not a problem as these teeth are continuously growing.

A cheetah tearing at its prey with its specialised teeth

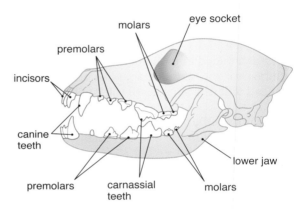

The skull of a dog showing the canine and carnassial teeth

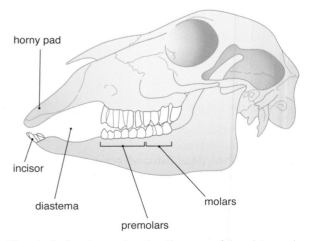

The skull of a sheep showing the powerful molars and premolars

▶ The herbivore gut

The main adaptation herbivores have to their high cellulose diet is in the design of their digestive system. Cellulose is a valuable source of energy, but it is also difficult to digest.

Like most mammals, herbivores do not have an enzyme that will breakdown cellulose (cellulase). What they do have, however, are cellulose digesting bacteria in their gut.

Ruminants, like sheep and cattle have these bacteria in a section of the stomach called the **rumen**. This is found between the gullet and the small intestine.

These animals take partially digested food from the rumen back into their mouth. Here it is re-chewed before it passes back through the rest of the stomach. This is commonly called 'chewing the cud'.

Rabbits have a slightly different system for coping with cellulose. Their bacteria are found in a large appendix and caecum between the small and large intestines.

Why are rabbits often seen eating their own faeces?.
Soft pellets of faeces contain a lot of undigested food.
By eating them the rabbits give the bacteria another go at it.

What's in it for the bacteria?
It is not just the herbivores that gain from this relationship with the bacteria. The bacteria themselves gain a ready source of cellulose and other nutrients.

This is an example of **mutualism**, which is a relationship where both partners benefit.

The bacteria in the rumen work best in anaerobic (low oxygen) conditions. As a result, cattle in particular release large quantities of methane gas as a waste product.

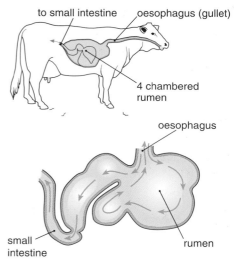

The stomach of ruminants has a special bacteria-containing chamber called the rumen

A cow chewing the cud

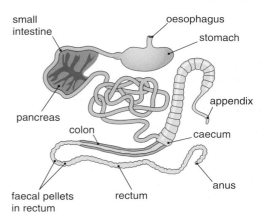

The gut of a rabbit showing the enlarged caecum that contains cellulose-digesting bacteria

► Feeding in invertebrates

We have already seen that mammals have teeth adapted to deal with a wide range of foods. Invertebrates like mussels and mosquitoes don't have teeth. Instead they have mouthparts specially adapted to the food they eat.

A mussel bed

Filter feeding in mussels

Mussels are bivalve molluscs (like the cockle on page 261). They live in the water and feed on microscopic organisms called **plankton**. A current of water is drawn in through a gap between the two shells (or valves). This current is created by the beating of tiny hair-like **cilia**.

(Look on page 74 to see how cilia help to keep the human breathing system clean.)

The current of water now passes over the gills inside the mussel. These gills act like a sieve and trap the plankton. Other cilia now move this trapped food to the mouth of the mussel, from where it enters the digestive system.

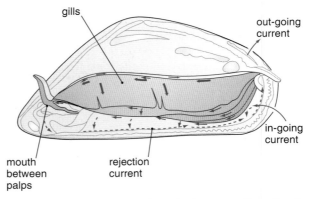

A current carries water containing plankton over the gills of the mussel

Feeding in the honeybee

In the summer you can see honeybees moving from flower to flower.
At each flower they are collecting **nectar**.
This sugary solution is used both as a food source and to make honey.

Like aphids, butterflies and houseflies, the honeybee feeds by sucking fluid (in this case nectar) into its mouth.
It sucks up the nectar through a long hollow tube called a **proboscis** which enables the bee to reach the **nectary** at the base of the flower.

Bees also collect **pollen** which is a source of protein. When the bee visits a flower, pollen grains stick to the hairs on the bee's body.
Bristles on the front legs comb the pollen grains from the body before they are mixed into a paste with some nectar.
This paste is then stored in the hive and eaten when other food is scarce.

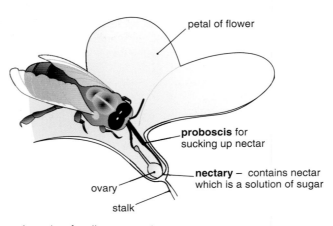

A worker feeding on nectar

A bee collecting pollen

The blood sucking mosquito

The mosquito is also an invertebrate that feeds by sucking, but in this case its mouthparts are adapted for piercing as well as sucking.

Mosquitoes suck sugary liquids, but prior to egg-laying the female *Anopheles* mosquito needs to feed on blood.

It has sharp needle-like mouthparts called **stylets** which can pierce skin and the capillaries beneath. Along side these stylets are two tubes: a food tube and a saliva tube.
These tubes are pushed into the hole made by the stylet. Saliva containing a chemical that prevents blood clotting is pumped into the hole.
The mosquito then uses its throat muscles to draw up blood from the capillary.

This may be a very effective method of feeding, but it is also responsible for the transmission of **malaria** – a disease that kills 2 million people a year. You can find out more about malaria on page 183.

Plasmodium is a parasitic single-celled organism found in the saliva of the *Anopheles* mosquito.

When the mosquito injects saliva into the human bloodstream the parasite goes with it.
It then feeds and reproduces inside red blood cells. The infected cells burst releasing more parasites and causing the characteristic fever associated with malaria.

Malaria is a disease that may result in regular bouts of fever, or in its severest form may cause death within a few days.

Malaria is not the only disease transmitted by blood sucking insects. The tsetse fly also has mouthparts that can pierce human skin. As it is feeding it injects the tiny parasite that causes sleeping sickness.

Like malaria, this disease is common in warm tropical regions such as Africa. Unfortunately countries in these regions tend to be quite poor. This means that they lack the resources to control these diseases. Many of the methods of control involve chemicals, like insecticides or drugs. These chemicals can be expensive, and also the people need to be taught how to use them effectively.

The mosquito uses its sharp stylets to pierce blood vessels.

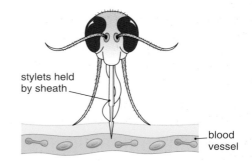

stylets held by sheath

blood vessel

The mosquito uses its sharp stylets to pierce blood cells

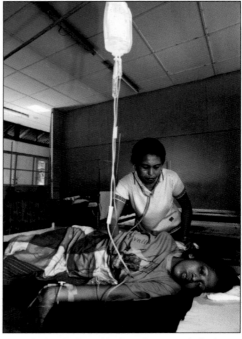

A malaria victim with the characteristic fever

▶ Biology at work : Pictures of the gut

X-rays

How can a doctor see inside your gut without
opening you up?
The answer is to use **X-rays**.

A machine sends a beam of X-rays through your body.
But the X-rays do not pass through dense material
like bone.
If the photographic film on the other side is then
exposed, it goes dark except where your bones are.

But what happens if we want to take pictures
of the gut?
Here there is no dense material.
The doctor gets the patient to drink a liquid that
will not let X-rays through.
The liquid drunk is barium sulphate and it is called
a **barium meal**.
The fluid fills the stomach and intestines so they
show up clearly when X-rayed.
The doctor uses the photograph to see if anything is
wrong with the patient's gut, such as a stomach ulcer.
An ulcer forms if the acid attacks the lining
of the stomach.

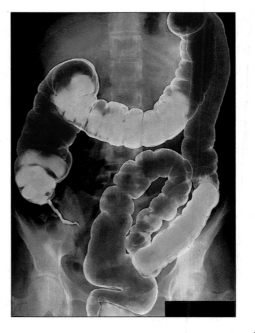

Optical fibres

Doctors use optical fibres to look inside the stomach.
Many optical fibres are held together in a bundle
that goes down the patient's throat.
Light passes down some of the fibres to illuminate
the stomach.
Reflected light passes back up the other fibres to
give the picture.

The doctor may find a stomach ulcer.
If so a laser beam can be sent down to burn
and seal the ulcer.

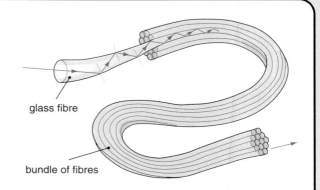

glass fibre

bundle of fibres

Summary

You need a balanced diet if you are to stay healthy.

Proteins are needed for growth.

Carbohydrates and fats are our energy foods.

We can measure the energy that these foods give in kilojoules.

Different people need different amounts of energy depending upon their age, size and activity.

It is important to get the balance right between our energy intake and our energy output.

We only need vitamins and minerals in small amounts but if they are missing we can be very ill. Water and fibre are also important in our diet.

Our teeth are important for digesting our food. We should take good care of them.

Digestion means breaking down large molecules like proteins into small, soluble molecules like amino acids. Chemical digestion involves enzymes.

Different parts of our digestive system have different functions.

In the stomach protease enzymes work best in acid conditions.

In the small intestine, bile from the liver makes conditions alkaline.

When digestion is complete, the soluble food is absorbed into the blood.

Water is absorbed in the large intestine before waste food is passed out of the body.

▶ # Questions

1. Copy and complete:
   a) Starch and sugar are examples of ..... .
   b) Foods rich in .... supply you with a quick source of energy.
   c) .... are body-building foods. They are made up of about 20 different ....
   d) Citrus fruits contain plenty of ..... .
   e) Bran cereal and wholemeal bread contain lots of ..... .
   f) Fats provide the body with a .... of energy.

2. Copy and complete the table of vitamins and minerals:

Nutrient	Rich source	Deficiency disease
	citrus fruits	scurvy
iron		
		goitre
Vit. B$_1$	yeast, cereals	
calcium		
		poor night vision, unhealthy skin

3. The table shows the energy content (in kJ per 100 g) of some common foods. The columns A, B, C and D show the percentage of either protein, fat, carbohydrate or water in each food.

Food	Energy (kJ/100 g)	A (%)	B (%)	C (%)	D (%)
milk	290	3	89	4.5	3.5
butter	3000	0.5	16.5	–	83
potatoes	370	2	82	16	–
beef	1300	25	55	–	20
tuna	700	18	70	–	12

a) Which food has:
   i) the highest energy content
   ii) the lowest energy content?
b) Look carefully at the figures and try to work out which of A, B, C or D is carbohydrate, which is water, which is protein and which is fat. For each choice you make give a reason.
c) Give 2 important food materials which are not in the table, but are essential for a balanced diet.

4. a) Which food in the table below contains
   i)   most protein   ii) least carbohydrate?
   What do you need protein and carbohydrates
   for?

b) Which foods have no fibre?
   What do you need fibre for?

c) Which food gives
   i)   most energy   ii) least energy?

d) Which food has most iron?
   Why do you need iron?

e) Which foods contain no vitamin C?
   Why do you need vitamin C?

f) How much energy is there in
   i)   50 g of milk   ii) 200 g of sausage?

7. Match up each of the parts of the body in the
first column with its function in the second:

a) mouth
b) colon
c) pancreas

d) liver
e) small intestine
f) stomach

1) is very acidic
2) makes bile
3) most food is absorbed
   here
4) food is chewed here
5) makes pancreatic juice
6) most water is absorbed
   here.

Food	Energy (kJ per 100 g)	Protein (%)	Fat (%)	Carbohydrate (%)	Fibre (%)	Iron (mg per 100 g)	Vitamin C (mg per 100 g)
milk	272	3.3	3.8	4.7	0	0.1	2
sausage	1520	10.6	32.1	9.5	0	1.1	0
chicken	599	26.5	4.0	0	0	0.5	0
cabbage	66	1.7	0	2.3	54	0.4	23
watercress	61	2.9	0	0.7	25	1.6	60
apples	196	0.3	0	11.9	20	0.3	5

5. a) Why is enamel the hardest substance in your
       body?

b) What are the 4 main types of teeth?

c) Which teeth are not present in your milk set,
   but present in your permanent set?

d) What causes tooth decay?

6. Look at the diagram of the digestive system:

a) Name the parts labelled A–J.

b) Match the labels on the diagram to these
   functions:
   i)   absorbs a lot of water
   ii)   contains acid
   iii) stores faeces
   iv)   makes bile
   v)   stores bile
   vi)   joins the throat and stomach
   vii) most absorption takes place here
   viii) has no function in humans
   ix)   faeces pass out here
   x)   makes pancreatic juice

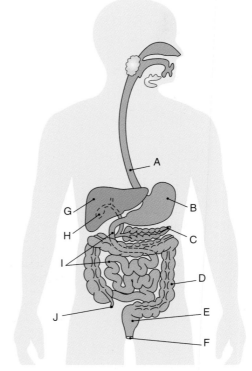

Further questions on page 195.

chapter 5

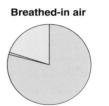

How long can you hold your breath for?
After about a minute it becomes too difficult and –
gasp! – you have to breathe in.
But why is breathing so important to you?

If you look at the pie-charts, they will give you a clue.
They show the proportions of the gases that we breathe.
What do they tell you about the amounts of oxygen that
you breathe in and out?
What do they tell you about the amounts of carbon dioxide
that you breathe in and out?

We use up oxygen in our bodies and produce carbon dioxide.
But why?

Breathed-in air   **Breathed-out air**

☐ oxygen ☐ nitrogen ☐ carbon dioxide

▶ Releasing energy

What happens when we burn a fuel like petrol?
Oxygen is used up and carbon dioxide is made.
The flame gives off a lot of light and heat.

The same sort of thing happens in your body.
Your fuel is glucose from your food.
Oxygen is needed to break the glucose down
and release the energy.

Look at this equation:

glucose	+	oxygen	⟶	carbon dioxide	+	water	+	energy
$C_6H_{12}O_6$		$6\,O_2$		$6\,CO_2$		$6\,H_2O$		

The most important point is that energy is released.

We call this process **respiration**.
Because we need oxygen for it to happen,
it is called **aerobic respiration**.

Burning petrol

▶ Using energy

Your body needs energy for many different things.
Energy is used up:

- working your muscles
- transporting chemicals
- absorbing food (active transport)
- sending messages along nerves
- building cells for growth
- keeping your body temperature constant.

Respiration takes place in **all** our cells **all** the time.

Our cells contain tiny structures called **mitochondria**.
This is where energy is released from glucose.

Muscle cells use up lots of energy.
They have lots of mitochondria.

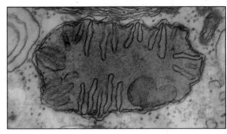

An electron micrograph of a mitochondrion

> **Living things need energy to keep alive.**
> **They transfer chemical energy from the food they eat.**
> **The energy is released to do work during respiration.**
> **You use this energy to keep going.**

Experiment 5.1   Measuring the heat energy from germinating seeds

During respiration a lot of energy is lost as heat.

You can show that heat energy is released as follows:

Set up the 2 thermos flasks as shown.
Use surface-sterilised germinating peas or beans.
Measure the temperature of each flask at the beginning
of the experiment and each day for a week.

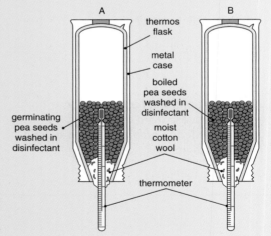

- How was the heat produced in flask A?

- Why was there no rise in temperature in flask B?

  Microbes respire too.
- So why was it important to sterilise the surfaces of
  both sets of peas?

  A thermos flask keeps heat energy in.
- Why was this important in this experiment?

  The cotton wool lets gases pass in and out of
  the flask.
- Why was this important for respiration?

	Day 1	Day 2	Day 3	Day 4	Day 5
flask A (°C)					
flask B (°C)					

▶ Breathing out carbon dioxide

Carbon dioxide is a waste gas made in respiration.
It can become toxic if it builds up in our cells.
The more exercise we do, the faster and deeper
we breathe to get rid of the carbon dioxide.

Experiment 5.2   Testing for carbon dioxide

You can show that you breathe out carbon dioxide.

Breathe out gently through a straw into a test-tube
of lime water.
Carbon dioxide makes lime water go cloudy.

⚠ **eye protection**

Now try doing the same thing, but this time breathe
into hydrogencarbonate indicator in a clean test-tube.
Carbon dioxide changes hydrogencarbonate indicator from
red to yellow.

Respiration for all

All living things carry out respiration.
Animals, plants and bacteria all respire.
So all living things give out carbon dioxide.
You can find out about respiration in plants
on pages 215–16.
You can find out how fish breathe on page 147.

Your teacher may show you this demonstration:

*Demonstration 5.3   To show that germinating seeds release
carbon dioxide during respiration*

Set up the apparatus as shown in the diagram:
A filter pump is used to suck air through
the apparatus.

⚠ **eye protection**

- How long does it take before the lime water
  in boiling-tube C turns cloudy?

- Why did the lime water in boiling-tube C turn cloudy
  before the limewater in boiling-tube B?

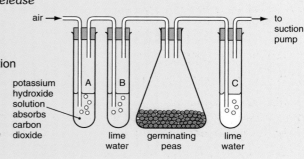

air →

to suction pump

potassium hydroxide solution absorbs carbon dioxide

A   B   C

lime water   germinating peas   lime water

More carbon dioxide out?

Look at the table:

Gas	Inspired air (breathing in)	Expired air (breathing out)
oxygen	21%	16%
carbon dioxide	0.04%	4%
nitrogen	78%	78%
water vapour	variable	saturated

It shows that we breathe out more carbon dioxide
than we breathe in.
How could you prove this is true?

Experiment 5.4   Carbon dioxide in breathed-in and breathed-out air

Set up the apparatus as shown in the diagram:
Breathe gently in and out of the mouth-piece
several times.
- When you breathe in, does the air come in through A
  or through B?
- When you breathe out, does the air go out through A
  or through B?
- In which tube did the lime water turn cloudy first?

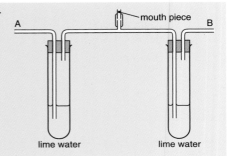

Less oxygen out?

When we breathe in our bodies use some of the
oxygen for respiration.
The rest is breathed back out again.

Our cells use up the oxygen to break down the
glucose and release energy.

The table shows that we breathe out less oxygen
than we breathe in.
How could you prove that this is true?

Experiment 5.5   Oxygen in breathed-in and breathed-out air

Time how long it takes before the candle
goes out in:
i) fresh air
ii) breathed-out air
(you can collect this by breathing out through a
rubber tube as shown in the diagram).

- What does this experiment tell you about
  the amount of oxygen in fresh air and in
  breathed-out air?

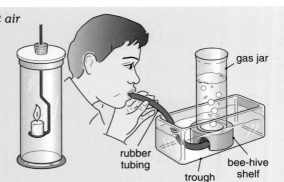

▶ How fast ?

You can measure how fast respiration takes place.
This is the **rate of respiration**.
We measure either the rate at which oxygen is used up,
or the rate at which carbon dioxide is produced.
To do this we use a **respirometer**.

Experiment 5.6   A simple respirometer

You could use the simple respirometer in the diagram :
It will tell you how quickly germinating seeds use
up oxygen.

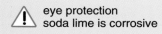
eye protection
soda lime is corrosive

- How do you think it works ?

- What does the soda lime do ?

- Why is it important to keep the apparatus at a
  constant temperature ?

- How could you find out the effects of different
  temperatures on the rate at which oxygen is
  used up by the seeds ?

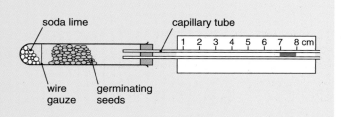

Experiment 5.7   A more accurate respirometer

You can measure the rate of respiration more
accurately with this apparatus :

⚠ eye protection

Put some mealworms or woodlice into the boiling-tube.

Set up the rest of the apparatus as shown.
Be very careful not to touch yourself or the
animals with the soda lime. It is corrosive.

Close the clip and find out how much
the coloured liquid rises in 30 minutes.

Soda lime absorbs carbon dioxide.

- Explain how you think the apparatus works.

- Can you think of a control for the experiment ?

- Why was the boiling-tube kept at a constant temperature ?

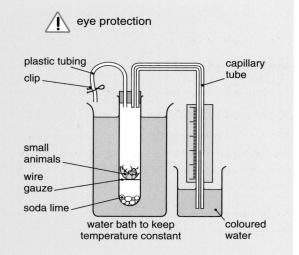

> **Respiration is the release of energy from glucose
> in living cells.**
> **This energy release takes place all the time.**
> **The more energy that is needed, the faster
> the rate of respiration.** .

▶ Your breathing system

You need to breathe in air to get oxygen.
You breathe air out to get rid of carbon dioxide.
We call this **gas exchange**.

In humans it takes place in our lungs.
But there are other important parts of
our breathing system.

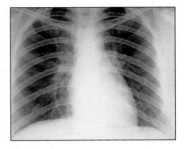

A chest x-ray

Finding your lungs

Where do you think your lungs are?

You'll find them inside your chest or **thorax**.
They are surrounded and protected by your ribs.

Many people don't realise how big their lungs are.
Each of your lungs is as big as a rugby ball.
They fill the whole of your chest space.

Below your lungs is a sheet of muscle called the
diaphragm (dia-fram).
It separates your thorax from your **abdomen** below.

Your diaphragm and ribs help you to breathe.

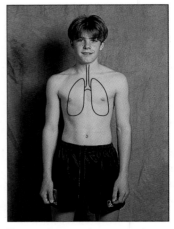

Do you know where your lungs are?

Air-conditioning

Air enters through your nose and mouth.

It then passes down your windpipe or **trachea**.

This first part of your breathing system treats
the air before it reaches your lungs.
Cold, dry and dirty air might damage your lungs so
it is:
- warmed
- moistened
- filtered and cleaned.

The cells lining the nose and trachea make slimy **mucus**.
Dust and germs get trapped in the slime.
The cells have tiny hairs or **cilia** on them.
These beat to carry the mucus up to your nose and throat.
What happens to it then?

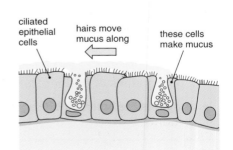

▶ Two-way trip to your lungs

Before going down your windpipe, air enters
your **larynx** (voice-box).
This is sometimes called your Adam's apple.
Can you feel it?

Your larynx contains your vocal cords.
When air blows over these you make sounds.
It's a bit like blowing through a mouth-organ.

You can't breathe and swallow at the same time.
This is because when you swallow, a flap of skin
called the **epiglottis** drops over the opening
to your larynx.
This stops any food from going down your windpipe.

Air is sucked down your windpipe.
So why doesn't it collapse?

It is kept open by rings of **cartilage**.
The cartilage rings are C-shaped.

Your windpipe branches many times,
a bit like a tree.
The branches end up at tiny air sacs called
alveoli (al-v-o-lee).
It is here that gas exchange takes place.

Your lungs are spongy.
They are surrounded by
the **pleural membrane**.
This makes a slippery fluid.
How do you think that this helps when
your lungs rub against your ribs?

Your ribs protect your lungs.
They also move during breathing.
Can you find the muscles that
move your ribs?
Look at the diagram to find their name.

Your diaphragm forms the floor of
your thorax.
What is it made of?

The diaphragm also moves
during breathing.

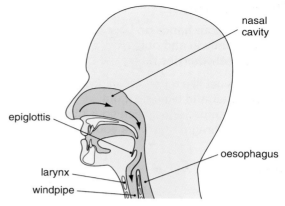

The pathway of air to your windpipe

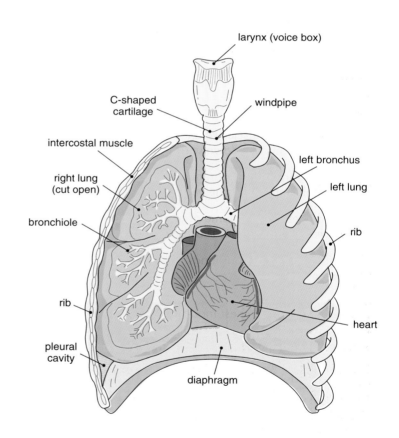

▶ Muscles without oxygen

Your muscles need oxygen and sugar to respire aerobically.
These are brought to your muscles by your blood system.

During vigorous exercise your heart and lungs can not get enough oxygen to your muscles quickly enough.
When this happens your muscles start to carry out anaerobic respiration.
Glucose is broken down to **lactic acid**, when there is no oxygen

glucose ⟶ lactic acid + energy

Lactic acid can slowly poison your muscles.
This causes cramp.
We must get rid of the lactic acid.

Have you noticed that we carry on breathing faster and deeper after vigorous exercise?
The extra oxygen breaks down the lactic acid.
This extra oxygen is called the **oxygen debt**.
Our oxygen debt builds up after we exercise hard.
It has to be 'paid back' straight away.

Sprinters build up lactic acid in their muscles.
They often hold their breath during a 100 metre race.
Afterwards they need about 7 litres of oxygen to get rid of the lactic acid.
They breathe deeply after the race in order to repay their oxygen debt.

Long-distance runners could not stand such a build up of lactic acid.
They run at a much slower speed.
They build up some lactic acid in the early stages of the race, but get rid of this while they are running.

Anaerobic respiration produces less energy than aerobic respiration.
Without oxygen, glucose is only partly broken down into alcohol or lactic acid.
A lot of energy remains in the molecules of alcohol and lactic acid.

	Energy released (kJ/g glucose)
aerobic respiration	16.1
fermentation by yeast	1.2
anaerobic respiration in muscle	0.8

▷ Smoking and health

Smoking can damage your health.
It can cause diseases of the lungs and heart.
It is estimated that every cigarette shortens
a smoker's life by 14 minutes.
Most heavy smokers die from diseases caused by
smoking.

Toxic chemicals

Tobacco smoke contains lots of chemicals.
Many of these are harmful :

Nicotine is a drug.
It acts upon the brain and nervous system.
Smokers become addicted to it.
That's why they find it so hard to give up.
Nicotine makes the heart beat faster and
narrows the blood vessels.
This can cause heart disease.

Tar collects in the lungs when the smoke cools.
It contains over a thousand chemicals.
Some of these can cause cancer.
Tar also irritates your air passages and makes
them narrower. It gives you 'smoker's cough'.

Carbon monoxide is a poisonous gas.
It is taken up by the blood instead of oxygen.
So carbon monoxide stops the blood carrying
as much oxygen as it should.

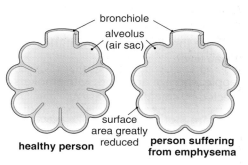

No wonder smokers cough.

The tar and discharge that collects in the lungs
of an average smoker.

Diseases caused by smoking

Bronchitis is when the air passages become inflamed.
The cilia lining your air passages stop beating.
So the mucus, dirt and bacteria stay in your lungs.

Emphysema is when chemicals in tobacco smoke
weaken the walls of the air sacs.
Coughing can burst them damaging the lung tissue.
Your lungs can not take in enough oxygen and you
get breathless.

bronchiole

alveolus
(air sac)

surface
area greatly
reduced

healthy person

person suffering
from emphysema

*Someone with emphysema can get very short
of breath. Their air sacs have less surface
area. So there is less gas exchange,*

Summary

Respiration involves the breakdown of glucose to release energy.

Aerobic respiration uses oxygen to do this.

Carbon dioxide is made as a waste product and must be removed.

The rate of respiration can be measured with a respirometer.

Air entering your lungs is warmed, cleaned and moistened.

Exchange of gases takes place in the air sacs.

Your intercostal muscles and diaphragm are used in breathing.

Your breathing rate is controlled by your brain and increases with exercise.

Yeast and muscles are able to respire without oxygen.

Smoking can seriously damage your health.

▶ Questions

1. Copy and complete:
   Respiration takes place in all our . . . . . The fuel for respiration is . . . . . It is broken down to release . . . . . Also produced are water and the waste gas . . . . When it takes place in the presence of . . . . we call it . . . . respiration. These reactions take place in every living cell, inside tiny structures called . . . . .

2. Look at the apparatus used in this experiment:

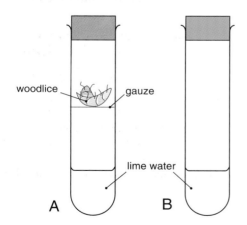

woodlice · gauze

lime water

A   B

a) Suggest a title for the experiment.
b) After 12 hours the tubes were examined. What results would you expect?
c) What was tube B for?
d) What would have happened if the lime water had been replaced by bicarbonate indicator?

3. Give an explanation for each of the following:
   a) When you breathe on a cold window, water droplets form.
   b) Breathed-out air turns lime water cloudy quicker than breathed-in air.
   c) Alveoli (air sacs) are very thin and have a large surface area.
   d) Plants give out carbon dioxide in the dark, but take it up in the light.

4. Look at the diagram of the respirometer:

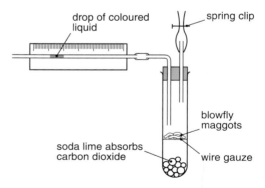

drop of coloured liquid   spring clip

soda lime absorbs carbon dioxide

blowfly maggots

wire gauze

a) In which direction will the drop of coloured liquid move?
b) What makes this happen?
c) Why must the spring clip be closed at the start of the experiment?
d) You are given identical sets of this apparatus. How could you investigate the effects of temperature on the rate of respiration of the maggots?

5. The diagram shows the human breathing system:

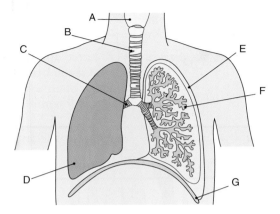

a) Write out letters A to G with the correct labels.
b) Match parts A to G with these descriptions:
  i)   sheet of muscle forming the floor of the chest
  ii)   one of these enters each lung
  iii) contains the vocal cords
  iv)   flexible tube kept open by rings of cartilage
  v)   where exchange of gases takes place
  vi)   a slippery membrane
  vii) made of spongy tissue and found in the chest.

6. The diagram shows some alveoli (air sacs) and a blood capillary in the lung.

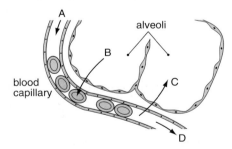

a) Which arrow shows:
  i)   blood high in oxygen
  ii)   blood low in oxygen
  iii) the diffusion of oxygen
  iv)   the diffusion of carbon dioxide?
b) Give 2 features of the air sacs that help gas exchange.

7. Write down a function for each of the following:
a) the C-shaped rings of cartilage in the trachea
b) the epiglottis
c) the pleural membrane
d) the mucus in the windpipe
e) the diaphragm.

8. The apparatus was set up as shown:

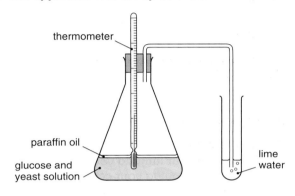

The flask was kept at 35 °C. After 15 minutes the lime water had turned cloudy.
a) What gas was given off?
b) What process produced the gas?
c) Why was the flask kept at a constant 35 °C?
d) What was the paraffin oil for?
e) Suggest a control for this experiment.

9. The table shows the units of lactic acid produced in the leg muscles of an athlete.

Time (minutes)	0	10	20	30	40	50	60	70	80
Lactic acid units	0	1	7	12	9	6	3	1	1

a) Draw a line-graph using the data.
b) When did the lactic acid reach a maximum? Try to explain this.
c) What happened to the lactic acid after this time? Try to explain this.

Further questions on page 195.

▶ A double circulation

Your heart is divided into two halves: the **right** and the **left**.
The blood in the right side does not mix with the blood in the left side.
So your circulation is really in two parts:

- The right side of your heart pumps blood to
  your lungs and then back to the heart again.
  How does the blood change when it gets to your lungs?
  What does it pick up? What does it drop off?

  In your lungs the blood picks up oxygen.
  We say that it becomes **oxygenated**.
  The blood also gets rid of carbon dioxide.

- The left side of your heart pumps blood to the
  rest of your body and then back to the heart again.
  How does the blood change when it gets to your body cells?
  What does it drop off? What does it pick up?

  The blood gives up its oxygen to your body cells.
  We say that it becomes **deoxygenated**.
  Carbon dioxide passes into the blood from the body cells.

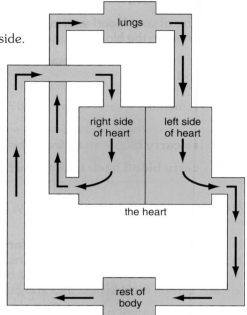

Look at the diagram:

How many times does the blood pass through the heart on one circuit
of the body?

That's why it's called a **double** circulation.

William Harvey, was an English physician.
He used his knowledge of anatomy to make a unique
discovery about the circulation of blood around the body.
As a result of careful observation and carrying out
experiments,he was able to explain how blood moves
around the body in a circle – travelling from the left
side of the heart in arteries and then back to the right
side of the heart in veins.

In 1623, he published his book *On the Motions of the
Heart and Blood*. In it he showed how the evidence from his
experiments disproved many of the long-held ideas of the time.

Harvey also predicted that there were thousands of tiny
capillaries connecting arteries to veins, despite being unable
to see them.

Why was Harvey unable to observe blood capillaries?

*Harvey demonstrating the action of valves to a
group of physicians in London*

▶ Arteries

When your heart muscles contract they force
the blood into your arteries.
What do you think the pressure of blood is like
in arteries?
Each beat of the heart pumps the blood along
under high pressure.

The artery walls are elastic and stretch to take the blood.
Then they contract and bounce back to force the blood along.
This bouncing back can be felt as a **'pulse'** as the blood
flows through.

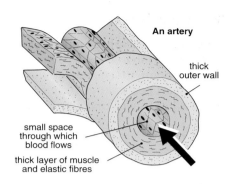

An artery

thick outer wall

small space through which blood flows

thick layer of muscle and elastic fibres

Experiment 6.1   Taking your pulse

Can you feel your pulse?
Try to feel an artery at your wrist or at the side
of your neck.

The number of pulses per minute shows how fast
your heart is beating.

How does your pulse rate compare with other people's?

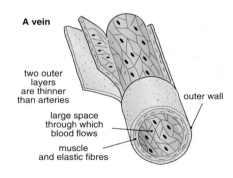

▶ Veins

Capillaries join up to eventually form veins.
Veins are wider than arteries and have thinner walls.
The pressure inside veins is much lower.
So the blood flows much more slowly in them.
The blood is often squeezed along by your muscles.

The flow of blood in veins is helped by **valves**.
Valves are like double doors that will only open in
one direction.
If you try to go back in the other direction the
doors won't open.
Valves stop your blood from flowing backwards.

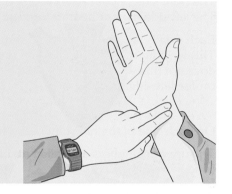

A vein

two outer layers are thinner than arteries

outer wall

large space through which blood flows

muscle and elastic fibres

Valves open to let the blood flow towards the heart

Valves close to stop blood flowing backwards

▶ Control of heartbeat

If the heart was removed from the body it would
continue to beat!
What does this tell you about what makes the heart beat?

The beating of the heart is controlled by the **pacemaker**.
This is a group of cells in the right atrium.
The pacemaker sends electrical messages to the
heart muscle.
These messages stimulate the heart muscle to contract.

The pacemaker also receives information from the brain.
Some nerves slow down the heart rate, others speed it up.
So the brain is able to adjust the heart rate to the needs
of the body.

What might cause your heart to beat faster?

During exercise you need to get more oxygen and
food to your muscles.
Your heart beats faster to help you to do this.
What substances need to be taken away from
the muscles during exercise?

You can find out about the artificial pacemaker
on page 102.

Throb,
throb,
throb.

The heart's blood supply

Despite being full of blood, the heart needs a blood
supply of its own.

Coronary arteries carry oxygenated blood to
the heart muscle.

Why does the heart muscle need a good oxygen supply?

What else does it need from the blood to give energy?

What might happen if a coronary artery became blocked?

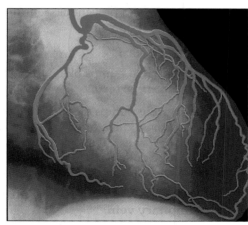

Angiogram of the coronary arteries

▶ Heart disease

Heart disease causes a quarter of all deaths in Britain.
It is the biggest single killer of middle-aged men in
the developed world.

You need a healthy heart to pump blood around your body.
Heart muscle needs food and oxygen for it to keep
contracting.
These get to the heart in the **coronary arteries**.
If these get blocked then it can cause **heart disease**.

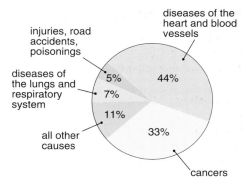

Causes of death in people under 75 in the
UK (total deaths = 267 500)

Slowing the flow

Healthy arteries have a smooth lining.
They let the blood flow through easily.

But saturated animal fats like *cholesterol* can stick to the walls.
This can narrow the artery and slow down the flow of blood.

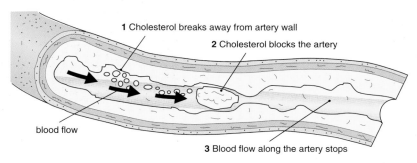

1 Cholesterol breaks away from artery wall
2 Cholesterol blocks the artery
blood flow
3 Blood flow along the artery stops

The artery walls can become rough.
This can cause the blood to clot and block the vessel.
The blockage is called a **thrombosis**.

Narrowing of the coronary artery causes serious problems:

- If the coronary artery gets partly blocked it can cause chest pains,
  especially if activity or emotion makes the heart work harder.
  This is called **angina**.
  It is caused by not enough oxygen getting to the heart muscle.
  Angina should act as a warning to the sufferer.

- A total blockage or thrombosis can cause a heart attack.
  The supply of oxygen is cut off.
  It causes a severe pain in the chest.
  The affected part of the heart is damaged.

The heart may stop beating altogether – this is called
cardiac arrest.
Death will follow unless the heart starts beating again
within minutes.

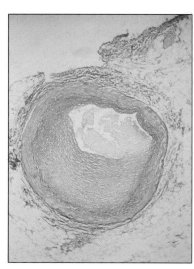

A blocked artery in section

Risk factors

These are things that are thought to increase the
chances of getting heart disease.
Some of them you can't avoid like :

- **Inherited genes** – heart disease tends to run in families.
- **Age** – the chances of getting heart disease increase with age.
- **Sex** – men are more likely to get heart disease than women.

Some of the other risk factors you can do something about are :

- **Eating fatty foods** – these can increase cholesterol
  in the blood.
- **Being over-weight**.
- **Smoking**.
- **Taking little or no exercise**.

Avoiding heart disease

- **Take care of your diet :**
  - Eat more poultry and fish – they are less fatty.
  - Cut down on fried foods.
  - Eat less red meat.
  - Eat more fresh fruit and vegetables.

- **Take some regular exercise**.

- **Do not smoke**.

Experiment 6.2   Dissecting a sheep's heart

Look at a dissected sheep's heart.
(The heart is cut open by two vertical cuts,
one through the left atrium and ventricle,
the other through the right atrium and ventricle.)

Notice the differences in the thickness of the walls.

If the blood vessels are still intact, try to find out
which is which.

Look for the coronary vessels on the surface.

Look inside for :
- the valves between the atria and the ventricles,
- the valves at the base of the pulmonary artery and aorta.

Try running a stream of water against the valves.
Do they open ? How does this help the heart ?

Wash your hands with soap and water
when you have finished.

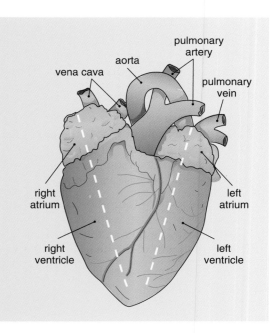

▶ Your blood

If someone has an accident or a major operation,
they often lose a lot of blood.
The blood is vital for life.
It has to be replaced quickly.
The person has to have a **blood transfusion**.

So why is your blood so important to you?

Your blood does two important things:

- it transports things from one part of your body to another.
- it helps to protect your body from disease.

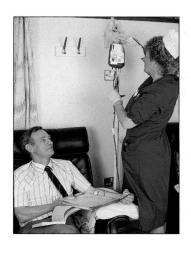

What's blood made of?

You have about 5 litres of blood in your body.
That's a bucket full.
Blood looks like a red liquid, but there's more to it than that.

What happens if you leave a sample of blood to stand?

Look at the test-tubes:
Can you see it has separated into two parts?

- The yellow liquid is called **plasma**.
  It is mainly water with chemicals dissolved in it.
  Some of these are:

  - Food, such as sugars, amino acids, vitamins and minerals.

  - Chemical waste like urea.

  - Blood proteins like antibodies.

  - Hormones – chemicals that control things like our growth.

- At the bottom of the test-tube the cells
  have settled out.

  There are three main types of blood cells:

  - Red cells have no nucleus.
    They look red because they have a red pigment
    called **haemoglobin**.

  - White cells do have a nucleus.
    There are two main types:
    lymphocytes and **phagocytes**.
    White cells do not have haemoglobin
    so they don't look red.

  - **Platelets** are tiny bits of cells.

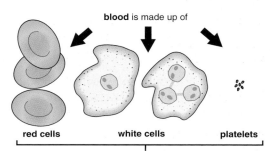

blood is made up of

red cells   white cells   platelets

floating in a yellow watery liquid called **plasma**

▶ Red cells

There are about a million red cells in each drop of blood.
They are made in the bone marrow.

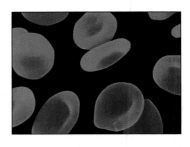

Red cells carry oxygen.
How does their shape help them to do this?

Red cells are disc-shaped with the middle pushed in.
They have a large surface area to volume ratio.
This helps them to absorb a lot of oxygen.

Red cells have no nucleus.
Instead the cell is filled with **haemoglobin**.
This is a special protein that contains iron.
You must have enough iron in your diet to make
enough haemoglobin for your red cells.

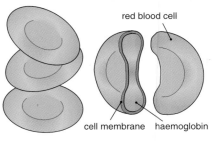

red blood cell

cell membrane   haemoglobin

Haemoglobin combines easily with oxygen.
If forms **oxyhaemoglobin**.

Haemoglobin + oxygen ⟶ oxyhaemoglobin

Look at the diagram:
Where does oxyhaemoglobin form?
Where does oxyhaemoglobin break down to give
oxygen and haemoglobin?

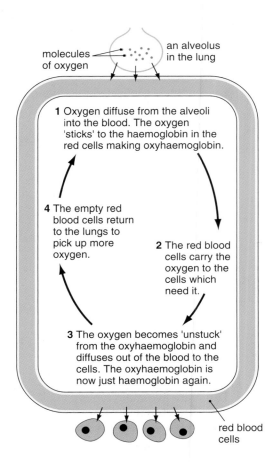

molecules of oxygen — an alveolus in the lung

1 Oxygen diffuse from the alveoli into the blood. The oxygen 'sticks' to the haemoglobin in the red cells making oxyhaemoglobin.

4 The empty red blood cells return to the lungs to pick up more oxygen.

2 The red blood cells carry the oxygen to the cells which need it.

3 The oxygen becomes 'unstuck' from the oxyhaemoglobin and diffuses out of the blood to the cells. The oxyhaemoglobin is now just haemoglobin again.

red blood cells

Demonstration 6.3   Transporting gases in the blood

Your teacher will give you some blood that is safe to use.
Pour equal amounts into two boiling-tubes A and B.
Bubble oxygen through tube A and carbon dioxide
through tube B.

- Why does the blood in A go bright red?

- Does the blood in tube B have less oxygen?

Now try bubbling oxygen through the blood in tube B
and carbon dioxide through the blood in tube A.
Try to explain your observations.
Wash your hands with soap and water
when you have finished.

CO_2 too!

The red cells also carry some carbon dioxide.
But most of it is carried dissolved in the plasma.

Where do you think carbon dioxide *enters* the blood?
Where do you think carbon dioxide *leaves* the blood?

► White cells

The white cells fight disease.
There are far fewer of them than red cells.
They also look different.
Can you see how they are different?

White cells are not disc-shaped.
They do not have haemoglobin.
They do have a nucleus.

Like red cells, the white cells are made in the bone marrow.
Their job is to protect the body from any germs that
get into the blood.
The two types of white cells do this in different ways.

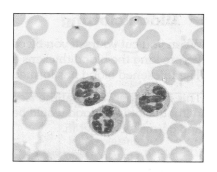

Lymphocytes

When a bacterium or virus enters the body the white cells
recognise that it is 'foreign' and should not be there.
The lymphocytes make chemicals called **antibodies**.
These attack the germs in a number of ways:
- They make them stick together.
- They dissolve them.
- They destroy the toxins (poisons) that the germs make.

After you have had a disease the antibodies stay in your blood.
They make you **immune** to the disease.
There is a different antibody for each type of germ.
You can learn more about immunity in Chapter 11.

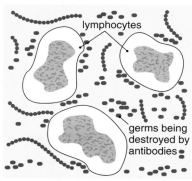

lymphocytes

germs being
destroyed by
antibodies

Phagocytes

These are the 'cell-eaters'. They swallow up germs and take
them into the cell. They then digest them and kill them.

When germs invade the body white cells move towards them.
They can squeeze through capillary walls.

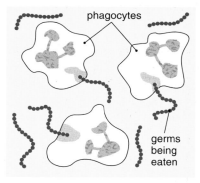

phagocytes

germs
being
eaten

Experiment 6.4   Making a blood smear
Your teacher will give you some blood that is safe to use.

Put a few drops on one end of a microscope slide.
Use another slide to draw the blood over the surface.
This gives a **blood smear**.

When it is dry put a few drops of Leishman's stain
on the smear. After 5 minutes wash the stain off.

When it is dry, look at your slide under the microscope.
Identify and draw any white blood cells.

When you have finished, dispose of your slide
into a beaker of disinfectant.

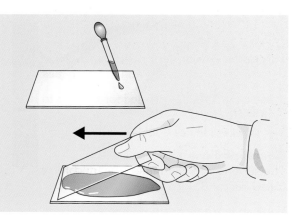

▶ Biology at work : Artificial pacemaker and blood pressure

Artificial pacemaker

Disease and ageing can affect the pacemaker in the heart.
The heartbeat can become too slow.
The artificial pacemaker works by mimicking the natural
pacemaker in the heart.

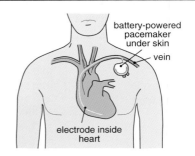

The artificial pacemaker consists of a pulse generator and two
leads or electrodes.
It can be implanted under the patient's skin, on the chest wall.
The electrodes are connected to the right atrium and
right ventricle through a vein.
Each electrode can sense the electrical activity of the heart muscle.

If the heart misses a beat, the artificial pacemaker generates
small electrical impulses.
These stimulate the atria and ventricles telling them to contract.

Blood pressure

The pumping heart produces a high pressure in your arteries.
We call this the **blood pressure**.
It rises if you do anything to make your heart beat faster,
or if the arteries become narrower.

Constant high blood pressure is harmful.
It puts a strain on the heart and makes it work harder.
It can also cause an artery to burst open.
If this happens in the brain it can cause a **stroke**.
A stroke can leave someone partly paralysed and
unable to speak. Even worse, it can kill them.

The causes of high blood pressure are not fully understood.
But things that can affect it include stress and tension,
over-eating, lack of exercise, smoking and drinking too
much alcohol.

Measuring someone's blood pressure

The blood pressure can be measured with this instrument :
It measures the blood pressure when the heart contracts
and when it relaxes.
The first figure is put over the second to give a fraction.
A healthy young adult's blood pressure is about 120/75 mmHg.

Biology at work : Blood transfusions

People who are ill or injured may need a blood transfusion.
The blood drains into a vein in the arm from a plastic bag.

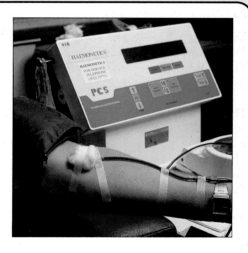

But not just any blood will do.
If someone is given blood of the wrong group it may make
their red cells stick together.
This can be fatal if blood vessels become blocked.

The main **blood groups** are called **A, B, AB** and **O**.

Your blood group is determined by the **antigens** present
on your red cells.

There are two types of antigens : **A** and **B**.

People with blood group **A** have **A** antigens only.

People with blood group **B** have **B** antigens only.

Blood group **AB** has both **A** and **B** antigens.

Blood group **O** has neither **A** nor **B** antigens.

In the plasma there are **antibodies**.
But these antibodies do not attack antigens on their *own* red cells.

For instance, the antibodies in blood group A plasma do not attack
the A antigens on blood group A red cells, but they will attack B antigens.

The antibodies in group B plasma do not attack the B antigens on
blood group B red cells, but they will attack A antigens.

The antibodies in group AB plasma do not attack the A or B antigens
on blood group AB cells.

The antibodies in group O will attack both A and B antigens.

The table shows which groups are safe for transfusion :

Group	Can donate to	Can receive from
A	A and AB	A and O
B	B and AB	B and O
AB	AB	all groups
O	all groups	O

To which blood groups can group O donate their blood ?
Group O people are called universal donors.

From which blood groups can group AB receive blood ?
Group AB people are called universal recipients.

Summary

- Larger animals need a transport system to circulate chemicals around the body.

- Arteries carry the blood to the body cells. Veins return blood to the heart.

- Capillaries link up arteries and veins.

- Chemicals are exchanged between the blood and the body cells across capillaries.

- The heart is our muscular pump that keeps our blood circulating.
  Both sides of the heart contract and relax at the same time.

- The blood is made up of plasma, red cells, white cells and platelets.
  Red cells carry oxygen around the body.
  White cells protect us from germs.
  Platelets are involved in the process of blood clotting.
  The plasma transports carbon dioxide, dissolved food, urea, hormones and blood proteins.

- Tissue fluid leaks out of the blood at capillaries. It enables exchange of materials to take place efficiently.

▶ Questions

1. Copy and complete:
   Blood is pumped around the body by a muscular . . . . .
   Blood travels away from the heart in . . . . .
   These contract and . . . . the blood along. This can be felt as a . . . . .
   Blood returns to the heart in the . . . . . These have . . . . walls than arteries.
   Blood is prevented from flowing backwards in them by . . . . .

2. Look at the diagram of the blood:

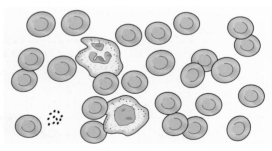

   a) Name 3 ways in which the white blood cells are different from the red blood cells.
   b) Name 2 things about red cells that adapt them for carrying oxygen.
   c) What are the 2 types of white cell? Explain how they act to protect the body from disease.

3. Look at the diagram of the human heart in section:

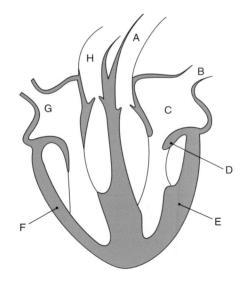

   a) Name the parts labelled A to H.
   b) Why do you think that E is thicker than F?
   c) What is the function of D?
   d) Which side of the heart carries oxygenated blood?

4. Look at the diagram of the heart:

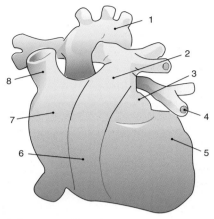

a) Label the parts 1 to 8.
b) Which 2 blood vessels in the diagram carry oxygenated blood?
c) In which blood vessel is the blood under the greatest pressure?
d) Which part of the heart contracts to send blood to the lungs?

5. a) What happens to the heart during:
   i) diastole   ii) systole
b) Explain how the heart is able to control the actions in i) and ii) above.

6. The graph shows the change in pressure in the ventricles during a heartbeat.

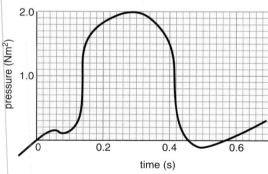

a) What is the maximum pressure in the ventricles?
b) How are the ventricles able to produce this high pressure?
c) Why is this important?
d) At what time is the pressure falling most rapidly?
e) What is causing this drop in pressure?

7. The diagram shows a blood capillary lying next to some muscle cells:

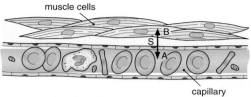

a) What fluid is found in S?
b) Name 2 substances that would pass from A to B.
c) Name 2 substances that would pass from B to A.
d) What is the capillary wall like to enable this to happen?

8. Copy and complete the table:

Arteries	Capillaries	Veins
Carry blood .... from the heart	Connect .... and	Carry blood .... the heart
Have a .... wall	Walls are very	Have a .... wall
Blood flows through at .... pressure	Low pressure allows exchange of materials	Blood flows through at .... pressure
No	No	Valves stop backflow of blood

9. At high altitude there is less oxygen in the air. People who live at altitude make more red cells to get what oxygen they can from the air. The table shows the parts of the blood of 3 people:

	Person A	Person B	Person C
red cells (mm³)	7 500 000	5 000 000	2 000 000
white cells (mm³)	5000	6 000	5 000
platelets (mm³)	250 000	255 000	500

a) Which person lives at high altitude? Give a reason for your choice.
b) Which person is suffering from anaemia (lack of iron)? Give a reason for your choice.
c) Which person has blood that will not clot properly? Give a reason for your choice.

Further questions on page 197.

Homeostasis

chapter 7

Have you ever cooked something in an oven?

You turn the dial to the temperature that you want.
When it reaches that temperature, you put in whatever you are cooking.
You don't have to re-adjust the temperature.
It keeps more or less the same.

How do you think that this happens?

Inside the oven there is a **thermostat**.
It keeps the oven at the temperature you want.

If the thermostat detects that the oven is getting too hot, it switches the heater off.
The oven temperature drops.

If the temperature falls too low then the thermostat switches the heater back on again.
The oven temperature rises again.

This is an example of **feedback**.
Information about the oven temperature is fed back to the thermostat.
It acts by either switching the heater on or off.

There are feedback systems at work in your body.

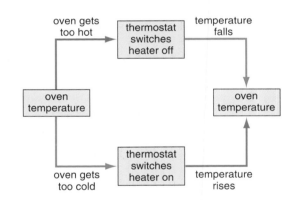

Keeping things steady

Many chemical reactions are going on inside your body.
Molecules are being built up and broken down in your cells.
Can you remember what controls these reactions?

Enzymes work best in particular conditions.
Can you remember what they are?

Any slight change in the conditions can slow down or stop the enzyme from working.
It is important that things like temperature, pH and water content are kept as steady as possible.

▶ Controlling conditions

Keeping conditions steady inside the body
is called **homeostasis**.
Which part of the body do you think acts as
the thermostat?

The brain has overall control of our body
processes.
When blood flows through the brain, it checks:
- the temperature,
- the concentration of chemicals, such as
  carbon dioxide.

So what happens if the temperature of the blood
reaching the brain is too high?
It sends out messages along nerves to parts of
the body that lower our temperature. For instance,
we start to sweat.

Can you guess what happens if we get too cold?
The brain detects the blood temperature again.
This time it sends out messages along nerves to
parts of the body that raise our temperature.
So this time we would stop sweating.

The control of body temperature is an example
of homeostasis.
Our blood is providing the feedback to our brain.

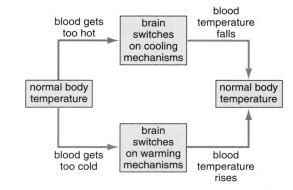

Exercise makes us sweat

▶ Other control systems

The best temperature for the body is 37 °C.
But what about other conditions?

- Our **blood sugar** level has to be kept
  constant.
  It has to be carefully controlled by our
  liver and pancreas.

- Our **water level** is controlled by our
  kidneys.

- The **pH** of our blood is kept constant at 7.4.
  Our kidneys control this by getting rid of
  excess ions.

- The **carbon dioxide** concentration of the
  blood is controlled by our lungs.

All these things rely on feedback if they are
to be kept constant.

The brain controls many conditions in the body

▷ Controlling blood sugar

Your body cells need glucose for energy.
They need it in controlled amounts.

What happens when you eat a high carbohydrate meal ?
Your blood glucose can go up 20 times.
But it does not stay high.

Special cells in your **pancreas** detect
the high glucose level in your blood.
The pancreas makes a hormone called **insulin**.
The insulin tells the liver to take glucose out
of your blood.
It is changed into **glycogen** in the liver.
So insulin **lowers** your blood glucose level
back to normal.

A high-carbohydrate meal

What happens when you run a race or carry out
some other type of exercise ?
Your muscles use up lots of glucose.
Your blood sugar level falls.
But it does not keep falling.

This time your pancreas makes another hormone
called **glucagon**.
When this gets into your blood, it travels to your liver.
Glucagon tells the liver to break the glycogen down
to glucose again.
The glucose is released into the blood.
So glucagon **raises** your blood sugar level back
to normal.

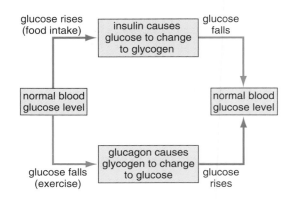

Built-in control

In this case, blood sugar level is controlled by the pancreas.
It **monitors** the glucose level in the blood.

As a result of the feedback that it gets, it either:

• makes insulin to decrease the blood sugar, **or**
• makes glucagon to increase the blood sugar.

Insulin and glucagon are important hormones.
They act by switching off or switching on
the supply of glucose.

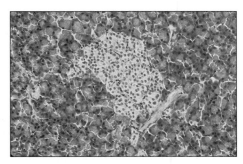

These are pancreas cells.
The ones in the middle make insulin and
glucagon.

▶ Your skin

Your skin has many important jobs:

- it protects your body from damage,
- it stops germs getting in,
- it stops too much water loss,
- it lets you feel touch, pain, temperature and pressure,
- it helps keep your body temperature constant.

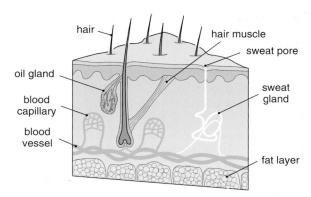

A section of the skin

▶ Hot or cold?

We are **warm-blooded**.
This means that we can keep our body temperature constant all the time.
On a cold winter's day or in the hot summer, our body temperature stays around 37 °C,

Cold-blooded animals like lizards can't do this.
On a hot day their body temperature is high.
On a cold day their body temperature is low.
Cold-blooded animals are inactive in winter because their body temperature is too low.

Many warm-blooded animals like us have a layer of fat beneath their skin.
This helps to insulate their body.
Animals like seals and polar bears have a very thick layer of fat.
Why do you think this is?

A hair-raising experience

Many warm-blooded animals have fur or hair.
This traps a layer of air close to the skin.
Air is a poor conductor of heat.
So it cuts down the amount of heat lost.

In cold weather the hairs stand up.
They do this when the hair muscles contract.
This traps a thicker layer of air.
So it cuts down even more on heat loss.

In hot weather the hairs lie flat.
The hair muscles are now relaxing.
Less air is trapped close to the skin.
So more heat is lost by radiation.

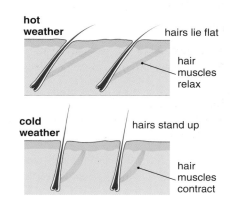

▶ Controlling body temperature

No matter what the weather is like, your body temperature
stays at 37 °C – unless you have a fever.
Your brain monitors the temperature of the blood
running through it.
Nerves bring information to the brain about the temperature
of your skin.
Your skin helps you to keep your body temperature constant.

When it's hot :

What is your skin like when it is hot?
Why do you sweat and look red-faced?

- **Blood vessels** at your skin surface widen.
  They allow more blood to flow to the surface.
  So more heat is lost by radiation.

- **Sweat glands** in your skin make sweat.
  The sweat evaporates and this cools you down.

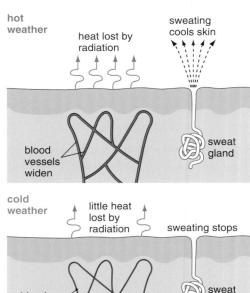

Getting colder :

What is your skin like when it gets cold?
Why do you look pale and shiver?

- **Blood vessels** at your skin surface close up.
  They cut down the flow of blood to the surface.
  So less heat is lost by radiation.

- **Sweat glands** stop making sweat.

- **Shivering**
  Your muscles start to contract quickly.
  This produces extra heat that warms your body.

Hypothermia

This is a gradual cooling of the body.
Eventually the temperature deep inside
your body will also drop.
A drop of 2 °C starts to affect the brain.
Body movements and speech start to slow down.
The person may go into a coma and eventually die.

Why do you think that babies and old people are
particularly at risk?
Why do you think a hot meal and warm clothes
would help?

Damp clothes and cold winds can also cause hypothermia.
Why do you think that pot-holers and climbers might
be at risk?

▶ Excretion

Chemical reactions in your body cells produce waste. This waste includes carbon dioxide and urea.

These chemical wastes have to be removed. Otherwise they would poison us.

Removing waste made in our cells is called **excretion**.

What are the organs that remove carbon dioxide?

If your lungs did not excrete carbon dioxide you would not survive long. Why not?

Your body cannot store excess amino acids. So they are broken down in the liver to make a waste chemical called **urea**.

This is called **deamination**.

The urea is taken from the liver to the kidneys. The kidneys excrete the urea.

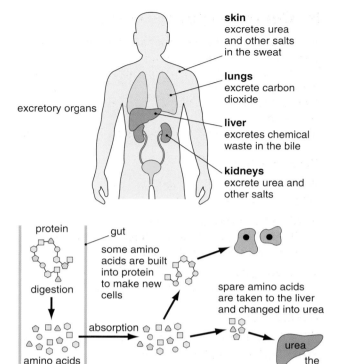

skin excretes urea and other salts in the sweat

lungs excrete carbon dioxide

liver excretes chemical waste in the bile

kidneys excrete urea and other salts

excretory organs

protein

gut

digestion

amino acids

absorption

some amino acids are built into protein to make new cells

spare amino acids are taken to the liver and changed into urea

urea

the liver

▶ Your kidneys

Do you know where your kidneys are?

They are at the back of your body. Try putting your hands on your hips. Your kidneys should be where your thumbs are.

Waste chemicals like urea are carried to your kidneys in the blood. The kidneys take these chemicals out of the blood as it flows through them. They are then excreted as **urine**. So your kidneys 'clean' your blood.

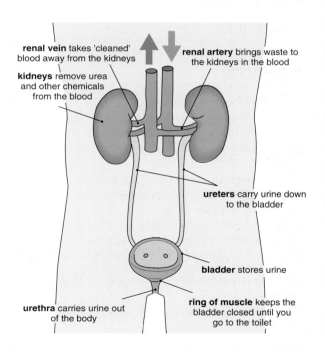

renal vein takes 'cleaned' blood away from the kidneys

renal artery brings waste to the kidneys in the blood

kidneys remove urea and other chemicals from the blood

ureters carry urine down to the bladder

bladder stores urine

urethra carries urine out of the body

ring of muscle keeps the bladder closed until you go to the toilet

▶ Inside the kidneys

If you cut open a kidney lengthways, you can see what is inside.

You should be able to make out 2 areas:
a dark outer area – the **cortex**
and a light inner one – the **medulla**.

Inside each kidney are thousands of tiny tubes called **nephrons**.
These **filter** your blood and remove waste chemicals.
The filtering is done in the outer area.

The waste chemicals are turned into urine.
This drains down the ureter to the bladder.

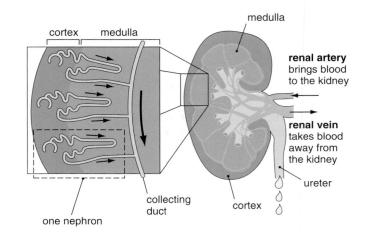

▶ How the kidneys work

Blood is brought to each kidney in the renal artery.
It contains a lot of waste chemicals like urea.

The renal artery branches many times.
Each branch ends in a bunch of capillaries called a **glomerulus**.

The glomerulus is inside part of the nephron called the **Bowman's capsule.**

The capillaries then carry blood away from each nephron.
They join up and eventually form the renal vein.

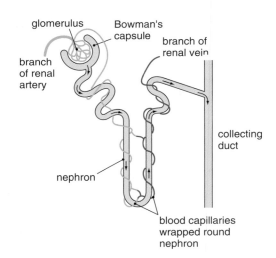

As blood passes through each glomerulus it is filtered.
The filter is like a net with tiny holes in it.
Large molecules, like blood proteins, are too big to pass through the filter.
Small molecules, like urea, glucose, salts and water, pass out of the glomerulus and into the nephron.

All the glucose, some salts and much of the water are needed by the body.
They have to be **reabsorbed** back into the blood from the nephron. This takes place by active transport.
Energy from respiration is needed for reabsorption

What is left is urea and waste salts dissolved in water.
This is now called urine.
It flows down the ureter to the bladder.

The 'cleaned' blood leaves the kidney in the renal vein.

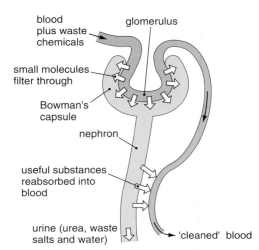

► Controlling body water

You take in water and lose it every day.
Look at the pie-charts:

Your body needs a constant amount of water in the cells.
Your body has to balance the amount of water it takes in with the amount it gets rid of.
This is also the job of the kidney.

What happens when you drink a lot of fluids?
Of course, you need to urinate more.

The blood becomes diluted.
Your kidneys remove more water from it.
This extra water makes a lot of dilute urine.

What happens when it is hot and you do not drink much fluid?
You tend to urinate less.

Your blood becomes more concentrated.
Your kidneys remove less water from it.
You make a small amount of concentrated urine.
But how is this all controlled?

Controlling the kidneys

The amount of water in your urine is controlled by a hormone.
It's called **antidiuretic hormone – ADH** for short.
ADH is made by a gland in your brain.
It is made when you need to keep water in your body.

Let's imagine that you haven't had a drink for a while:

- your blood becomes more concentrated;
- ADH is produced;
- it tells the kidneys to reabsorb most of the water from the nephrons back into the blood;
- you make a small amount of concentrated urine.

So what happens if you drink lots of fluids?

- your blood becomes dilute;
- no ADH is produced;
- the kidneys don't reabsorb much water from the nephrons back into the blood;
- you make lots of dilute urine.

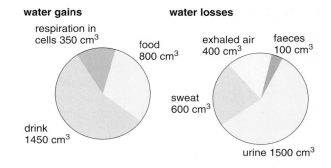

water gains   water losses

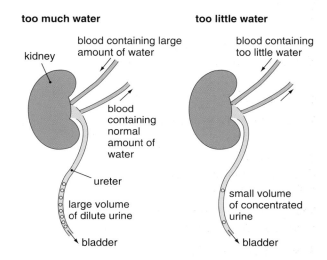

too much water   too little water

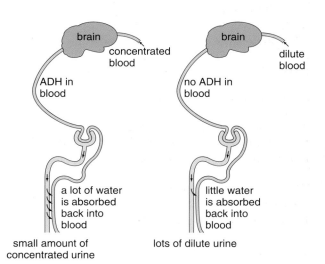

▶ Biology at work : Diabetes

Some people have a high level of glucose in their blood.
Their pancreas can not make enough insulin.
So they do not convert enough glucose to glycogen.
Their blood sugar level becomes dangerously high.
This can often make them tired and thirsty.
If it goes untreated it can lead to weight loss and
even death.

The strip will turn blue if glucose is present in the urine sample

Diabetes can be detected if glucose is found in the urine.
There is so much glucose in the blood that the kidneys
can not reabsorb it all.
They have to excrete some of it.

How could you detect the presence of
glucose in urine?
Look at the photograph:
What does it tell you if the urine
turns the glucose-detecting strip blue?

Is the person a diabetic or not?

Can you think of another chemical test
for the presence of glucose in urine?

Diabetes can be controlled in a number of ways:

- A special low-glucose diet can help if the condition is not
  too severe.

- Special tablets can reduce the blood sugar level.

- Diabetics may have to inject themselves with insulin:
  The insulin reduces the glucose by
  changing it to glycogen.
  The glycogen is stored in the liver so
  the level of glucose in the blood falls just as it would
  in a healthy person.

It is difficult to get the dose of insulin exactly right.
If too much insulin is injected, the blood sugar can fall
too low. Why do you think this is?
It can cause trembling, sweating and general weakness.
Diabetics learn to notice these symptoms and eat
a little sugar to raise their blood sugar level.

► Biology at work : The kidney machine and kidney transplants

The kidney machine

You can survive on one kidney.
But if both kidneys become diseased or damaged,
it can be fatal.

Fortunately a kidney machine can be used to remove
the waste chemicals from a patient's blood.
The patient has to use the machine for about 5 hours,
2 or 3 times a week.

- First a tube is connected to one of the patient's veins.

- The blood flows along the tube and into the machine.

- Inside the machine the blood is pumped over the
  surface of a **dialysis membrane**.
  This separates the patient's blood from the
  dialysis fluid.

- Urea diffuses out of the blood, across the dialysis
  membrane and into the dialysis fluid.

- The dialysis fluid already has sugars and salts
  in it. So sugars and salts from the blood
  will not diffuse across into the fluid.

- Urea and other wastes leave the machine in the
  dialysis fluid.

- The patient's 'cleaner' blood passes back into
  the vein.

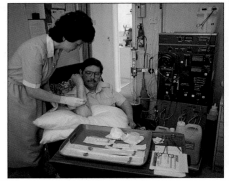

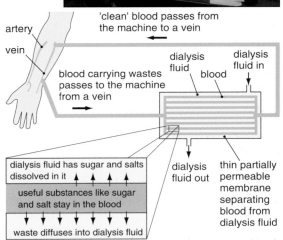

Kidney transplants

A person with failed kidneys may have a kidney transplant.
This involves replacing the diseased kidney with a healthy
one from a donor

Sometimes a close relative wants to donate one of their
kidneys. A near relative would have a 'tissue-type' similar
to the patient. This would reduce the chances of the
patient's body rejecting the transplant.

Also to prevent rejection, the bone marrow of the patient
is treated with radiation to stop white blood cell production.
Along with the use of drugs, this helps to suppress the
patient's immune system.

The surgeon attaches the transplant kidney close to the
patient's bladder. After the operation the patient has to
rest in sterile conditions for some time and is then able
to lead a normal life.

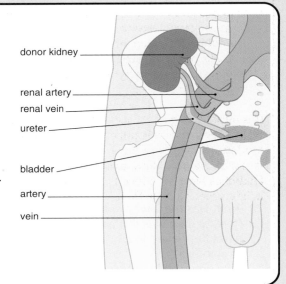

Summary

- Homeostasis means keeping conditions constant inside the body.

- The pancreas produces insulin and glucagon.
  Insulin lowers blood glucose by converting it to glycogen in the liver.
  Glucagon raises blood sugar by converting stored glycogen back to glucose.

- The brain has a major role in homeostasis.

- The kidneys carry out excretion by getting rid of urea and other wastes.
  The kidney also regulates the amount of water in your blood.

- The skin is important in keeping your body temperature constant.
  The sweat glands, blood vessels and hairs in the skin are involved.

▶ Questions

1. Copy and complete:
Keeping conditions steady inside the body is called . . . . .
After a . . . . meal our blood sugar rises. The pancreas produces a hormone called . . . . .
This converts glucose to . . . . and it is stored in the . . . . .
During a race our blood sugar level may get . . . . . The pancreas makes another hormone called . . . . . This converts stored . . . . back to glucose so the muscles can use if for . . . . .

2. The graph shows the effect of injecting 1 unit of insulin into a person.
The concentration of glucose in the blood was measured at regular intervals.

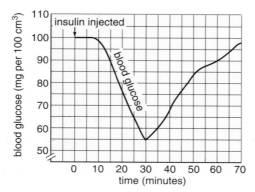

a) What was the lowest value of blood glucose?
b) At what time was this recorded?
c) What happened to cause the blood glucose level to fall?
d) Why does the blood glucose level start to rise again?

3. The graph shows the effect of changing outside temperature on the body temperature of a human (warm-blooded) and a lizard (cold-blooded):

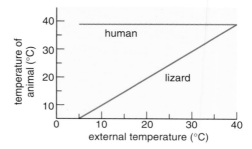

a) What happens to the body temperature of the human as the outside temperature increases? Explain why this happens.
b) What happens to the body temperature of the lizard as the outside temperature increases? Explain why this happens.
c) Why are lizards most active in warm weather?
d) How do you think lizards cope with very hot weather?

4. Look at the diagram of the skin section:
a) Name the parts A to D.
b) What do parts B and D do if you get too hot?
c) What do parts B and D do if you get too cold?
d) Explain how parts A and C react in the cold.

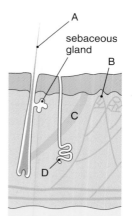

5. a) Which parts of the body lose most heat energy?
   b) Which groups of people are most at risk from hypothermia?
   c) What advice would you give elderly people about preventing hypothermia?
   d) Why are several layers of thin clothing better for keeping you warm than one layer of thick clothing?

6. The diagram shows a simple version of a kidney machine.
   The patient's blood is separated from the dialysis fluid by a partially permeable membrane.

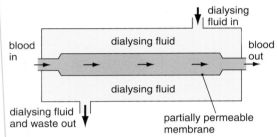

   a) By what process do chemical wastes pass from the blood into the dialysis fluid?
   b) Why do proteins not pass out of the blood?
   c) Why would the presence of protein in the urine indicate kidney damage?
   d) Why should the presence of glucose in the urine cause concern?

7. The table shows 5 substances which are present in the blood supply to the kidney, in the nephron, and in the urine. (All values are in mg per dm^3.)

Substance	Blood entering kidney	Nephron	Urine
urea	0.4	20	20
glucose	1.5	1.5	0
amino acids	0.8	0.8	0
salts	8.0	8.0	16.5
protein	82	0	0

   a) Which substances pass from the blood into the nephron?
   b) How do they pass into the nephron?
   c) Which substances are reabsorbed into the blood from the nephron?
      Explain why this happens.
   d) Explain the results for protein.

8. a) Name the parts of the excretory system A to D:

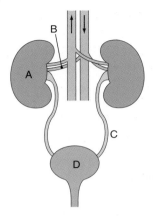

   b) Match each part with one of these functions:
      1. Stores urine.
      2. Filters urea and other waste chemicals out of the blood.
      3. Carries blood with a high concentration of urea.
      4. Carries urine down to the bladder.

9. The graph shows how the quantities of sweat and urine vary with temperature:

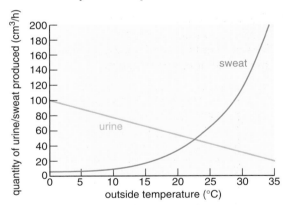

   a) At what temperature is the amount of sweat and urine the same?
   b) What happens to the amount of sweat as the temperature rises?
      Explain why this happens.
   c) What happens to the amount of urine as the temperature rises?
      Explain why this happens.

Further questions on page 198.

NERVOUS SYSTEM

chapter 8

Things are happening around you all the time.
You have to detect and respond to many changes.
But how does your body do this?

Your body responds to changes in 2 ways, with your
nervous system and your **hormonal system**.

Your nervous system sends electrical messages along
nerves to and from different parts of your body.

Your hormonal system sends chemical messages around
your body in the blood.

The electrical messages and the chemical messages tell
your body what to do.

Getting a reaction

All our reactions happen in a similar way.
There are always stimuli, receptors and effectors.

- **Stimuli** are changes that can be detected.
  A stimulus is just one of these changes.
- **Receptors** detect the changes.
- **Effectors** bring about the responses.

What happens if you sit down on a drawing pin?
The stimulus is the drawing pin.
The receptors are pain sensors in your skin.
The effectors are the muscles in your legs.
Your response is to get up quickly!

The chain of events is:

stimulus $\longrightarrow$ receptor $\longrightarrow$ coordinator $\longrightarrow$ effector $\longrightarrow$ response

The coordinator is the part of the body that decides
what to do.
What do you think the coordinator is in our example?

This type of action involves the nervous system.
Can you think of some other examples?

▶ Your nervous system

The nervous system **controls** your actions.
It **coordinates** different parts of your body so that
they work together and are able to bring about the
correct responses.

Your nervous system coordinates your muscles,
so that you can walk, write, read this book
or do exercise.

When you smile, the nervous system coordinates the
muscles of your face.

Your nervous system also coordinates things that
you don't even think about, like swallowing,
blinking and breathing.

The main parts of the nervous system are the **brain**
and the **spinal cord**.
Together they are called the **central nervous system**.
They are both made of delicate nervous tissue.
The brain is protected inside the skull.
The spinal cord is protected inside your backbone.

The central nervous system is connected to different
parts of the body by **nerves**.
Each nerve is made up of lots of **nerve cells** or **neurones**.

Sense organs are our receptors.
They send messages to the central nervous system
telling it what has happened.
These messages are sent along **sensory neurones**.

Muscles and glands are our effectors.
The central nervous system sends messages telling
them what to do.
These messages are sent along **motor neurones**.

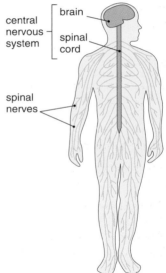

The main parts of the human
nervous system

Experiment 8.1.   Inside the spinal cord

Hold a slide of a section of the spinal cord up the light.
Can you see 2 areas?

The middle area is the grey matter.

Look at this part under the microscope.
Can you see any nerve cells?

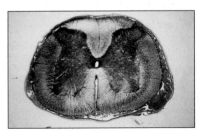

A section of the spinal cord

▶ Neurones

Nerve cells are different from other cells.
They do have a cell membrane, cytoplasm and nucleus,
but they are a different shape.
Part of the cell is stretched out to form the **axon**.
The axon can be over a metre long.

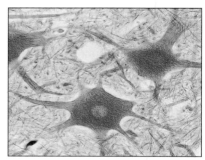

Neurones in the brain

Sensory neurone

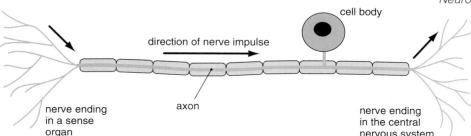

cell body

direction of nerve impulse

nerve ending
in a sense
organ

axon

nerve ending
in the central
nervous system

Motor neurone

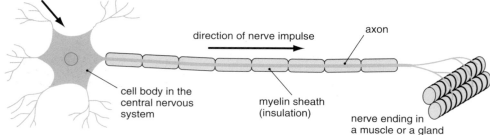

direction of nerve impulse

axon

cell body in the
central nervous
system

myelin sheath
(insulation)

nerve ending in
a muscle or a gland

How the messages are carried

The messages that nerves carry are called **nerve impulses**.
They are electrical signals.
They pass very quickly along the axon of the neurone.

An impulse travels along the axon like a train along a track.
Each one is separate from the next.
They travel along one after another.
Some axons have a **fatty sheath** around them.
This insulates the axon and makes the impulse travel along faster.

In **multiple sclerosis** the fatty sheath breaks down.
Impulses slow down or may even stop.
People with this disease gradually lose the use of their muscles
because the messages never reach them.

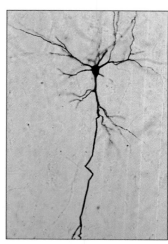

This neurone has a long axon

▶ Coordination

Your nervous system helps you to react to different situations.
Let's use an example to see how this happens.

What happens when you get an itch on your elbow?
Look at the diagram and follow the chain of events:

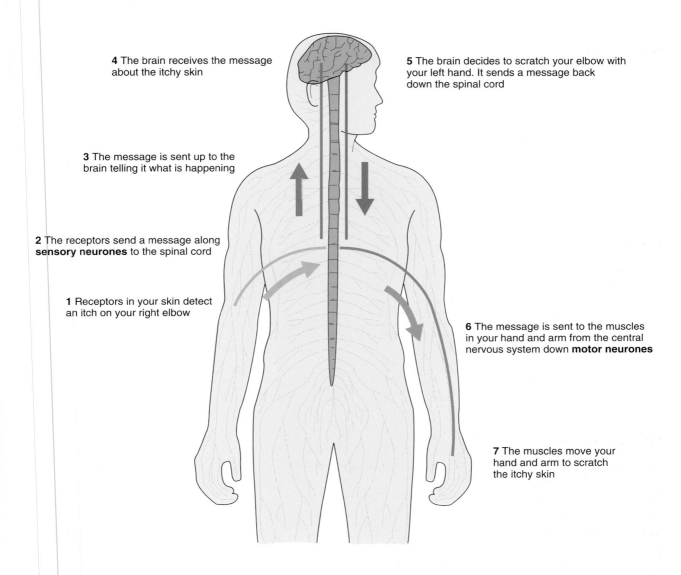

4 The brain receives the message about the itchy skin

5 The brain decides to scratch your elbow with your left hand. It sends a message back down the spinal cord

3 The message is sent up to the brain telling it what is happening

2 The receptors send a message along **sensory neurones** to the spinal cord

1 Receptors in your skin detect an itch on your right elbow

6 The message is sent to the muscles in your hand and arm from the central nervous system down **motor neurones**

7 The muscles move your hand and arm to scratch the itchy skin

What is the stimulus in this reaction?

What is the response?

Which parts of the body are the receptor, the effector and the coordinator?

▶ Synapses

The end of one neurone is not connected to the next.
There is always a small gap between them.
The gap is called a **synapse**.

When an impulse reaches the end of an axon,
a chemical is produced.
The chemical diffuses across the gap.
It starts off an impulse in the next neurone.

Only one end of a neurone can make this chemical.
So synapses make sure an impulse can only travel
in **one** direction.

Synapses have 2 other functions.
They act as:

- **a resistor** – it may take a number of impulses
  before enough chemical is made to start the
  impulse in the next neurone.

- **a junction box** – one neurone may pass on its
  impulse to a number of other neurones.

Our synapses are easily affected by drugs.
Some drugs can block them.
Others can make them work too quickly.
Alcohol is thought to affect synapses in the brain.
This can slow down people's reactions.

To the muscles

We use nerves to control our muscles.
Motor neurones end in synapses in muscle cells.
A chemical passes across the synapse and the muscle
cell contracts.

Motor neurone disease affects the neurones that
join with muscles.
The neurones start to break down and can not carry
impulses any more.
So the muscles can not contract and the person is
paralysed.

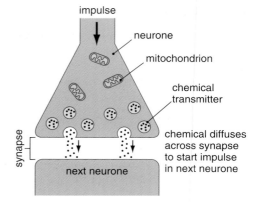

How a synapse works

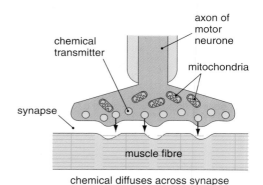

chemical diffuses across synapse
to make muscle contract

How an impulse reaches a muscle

Nerve - muscle connections

▶ Reflex arcs

You take your hand away from a hot object very fast.
You do it automatically – without thinking.
Why do you think this is?

Many reflexes protect you.
They happen very quickly, so you don't harm yourself.

Look at the diagram below.
Try tracing the pathway of the impulse along the neurones.
This pathway is called a **reflex arc**.

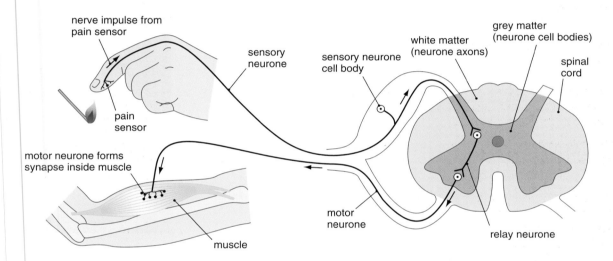

The **stimulus** in our example is the hot flame.

The **receptor** is the heat sensor in the skin.

- The impulse travels to the spinal cord along the **sensory neurone**.
- In the spinal cord the impulse is passed on to the **relay neurone**.
- This passes the impulse on to the **motor neurone**.

The motor neurone carries the impulse to a muscle in the arm. The muscle is the **effector**.

The muscle contracts to remove the hand from the hot object. This action is the **response**.

How many synapses are there in this reflex arc?
There is one between each neurone and one between the motor neurone and the muscle – that makes three!

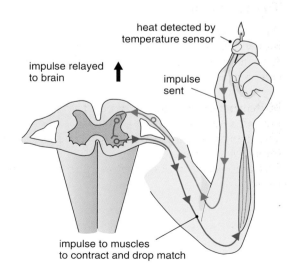

▶ Your reflexes

- Pulling your hand away from a hot object.
- Blinking when dust gets into your eye.
- Coughing when food goes down the 'wrong way'.
  What have all these reflexes got in common?

Well for one thing you can not stop yourself reacting.
These reflexes are automatic and often protect you.

Experiment 8.2   Testing your reflexes

Try to test some of your reflexes with a partner.
What happens with each of these:
- Sit on the bench with your legs relaxed.
  Your partner taps you just below the knee.
- Look straight ahead.
  Your partner suddenly waves a hand in front of your eyes.
- Kneel on a chair and let your feet hang loose.
  Your partner taps the back of your foot, just above the heel.
- Your partner shines a torch into your eye?

How fast?

Lots of sportsmen and sportswomen need fast reflexes.
What sports do you think need quick reactions?

You can see how quick your reflexes are by measuring
your **reaction time**.

Experiment 8.3   Measuring your reaction time

You can measure your reaction time with a falling ruler.
Place your arm on the bench as in the diagram:
Your partner holds the ruler with zero next to your
little finger, but **not** touching it.
When your partner decides to let the ruler go, try
to catch it as quickly as possible.

Read off the scale next to your little finger.
Try the test 10 times.
Record your results in a table.

Now repeat the test but with the ruler touching your hand.

- Does your reaction time improve with practice?
  Why do you think this is?

- Was your reaction time quicker with or without the ruler
  touching your hand? Why was this?

Try to change the test so that you use only your hearing.

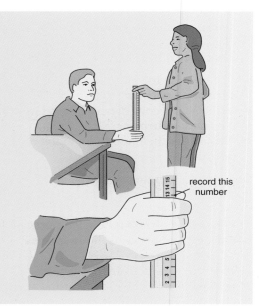

record this
number

▶ Your brain

Your brain **coordinates** your actions.
Many of them are complicated.
Riding a bike, dancing or playing soccer, for example.

Your brain is at the top of the spinal cord.
It contains more than ten billion neurones.
These link up to enable you to coordinate
incoming and outgoing impulses.
This is how you control your actions.

The brain is very complex.
We still have a great deal to discover about how
it works.

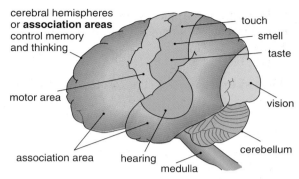

Different parts of the brain have different jobs to do

Three important parts are:

- The **cerebral hemispheres** control complex behaviour.
  They are responsible for thought, memory and intelligence.
  They link the senses such as seeing and hearing with
  muscles that bring about movement.
  This front part of our brain is responsible for our
  feelings and emotions.

- The **medulla** is the part that attaches to the spinal cord.
  It controls automatic actions like our heartbeat, breathing
  and blood pressure.

- The **cerebellum** controls our sense of balance and
  muscular actions.
  It allows us to make precise movements such as walking,
  running or riding a bike.

People have often said that the brain is like a very
complicated computer.
But they can not explain how it controls our thinking,
feelings and emotions.

Conditioning

Your brain can influence your reflexes.
You make saliva when food is in your mouth.
But other things can make your mouth water.
The smell of food or the bell ringing for lunchtime.
This type of reflex involves the brain.
It is called **conditioning** and is a type of learning.
Can you think of other examples of conditioning?

▶ Your senses

We are aware of things around us.
Our senses detect stimuli and we respond.

Humans have receptors or **sense organs** :

- The **skin** responds to touch, pressure, pain, heat and cold.

- The **tongue** responds to chemicals in our food and drink.
  It gives us our sense of taste.

- The **nose** responds to chemicals in the air.
  It gives us our sense of smell.

- The **ears** respond to sound vibrations and movements.
  They give us our sense of hearing and also our balance.

- The **eyes** respond to light rays.
  They give us our sense of sight.

Which senses are being used here ?

Reading braille

▶ Your skin

There are many different types of sensors in the skin.
The number of sensors varies in different parts of the body.

The greatest number of skin sensors are at our fingertips.
They enable us to feel lots of different things.

The lowest number of skin sensors are in the middle of the back.

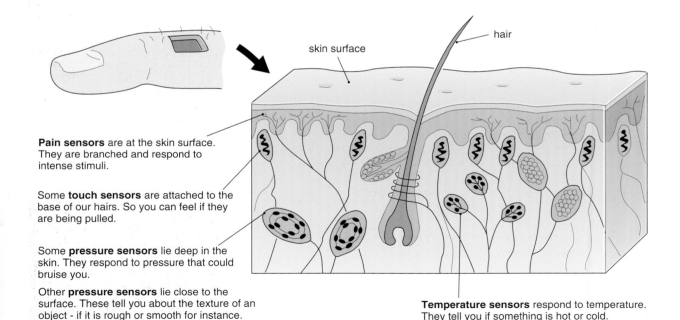

skin surface

hair

Pain sensors are at the skin surface.
They are branched and respond to
intense stimuli.

Some **touch sensors** are attached to the
base of our hairs. So you can feel if they
are being pulled.

Some **pressure sensors** lie deep in the
skin. They respond to pressure that could
bruise you.

Other **pressure sensors** lie close to the
surface. These tell you about the texture of an
object - if it is rough or smooth for instance.

Temperature sensors respond to temperature.
They tell you if something is hot or cold.

126

▶ Your tongue

Your senses of taste and smell are closely linked.
They are both chemical senses.

What things can you taste?

You can only taste sweet, sour, bitter, and salty things.
People think that they can taste other things but they are
really using their sense of smell.

The sensors that give you your sense of taste are
found in little grooves on your tongue.
They are called **taste buds**.
Each taste bud can only detect one taste.
The different types of taste buds are found in
particular areas on the tongue.

The chemicals in your food must dissolve in saliva
before you can taste them.
The taste buds then send impulses to the brain.
The brain interprets the sensation of the taste.

If food has gone off it tastes horrible.
Why do you think that this is useful?

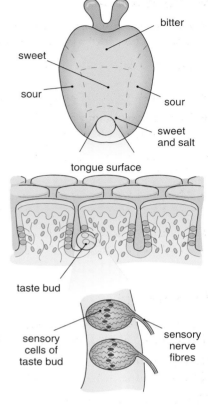

▶ Your nose

Your nose also senses chemicals.
But it is thousands of times more sensitive than
your sense of taste.
We can detect a lot of different smells.

Smells are chemicals in the air.
The chemicals dissolve in the moist lining of your nose.
They stimulate sensors in your nose to send impulses to
your brain.
The brain interprets these impulses as different smells.

Can you think of jobs that rely on a keen sense of smell?
How about people who test perfumes or wines?

Have you noticed how you can not taste your food if you
have a heavy cold? Why do you think this is?
It proves that a lot of tastes are really smells!

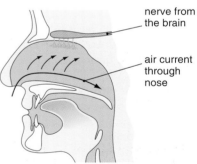

Sensors in the nose

▶ Your ears

Where are your ears?
Not just at the side of your head.
The important bits are inside your skull.

If you look at the diagram below you can see
how complicated the ear is.
But how do you hear?

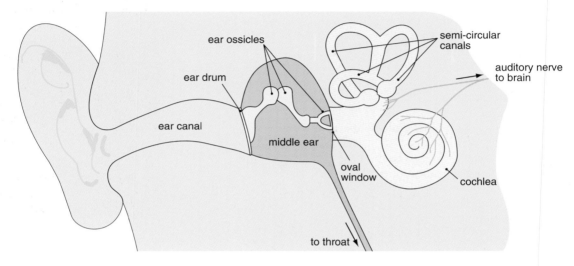

Hearing

The air around you is full of sound waves.
Your ears work by converting these sound waves into nerve impulses.
This is how it happens:

- The outer part of your ear funnels the sound
  waves into the **ear canal**.
- The sound waves travel along the ear canal to
  the **eardrum**.
- The eardrum starts to vibrate when sound waves
  hit it.
- The vibrations are passed on to 3 little bones
  called the **ear ossicles**.
- The ear ossicles pass the vibrations on to the
  inner eardrum or **oval window**.
- When the oval window vibrates it causes fluid in
  the **cochlea** to move.
- Inside the cochlea are lots of tiny, sensory hairs.
  Movement of the fluid sets these hairs vibrating.
  They send off nerve impulses to the brain.
- The brain interprets these impulses as sounds.

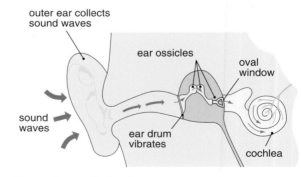

The pathway of vibrations

Your balance

Your ears have 2 jobs to do.
As well as hearing they help you to keep your balance.

The **semi-circular canals** detect movement.
They are found inside the skull just above the cochlea.
The 3 canals are filled with a fluid.
Each one lies at right angles to the other two.

Inside each canal there are sensory hairs.
These are sensitive to movement of the fluid.

When you move your head the liquid in the canals moves.
This pulls on the sensory hairs.
They trigger off impulses to the brain.
Your brain makes you aware of the movement.

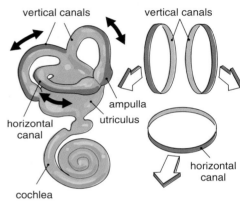

Relative positions of the 3 semi-circular canals

Experiment 8.4   *Varying the pitch*

Connect a loudspeaker to a signal generator
(this produces different frequencies).

Turn the pointer to lower and lower frequencies.

- What happens to the pitch of the note?
- What is the lowest frequency that you can hear?
- What is the highest frequency that you can hear?
  Did this vary from one person to another?

Deafness

Your ear is very delicate and can easily be damaged.

There are several causes of deafness.

Wax can build up in the ear canal and block sound waves.
The eardrum may become damaged.

Damage to the ear ossicles is more serious.
Bone tissue can form around them so they
can't vibrate.

Damage to the cells in the cochlea can cause
permanent deafness.
This can happen if you listen to very loud sounds
at a particular pitch.
Listening to very loud music on personal stereos can
cause this kind of damage.

Hearing aids have become less conspicuous

Relaxing with a personal stereo

129

▶ Your eyes

Sight is one of your most important senses.
Just think what it must be like to live in darkness
all the time.

Each eye lies in a socket in the skull.
It is moved by the actions of 3 pairs of **eye muscles**.
These swivel your eyes in their sockets.

At the front of the eye is the transparent **cornea**.
Light enters your eye through here.
It then passes through the **pupil**.
This is surrounded by the coloured **iris**.

At the front of the cornea is the **conjunctiva**.
This is a delicate, transparent layer.
It is kept moist by the **tear glands**.
These make the tears that wash your eye clean
every time you blink.

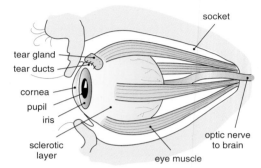

Inside the eye

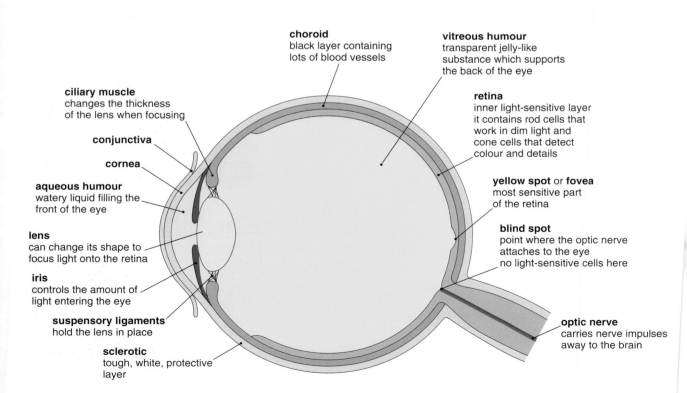

choroid
black layer containing
lots of blood vessels

vitreous humour
transparent jelly-like
substance which supports
the back of the eye

ciliary muscle
changes the thickness
of the lens when focusing

retina
inner light-sensitive layer
it contains rod cells that
work in dim light and
cone cells that detect
colour and details

conjunctiva

cornea

yellow spot or **fovea**
most sensitive part
of the retina

aqueous humour
watery liquid filling the
front of the eye

blind spot
point where the optic nerve
attaches to the eye
no light-sensitive cells here

lens
can change its shape to
focus light onto the retina

iris
controls the amount of
light entering the eye

suspensory ligaments
hold the lens in place

optic nerve
carries nerve impulses
away to the brain

sclerotic
tough, white, protective
layer

Seeing things

Light enters your eye through the transparent cornea, it passes through the lens and is focused on the retina.

In the retina there are cells which are sensitive to light called rods and cones.

When light stimulates them they send impulses to the brain along the optic nerve. Your brain interprets these impulses to make a picture.

Notice that the image on the retina is **inverted**. But your brain has learned to turn the picture the right way up. In the retina **rod cells** respond to dim light and **cone cells** detect colour and details.

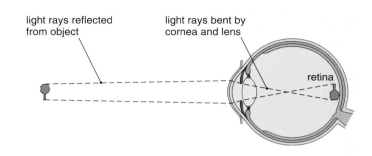

light rays reflected from object

light rays bent by cornea and lens

retina

Focusing

Most of the bending of the light rays is done by the curved cornea. But your lens can bend the light rays slightly.

The shape of the lens is controlled by the ciliary muscles. If you are looking at a distant object:

- the ciliary muscles **relax**,
- this **tightens** the suspensory ligaments
- so the lens is pulled into a **thin** shape.
- The distant object is focused on the retina.

If you are looking at a near object:

- the ciliary muscles **contract**,
- this **slackens** the suspensory ligaments
- so the elastic lens goes **fatter**.
- The near object is focused on the retina.

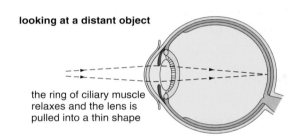

looking at a distant object

the ring of ciliary muscle relaxes and the lens is pulled into a thin shape

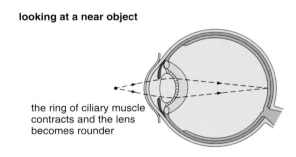

looking at a near object

the ring of ciliary muscle contracts and the lens becomes rounder

Experiment 8.5   Finding your blind spot

Hold this book up in front of you at arm's length. Cover your **right** eye and keep staring at the magic wand. Move the page slowly towards you until the rabbit disappears.

This happens because the light rays from the rabbit are falling on to your blind spot where there are no light-sensitive cells.

► Hormones

The **hormonal system** also coordinates the body.
Hormones are chemicals produced by glands.
Small amounts of these chemicals are carried
around the body in the blood.
They tell different parts of the body what to do.

The body responds to these hormones.
Responses may last a few minutes or go on for years.
Hormones can affect things like the rate of metabolism,
growth and sexual development.

You already know about some hormones.
Do you remember what the hormone insulin does?

Thyroid makes **thyroxin.**
This regulates the rate of metabolism.
Too little and our chemical reactions
slow down.

lungs

heart

Adrenal glands make **adrenaline** when
you are frightened or angry. Adrenaline
helps your body cope with an
emergency.

kidney

Testes make **testosterone** in males.
This develops male features during
puberty.

Pituitary is a gland at the base of the
brain. It makes many hormones and
controls things like growth, water balance
and sperm and egg production. The
pituitary also makes hormones
that control other hormonal glands.

stomach

Pancreas makes **insulin** and **glucagon.**
Insulin lowers blood sugar by changing
it to glycogen. Glucagon increases
blood sugar.

Ovaries make **oestrogen** and
progesterone in females. These control
the menstrual cycle and develop female
features during puberty.

Hormones are involved in homeostasis.
Hormonal glands are affected by feedback.
If the level of hormone in the blood is too high
the gland detects it and makes less hormone.

Sometimes things can go wrong.
A gland may make too much or too little of a hormone.
For instance, too much pituitary growth hormone
can make a person become a giant, too little can make
a person become a dwarf.

What happens if too little insulin is produced by the pancreas?
How is diabetes treated?

Adrenaline

Adrenaline is produced by the adrenal glands
which are located above each kidney.
Adrenaline is released during times of excitement,
fear or stress.
Often called the 'flight or fight' hormone, adrenaline helps
the body prepare for action in the following ways:

- Glycogen is converted to glucose in the liver,
  so more glucose reaches the muscles as a source of energy
  for the rapid contractions needed for sudden action.
- Heart rate increases so that more glucose and oxygen
  are delivered to the muscles for energy release.
- The bronchioles widen so more air reaches the lungs.
- Blood vessels to the brain and muscles widen,
  so more glucose and oxygen are delivered to these organs.
- Blood vessels to the gut and other organs narrow,
  allowing blood to be diverted to more life-saving organs.
- Hairs are raised ('goose pimples' in humans).
  This makes furry animals look larger to deter attackers.

The production of adrenaline has evolved to protect us
and other animals from danger.
If too much adrenaline is produced, as a result of prolonged stress,
constant high blood pressure and heart disease may result.
Beta-blockers are drugs that combine with adrenaline and so
reduce its effects.

Other hormones

Hormones are covered in other chapters of this book:

Insulin and **glucagon** control blood sugar levels (page 105).

ADH controls the level of water in your body (page 113).

Testosterone (the male hormone) ands **oestrogen**
(the female hormone) bring about the changes to
our bodies that occur at puberty (page 166).

Look at the table to see how the nervous system
and the hormonal system work together to control
the activities of our body.

Nervous system	Hormonal system
information passes as electrical impulses along neurones	information passes as chemical messengers in the blood
effects are rapid and short-lived	effects are usually slow and longer lasting
affects particular organs	affects the whole of the body
often involves reflexes	controls growth, development, metabolism and reproduction

▶ Biology at work : The misuse of drugs in sport

Some sports people take drugs to improve their performance.
They do this because:
- Media pressure is put on them to be successful.
- They think that their sporting successes will make them rich.
- They think everyone else is doing it.
- They do not think that they will get caught.

Performance-enhancing drugs have been banned by the
International Olympic Committee (IOC) to ensure that competition
in sport is fair and to protect the health of sports people.

Ben Johnson won the 100 m title at the 1992 Olympics but was disqualified for taking drugs

Types of drug

Anabolic steroids are substances similar to the male sex hormone
testosterone.
They work by mimicking the protein-building effects of this hormone.
The result is muscle growth, which gives the athlete increased strength
and endurance.

There are a number of harmful side-effects resulting from the excessive
use of anabolic steroids.
In men, use of these drugs can bring about increased aggression,
impotence, baldness, kidney and liver damage and even the
development of breasts.
In women, there is a development of male features, facial and body hair
and irregular periods.

Beta-blockers are drugs used to treat people with heart problems.
When taken, they lower the heart rate and reduce blood pressure.
They are able to reduce the effects of stress on the body.
The IOC has banned them in such sports as archery, shooting,
ski-jumping, bobsleigh, biathlon and modern pentathlon.

Canadian snooker player Bill Werbeniuk took beta-blockers to steady his aim

Stimulants, such as amphetamines and cocaine, can give the athlete
a lift, keeping them awake and competitive.
They speed up the reflexes and reduce the feeling of fatigue.

They can be harmful to the body since they increase heart rate
and blood pressure and reduce the feelings of pain.
They can also be addictive and give rise to panic attacks and
increased aggression.

Narcotic analgesics include methadone, codeine and heroin.
These drugs act as pain killers that are able to mask an injury.
The problem is that if the athlete continues to compete,
the injury may become much worse or even permanent.
Some narcotic analgesics can be highly addictive.

Diane Mohdahl successfully proved that she was innocent of drug-taking

Summary

- Sense organs (receptors) detect stimuli and bring about responses in effectors.

- The nervous system controls and coordinates your actions.

- Neurones carry nervous impulses around your body.
  Between 2 neurones is a gap called the synapse.

- A reflex arc is a nerve pathway. Reflexes are automatic, fast and often protective.

- The brain is the controlling centre of the nervous system.

- Senses include touch, taste, smell, sight, hearing and balance.

- Sensory cells send impulses to the brain along nerves.

- The ear can convert sound waves into nerve impulses and control your balance.
  The eye can convert light rays into nerve impulses.

▶ Questions

1. Copy and complete:
   The brain and .... make up the central nervous system.
   The brain is protected by the .... and the spinal cord by the .... column. Impulses are carried to the spinal cord by the .... neurones. Inside the . ... matter of the spinal cord the impulses are passed on to .... neurones. The impulses leave the spinal cord along .... neurones. There is a gap between 2 neurones called a .....

2. a) What is meant by:
   i) a stimulus   ii) a receptor   iii) a response?

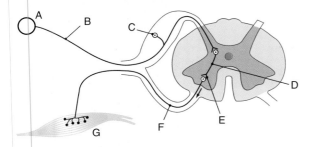

   b) Name the parts labelled A to G.
   c) Explain what is happening at the points A to G.

3. Look at the diagram of the motor neurone:
   a) Name the parts labelled A to D.
   b) Give the functions of parts B, C and D.

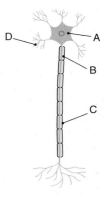

4. Match each of the following in column A with their function in column B:

Column A	Column B
• synapse	• carries impulses from the spinal cord to a muscle
• cerebellum	• controls learning and memory
• sensory neurone	• a gap between neurones
• cerebral hemispheres	• controls balance
• motor neurone	• controls heartbeat, breathing and blood pressure
• medulla	• carries impulses from a sense organ to the spinal cord

5. a) What is meant by a reflex action?
   b) Which reflex action happens when you:
      i)   get dust into your windpipe
      ii) have a bright light shone into your eye
      iii) see or smell some nice food
      iv) stand out in a cold wind?
   c) How does each of these reflexes help you?

6. The diagram shows the structure of the human ear:

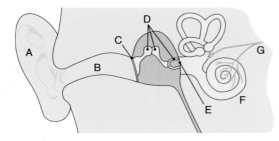

   a) Name the parts labelled A to G.
   b) What are the functions of the parts labelled:
      i) D   ii) E   iii) F?
   c) Explain how vibrations from part C reach part F.

7. Give the proper biological names for each of these parts of the eye:
   a) Light-sensitive layer.
   b) Controls the amount of light entering the eye.
   c) Delicate, transparent layer at the front of the eye.
   d) Tough, white, outer layer of the eye.
   e) Jelly-like substance that keeps the eye in shape.
   f) Carries nerve impulses to the brain.
   g) Black middle layer.
   h) Controls the shape of the lens.
   i) Attaches the lens to the ciliary muscles.

8. The diagram shows a section through the human eye:

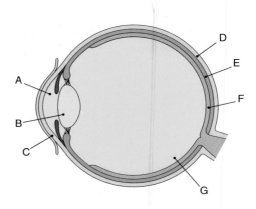

   a) Name the parts labelled A to G.
   b) Which of these parts help in the focusing of light on to F?
   c) Write out the sequence to show the pathway of light from C to F:
   d) How are nerve impulses carried away from the eye to the brain?

9. a) Name 4 ways in which the hormonal system is different from the nervous system.
   b) Which hormone:
      i)   prepares the body for action
      ii) reduces the amount of glucose in the blood
      iii) controls the rate of chemical reactions in the body
      iv) is produced in the testes of the male
      v)   is produced in the ovaries of the female?

Further questions on page 200.

chapter 9

All animals need to support their bodies.
They also need to move about.
Most animals need a supporting framework –
they need a **skeleton**.

Skeletons are used for:

- **Supporting** the body and giving it shape.

- **Protecting** soft parts of the body.

- **Moving** the body with the help of muscles.

I FEEL RATHER LET DOWN!

▶ Liquid skeletons

Some animals don't seem to have a skeleton at all.
Look at the jellyfish in the photograph:
How does it support its body and move about?

Its soft body is filled with water.
It moves its muscles against the water.
This opens and closes its umbrella.
So it propels itself along.

Worms also have a liquid skeleton.
The liquid is trapped in spaces inside the body.
The muscles squeeze against the liquid.
This keeps the body firm.

Muscles can squeeze in different parts of the
worm's body.
This changes its shape and helps it to move along.

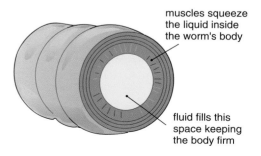

muscles squeeze
the liquid inside
the worm's body

fluid fills this
space keeping
the body firm

▶ Exoskeletons

Many animals have a skeleton on the *outside*.
This is called an exoskeleton.
Can you think of an animal with an **exoskeleton** ?

All the arthropods have exoskeletons.
Arthropods include insects, spiders and crabs.

Look at the crab in the picture :

Its exoskeleton is like a suit of armour.
There are flat plates to protect the body.
Hollow tubes form the limbs and allow
movement at **joints**.

Exoskeletons give good support and protection,
just like armour does.
But also, like armour, they can be very heavy
to carry around.
Animals with exoskeletons never grow very large.
If they did their exoskeletons would become too
heavy for their muscles to move.

The soft parts of these animals are *inside*
the skeleton.
But an exoskeleton can not grow as the rest of
the body does.
Every so often the hard covering is shed and
a new one grows. This is called **moulting**.

Metamorphosis is the change in body form as an animal grows.
In insects such as butterflies, blowflies or this dragonfly, the young
are called **larvae**. They do not look like the adult.
Each time the larva moults it gets bigger until it forms a resting stage
called a **pupa**.
Eventually the adult emerges from the pupa and flies off.
This dramatic change from young to adult is called **complete
metamorphosis**.

In metamorphosis, the young and the adult have different food sources.
For example, caterpillars eat vegetation whilst butterflies eat nectar.
How is this an advantage to the insect?

Young and adult insects often have different habitats.
This also would reduce competition for scarce resources.

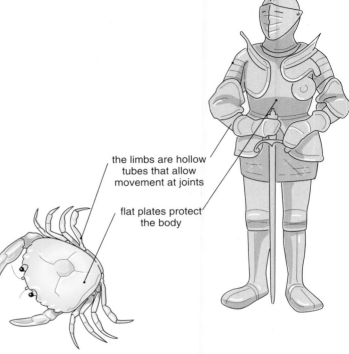

the limbs are hollow
tubes that allow
movement at joints

flat plates protect
the body

A dragonfly larva moulting its exoskeleton

▶ Endoskeletons

Your skeleton is *inside* your body, so it is
called an **endoskeleton**.
It is made of hard bone and cartilage.

Fish, amphibians, reptiles, birds and mammals
all have endoskeletons.
They are all **vertebrates**.

Look at the drawing of a section of bone
under the microscope:
Can you see cells in the bone?

Bone and cartilage are both living tissues.
So the skeleton can grow as the rest of the
animal does.
The living cells are also able to repair
broken bones.

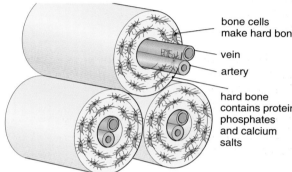

bone cells
make hard bone

vein

artery

hard bone
contains protein,
phosphates
and calcium
salts

All vertebrate skeletons have the same
basic parts:

- A **skull** which contains and protects the brain.
- A jointed **backbone** made up of small bones
  called **vertebrae**.
- A **rib-cage** protecting the thorax.
- **Limbs** (arms and legs) and **limb girdles**
  (shoulders and hips).

Look at the 2 skeletons below.
See if you can pick out the basic parts
in each one.
Which animal does each skeleton belong to?

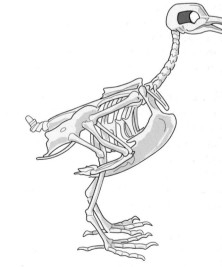

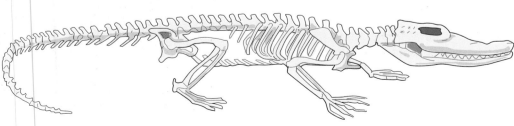

▶ The human skeleton

Your skeleton is made up of more than 200 bones.

Look at the diagram:

Can you pick out the four basic parts of the vertebrate skeleton:

How many of these bones can you name?

How is **this** skeleton different from the ones on the last page?

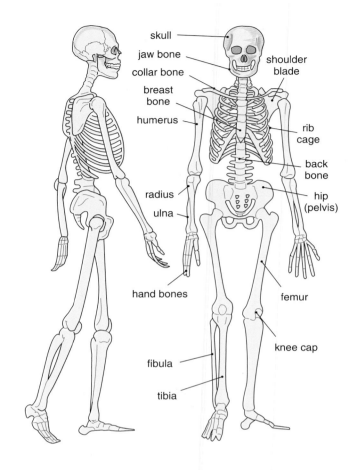

Our skeleton has 4 main functions:

- **Support** – it holds us upright and provides a framework for tissues and organs.

- **Protection** – the heart and lungs are protected by the rib-cage.
  What protects the brain and the spinal cord?

- **Movement** – takes place when muscles move bones at joints.

- **Making blood cells** – red and white blood cells are made inside the bone marrow.

Experiment 9.1   Parts of a skeleton

Look closely at the different bones of a human skeleton.

- How is the skull attached to the backbone?

- How are the ribs attached to the backbone?

- How are the limbs attached at the shoulders and hips?

- Can you find a common pattern to the bones of the arm and the bones of the leg?

▶ The backbone

Humans are different from most other vertebrates.
We do not walk on all fours.
We stand upright, walk on our legs and so are
free to use our hands.
But this sometimes gives us backache.

Your backbone is made up of 33 separate bones
called **vertebrae**.
They have joints between them,
so you can bend and twist.

Your vertebrae are supported by strong muscles –
try feeling the ones in your back.

Each vertebra is hollow.
Inside the space is the spinal cord.
The surrounding bone of the vertebrae protects
the soft tissue of the spinal cord.

At the top of the backbone the spinal cord passes
through a hole into your skull.
Here the spinal cord is joined to your brain.

Between your vertebrae are discs of cartilage.
They stop your vertebrae rubbing together
when you move.

A slipped disc happens when the disc bursts or moves
out of position. The pressure on the spinal cord can
be extremely painful.

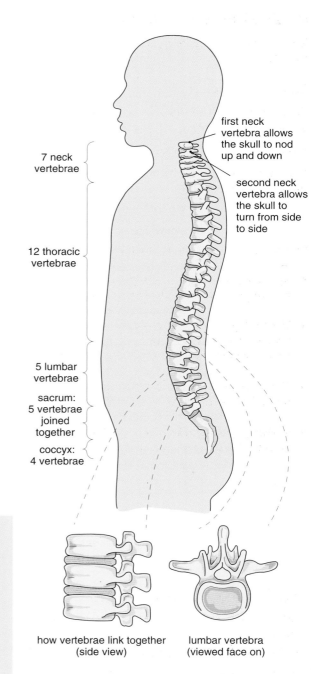

7 neck
vertebrae

first neck
vertebra allows
the skull to nod
up and down

second neck
vertebra allows
the skull to
turn from side
to side

12 thoracic
vertebrae

5 lumbar
vertebrae

sacrum:
5 vertebrae
joined
together

coccyx:
4 vertebrae

how vertebrae link together
(side view)

lumbar vertebra
(viewed face on)

Experiment 9.2   Looking at vertebrae

Look carefully at the vertebrae on a human skeleton.

- Do they all look the same?
  What differences are there?

- Can you put them into 5 groups that look alike?

- What different jobs do these vertebrae do?

- Can you see the discs of cartilage between the
  vertebrae?

Now look at some separated vertebrae.

- Can you see where one moves on the next?

- Can you see where the spinal cord lies?

▷ Joints

Joints occur where 2 bones meet.
Joints allow movement to take place.

Some joints allow more movement than others.
Some don't allow any movement at all.

Look at the different types of joint in the X-rays:
Then look at the table to see how they move.

Joint	Where found in body	Type of movement
hinge	elbow, knee, finger	in only one plane – like the hinge on a door
ball-and-socket	hip and shoulder	in all directions
pivot	neck	nodding or turning
fixed	skull and pelvis	no movement
gliding	backbone	slight movement

Synovial joints

Most movement occurs at **synovial joints**.
Hinge and ball-and-socket joints are both
types of synovial joint.

Movement at these joints could cause friction.
A synovial joint is built to cut down friction:

- The ends of the bones are covered with
  cartilage. This acts as a shock-absorber and
  stops the 2 bones rubbing together.

- The **synovial membrane** encloses **synovial
  fluid**. This lubricates or oils the joint and makes
  movement easy.

- The bones are held together at a joint by tough
  ligaments.

- Muscles are connected to the bones by **tendons**.
  When muscles work, they pull on tendons and move
  the bone.

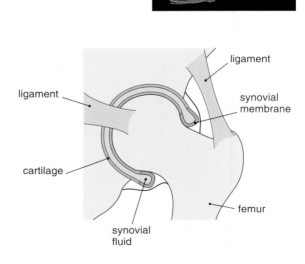

Experiment 9.3   Human joints

Look carefully at a model of the human skeleton.
Try to find the different types of joints shown
in the table above.

▶ Muscles

You have over 350 muscles in your body.
Without your muscles you couldn't move.

Your muscles provide the force to pull or
to squeeze things.
They work by shortening or **contracting**.
A resting muscle is long and thin. When it
contracts it becomes short and fat.

There are 3 main types of muscle :

- **Voluntary muscles** are attached to
  bones by tendons.
  They bring about movement at joints.

  These muscles can be controlled at will.
  If you decide to lift your hand up, muscles
  in your arm contract.
  This pulls on the tendon which pulls up the
  lower arm bone.

  Voluntary muscles are powerful.
  They can contract quickly but soon get tired.

- **Involuntary muscles** move food down
  your gut, blood along blood vessels, and urine
  down the ureters.

  You can not control them – they work on their
  own.
  They contract slowly and do not tire.

- **Cardiac muscle** is only found in the heart.
  It is very powerful and never gets tired.
  It contracts on its own but your nerves and
  hormones can change the number of contractions
  to make your heart beat faster or slower.

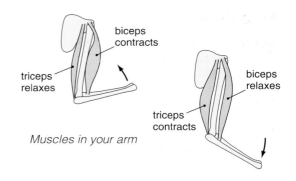

biceps contracts

triceps relaxes

biceps relaxes

triceps contracts

Muscles in your arm

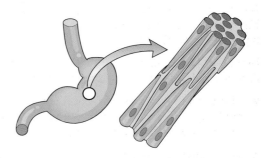

Voluntary muscles move your skeleton

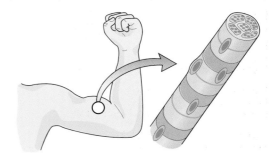

Involuntary muscles churn up your food

Experiment 9.4   Looking at muscle fibres

Look carefully at a small piece of raw steak.
Can you see how the muscle fibres are in groups ?

Try separating some of these fibres out in some
salt solution on a slide.
Look at the muscle fibres under the microscope.

Wash your hands with soap and water
when you have finished.

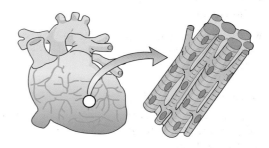

Cardiac muscle keeps your heart pumping

▶ Muscles at work

Your muscles provide the force needed to
move bones at joints.
Muscles can not *push* – they can only *pull*.

Try pushing up against the underside of a
table with the palm of your hand.
What does your **biceps** muscle feel like?
What does your **triceps** muscle feel like?

When a muscle **contracts** it gets shorter
and fatter.
When a muscle is not contracting it returns
to its normal size – we say that it **relaxes**.

Now push down with the back of your hand
against the table-top.
What does your triceps muscle feel like?
What does your biceps muscle feel like?

Muscles like your biceps and triceps work
in pairs.
When one contracts, the other relaxes.
They form an **antagonistic pair** of muscles.

What happens to your muscles when you pick
up a book?

Nerves carry impulses from your brain to
the muscles in your arm.
They tell your biceps to contract and your
triceps to relax.
As your biceps shortens it pulls on the tendon
that pulls up your lower arm.
Your arm bends at the hinge joint at the elbow.

What do you think happens to your arm muscles
when you put the book back onto the table?

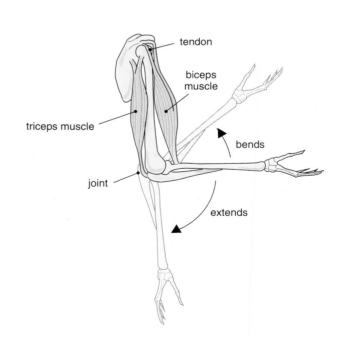

How muscles work

Muscle is meat.
The muscle that moves bones is the steak
that we may eat with our chips.

Each muscle is made up of lots of **muscle fibres**.
These fibres are bound together into bundles.
At each end of the bundles are tendons.
Tendons connect muscles to bones.

When a muscle contracts, each individual muscle
fibre shortens.
The whole muscle contracts, pulling on the tendon
which pulls the bones closer together.

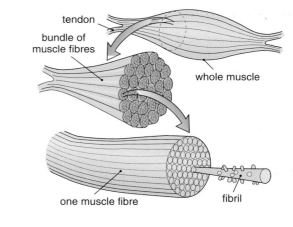

Human moves

Look at the picture of the athlete:

Her **thigh** and **hamstring** muscles bend
and straighten her knee joint.
Her **calf** and **shin** muscles bend and straighten
her ankle joint.

Try to work out which muscles contract and
which ones relax in the first 2 strides of a race.

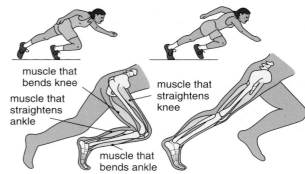

Experiment 9.5   Testing your finger strength

Set up the clamp stand as shown:
Place your hand flat on the table and put your
middle finger through the elastic band.
Now move your finger down to touch the table.
Count the number of finger movements that
you can do **continuously** for 2 minutes.
Record the number of finger movements for
each 20-second period in a table like this:

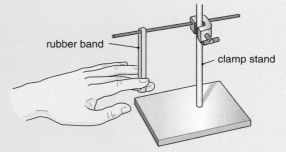

Time interval (seconds)	0–20	20–40	40–60	60–80	80–100	100–120
Number of finger movements						

Plot a line-graph with axes like this:

Try to explain your results.

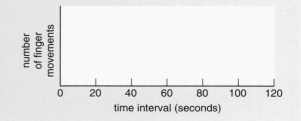

▶ Movement in fish

As we saw earlier in this chapter,
movement is brought about in humans
by muscles that occur in antagonistic pairs.

This applies to fish as well as other animals.

In a fish, the muscles that allow it to swim
are found in blocks on either side of the spine.

These blocks of muscle contract on one side
and relax on the other. This moves the body from
side to side – in a zig-zag pattern.

How does this help the fish to move forward?.

This is where the **tail fin** plays a role.
This vertical fin pushes against the water as the body zig-zags,
and the force pushes the body forwards.

It is not just muscle action that helps fish to swim.
So what other special features do fish have to aid locomotion
in water?.

Water is a lot denser than air. So to make movement easier
most fish have a streamlined shape.
This reduces their resistance and allows them to glide
through the water.

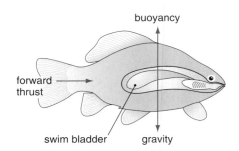

Blocks of muscle help fish swim

What happens if a fish stops swimming?

Bony fish (those with a skeleton made of bone) like salmon, trout
and stickleback, have a buoyancy aid called a **swim bladder**.

This is a gas-filled sac. When it is full, the fish rises in the water.
If on the other hand the gas is removed,
then the density of the fish increases and it sinks.

The **cartilaginous fish** (those with a skeleton made of cartilage)
like sharks and the dogfish do not have a swim bladder.
If they stop swimming they sink!.

Fins other than the tail fin also assist swimming.
Not by pushing the fish along, but by maintaining stability
and altering direction.

The **dorsal** and **ventral** fins give the fish a bigger vertical surface area.
This makes the fish more stable – less likely to topple over.

Other fins are found in pairs on either side of the body.
e.g. the **pectoral** and **pelvic** fins.

By altering the angle of these fins, the fish can move up,
down and even backwards.
This very effective way of manoeuvring
has been adapted by man for use in submarines.

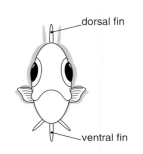

The swim bladder is a buoyancy aid

Movement and gas exchange

The forward movement of fish through the water helps to make gas exchange as efficient as possible.

Fish breath using special organs called **gills.** These have lots of folds and so provide a large surface area for gas exchange.

The gills are found near the front of the fish in an area called the **pharynx.**
At the front of the pharynx is the mouth and at the back is the gill cover or **operculum.**
This cover is only found in bony fish, such as trout and salmon. Cartilaginous fish do not have gill covers.

Water passes in when the mouth is open and the operculum is closed.
Water then passes out when the operculum opens. As it leaves, the water is forced over the surface of the gills.
Gas exchange now takes place between the water and the many small blood vessels in the gills.

The flow of water over the gills is not just caused by the fish moving forward.

When the fish 'breathes in' it lowers the floor of its pharynx. This increases the volume of the mouth cavity and water enters through the open mouth.
When it 'breathes out' the floor of the pharynx rises and the mouth closes.
This creates a pressure that pushes the water out over the gills.
This is called the **respiratory current**.

How good is gas exchange in fish?.
With the aid of a continuous supply of water flowing over the gills, fish breathe very efficiently.
They can in fact extract 3 times more oxygen from water than we can from air!

Other animals with gills

You can easily see the action of the gills on animals like the mayfly nymph.
This freshwater invertebrate has gills sticking out from its body.
These gills can be seen vibrating rapidly.
This vibration helps to keep a flow of water over their surface

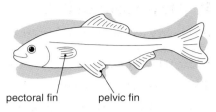

Other fins assist swimming

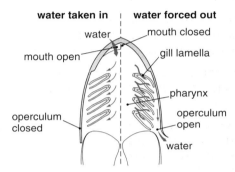

Breathing in fish

The mayfly larva lives in fast-flowing streams, which ensures that its gills are well aerated.

▶ Flight in birds

Birds have a number of adaptations to flight.

In order to keep weight to a minimum, their bones have a honey-combed structure. This means that they are nearly hollow and therefore light in weight, but at the same time they remain very strong.

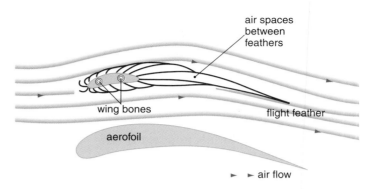

The wing has a large surface area and a special aerofoil shape

A major adaptation to flight is obviously the wing.

Wings assist flight in two ways:

- They provide a large surface area to push downwards on the air and lift the bird upwards.
- They also have a special curved shape known as an **aerofoil**.

The aerofoil wing is more strongly curved on the upper surface than the lower surface. This means that the air travelling over the top of the wing, travels faster than the air moving underneath (simply because it has further to travel).

Aircraft wings share the aerofoil shape with birds

How does this help a bird to fly?. The slower moving air underneath the wing exerts more pressure than the faster air above it. The result is an upward force known as **lift**.

Not surprisingly, this same shape is used in aeroplane wings.

Another feature that aircraft and birds have in common is their streamlined shape. This reduces air resistance and cuts down on the energy needed for flight.

One example of this streamlining is the long, narrow wings possessed by fast-flying birds like swallows and swifts. These birds have been timed at up to 160 km/h (nearly 100 m.p.h.!).

The swallow with its streamlined wings

Feathers

As everyone knows wings are covered in feathers, and these structures play an important role in assisting flight.

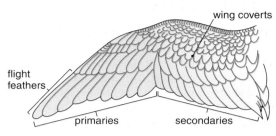

There are two main types of wing feathers:

- the long stiff **flight feathers** on the wing edges.
- the smaller **wing coverts**

The coverts overlap the flight feathers on the top and bottom of the wing.

Wing feathers

It is important that the feathers have a smooth flat surface. This is maintained by each feather being composed of hundreds of interlocking **barbs** fixed to a hollow **quill**.
The quill being hollow is obviously another adaptation for flight – being light and strong.

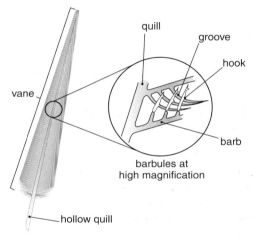

Birds can often be seen preening their feathers. This action of drawing the feather through the beak helps to keep the barbs 'zipped' together.

Flight involves two main movements:

- On the **downstroke** (powerstroke), the wing moves downwards and forwards. The smooth flat flight feathers push down on the air and support the weight of the bird. At the same time, the ends of the primary flight feathers curve into a propeller shape which pulls the bird forward.

- During the following **upstroke** (recovery stroke) the primary feathers twist open. This means that air can pass through them as the wing prepares for the next downstroke. The upstroke needs much less effort than the downstroke.

The barbs interlock with a series of hooks and grooves

Flight needs very powerful muscles and these can account for up to a third of the bird's body weight. These muscles also need strong points of attachment. As a result birds have an enlarged breast bone with an extension called the **keel.** This gives a strong and large surface area for muscle attachment.

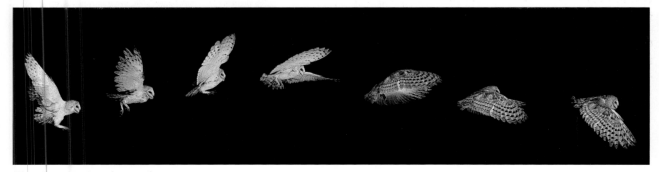

The downstroke of an owl

▶ Biology at work : Artificial hips

As we get older our joints don't work as smoothly. Sometimes they rub and grind against each other. This friction causes pain and makes it difficult to move.
Arthritis is a disease that can make things worse.

Rheumatoid arthritis is when the smaller joints of the body become inflamed.
Tissue grows across the joint and makes movement difficult.
The joint can become permanently fused so there is no movement at all.
The disease is usually inherited.

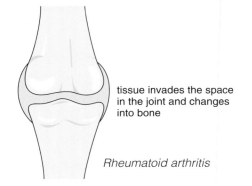

tissue invades the space in the joint and changes into bone

Rheumatoid arthritis

Osteoarthritis usually affects older people.
The cartilage at the end of the bones becomes worn away. The cartilage acted as a shock-absorber. Without it there is a lot more friction so movement of the joint can be very painful.
Sometimes the diseased joint is replaced by an artificial one.

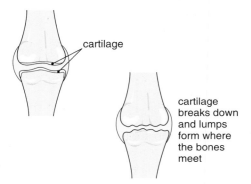

cartilage

cartilage breaks down and lumps form where the bones meet

Normal joint (left); osteoarthritis (right)

An **artificial joint** can be used to replace the ball-and-socket joint at the hip.
It is made up of 2 parts.

- a stainless steel ball which replaces the head of the femur bone, and

- a plastic cup in which the ball swivels.

The artificial joint must have all the important properties of the real one.
It must :

- allow movement in all 3 directions,

- be lubricated to cut down friction,

- be strong and able to absorb knocks.

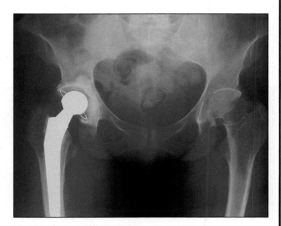

X-ray of an artificial joint

Biology at work : Sports injuries

Many sportsmen and sportswomen run the risk of injury.
The commonest injuries occur to muscles, ligaments, bones and joints.
These sorts of injuries often happen early in the season when training sessions start.

Pulled muscle

This happens when a muscle is over-stretched.
Some of the muscle fibres may tear causing the muscle to contract.
The muscle swells up due to internal bleeding.

Sprains

Ligaments join the bones together at joints.
If a joint bends beyond its normal limits
the ligament can tear.
A strain like this needs rest and the pain can be eased by an ice-pack and a supporting bandage.
If many ligaments tear, a bone can come out of place.
We say that the bone is **dislocated**.
A doctor can put the dislocated bone back in place.

Displaced cartilage

The knee has to withstand a lot of strain.
There are 2 pads of cartilage in the knee joint
that act as shock-absorbers.
One of these may become damaged or pushed out of place if the knee is suddenly twisted.
Soccer players sometimes have to have an operation to remove a displaced cartilage.

Fractures

Bones can become broken or fractured.
- A **simple fracture** is when the bone breaks cleanly in two.
- A **greenstick fracture** is when the bone breaks on one side only.
- A **compound fracture** is when there is more than one break.
- An **open fracture** is when the broken bone pierces the skin.

Fractures are treated by resetting the bone.
After checking with an X-ray, the injury is put in a splint or a plaster cast.

A dislocated shoulder

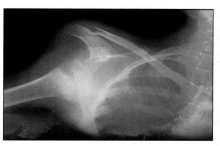

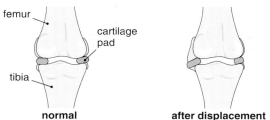

femur
cartilage pad
tibia
normal   **after displacement**

Displaced cartilage in the knee

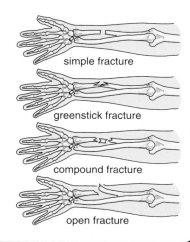

simple fracture

greenstick fracture

compound fracture

open fracture

REPRODUCTION and GROWTH

chapter 10

Reproduction means producing new living things.
Animals and plants reproduce to make new individuals
of the same species.
What would happen if living things didn't reproduce?

There are 2 main ways of reproducing:
- **asexual reproduction**, and
- **sexual reproduction**.

▶ Asexual reproduction

In asexual reproduction there is only **one** parent.
All the offspring are **identical** to the parent.
They have exactly the same genes.
They are called **clones**.

The potato plant
makes potato
tubers.
These separate
and form new
plants.

This saxifrage
makes lots of
little plantlets.
They become
detached to
make new
plants.

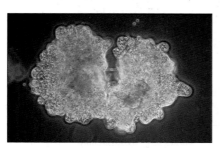

Microscopic organisms like Amoeba
are made of one cell.
They reproduce asexually by
the cell dividing into two.

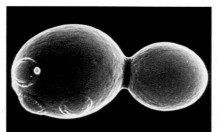

Yeast also divides to make new cells.
Each cell separates to form a new
individual.

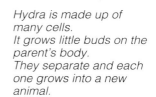

Hydra is made up of
many cells.
It grows little buds on the
parent's body.
They separate and each
one grows into a new
animal.

In all these plants and animals all the offspring
produced have come from **one** parent.

▷ Sexual reproduction

In sexual reproduction there are *two* parents.
The parents have **sex organs**.
The sex organs make **sex cells** or **gametes**.

In male animals the sex cells are called **sperms**.
The sperms are made in sex organs called **testes**
(testis is the singular of testes).

In female animals the sex cells are called **eggs**.
The eggs are made in sex organs called **ovaries**.

During sexual reproduction the sperm and the egg
join together.
This is called **fertilisation**.
A fertilised egg or **zygote** is produced.

The fertilised egg divides many times to form
a ball of cells.

Soon it will grow into an **embryo**.

Eventually it develops into a separate individual.

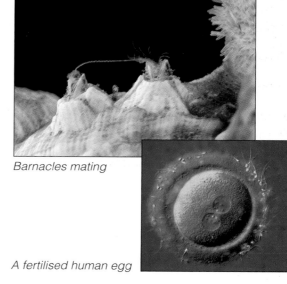

Barnacles mating

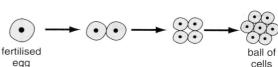

A fertilised human egg

fertilised
egg

ball of
cells

Getting it together

The sperm contains genes from the father.
The egg contains genes from the mother.
The fertilised egg has a mixture of genes
from both parents.

So sexual reproduction brings about greater **variation**
in the offspring.

Fertilisation can take place *outside* the body – in water.
This is called **external fertilisation**.

Can you name some animals that reproduce like this?

In mammals, birds and reptiles the sperm and the egg
join *inside* the body of the female.
This is called **internal fertilisation**.

Can you name some animals that reproduce like this?

155

▶ The female reproductive system

The ovaries are the female sex organs.

They produce the female gametes – the **eggs**.

The ovaries also make the female hormones **oestrogen** and **progesterone**.
This starts to happen between 10 and 15 years.

Oestrogen brings about the changes in a girl's body as she starts to develop into an adult.

For instance, the breasts develop and periods start.

Progesterone prepares the womb so that it could receive a fertilised egg if the girl was pregnant.

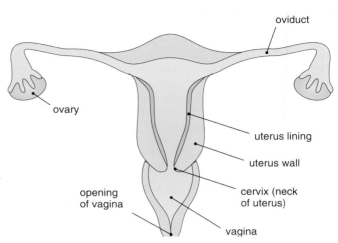

Female reproductive system : front view

- The ovaries are attached to the inside of the abdomen just below the kidneys.

- An egg is released about every 28 days.

- The egg passes out of the ovary and into the funnel-shaped openings of the **oviduct**. This is called **ovulation**.

- The egg moves slowly down the oviduct towards the **uterus** (womb).

- If sperms are present in the oviduct the egg will be fertilised. If the egg is not fertilised it will die after about a day.

- If the egg is fertilised it will attach itself to the lining of the uterus and develop into a baby.

- The lower end of the uterus has a ring of muscle called the **cervix**. It leads to a muscular tube called the **vagina** that opens to the outside of the body.

- Above the opening of the vagina is the urethra opening.
Urine passes out of the urethra.
Above the urethra is the sensitive **clitoris**.

- The outer opening of the vagina is called the **vulva**.

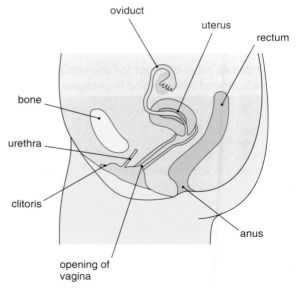

Female reproductive system : side view

▶ Sexual intercourse

Sperms are placed inside the woman's body during sexual intercourse.

- The erect penis is placed into the vagina.

- Fluid made by the walls of the vagina lubricates the passage so that the penis can slide in and out.

- This movement stimulates the penis. Sperms leave the testes and mix with fluid from the glands to make semen.

- Eventually the semen is ejaculated into the vagina. The man experiences feelings of pleasure called an orgasm. Repeated movements of the erect penis against the clitoris or against the vagina may also produce an orgasm for the woman.

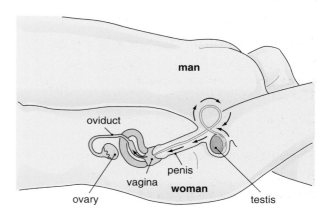

▶ Fertilisation

There are millions of sperms in the man's semen. If one of them is to meet an egg it must swim from the vagina to the oviduct.

They swim through the cervix into the uterus, then up through the mucus lining the uterus all the way to the oviduct.

Many sperms do not survive this difficult journey. Why are so many sperms produced?

If there is an egg in the oviduct, one sperm may succeed in penetrating it.

The sperm's tail is left outside the egg. The sperm nucleus fuses with the egg nucleus. This is **fertilisation**.

A membrane immediately forms around the fertilised egg or **zygote**. This stops other sperms from entering.

If there is no egg in the oviduct no fertilisation can take place. But the sperms can stay alive for 2 or 3 days, so if an egg is released from the ovary during this time it may be fertilised.

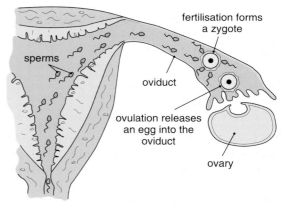

Ovulation and fertilisation

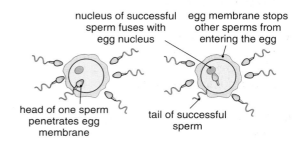

▶ Implantation

Fertilisation takes place in the oviduct.
The fertilised egg or **zygote** begins to
divide.

Eventually it forms a ball of cells.
This starts to move down the oviduct.
It may take several days to reach the uterus.
It is now called the **embryo**.

The embryo sinks into the soft lining of
the uterus. This is called **implantation**.

The embryo gets food and oxygen from
the blood vessels in the uterus lining.
This allows it to grow.

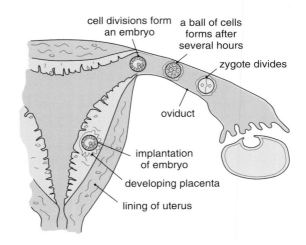

cell divisions form an embryo

a ball of cells forms after several hours

zygote divides

oviduct

implantation of embryo

developing placenta

lining of uterus

▶ The placenta

How does the embryo get food and oxygen
and get rid of waste?

It grows finger-like projections or **villi**
into the uterus lining.
This eventually forms a plate-like structure
called the **placenta**.
The embryo has now developed into a **fetus**.

The **umbilical cord** joins the fetus to the
placenta. The cord contains an artery and a vein that
take the fetus blood to the placenta and back again.

In the placenta the blood of the fetus flows
close to the blood of the mother.
But they do not mix. Why is this?

The mother's blood flows under high pressure.
Do you think it would damage the delicate blood
vessels of the fetus?
What would happen if they were different blood types?

In the placenta food and oxygen diffuse from the
mother's blood into the blood of the fetus.
Carbon dioxide and waste products diffuse from
the blood of the fetus into the mother's blood.

This gives a stable environment for the fetus to grow.

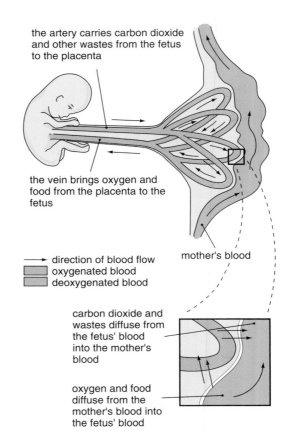

the artery carries carbon dioxide
and other wastes from the fetus
to the placenta

the vein brings oxygen and
food from the placenta to the
fetus

→ direction of blood flow
■ oxygenated blood
■ deoxygenated blood

mother's blood

carbon dioxide and
wastes diffuse from
the fetus' blood
into the mother's
blood

oxygen and food
diffuse from the
mother's blood into
the fetus' blood

▶ Pregnancy

Pregnancy lasts from fertilisation to birth
– that's about 9 months.

The fetus becomes surrounded by a membrane
called the **amnion**.
It contains a fluid in which the fetus floats.
This cushions the fetus and stops it from
being bumped.

At about 4 weeks the heart is beating.
By 8 weeks it has a face, limbs and
fingers and toes.
The mother feels the fetus start to kick
after about 16 weeks.

It is important that the mother looks after
her diet during this time.
Smoking, drinking alcohol and taking drugs
can all harm the fetus.

The placenta protects the baby from
some harmful substances and germs.
Rubella is caused by a virus that can get across
the placenta and damage the fetus.
This is why all young women should be
vaccinated against rubella **before** they
become pregnant.

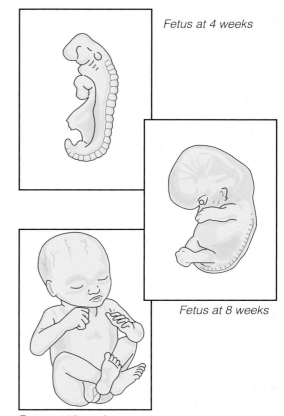

Fetus at 4 weeks

Fetus at 8 weeks

Fetus at 16 weeks

▶ Birth

After about 9 months the baby is ready
to be born.
Its head usually lies above the cervix :

The mother starts to feel small contractions
of the uterus wall. Eventually these become
stronger and happen more often.
The amnion breaks and the fluid escapes.

The muscles of the uterus wall now contract
very strongly and start to push the baby out.

The cervix widens or dilates and the baby's
head is pushed through the vagina.

As the baby is born it breathes air for the
first time.
The cord is tied and cut.

After a few minutes the placenta comes
away from the uterus wall.
This is pushed out as the **afterbirth**.

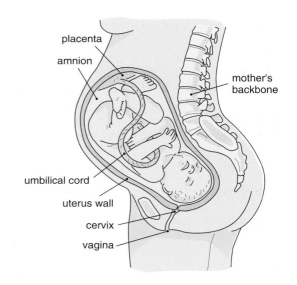

placenta

amnion

mother's backbone

umbilical cord

uterus wall

cervix

vagina

► Ovulation and the menstrual cycle

One change that happens to girls at puberty
is that they start to have periods. This usually
happens when a girl is between 8 and 15 years old.

During a period the lining of the uterus breaks down
and a small amount of blood and cells passes out
of the vagina.
This is called **menstruation**.

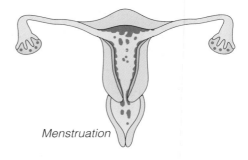

Menstruation

As soon as the girl's period has finished a new egg
starts to develop in the ovary.

It grows inside a fluid-filled ball called a **follicle**.

As the follicle gets bigger it moves to the edge of
the ovary.

Eventually the follicle bursts releasing the egg into
the oviduct.
This is **ovulation**.

The empty follicle forms the **yellow body**.

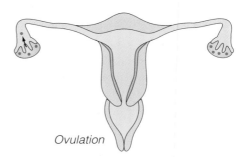

Ovulation

While the egg is developing in the ovary the lining
of the uterus starts to thicken.
In the week after ovulation it has a thick lining
of blood vessels and glands.
If fertilisation occurs the fertilised egg **implants**
in the thick uterus lining.
The woman is pregnant.

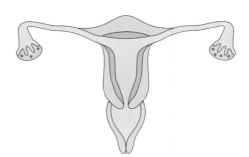

If fertilisation does not occur the egg dies and
passes out of the vagina.

The yellow body also breaks down in the ovary.

The thick lining of the uterus breaks down and
is lost during menstruation.

The cycle now begins again.

Uterus ready for implantation

What happens to the lining of the uterus if a pregnancy
does occur?

Why does a thickened lining of the uterus help
the embryo develop?

Between the ages of 45 and 55 years a woman's
periods stop. This is called the **menopause**.

Ovulation and menstruation are controlled by hormones.

▶ Control of the menstrual cycle

Hormones from the **pituitary** control the cycle.

A pituitary hormone called **FSH (Follicle Stimulating Hormone)** starts the cycle off.
It tells the ovary to make an egg.

The follicle and egg start to develop.
This gives a signal to the ovary telling it to make **oestrogen**.

Oestrogen causes the lining of the uterus to thicken and prevents more eggs developing.

Oestrogen passes to the pituitary in the blood.
It stops the pituitary from making any more FSH.

Instead it gives the signal for another pituitary hormone to be produced.
This is called **LH (Luteinising Hormone)**.

LH makes the ovary release an egg (ovulation).
It also turns the empty follicle into a **yellow body**.

The yellow body starts to make **progesterone**.
Progesterone makes the uterus lining thicken even more.

Both oestrogen and progesterone make sure the lining of the uterus is ready for implantation of the fertilised egg.

If pregnancy occurs these two hormones continue to be produced.
They make sure that the lining of the uterus stays thick and they stop the woman's menstrual cycle.

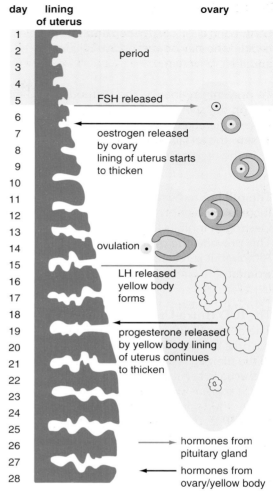

How hormones control ovulation and menstruation

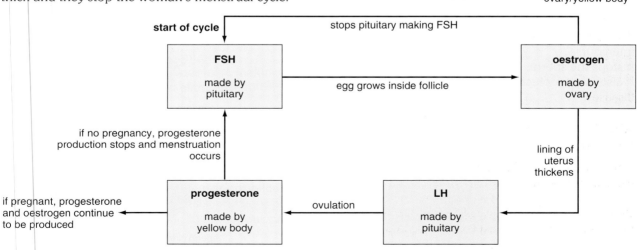

▶ Adolescence

You are born with a complete set of sex organs.
But they only become active later in life.

Between the ages of about 10 and 14, the testes start
to make sperms and the ovaries start to make eggs.
This time of development in your life is called **puberty**.

Girls usually develop earlier than boys do.
But how early varies from person to person.

What do you think starts these changes off?
The answer is 'hormones'.

The **pituitary gland** at the base of the brain
starts to make hormones.
These make the sex organs active.
The sex organs start to produce sex hormones.

The testes start making **testosterone**.
This hormone brings on other changes in boys:
- the testes start to make sperms,
- hair starts to grow on the face and body,
- the voice deepens,
- the muscles develop.

The ovaries start making **oestrogen**.
This hormone brings on other changes in girls:
- the ovaries start to release eggs,
- hair starts to grow on parts of the body,
- the breasts develop,
- the hips widen,
- periods start.

You become an **adolescent** when puberty starts.
Adolescence finishes when you stop growing at
about 18 years.
Adolescence can be an emotional time.
Hormones can bring about mood changes and
increase sexual urges.
Most people cope well and develop into responsible
young adults.

Biology at work : In vitro fertilisation

Some couples are unable to have children.
This may be because the man can not make enough sperms.
Another reason may be that the woman's oviducts are blocked.
Both these problems prevent sperms and eggs from meeting.

In vitro fertilisation can often help these couples.
'In vitro' means 'in glass'.
It involves fertilisation of a human egg outside the body.
This used to be called making 'test-tube babies'.

First the woman is injected with FSH (Follicle
Stimulating Hormone).
This makes her produce eggs.
The doctor makes a small incision in the body wall.
A fine tube is then inserted and the eggs are sucked out.

The eggs are kept alive in a solution containing
food and oxygen.
Some semen from the father is mixed with the eggs.
The fertilised eggs are kept in the solution for a few days.
They are watched under the microscope as they develop
into embryos.

The doctor then places an embryo into the mother's uterus.
The embryo develops normally into a baby.

Why do you think the eggs were placed into a solution
containing food and oxygen?

Why do you think that fertilised eggs are left for a few
days before implanting them into the uterus?

Sometimes more embryos form than can be
used.
Many people think that it is wrong to destroy
these extra embryos.
What do you think?

Sometimes these extra embryos have been
frozen.
They can then be used later if the first
embryos do not grow.
Do you think that it is right to do this?

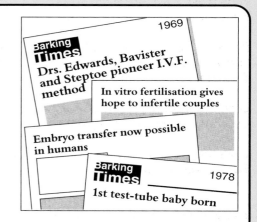

1969
Barking Times
Drs. Edwards, Bavister
and Steptoe pioneer I.V.F.
method

In vitro fertilisation gives
hope to infertile couples

Embryo transfer now possible
in humans

Barking Times
1978
1st test-tube baby born

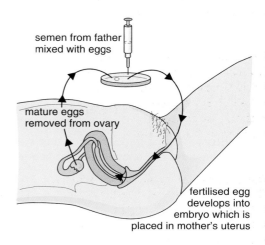

semen from father
mixed with eggs

mature eggs
removed from ovary

fertilised egg
develops into
embryo which is
placed in mother's uterus

▷ Biology at work: Fertility drugs

Women who are not producing eggs can be given a
fertility drug.
This contains Follicle Stimulating Hormone to get
the ovaries to make eggs.
This can cause more than one egg to be produced
at the same time.
This can result in twins, triplets, quadruplets or
even more!

What do you think are the benefits and the problems in
the use of hormones to control fertility?

Twins

Normally only one fetus develops in the uterus
at a time. If two develop then the result is **twins**.

If two eggs are released from the ovary at the
same time they may both be fertilised.
This will result in **non-identical twins**.
The two babies will be born together but they will
look no more alike than brothers and sisters.
This is because they have different genes.
They may also be of different sexes.

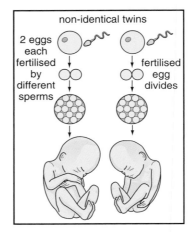

Identical twins look exactly alike.
An egg is released from the ovary and fertilised
as normal.
The fertilised egg or zygote splits into two separate
cells.
Each of these develops into a baby.

Since they have both come from the same fertilised
egg cell they will have the same genes.
For this reason they are always the same sex.

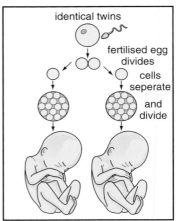

Summary

- Asexual reproduction results in offspring that are identical to the parent (clones).

- Sexual reproduction involves 2 parents and the production of sex cells.

- Fertilisation involves the joining together of a sperm and an egg.

- Sexual reproduction results in greater genetic variation.

- Sperms are produced in sex organs called testes and eggs are produced in sex organs called ovaries.

- During sexual intercourse semen from the male is put into the female's vagina.

- Fertilisation occurs in the oviduct and the fertilised egg implants into the uterus wall.

- The placenta controls the exchange of materials between the fetus and the mother. During pregnancy the fetus grows inside the uterus of the mother.

- The menstrual cycle is controlled by hormones. Hormones also result in the development of male and female features during puberty.

▶ Questions

1. Copy and complete:
   An egg is made in one of the . . . . about every 4 . . . . . It passes into the . . . . where fertilisation may take place if . . . . are present. The sperms are made inside the . . . . of the male. They are put into the . . . . of the female during . . . . intercourse. The sperms have to swim through the cervix and up through the . . . . before they reach the oviduct. If . . . . takes place in the oviduct, the fertilised egg passes down to the uterus where it . . . . into the wall. Eventually a . . . . forms to which the embryo is attached by an . . . . cord.

2. a) Give 3 examples of living things that reproduce asexually.
   b) Give 3 examples of living things that reproduce sexually.
   c) Give 3 examples of animals that carry out external fertilisation.
   d) Give 3 examples of animals that carry out internal fertilisation.

3. Look at the diagram of the female reproductive system:

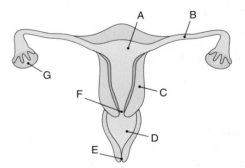

   a) Name the parts labelled A to G.
   b) Where on the diagram do each of the following take place:
      i) the release of an egg,
      ii) fertilisation,
      iii) implantation,
      iv) the baby passing through here during birth?
   c) What happens to the wall of the uterus
      i) before release of an egg
      ii) if no fertilisation occurs?
      How are these events controlled?

4. a) How many sperms are needed to fertilise an egg?
   b) Why does a membrane form around the egg after fertilisation?
   c) Give 3 differences between a sperm and an egg.
   d) Why is it important that the sperm and the egg each have half the normal number of chromosomes?

5. Look at the diagram of the male reproductive system:

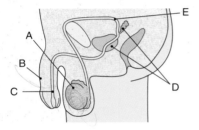

   a) Name the parts labelled A to E.
   b) Which of the structures on the diagram is responsible for the following:
      i) making sperms
      ii) adding fluids to the sperms to make semen
      iii) passing semen into the vagina of the female
      iv) carrying sperms from the testis to the penis.
      v) carrying semen and urine at different times?

6. An egg is released from a woman's ovary on 7th March.
   a) Over which days would fertilisation be most likely to occur?
   b) The egg was not fertilised. How soon after 7th March will the woman's period start?
   c) How long does a period usually last?
   d) When is the next egg likely to be released?

7. a) What is the female hormone produced by the ovaries during puberty?
   b) What changes does this hormone make in a girl's body?
   c) What is the male hormone produced by the testes during puberty?
   d) What changes does this hormone make in a boy's body?

8. Look at the diagram showing the baby in the uterus:

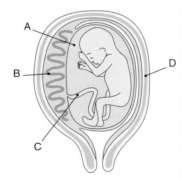

   a) Name the parts labelled A to D.
   b) How does the baby get the food and oxygen that it needs?
   c) How does the baby get rid of waste products?
   d) What is the function of the fluid A?
   e) Why should the mother not smoke while she is pregnant?

Further questions on page 201.

chapter 11

▶ Microbes and disease

In the 19th century **Louis Pasteur** showed that
microbes made food go bad.
He thought that microbes could also caused disease.
He was able to show that infectious disease was caused
by cholera in hens and by anthrax in sheep.

About the same time, **Robert Koch** was able to prove
that diseases such as tuberculosis were caused by microbes.
Pure cultures of microbes when injected into healthy animals
brought about the symptoms of the disease.

Pasteur and Koch could not have imagined that one day
not only a particular disease organism would be identified,
but that we could vaccinate against it and even eradicate it
from the world,as in the case of smallpox.

Louis Pasteur

Robert Koch

What are germs?

Bacteria,viruses and fungi are all microbes.
Not all of them are harmful.Some are useful
and help us to make bread,cheese and wine.
The microbes that cause disease are called **germs**.

(*Remember* : Not **all** diseases are caused by microbes,
for instance,diabetes is a disease caused by the
pancreas not being able to make enough insulin).

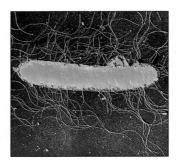

A bacterium found in the gut

Bacteria

Bacteria are cells that are big enough to be seen
under the light microscope.
Bacteria are found everywhere - in the air,
in water and in the soil.
They can also be found inside living organisms.
Some bacteria are useful, but others can cause diseases
such as pneumonia,scarlet fever and tuberculosis.

The basic structure of a bacterial cell is shown here.
Can you see the differences between this cell
and an animal cell or a plant cell?

The bacterial cell has a cell wall,but not made out
of cellulose as in plant cells.
There is no proper nucleus,just a loop of DNA.
Many of the structures found inside other cells
such as mitochondria,are missing in bacteria.
Bacteria often have additional loops of DNA
inside their cytoplasm called **plasmids**.
You can find out more about plasmids on page 289.

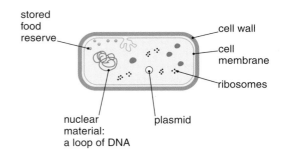

stored
food
reserve

cell wall

cell
membrane

ribosomes

nuclear
material:
a loop of DNA

plasmid

Bacterial growth

Bacteria can be grown in sterile conditions in the laboratory (page 309).
A colony of bacteria starts with just 1 cell.
In the right conditions, the cell divides to give 2 cells, 2 cells become 4, 4 become 8, 8 become 16, and so on.
Bacteria can multiply very quickly to form a **colony**.

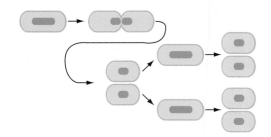

If you look at the graph you can see 4 main phases in the growth of a bacterial colony:

- The **lag phase** when little growth occurs since the cells are taking up water and starting to make enzymes.
- The **log phase** when the population is increasing rapidly. The population increases by doubling and there is no shortage of food or water.
- The **stationary phase** when bacterial cells are dying at the same rate at which they are being produced. This may be because of shortage of food or because waste products are building up.
- The **death phase** when more cells are dying than are being produced,so the population declines. Cause of death may be lack of food, shortage of oxygen or a build up of toxic waste products.

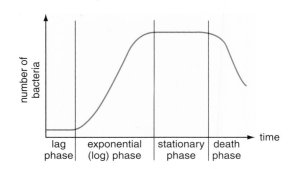

Bacteria which cause disease can survive harsh conditions such as heat,cold and drought.
They can rest for a long time as **spores**.
When good conditions return,they germinate and multiple rapidly again.

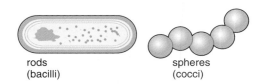

rods
(bacilli)

spheres
(cocci)

There are 3 main shapes of bacteria – **bacillus** (rods), **coccus** (spheres) and **spirillum** (spirals).

spirals
(spirilla)

Fungi

Some fungi can also cause disease such as athlete's foot and ringworm.
Fungi are not plants since they do not have chlorophyll.
The main fungus body is called the **mycelium.**
It consists of a branching network of threads or **hyphae.**
The hyphae grow over the surface of their food source.
They releases enzymes which digest the food outside the fungus.
The digested food is then absorbed by the hyphae.
Fungi reproduce by making spores that can be carried to infect another person or animal.
Fungi are visible under the light microscope and the spread of fungal disease increases in poor hygiene conditions.

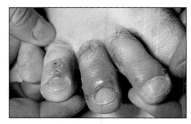

Athlete's foot

Viruses

Like some bacteria and fungi, viruses are **pathogens**.
This means that they can cause disease.
Viruses are **parasites** – this means that they rely upon the cells
of another organism (the **host**) for food and to be able to reproduce.

Viruses are extremely small, far smaller than bacteria or fungi.
They are only visible under an electron microscope.

A virus consists of a **protein coat** which surrounds
a core of either DNA or (less often RNA). (See pages 273, 275.)
In fact, viruses are not proper cells at all.
They have no cell membrane and no nucleus.
So how do they exist and reproduce?

Viruses can only exist *inside* living cells.
Once they enter the host cell, they hijack its enzymes
and use them to make new viruses.
This takes place as follows:

- The virus enters the body.

- The viral DNA is injected into the host cell.

- The viral DNA instructs the enzymes in the host cell
  to make new virus protein coats.

- The viral DNA also multiplies inside the host cell.

- The new viral DNA and protein coats join together
  to make new viruses.

- The host cell bursts releasing the new viruses.

- The new viruses are now free to infect other cells.

Viruses can be very harmful and are the cause of
many diseases because they reproduce so quickly.
They do not respond to antibiotics and are constantly
changing to produce new resistant strains.

Diseases caused by viruses include influenza, the common cold,
measles, chickenpox and AIDS.
You can find out more about how the HIV virus
can cause AIDS on page 184.

Foot-and-mouth disease is a virus that can devastate livestock

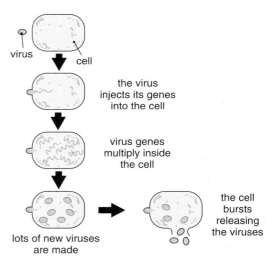

virus
cell

the virus injects its genes into the cell

virus genes multiply inside the cell

lots of new viruses are made

the cell bursts releasing the viruses

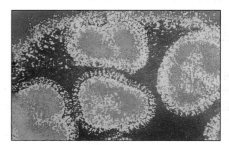

Influenza viruses

▶ How do germs affect us ?

Germs have to enter our body before they can do us any harm.
They can get in through the nose and mouth and through any cuts in our skin.

Once inside the body the germs start to multiply.
Conditions inside our body are just right for them and numbers can increase rapidly.
But it takes some time before we start to feel ill.
This early stage of the disease is called the **incubation period**.

So how do germs affect us ?

Germs can cause disease in 2 ways :

- They destroy living tissue, for example, lung tissue can be destroyed by tuberculosis bacteria.

- They make poisonous waste called **toxins**, for example, salmonella bacteria make the toxins that cause food poisoning.

The **symptoms** of a disease are the effects that it has on the body.
These symptoms are often caused by the toxins that the germs make.

Diseases are spread when the germs from one person are passed on to another person.
A person who has the disease is **infectious**.
They may pass the disease on to other people.

Can you think of any ways in which diseases are spread ?

Death toll rises in food bug outbreak

Five people have died of food poisoning in Britain's worst case of *E. coli bacteria* contamination.

A hospital has been closed to all GP-arranged admissions except suspected cases of the *E. coli 0157* food poisoning outbreak.

The butcher's shop thought to be the source of the outbreak announced yesterday that it was temporarily closing.

Seven members of staff linked to the food poisoning outbreak in Scotland are infected.

Thirty-two adults and a child were being treated yesterday in the hospital, where the Lanarkshire Infectious Disease Unit is based. The number giving cause for concern rose from ten to 15 over the weekend, and the number showing symptoms rose from 189 to 209.

symptoms

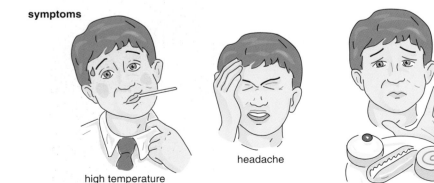

high temperature

headache

loss of appetite

sickness

all are caused by the body trying to fight, or resist, the microbes causing the infection

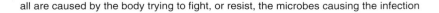

▶ How are germs spread ?

Here are some ways in which people can be infected with germs.

In the air
Germs can enter our body in the air we breathe. The germs can stick to dust floating in the air.

The bacteria causing diphtheria can be spread like this.

What happens when an infected person sneezes or coughs ?

Tiny drops of liquid are showered into the air. This is why you should cough or sneeze into a handkerchief.

Viruses that cause flu and the common cold are spread in this way.

By touching
You can pick up some germs by touching an infected person.
You can also become infected by touching things that an infected person has used such as towels, combs or cups.

The fungus that causes athlete's foot is spread by walking on wet floors after infected people.

A disease that is spread by touch is **contagious**. Very few diseases are contagious.

In food and water
Food and drink can be infected with germs.

Typhoid and cholera are spread when infected faeces get into drinking water.

Infection can be passed onto food by a person with dirty hands.
This is why you should always wash your hands after going to the toilet and before you have a meal.

Some food products that come from animals contain bacteria which are only destroyed by cooking thoroughly.
Salmonella bacteria are found in some poultry products.

By animals

Many animal pests can carry germs that
they pick up from faeces.
Flies will settle on animal dung.
If they crawl over uncovered food they will
spread the germs from the faeces like the dysentary bacterium.

Mosquitoes can spread malaria if they bite
an infected person.
They carry the germs to the next person that they bite
and so the disease is spread.

By infected needles

Drug addicts should never share needles.
If an infected person uses a needle the disease
can be passed on to anyone else who uses it.

Viruses causing diseases such as AIDS and
hepatitis can be passed into the blood in this way.

Preventing infection

Good hygiene is often the key to preventing
the spread of disease :

- Wash your hands
  - before meals,
  - after going to the toilet, and
  - before handling food.

- Wash your hair regularly – special shampoos
  can get rid of dandruff and head lice.

- Have a regular bath or shower especially in
  hot weather.

- Clean your teeth at least twice a day – first
  thing in the morning and last thing at night.

- Thoroughly wash any cuts or scratches.
  A plaster will help to stop microbes getting in.

- *Food* should be covered to keep flies away.
  Cook food thoroughly and eat it straight away
  or keep it in the fridge or freezer.
  Keep cooked food away from raw food.

- *Water* should be boiled (or chemically sterilised)
  before drinking if there is any risk of
  contamination.

How many ways of spreading disease can you find here ?

▷ Destroying germs

If something is **sterile** it is free from germs.
Can you think of any ways of killing germs
outside the body?

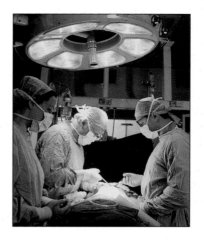

- **Heating** is one way of sterilising.
  Hospitals use heat to sterilise instruments.
  They are heated to 120 °C in a type of pressure
  cooker called an **autoclave**.

- Dressings can be treated with **radioactivity**
  to kill all microbes.

- **Disinfectants** are chemicals that kill germs.
  They are often used on non-living surfaces.
  Disinfectants are used on kitchen work surfaces
  and in toilets.

- **Antiseptics** are chemicals that kill germs
  on living tissue.
  They are weaker than disinfectants which would
  damage our cells.

In the 1860s the British surgeon **Joseph Lister**
used the first antiseptic.
Lister noticed that patients' wounds often went
bad or **septic** after operations.
He concluded that the microbes entered the
wounds from the air.
Lister sprayed wounds with an antiseptic called
carbolic acid during the operation.
He also washed scalpels and dressings with it.
Far fewer patients died from infected wounds.

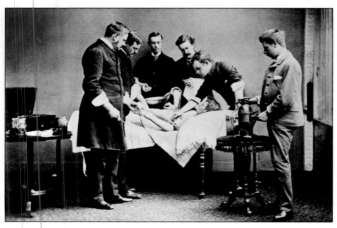

Joseph Lister performing an operation using the first antiseptic

▶ Barriers

How does your body defend itself from germs?

Your body has a number of ways of stopping microbes from getting in.

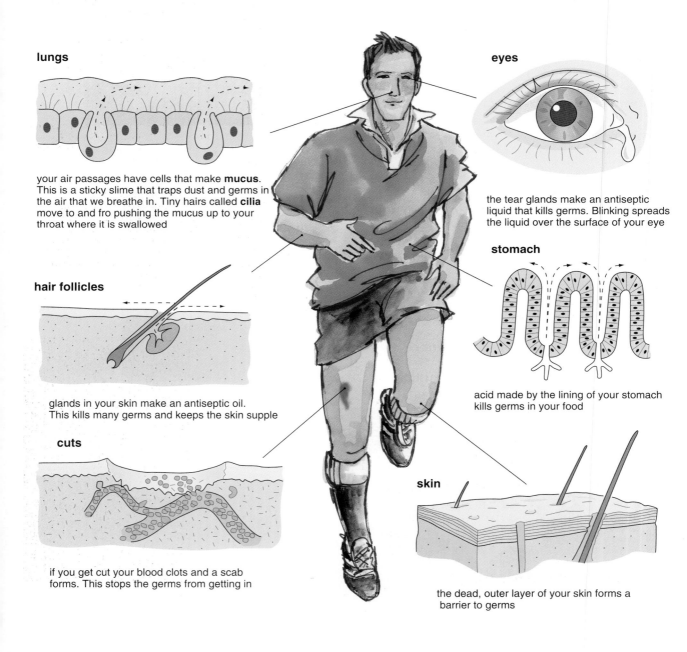

lungs

your air passages have cells that make **mucus**. This is a sticky slime that traps dust and germs in the air that we breathe in. Tiny hairs called **cilia** move to and fro pushing the mucus up to your throat where it is swallowed

hair follicles

glands in your skin make an antiseptic oil. This kills many germs and keeps the skin supple

cuts

if you get cut your blood clots and a scab forms. This stops the germs from getting in

eyes

the tear glands make an antiseptic liquid that kills germs. Blinking spreads the liquid over the surface of your eye

stomach

acid made by the lining of your stomach kills germs in your food

skin

the dead, outer layer of your skin forms a barrier to germs

▶ Immunity

Do you know how germs are killed *inside* the body?.

All germs have chemicals on their surface called **antigens**.
These chemicals are largely made of protein.
When you catch a disease like measles your body makes chemicals called **antibodies**.
These antibodies stick to the antigens on the surface of the microbe.
Antibodies make the germs stick together.
White blood cells are then able to attack and destroy them more easily.

Each type of germ has a different antigen.
So each kind of germ can only be destroyed by a certain kind of antibody.
Once you have made a particular antibody it stays in your blood for a long time.
It is ready to kill any more germs if you get the same disease again.
You are now **immune** to that particular disease.

White blood cells can also make chemicals called **antitoxins**.
These destroy the toxins(poisonous wastes) made by the germs.

You don't have to catch a disease to become immune to it.
You can be **immunised** with a **vaccine**.
A vaccine contains dead or inactive germs.
These germs still have antigens and they stimulate your white cells to make antibodies.
These antibodies will now destroy the antigens.

Once you have been **vaccinated**, your immune system will be able to react very rapidly if you are infected by the same germs again.
Antibodies will be made, and the antigens destroyed possibly without you having any symptoms.

This is called **active immunity**.

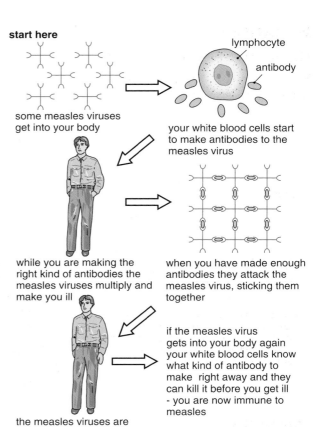

start here

lymphocyte

antibody

some measles viruses get into your body

your white blood cells start to make antibodies to the measles virus

while you are making the right kind of antibodies the measles viruses multiply and make you ill

when you have made enough antibodies they attack the measles virus, sticking them together

if the measles virus gets into your body again your white blood cells know what kind of antibody to make right away and they can kill it before you get ill - you are now immune to measles

the measles viruses are made harmless and you get better

A rubella vaccination

Passive immunity.

With **passive immunity** you are not injected with weakened germs but with antibodies themselves.
This treatment is used to give rapid protection against particularly dangerous germs.
A good example is the disease **rabies** which you might catch if bitten by an infected dog.

How does the immune system work?

Two types of white blood cells (**lymphocytes**) are involved in giving us immunity.
They are called **T cells** and **B cells**.

The T cells recognise the antigens on the surface of the germs.
To do this they have special **receptors** on their surface.
These receptors allow the T cells to attach to the antigens, and they can then destroy them.

T cells also have another important job.
They stimulate the B cells to multiply.
The B cells produce **clones** (genetically identical copies) of themselves.
These cells are then able to produce antibodies against any specific antigens.

There are as many as 10 million different B cells.
So for every antigen that enters the body, there will almost certainly be a B cell to produce antibodies against it.

Some B cells are known as **memory B cells.**
These don't actually make antibodies but they are still very important.

They live in the blood for a long time and they **remember** particular antigens.
This means that the next time you pick up a particular infection your immune system can respond to it very rapidly.

These B cells give us what is called an **immunological memory.**

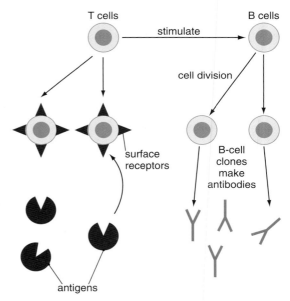

The production of lymphocyte T and B cells

► Vaccines

About 200 years ago smallpox was a deadly disease.
Edward Jenner was a doctor in Gloucestershire.
He noticed that people who caught cowpox were
immune to smallpox.
Cowpox is a mild disease which can be caught
from cattle.

Jenner scratched the skin of a young boy.
He then rubbed in pus from a person suffering
from cowpox.
The boy caught cowpox but soon recovered
and was immune to the disease.

Then he inoculated the boy with pus from a
smallpox victim.
The boy did not catch the deadly smallpox.
The boy had become immune to smallpox because the
virus had similar antigens to the cowpox virus.

Poliomyelitis ('polio' for short) is a virus that destroys
nerve cells.
It damages the spinal cord so much that victims
become paralysed.

In 1953 **Jonas Salk** made a vaccine to prevent polio.
He was able to kill samples of the virus.
Injecting the dead virus into people gave them
immunity to the disease.
Polio has now disappeared from developed countries.

In 1999 the UK became the first country to use a
new vaccine against Meningitis C.
This is a serious bacterial disease responsible for many
deaths amongst children.

First used in Britain in 1988, the combined MMR vaccine
gives protection against 3 diseases: measles, mumps
and rubella (German measles).
It is controversial because many people fear that the vaccine
will make their children more susceptible to a condition
called **autism** (a mental condition impairing responses).

What other diseases are vaccines available for?

Have you been inoculated against tetanus, whooping
cough, measles, diphtheria, rubella, mumps or influenza?

Jenner vaccinating his son

Epidemic feared after meningitis claims two adults

181

Boosters

There are some diseases that vaccines can
not be made for
If there is an outbreak of the disease people
need protection quickly.
They can be injected with ready-made antibodies.
These antibodies have been made in the body
of another person or animal.

But antibodies that we have **not** made inside
ourselves do not always last very long.
A further dose or 'booster' may need to be given.
Boosters are needed to protect against typhoid
and cholera.

▷ Medicines

Some chemicals can be used to relieve the
symptoms of a disease but they don't kill germs.
For instance, aspirin is used as a painkiller.
Other chemicals like **antibiotics** relieve the
symptoms by killing the germs.

The first antibiotic was discovered by
Alexander Fleming in 1928.
He was growing bacteria on agar plates.
But he left one of the plates open by accident.
A mould started to grow on the surface.

Fleming noticed that the mould was stopping
the bacteria from spreading.
It seemed to be making a substance that killed
the bacteria.
The mould was called *Penicillium notatum*.

10 years later **Howard Florey** and **Ernst Chain**
discovered how to extract large quantities of the
active substance found in the mould.

This substance was called **penicillin** and was the
first antibiotic. It was quickly put to good use in
treating soldiers' wounds in the Second World War.

Today when we talk about penicillin we are referring
to a large group of antibiotics. These are produced
by a variety of different strains of the penicillium
fungus.

Alexander Fleming at work in his laboratory

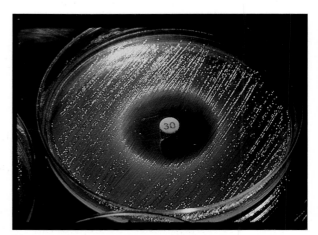

*No bacteria are growing around the
penicillin disc at the centre*

▶ Malaria

As we have already seen on page 65,
malaria is a disease spread by the bite of
the female *Anopheles* mosquito.

It is an example of a disease caused
by neither a virus nor bacteria.
The microbe responsible is a tiny single-celled
parasite called **Plasmodium**.

When a mosquito bites an uninfected person,
Plasmodium passes into the blood together with
saliva.
It then invades the red blood cells and liver cells.
In these cells it multiplies producing many more parasites.

What are the symptoms of malaria?

Malaria victims tend to suffer from regular bouts
of fever accompanied by chills and heavy sweating.
These bouts are associated with the bursting
of red blood cells and the release of more parasites.

The most dangerous form of malaria involves the
red blood cells sticking together. This blocks the
blood supply to important organs like the brain
and can cause death.

How can malaria be prevented?

Most effort goes into destroying the mosquito
and so preventing its transmission.
Some examples of control measures are:

- using insecticides to kill mosquito larvae in ponds
- stocking ponds with fish that eat the larvae
- draining the ponds that the mosquitoes use as
  breeding areas
- surrounding beds with nets treated with insecticide.

Other methods of control involve dealing with the humans
rather than the mosquito:

- use of anti-malarial drugs, like quinine, which prevent
  the parasite from spreading throughout the body
- development of vaccines
- use of insect repellents on the skin.

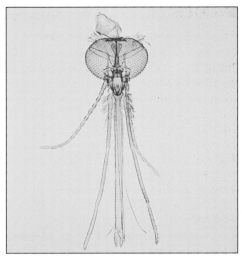

The mosquito has mouthparts adapted to
pierce skin

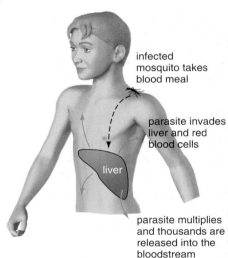

infected
mosquito takes
blood meal

parasite invades
liver and red
blood cells

liver

parasite multiplies
and thousands are
released into the
bloodstream

The development of malaria

Healthworker fumigates homes to
remove mosquitoes

▶ AIDS (Acquired immune deficiency syndrome)

Most people have heard of **AIDS**.
But how many know exactly what it is?.
AIDS is actually a collection of diseases
which result from a weakening of the
immune system.

AIDS is caused by a virus called **HIV**.
HIV (human immunodeficiency virus) attacks
and destroys the white blood cells that help
us to fight infection.
This reduces the body's ability to fight disease.

The early symptoms of AIDS are very much like flu,
with swollen glands and a high temperature.
Later symptoms might include weight loss, various
types of cancer and a decrease in brain function.

Catching HIV does not necessarily result in AIDS.
Some people simply remain as carriers, with no symptoms at all.

How is HIV transmitted?

HIV is transmitted in the blood or semen.
The virus can pass from one person to another
during sexual intercourse.
Either partner may infect the other.

The virus can also be passed via hypodermic needles
contaminated with infected blood.
In this way, HIV has spread very quickly amongst drug addicts.

Unborn babies are also at risk from HIV.
This is because the virus can pass across the placenta
to the fetus.

How can AIDS be prevented?

Although there is no cure for AIDS and as yet no
vaccine for HIV. There are precautions that can reduce
its spread. These include :
- the use of condoms during sexual intercourse
- setting up free needle exchanges to reduce the use of
  shared needles amongst drug users
- careful screening of donated blood used for transfusions.

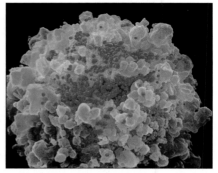

A white blood cell infected by the HIV virus (shown in red)

The HIV virus can be passed via dirty needles

A government leaflet warning about the dangers of AIDs

184

▶ Drug abuse

Drugs and solvents are powerful chemicals that can change how you think, feel and behave.

So far we have mentioned some useful medicines like antibiotics and painkillers.

Medicines contain at least one drug. That's why you should be very careful when you use them.

Medicines can help cure a disease but can be dangerous if you exceed the prescribed dose.

But there are other drugs that are not useful. Some like tobacco are legal, but others like cannabis and ecstasy are not.

Alcohol and tobacco are the two commonest drugs. They are easily available but can cause serious health problems.

There are many different drugs and solvents. Different drugs have different effects on people. The strength of the drug also affects what it does to you.

Some people take a drug without knowing what's in it or how powerful it is. This makes taking the drug even more dangerous.

Britain has strict laws against people who possess, sell or pass on certain drugs. Breaking these laws can mean a fine, caution or maybe a prison sentence. Some people are becoming so desperate to get drugs that they steal or commit other crimes to get the money to buy them.

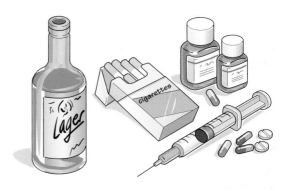

Piriton Tablets (chlorpheniramine maleate 4mg)
Fast relief from nettle rash, hives, heat rash, prickly heat or dermatitis; reactions to food, medicines or insect bites; hayfever symptoms of the eyes and nose
INGREDIENTS Active: chlorpheniramine maleate. Also contains: lactose, maize starch, magnesium stearate, colour: yellow iron oxide (E172)
DOSAGE Adults: Take one tablet every four to six hours (maximum 6 in one day). **Children aged 6-12:** Half a tablet every four to six hours (maximum 6 halves in one day). Not recommended for children under 6
If symptoms persist consult your doctor
DO NOT TAKE PIRITON TABLETS IF YOU ARE TAKING MAOI DRUGS
Please read the enclosed information leaflet carefully before use
KEEP ALL MEDICINES OUT OF THE REACH OF CHILDREN

WARNING: May cause drowsiness. If affected do not drive or operate machinery. Avoid alcoholic drink. P

PL10949/0106   Piriton is a Glaxo trade mark © 1994
p Glaxo Pharmaceuticals UK Ltd, UB11 1BT, England   Store below 30°C

▶ How do the drugs act ?

Drugs affect the brain and nervous system.

Drugs that slow down the nervous system
are called **depressants**.
Barbiturates and heroin are depressants.
Benzodiazepines have now replaced barbiturates
for most medical purposes – they are known
as **tranquillisers**.

Drugs that speed up the nervous system
are called **stimulants**.
Amphetamines and cocaine are stimulants.

Some drugs are taken by mouth.
Ecstasy tablets are stimulants.
They are swallowed to make people feel as if they
have more energy.
Some young people have died through using ecstasy.

Drugs like cannabis are smoked.
Users smoke it to feel relaxed.
But it is thought to cause respiratory
diseases like lung cancer and bronchitis.

Injecting a drug is the most dangerous way of taking it.
It is easy to 'overdose' and sharing needles spreads hepatitis
and HIV, the virus that causes AIDS.

The body gets used to some kinds of drugs.
To get the same effect a person has to take
an increasing amount of the drug.
The body has developed a **tolerance** to it.
A person can become dependent on the drug
if they start to have to take it regularly.
Addiction means that the person has become so
dependent on the drug that it is doing them serious harm.

If a person stops taking a drug they have become
addicted to, they develop **withdrawal symptoms**.
But if the drug is not taken these effects can fade
after 2 or 3 weeks.

Think about the use and misuse of drugs. You could include
antibiotics such as penicillin, pain killers like aspirin and heroin,
stimulants like caffeine and amphetamines and sedatives like
alcohol and barbiturates.

▶ Solvents

Solvents are everyday products like glues,
dry-cleaning fluid, aerosols and lighter fuel.
They give off fumes that **sniffers** breathe in.
Solvents contain dangerous chemicals that can kill you.

Solvent abuse is a growing problem among
youngsters aged 12 to 16.
It is against the law for shopkeepers to sell solvents to
people under 18 years of age.
But many of the solvents are easily available around
the home.

Solvent fumes are absorbed by the lungs and soon
get to the brain.
They slow down breathing and heartbeat rate.
Repeated or deep breathing can cause loss of
control and unconsciousness.

Solvent abuse claims more deaths than heroin
and cocaine put together.
Some people die immediately after inhaling some
chemicals like aerosols, cleaning fluids and butane gas.
These 'sudden sniff' deaths are often due to
heart failure.

Suffocation can occur if sniffers inhale from
large plastic bags.

Aerosol sprays squirted into the mouth can
freeze the air passages causing suffocation.

Sniffers can appear to be drunk.

They run the risks linked with being drunk, like :

- falling from a building or being involved
  in a road accident,
- passing out and choking on their own vomit.

There is also a risk of fire because
many solvents are flammable.

THE DAILY SKETCH
15TH FEBRUARY 1996

SOLVENT ABUSE
NEW DANGERS

The dangers of solvent abuse
were graphically illustrated
today as the teenage daughter of
a prominent local business man
was admitted to hospital near to
death. Rosie Simmons (14) was
taken to Gloucester Royal
Infirmary after collapsing in her
... after inhaling an

girls also present were taken under
observation but later released
without treatment.
Rosies father, Giles Simmons (44)
the owner of a local chain of
newsagents claimed that the sale of
solvents to young people was to
blame."

The best advice is ***never inhale solvents***.

Describe the harmful effects of solvents and tobacco
on the body and the dangers of contracting HIV
and hepatitis when injecting drugs.

▶ Alcohol

Alcohol is a socially acceptable drug.
It is a part of many people's social lives.

Alcohol is made when yeast is added to
a sugary solution such as grape juice.
The yeast breaks down the sugar to make
alcohol and carbon dioxide gas.
This is called fermentation.

Alcohol is a **depressant** – it slows down your
body's reactions.
As with many other drugs it can be **abused**.
Alcohol does not often kill – a person usually loses
consciousness before they can take a fatal amount.

Some people become **dependent** upon alcohol.
Their bodies develop a **tolerance** and they need
to take greater amounts to get the same effect.
People that become **addicted** to alcohol can not
face life without a drink
They are called **alcoholics**.

Alcohol is absorbed through the gut and carried
to the brain in the blood.
From there it affects the nervous system.
Many people find a little alcohol relaxing.
Increasing amounts make them dizzy.
Their judgement and reactions become affected.
For this reason a person should not drink and drive.

With greater amounts of alcohol people lose control
of their muscles and their speech becomes slurred.
A person in this state is more likely to get into
a fight or have an accident.
Their coordination becomes so poor that they can not
walk and end up passing out.

Look at the diagram :
How many units of alcohol are there in :
– a double whisky
– a pint of beer ?

Different brands of alcoholic drinks have
different strengths of alcohol.
Why are spirits served in smaller glasses
than beer ?
Some lagers are much stronger than others.
The strength of alcohol is shown on the label
as percentage volume of alcohol.

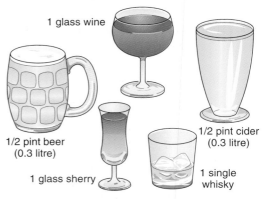

1 glass wine

1/2 pint beer
(0.3 litre)

1/2 pint cider
(0.3 litre)

1 glass sherry

1 single
whisky

All these drinks contain 1 unit of alcohol

▶ Long-term effects of alcohol

Drinking large amounts of alcohol over a number
of years can have serious effects on health.
It can lead to stomach ulcers, heart disease and
brain damage.

The liver is the part of the body that breaks
down alcohol.
Alcohol abuse over a number of years can lead
to **cirrhosis** of the liver.
The liver tissue becomes scarred and its healthy cells
become replaced with fat, or fibrous tissue.
The liver becomes less able to carry out its job
of removing the toxins from the blood.

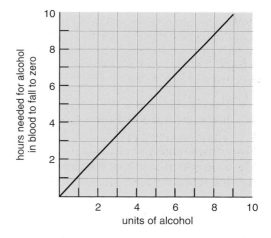

Even a healthy liver takes time to break down
alcohol and make it harmless.
It takes about *one hour* to remove *one unit* of
alcohol from the blood.
So depending upon the strength and quantity of
the drink, it may take several hours before the
body is free from alcohol.

Different drinks contain different amounts of alcohol.
Also a 'safe' amount of alcohol will depend upon age,
sex, body size and metabolic rate.
The safe amount for a woman is about two-thirds of
that for a man of the same weight.

Like many other drugs alcohol is habit-forming.
A social drinker can turn into a problem drinker.

Many people who become dependent on alcohol
do not think that they are.
They try to convince themselves that they do not
have a problem.
They feel tense and irritable and find it hard
to cope with everyday problems without a drink.

Alcoholics can cause their families pain and misery.
They can become aggressive after drinking and
spend a lot of money on drink.

Organisations like Alcoholics Anonymous can
help alcoholics.

▶ Biology at work : Preserving food

Do you know what makes food go off?

Bacteria and fungi get into the food from the air.
They attack the food and make it taste bad.
Some of these microbes can make us ill.

To stop food going bad we can **preserve** it.

To do this we must:
- kill the microbes in the food, and
- stop them from growing again.

Fancy these grapes?

What conditions do you think stops food from
going bad?

- **Heating** food to a high temperature sterilises it.
  It can then be sealed in clean *cans* or *bottles*.

- **Pasteurisation** kills the bacteria in milk.
  It was invented by **Louis Pasteur**.
  The milk is heated to 72 °C for 15 seconds, then
  cooled quickly.
  This kills most of the bacteria and does not affect
  the flavour.

- **Cooling** food stops microbes from growing and
  reproducing but it does not kill them.

  A refrigerator keeps food at about 5 °C.
  This will keep food fresh for a few days.

  A freezer preserves food at below −18 °C.
  This stops all microbe activity and food can be
  preserved for many months.
  But once the food thaws the microbes start
  to grow again.

  Frozen food should be fully defrosted before
  it is thoroughly cooked, otherwise the microbes
  will just be warmed by the cooking and will
  multiply quickly.

▶ Biology at work : Preserving food

- **Drying** is a way of preserving foods like fruit, vegetables and some meats.
  The microbes can not live without water.
  Some foods like coffee and soups
  are **freeze-dried**.
  The food is frozen and the ice
  is drawn off in a vacuum
  before sealing in packets.

- **Chemicals** can kill microbes in food.
  Many **food additives** act as preservatives, including sulphur dioxide, nitrates and nitrites.
  Each one is given an **'E number'**.

Freeze-dried foods

Other chemicals that have been used
for many years are :

Pickling foods in vinegar makes it too acid for microbes to live.

Adding **salt** takes water out of the food by osmosis so the microbes die.

The **sugar** in preserved jams also makes microbes lose water by osmosis.

Fish like kippers and salmon are
preserved by **smoking**.
The smoke kills the microbes in the foods.

- **Irradiation** kills the bacteria and fungi that cause food spoilage.

How are each of these foods preserved ?

The food is exposed to gamma radiation.
This kills the microbes but does not denature enzymes in the food.
So the ripening and texture of fruit and vegetables is not affected.
Food cannot be sold for a period of **24** hours after irradiation.
In the past there has been resistance to this technique.

Think about arguments for and against food preservation by:

– irradiation

– chemical preservatives.

▶ Biology at work : Antibodies and pregnancy testing

As we have seen earlier in this chapter, antibodies
play an important role in our immune system.
They also have a wide range of other uses,
e.g. in pregnancy testing and the inactivation
of poisons.

To use antibodies in this way, scientists have
found a way of creating pure samples
called **monoclonal antibodies**.

How are these pure samples produced?.
Firstly scientists take B cells that
produce a specific antibody.
They then combine them with a type of
rapidly dividing cancer cell.

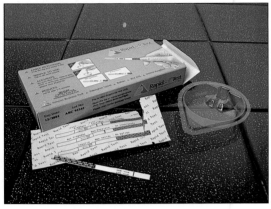

A commercial pregnancy testing kit

These **fused** cells then produce only
the antibody specific to the original
B cells.

In pregnancy testing kits, these antibodies
can be used to detect the presence of a hormone
called **human chorionic gonadotrophin (hCG)**.
This is found in the urine of women in the early
stages of pregnancy.

The test kit has a dipstick, which has a band of
the antibodies on its surface.
When this stick is dipped in a urine sample
these antibodies will bind with any molecules of hCG
that are present.

This combination of hormone and antibody then
moves up the stick.
Eventually it reaches another band of antibodies
which also bind to hCG, and at this point the
combination of antibodies and hCG will show up
as a coloured line.

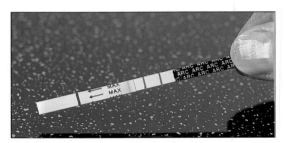

Test stick showing a positive result

If this line is seen on the dipstick then the test is positive,
the woman is pregnant.

Summary

- Germs are microbes that cause disease. They include bacteria, fungi and viruses. The symptoms of a disease are caused by the toxins made by the germs. Germs can be spread in the air, by touch, in food and water, and by animals. Good hygiene is the best way of preventing the spread of disease. Disinfectants and antiseptics help to prevent the spread of infection.

- The body's own defences include skin, blood and mucus lining the air passages of the lungs. When you catch a disease your body makes antibodies that give you immunity.

- A vaccine is a dead or harmless sample of a disease microbe.

- Antibiotic drugs have been very successful in the treatment of disease.

- Drugs and solvents are powerful chemicals that affect the way your body works.

- Like other drugs alcohol can cause tolerance, dependence and addiction.

▶ Questions

1. Copy and complete:
   Germs are . . . . that cause disease. Human diseases are caused by . . . ., bacteria and . . . . . The early stage of a disease is called its . . . . period. The symptoms of a disease are caused by the . . . . made by the germs. If something is germ-free we say that it is . . . . . Germs are *killed* on work surfaces by . . . . . Germs are killed on living tissues by using . . . . . Your air passages have cells that make . . . . . This traps dust and . . . . and tiny hairs called . . . . carry the mucus up to the throat.

2. Explain why you should:
   a) Always wash your hands before handling food.
   b) Never share a towel with someone.
   c) Always wash your hands after going to the toilet.
   d) Never let a dog lick your face.

3. a) What does it mean when you are immune to a disease?
   b) How is immunity brought about?
   c) What is a vaccine?
   d) How does a vaccine work?

4. The apparatus below was used in an experiment to find out the conditions which cause milk to decay.

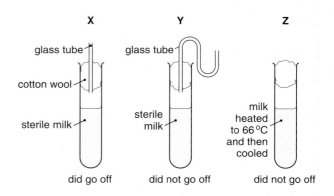

The milk in test-tubes **X** and **Y** was sterilised by boiling.
a) What kind of organisms make food go bad?
b) Explain why the milk in test-tube **X** went off but the milk in test-tube **Y** did not.
c) Milk is often preserved by the treatment in test-tube **Z**.
   Why is it better to use this method rather than boiling the milk?

5. Look at the graph. It shows a patient's temperature when suffering from a bacterial disease.

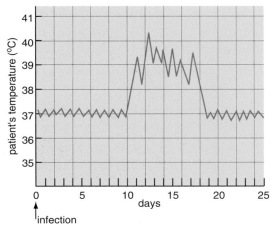

infection

a) What symptom of the disease is shown on the graph?
b) How long was the incubation period? What was happening during this time?
c) What caused the fever and how long did it last?

6. a) What is an antibiotic?
b) How was the first antibiotic discovered?
c) In the 1960s American soldiers in Vietnam were treated for syphilis with the antibiotic penicillin. But some of the syphilis germs became resistant to the penicillin. How do you think this could happen?

7. What do you think is the difference between each of these:
a) a disinfectant and an antiseptic
b) an antibody and an antibiotic
c) a stimulant and a depressant
d) dependence and addiction?

8. a) In what ways can a drug be taken?
b) What parts of the body does a drug affect?
c) What different effects can drugs have on the body?

9. Before going to lunch at 1.00 p.m., Dennis had a glass of sherry. During lunch he had 2 glasses of wine and a brandy. He returned to work at 2.00 p.m. and worked until 5.30 p.m. On leaving work Dennis drank 2 pints of beer and at 8.00 p.m. caught a taxi home.
   The graph shows the level of alcohol in Dennis' blood from lunchtime onwards.

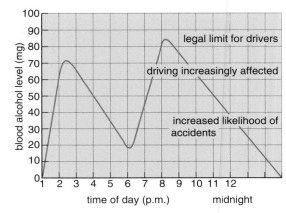

a) From the graph, state the time when:
   i) the blood-alcohol level was highest.
   ii) he was most likely to have an accident at work.
b) If Dennis had not drunk any beer, when would his blood-alcohol level probably have returned to zero?
c) At what time could he have driven his own car home legally?
d) When would his blood have had no alcohol in it?

10. Explain why the following are **not** true:
a) Drinking beer is less harmful than drinking spirits.
b) Alcohol is a stimulant drug.
c) It is safe to drive if you are below the legal limit.
d) Drinking heavily for many years does you no harm because your body gets used to it.

Further questions on page 203.

Food and digestion

1. The table below gives some information about the nutritional content of a traditional beefburger and of a similar non-meat vegetable burger. Vegetable burgers are made from a mycoprotein, coloured and flavoured to taste like beef.

Contents per 100 g	Beefburger	Vegetable burger
energy	1192 kJ	970 kJ
protein	15.0 g	18.5 g
carbohydrate	3.7 g	11.7 g
fat	23.8 g	12.7 g
sodium**	0.5 g	1.3 g
fibre	0.4 g	4.5 g

**mostly as sodium chloride

a) i) Which 'burger' has the higher protein content per 100 g? [1]
   ii) How much protein is present in 120 g of beefburger? [1]
   iii) In which organ of the body are carbohydrates stored? [1]
   iv) Name the carbohydrate which is stored in this organ? [1]
b) State **two** reasons why a person who is anxious to eat a healthy diet might choose the vegetable burger rather than the beefburger. Give an explanation for the choice in each case. [4] (OCR)

2. Food substances need to be digested before they can pass into the blood.
Many foods contain fat.
a) What are the products of fat digestion? [1]
b) The liver produces a chemical substance called bile which is added to food during digestion. Explain how bile helps in the digestion of fat. [3]
c) Describe **one** effect of eating too much food rich in animal (saturated) fat and explain the problems this may eventually produce in the body. [2] (EDEX)

3. The diagram shows the main regions of the alimentary canal in a human.

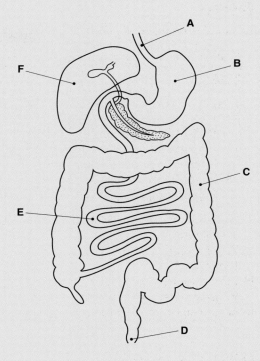

a) Name the parts labelled **A**, **B**, **C**, **D**, **E** and **F** on the diagram. [3]
b) In which of these structures
   i) are fatty acids and glycerol absorbed [1]
   ii) is most water absorbed; [1]
   iii) does egestion take place? [1] (OCR)

Breathing and respiration

4. a) Explain, as fully as you can, why respiration has to take place more rapidly during exercise. [2]
b) During exercise the process of respiration produces excess heat. Explain how the body prevents this heat from causing a rise in the core (deep) body temperature. [4]
c) In an investigation four groups of athletes were studied. The maximum rate of oxygen consumption for each athlete was measured and the mean for each group was calculated. The athletes then ran 10 mile races and the

mean of the best times was calculated for each group. The results are shown in the table below.

Group of athletes	Maximum rate of oxygen consumption (cm^3 per kg per min)	Best time in 10 mile race (minutes)
A	78.6	48.9
B	67.5	55.1
C	63.0	58.7
D	57.4	64.6

i) What is the relationship between maximum rate of oxygen consumption and time for a 10 mile race ? [1]

ii) Suggest an explanation for this relationship. [3] (AQA)

5. The diagram shows the breathing system of man.

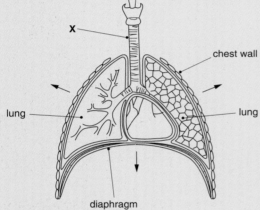

diaphragm

a) Name the tube **X**. [1]

b) Explain how tube **X** is kept open. [1]

c) Why is it necessary to keep tube **X** open ? [1]

d) Explain what would happen to the *volume* and *pressure* of air inside the lungs when the chest wall and diaphragm are moved in the direction shown by the arrows. [2]

e) What makes the diaphragm move in the direction shown ? [1]

f) The volume of air breathed during three different activities is shown on the graph.

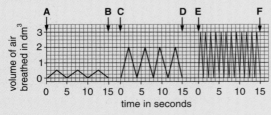

i) What was the number of breaths per minute during the activity between **C** and **D** ? [1]

ii) What was the volume of air exchanged per breath during the activity between **E** and **F** ? [1]

iii) Copy and complete the table by selecting from the list below the most appropriate activity.

running hard,   resting,   jogging

Activity between	Activity
A and **B**	
C and **D**	
E and **F**	

[3]   (OCR)

6. The information below was found on a cigarette packet.

> Warning : SMOKING CAN CAUSE FATAL DISEASES

a) Name **two** respiratory diseases which could be caused by cigarette smoking. [2]

b) The diagram below shows an alveolus (air-sac).

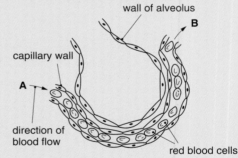

i) Through how many cell layers must oxygen pass to leave the air in the alveolus and reach a red blood cell ? [1]

The table below shows the relative concentrations of gases dissolved in the blood at the ends of the capillary shown in the diagram.

Gas	End A	End B
Carbon dioxide		
Oxygen	low	

ii) Copy and complete the table using the words **high** and **low**. [2]

c) i) Name a type of blood cell **not** shown in the diagram. [1]

ii) Explain how the cell named in c) i) is involved in the body's defence against disease. [1] (OCR)

7. a) Describe how the muscles, bones and their associated structures bring about smooth movement at the elbow hinge joint. [7]

b) During vigorous exercise a muscle builds up an 'oxygen debt'.

i) What happens to cause an 'oxygen debt' ? [3]

ii) How is the ability to build up an oxygen debt an advantage to the athlete ? [2]

c) Energy used in muscle cells originates from the sun.

i) Explain how the sun's energy is used in the production of food for animals. [5]

ii) It has recently been claimed that increased combustion of fossil fuels could lead to increased supplies of energy rich foods becoming available to animals. Suggest and explain a possible reason for this claim. [3] (OCR)

▷ **Blood and circulation**

8. The diagram shows the heart and pulmonary circulation of a human.

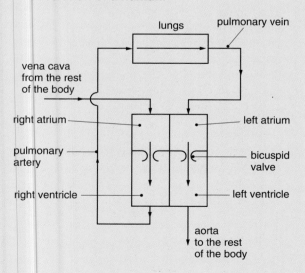

Using **only** the information given in the diagram, answer questions a) and b).

i) Name the blood vessel through which blood enters the heart from the body. [1]

ii) Name the blood vessel through which blood leaves the heart on its way to the rest of the body. [1]

b) Describe the path taken by the blood from the point where it enters the heart from the body, to the point where it leaves the heart for the second time. [8] (OCR)

9. The diagram represents a smear of blood on a microscope slide.

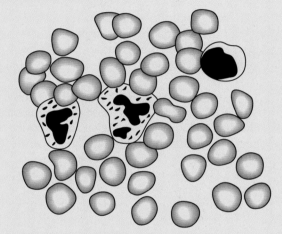

a) i) How many red blood cells can be seen on the slide ?

ii) How many white blood cells can be seen on the slide ? [2]

b) i) What is the function of the red blood cells ? [1]

ii) Give **two** ways in which red blood cells are adapted to carry out this function. [2]

c) Explain how carbon monoxide affects the way in which red blood cells function. [1]

d) Red blood cells survive on average about 100 days. New cells have to be produced in the bone marow.

i) Why are red blood cells not able to reproduce ? [1]

ii) 1 mm^3 of blood contains 5 million red blood cells.
How many red blood cells does 1 cm^3 (1000 mm^3) contain? [1]

iii) An adult has 5000 cm^3 of blood. How many red blood cells have to be made on average each day in the bone marrow? Show your working [2]

e) In some people the bone marrow is diseased and unable to produce enough red blood cells. These people may need a transplant of bone marrow from another person.
Explain how each of the following may help to prevent the rejection of the transplanted bone marrow.
  i) Use bone marrow from a brother or sister of the patient. [2]
  ii) Giving the patient drugs which stop the activity of the white blood cells. [2]
f) After the transplant operation the patient has to be isolated from other people for some time. Explain why. [2] (AQA)

10. The movement of blood through the circulatory system of a mammal is described as a double circulation. Explain how the structure of the heart maintains the double circulation and keeps the blood flowing under pressure. [9]
  b) i) Describe what is meant by coronary heart attack. [2]
  ii) How might diet and cigarette smoking make a heart attack more likely? [4]
  c) Describe how amino acids pass from the small intestine of a mammal to the heart via the liver. You should name the blood vessels through which the amino acids will be transported. [5] (OCR)

11. Three pupils were asked to find out who was the fittest. They decided to do this by measuring their pulse rates.
This is what they did.

1. They counted their pulse rates when sitting down.
2. They then exercised for three minutes in different ways:
   Peter ran up and down the stairs;
   Margaret did step-ups;
   John ran on the spot.
3. They counted their pulse rates as soon as the exercise stopped.

4. They counted their pulse rates three minutes after the exercise stopped and again six minutes after the exercise stopped.

Their results are shown on the graph below.

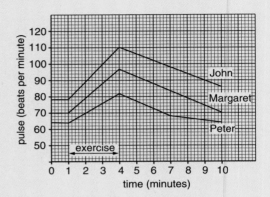

a) What was Margaret's pulse rate three minutes after exercise? [1]
b) They concluded that Peter was the fittest person.
Give one reason why they reached this conclusion. [1]
c) Suggest two ways they could have improved their investigation. [2] (AQA)

▶ Homeostasis

12. The regulation of body temperature is achieved by balancing energy release against energy loss. Energy release is greater during exercise.
a) The rate of metabolism changes during exercise. Describe how this influences energy release. [2]
b) Explain why, during exercise, the body attempts to lose more energy. [2]
c) What role does **negative feedback** play in regulating body temperature? [1]
d) During rest, excess sugar is stored. How is this achieved? [2]
e) The graphs opposite show how the blood glucose and the concentration of hormone involved in glucose storage vary over a 12 hour time period.

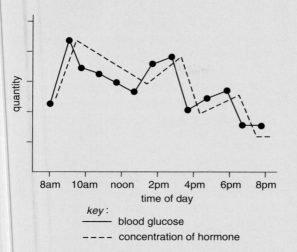

key :
——— blood glucose
---- concentration of hormone

i) Using these graphs explain why a single daily dose of hormone would not adequately control blood glucose concentration in diabetics. [2]

ii) Explain how physical exercise would influence the production of the hormone involved in glucose storage. [2] (OCR)

13. The graph shows the temperature of a monkey, a lizard and the air over a 24-hour period.

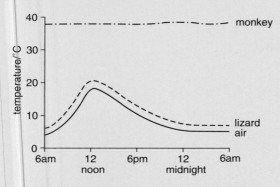

Using the information shown by the graph :

a) how does the body temperature of the monkey differ from that of the lizard? [1]

b) how do you account for this difference? [1]

c) i) At what time of day can the lizard be most active? [1]

   ii) Explain your answer. [1]

d) Suggest **one** way in which a mammal like the monkey could keep cool on a hot day. [1] (OCR)

14. The diagram shows the mean daily input and output of water for an adult.

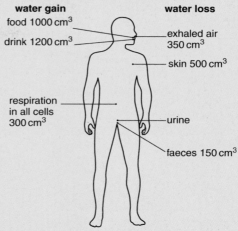

a) Respiration is a source of water. Copy and complete the equation for respiration
   sugar + ... → water + ... + energy [2]

b) The kidneys keep the water content of the body constant by controlling the volume of water passed out in the urine.

   i) Use data from the diagram to calculate the mean daily output of water in the urine. Show your working. [2]

   ii) Describe how the amount of water in the body is controlled by the kidneys. [3]

c) Sometimes kidneys fail. Two ways of treating kidney failure are the use of a dialysis machine and kidney transplants.
   Describe what happens to the composition of a patient's blood as it passes through a dialysis machine. [3]

d) In the treatment of kidney failure:

   i) Give **two** possible advantages of using a kidney transplant rather than a dialysis machine. [2]

   ii) Give **two** possible disadvantages of using a kidney machine rather than a dialysis machine. [2] (AQA)

15. The kidneys remove waste materials from the liquid part of the blood. The table overleaf shows the concentration of certain substances:
    ● in the liquid part of the blood
    ● in the liquid that has just been filtered from the blood in the kidneys
    ● in the solution in the bladder.

Further questions on Humans as organisms

II) Use the information in your graph and the table to help you explain your answer to part I) above. [2]

b) State **two** medical uses of sex hormones in humans. [2] (WJEC)

22. a) Describe how the needs of a human embryo are provided. [4]

b) The diagram shows part of the control system involved in the female reproductive cycle.

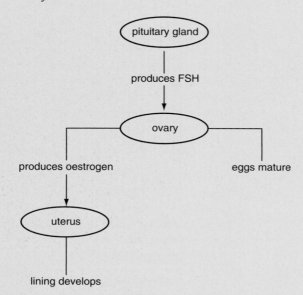

i) What type of substance are FSH and oestrogen ? [1]

ii) How does FSH get from the pituitary gland to the ovary ? [1]

c) High levels of oestrogen inhibit the production of FSH by the pituitary gland.

i) Explain how this is an example of negative feedback. [2]

ii) One drug that is used to treat female infertility is clomiphene. Clomiphene blocks the inhibitory effect of oestrogen on FSH production.
Explain how this may help in the treatment of infertility. [2] (AQA)

23. The diagram shows the normal menstrual cycle of a woman.

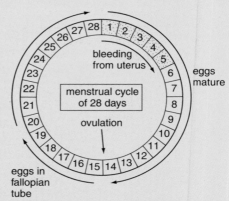

a) Where in the body are eggs produced ? [1]

b) What happens on day 14 of this cycle ? [2]

c) How do the eggs reach the uterus ? [1]

d) On which four days of this cycle is the egg **most likely** to be fertilised ? [2]

e) Male sperm can live in the female reproductive organs for up to seven days. Which is the earliest day in the cycle when sexual intercourse could produce a baby ? [1]

f) Write down the name of the type of contraception which

i) is **most** effective against the spread of AIDS. [1]

ii) stops eggs being produced [1] (OCR)

24. The graph shows how the uterus lining varies in thickness with time. Fertilisation took place on the 16th day of the second menstrual cycle.

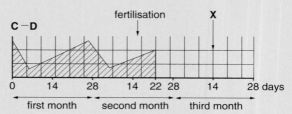

a) State the process which took place between **C** and **D**. [1]

b) Copy and complete the graph to point **X** to show what happens to the lining of the uterus after day 22 in the second month. [1]

c) Explain why it is important that the uterus lining changes in the way shown. [2]

d) Describe what happens to the zygote from the time it is formed until implantation occurs. [2]

e) If the oviducts (Fallopian tubes) are blocked, a woman cannot have a baby in the normal way, but may be able to have a 'test tube' baby. In order for this to happen, a doctor pushes a fine tube through the body wall and takes several eggs from the ovary.
Why can't the eggs be obtained through the vagina and uterus? [1]

f) The eggs are then put into a small glass dish and sperm are mixed with them. After a few days the developing zygotes are put back into the woman's uterus through the cervix.
  i) Why are sperm mixed with the eggs before they are put back into the woman? [2]
  ii) Explain why the zygotes are kept for a few days before they are put back into the woman. [1]

g) Give **two** reasons why the term **test-tube baby** is misleading. [2]

h) Name **three** changes which take place in the uterus to help protect and nourish the developing embryo. [3] (WJEC)

▷ Health

25. The diagram shows two Petri dishes and a wire inoculating loop. Petri dish **1** contains several colonies of bacteria from garden soil growing on agar jelly. Petri dish **2** contains sterile agar jelly only.

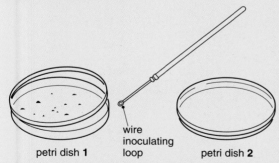

wire inoculating loop

petri dish **1**   petri dish **2**

a) Bacteria can be transferred from a colony in dish **1** to the agar jelly in dish **2** using the wire loop. The following precautions should be taken:

  1. The wire loop is heated to red heat in a Bunsen flame and then cooled before use.

2. The lid of each dish is raised just a little at one side for a short time to insert the wire loop.
3. The wire loop is used quickly after heating and cooling and is not allowed to touch any other object (e.g. hands or the bench).
4. The wire loop is re-heated and cooled again after use.
Explain the need for each of these **four** precautions. [4]

b) After the bacteria had been transferred to Petri dish **2**, the dish was placed in an incubator at 35 °C. Why was the Petri dish kept at 35 °C rather than at room temperature (20 °C)? [1] (AQA)

26. A person was given two vaccinations of an inactivated virus. The graph shows the person's primary and secondary immune responses.

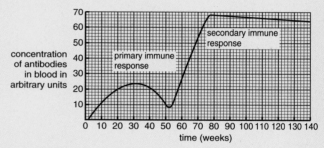

a) Draw an arrow on the graph to show when the second vaccination was given. [1]

b) Describe how proteins on the outside of inactivated viruses result in the production of antibodies. [3]

c) Give **three** ways in which the primary immune response is different from the secondary immune response [3]

d) Why is it important to use an inactivated virus? [1] (EDEX)

27. The hepatitis B virus causes a life-threatening disease. Vaccines for this virus can cost over £100 per dose. American scientists have genetically engineered bananas to produce an antigen, found on the hepatitis B virus. The banana 'vaccine' then produced costs a few pence per dose.
The hepatitis antigen has already been produced by genetically engineering potatoes. It has produced an immune response in rats which eat raw potatoes.

Further questions on Humans as organisms

a) If antigens are proteins, state why boiled potatoes would be of no use in giving immunity to humans. [1]

b) State an advantage of using genetically engineered bananas rather than normal vaccines in developing (Third World) countries. [1]

c) The following diagram shows how the immune response is stimulated by antigens.

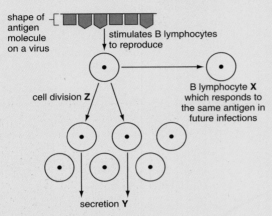

i) the type of B lymphocyte at **X**, [1]
ii) the product secreted at **Y**, [1]
iii) the type of cell division at **Z**. [1]

d) Copy and complete the following table to show **three** different ways of producing vaccines and the diseases to which they give immunity. [5]

Method of producing vaccine	Disease protected against
1 use of killed microbe	
2	
3	

(WJEC)

28. a) The conversion of proteins to amino acids can be represented as shown below.

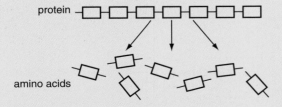

i) What name is given to the breaking down of proteins into amino acids in the body ? [1]
ii) State **one** use of amino acids in the body. [1]

b) Antibodies are proteins produced in the blood by the immune system when the body is infected.

i) Which part of the immune system produces antibodies ? [1]
ii) The effectiveness of a person's immune system can be reduced by the use of drugs. State **one other** way this can happen. [1]
iii) If a person has a kidney or other organ transplant, drugs are given to reduce the effectiveness of the immune system. Explain the reason for this. [2]

c) **Active** immunity is a permanent type of immunity gained as a result of the body reacting to an infection. **Passive** immunity is a temporary type of immunity where antibodies are given to the body, often by injection.

A baby may acquire passive immunity **other than** by means of an injection. State **one** way. [1]

d) A graph of a person's immunity is shown below.

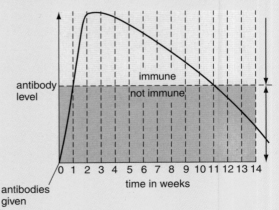

i) For how long was the person immune ? [1]
ii) Does the person to whom the graph refers have active or passive immunity ? Explain the reason for your answer. [2] (AQA)

Feeding in plants

What's the most common colour in nature?

Most of the green we see comes from leaves.
Why are they this colour?

If you look at some leaf cells under the
microscope what do you see?
Lots of round, green structures called
chloroplasts.
What do you think they are used for?

We call green plants the **producers**.
Why do you think this is?

Green plants are able to make their own food
from simple raw materials around them.
This process is called **photosynthesis**.

Energy is needed for photosynthesis.
This energy comes from sunlight.

Chlorophyll is a substance that absorbs sunlight.
Chloroplasts contain lots of chlorophyll.

The light energy is used to convert carbon dioxide
and water into sugars.
The sugars are the plant's food.
Oxygen is made as a waste product.

During photosynthesis the energy from sunlight
becomes converted into the chemical bond energy
in the sugars.

Photosynthesis is not a simple reaction.
It takes place in a number of small stages.
This is the equation for the whole process:

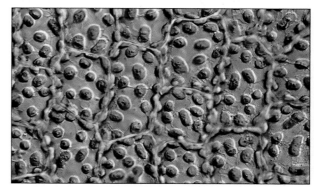

Chloroplasts in moss cells

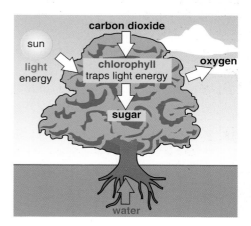

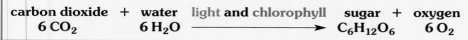

carbon dioxide	+	water	light **and** chlorophyll	sugar	+	oxygen
$6\,CO_2$		$6\,H_2O$	$\longrightarrow$	$C_6H_{12}O_6$		$6\,O_2$

▶ Investigating photosynthesis

Green plants make food from simple substances.
We can see from the equation on the previous page
that sugar is made.

*Starch grains provide an
insoluble store of food*

> *Experiment 12.1   Testing a plant for sugar*
>
> Put a piece of raw onion in a pestle and mortar.
> Grind it up with a little sand and 10 cm³ of water.
>
> ⚠ eye protection
>
> Filter the liquid into a test-tube.
>
> Heat the liquid with 10 drops of Benedict's solution
> on a water bath.
>
> Did the liquid turn orange?

If too much sugar is dissolved in the cell sap it
would make a strong solution. This would draw
water in from other cells by osmosis.
Starch is insoluble and does not cause this problem.

> *Experiment 12.2   Testing a leaf for starch*
>
> Dip a leaf into boiling water for about a minute
> to soften it.
>
> Turn off the Bunsen burner.
>
> ⚠ eye protection
>
> Put the leaf into a test-tube of ethanol.
> Stand the test-tube in a beaker of hot water
> for about 10 minutes.
>
> ⚠ ethanol is flammable
>
> Wash the leaf in cold water.
>
> Spread the leaf out flat on a petri dish and
> cover it with iodine solution.
> If the leaf goes blue-black, starch is present.
>
>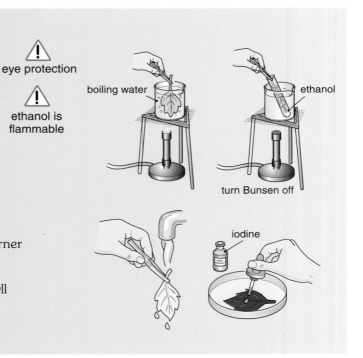
>
> • Why is it important to turn off the Bunsen burner
>   when you were heating the ethanol?
>
> • Why was it necessary to extract the chlorophyll
>   before you tested for starch?

▷ Raw materials for photosynthesis

What do plants need for photosynthesis?

We have already said that light energy is
needed to power the process.
If you look back at the equation on page 205
you will see what else is needed.

- **Chlorophyll** absorbs the light energy.
  Chlorophyll is in the chloroplasts of the leaf.

- **Carbon dioxide** gets into the leaves from the air.

- **Water** gets into the roots from the soil.

We can carry out experiments to show that these
raw materials are needed for photosynthesis.
We simply give the plant all the things that it needs
except for the one factor that we are investigating.

If the plant is unable to carry out photosynthesis
it will not make starch.
But we must make sure that the plant has no starch
to begin with.
We can **de-starch** as plant by leaving it in
the dark for 24 hours.

Experiment 12.3   Is chlorophyll needed for photosynthesis?

Take a de-starched, variegated geranium plant.
(Variegated means some parts of the leaves are
white because there is no chlorophyll there.)

Place the plant in sunlight for a few hours.

Draw one leaf to show the white and green parts.

Now test this variegated leaf for starch.

⚠️
eye protection

- Did only the green parts of the leaf go blue-black?
  Why did this happen?

- Why didn't you extract chlorophyll from the leaf
  and then see if it could carry out photosynthesis?

From air and water

How could you prove that a plant needs **carbon dioxide** to make its own food?

Provide it with everything it needs for photosynthesis *except* carbon dioxide. Then test to see if it has made starch.

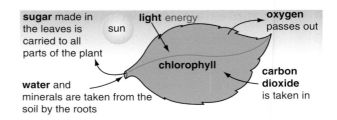

sugar made in the leaves is carried to all parts of the plant

light energy

sun

oxygen passes out

chlorophyll

carbon dioxide is taken in

water and minerals are taken from the soil by the roots

Experiment 12.4   Is carbon dioxide needed for photosynthesis?

Take a de-starched geranium plant.

Enclose it in a plastic bag with a chemical that absorbs carbon dioxide.
(**Soda lime** absorbs carbon dioxide.)

Leave the plant in sunlight for a few hours.

Test a leaf for starch.

 eye protection

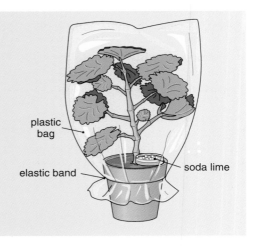

plastic bag

soda lime

elastic band

- Does the leaf contain starch? Why not?
- Has the plant carried out photosynthesis?
- What would be your **control** plant?
  A control plant should have everything it needs for photosynthesis *including* carbon dioxide.

Experiment 12.5   Is sunlight needed for photosynthesis?

Take a de-starched geranium plant.

Cover part of the leaf with some tin foil (this prevents light getting through).

Leave the plant in sunlight for a few hours.

Test the leaf for starch.

⚠ eye protection

aluminium foil

starch present

no starch

- Which parts of the test leaf go blue-black?
- Why do the parts that were covered **not** contain starch?

Plants also need water for photosynthesis.
Can you think up a simple experiment to prove this?
It's not easy is it?
If you remove all the water the plant will shrivel up.

Scientists can give plants a special form of water called 'heavy water'.
They can trace this water and see where it goes.
They can show that it is taken up and used in photosynthesis.

▷ Products of photosynthesis

Let's remind ourselves of the photosynthesis equation:

$$\text{carbon dioxide} + \text{water} \xrightarrow[\text{chlorophyll}]{\text{sunlight}} \text{sugar} + \text{oxygen}$$

So how are the products of the reaction useful?

Most photosynthesis takes place in the leaves.
So most of the food is made there.
But **all** parts of the plant need food.
Dissolved food is carried around the plant in its
transport system.
What happens to it then?

- Some of the **sugar** is used in respiration to
  give the plant energy.

- Some of the sugar is changed to starch and stored
  in the roots for future use.

- Some of the sugar is used to make **cellulose**.
  This is needed for plant cell walls.

Sugars can also be converted to other substances:

- Plants get nitrogen by absorbing nitrates from the soil.
  Sugars and nitrogen can form **amino acids**.
  Proteins are built up from amino acids.
  Plants need **proteins** for growth and cell repair.

- **Fats** and **oils** are used for storage in seeds.

Oxygen is also a product of photosynthesis.
This replaces the oxygen that is used up in respiration.

Cellulose strands in a plant cell wall

Experiment 12.6   Oxygen produced in photosynthesis

Set up the apparatus to collect bubbles of gas
given off by the pondweed.
Dissolve a little sodium hydrogencarbonate in the water.
Place the apparatus in the light.

Test the gas for oxygen with a glowing splint.

- Why was hydrogencarbonate added to the water?

- Why is it important to leave a gap between the beaker
  and the funnel?

Water rich in carbon dioxide circulates to the pondweed
and increases the rate of photosynthesis.

- Why is it essential that a water plant like Canadian pondweed
  is used in this experiment?
  (**Hint**: Think about how the gas is collected.)

- Why is the gas collected unlikely to be pure oxygen?

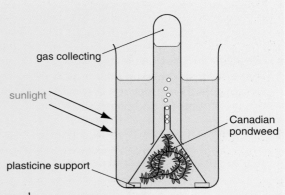

▶ Why is photosynthesis important?

Think about the food you've eaten in the
last 24 hours.
How much of it came from plants?

How about rice, potatoes, corn flakes and
peanuts for a start?

And what about the steak or the beefburger?
Where did they come from?
From animals that have eaten plants.

Then there are things like cooking oil and
low-fat margarine.
They are made from parts of plants.
Without plants we would soon get pretty hungry!

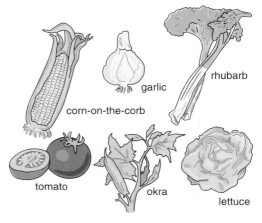

corn-on-the-corb
garlic
rhubarb
tomato
okra
lettuce

> *Experiment 12.7   Food plants*
>
> Look at some food plants like the ones shown here:
>
> Try to say what ***parts*** of plants they are.
> For instance, celery is a leaf stalk.
>
> Draw some parts of the plants that we eat.
> Write a note to say what each part does in a
> living plant.
>
> Carry out some food tests on different plant parts.
>
> Try testing carrot, onion, potato and different seeds.
> Test for sugar, starch, protein and fat.
> (See Experiments 4.1, 4.2, 4.3, 4.4, pages 45–7)

eye protection

- **Medicines** have been extracted from over 40
  species of flowering plants. Tropical rainforests
  are the main source of these plants.

- **Habitats** are provided by plants.
  The rainforests make up only 6 % of the Earth's land
  surface. But they support more than half the world's
  species of animals and plants.

- **Atmospheric gases** are kept stable by photosynthesis.
  Without green plants, carbon dioxide in the air would
  increase and oxygen would decrease.

These are powerful reasons why the destruction of
tropical rainforests should be stopped.

- Plants also provide us with building materials like wood.
  Fuels like oil, coal and peat have come from fossil plants.

▶ Rate of photosynthesis

Rate always involves time.
The rate of photosynthesis could be measured by how much sugar is made in a given time.

So why are people interested in this?
Well, the faster photosynthesis takes place, the more food is made and the bigger the plant will grow.
Scientists try to increase the rate of photosynthesis to increase the **yield** of a crop.

What sort of things would affect the rate of photosynthesis?

Sugar cane is a crop that grows well in the tropics.
Does the climate affect the rate of photosynthesis?

Cutting sugar cane

Light

Photosynthesis increases when light gets brighter – but only up to a point.
When a certain light intensity is reached the rate of photosynthesis stays constant. It can't go any faster even if the light intensity continues to rise.

Experiment 12.8   Photosynthesis and light intensity

You can use this apparatus to measure the effects of light intensity on the rate of photosynthesis:

Cut a piece of Canadian pondweed about 5 cm in length.
You can weigh down the other end with a paper clip.

Count the number of bubbles released with the lamp at different distances away from the plant.

● Did the number of bubbles increase when the lamp was nearer to the plant?
Why do you think this was?

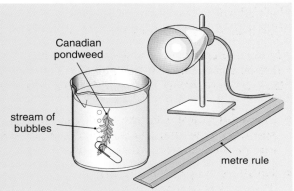

Canadian pondweed

stream of bubbles

metre rule

Many plants spread their leaves to catch as much light as as they can.

Light that is too strong can damage the chloroplasts.

Some woodland plants prefer dim light.
We call them **shade plants**.
They are able to make use of the limited amount of light that penetrates the tree canopy and reaches the woodland floor.

▶ Limiting factors

Things like light intensity can affect the rate of photosynthesis – we call them **limiting factors**.

It doesn't matter if the plant has lots of carbon dioxide and water and a nice warm temperature.
If light is in short supply, then light will *limit* the rate of photosynthesis.

Let's say light intensity is limiting photosynthesis.
The only way to increase the rate is to increase the limiting factor – in this case, light intensity.

Other limiting factors are carbon dioxide and temperature.
But only **one** factor can limit the rate at any one time.
It depends on which one is in the shortest supply.

Glasshouses can control limiting factors

Temperature

An increase in temperature usually increases the rate of photosynthesis.
Most chemical reactions increase with temperature.
But at about 40 °C the rate slows.
At temperatures above this, the rate drops quickly.
This is because the *enzymes* in photosynthesis are being destroyed.

Investigation 12.9   Plan an investigation into the effect of temperature on the rate of photosynthesis
(**Hint**: You could try the apparatus in Experiment 12.8 using different water baths.)

Remember that other factors like light intensity and carbon dioxide concentration must be kept constant.

Check your plan with your teacher before you start.

Why do you think that crops like grapes and melons grow better in a glasshouse?

The warm conditions inside the glasshouse increase their rate of photosynthesis.
In this way we can grow plants that would not normally grow in the UK.

Different types of plants have different temperatures at which they grow best.
Each has an **optimum** temperature for growth.

Carbon dioxide

The more carbon dioxide you give plants, the more
photosynthesis they carry out.
It is not possible to do this with crops outdoors.
The air usually contains about 0.03 % carbon dioxide.

Why do you think that carbon dioxide is often added
to glasshouse crops?

Look at the picture of lettuces grown in a
greenhouse:

Those in A are growing in air which has more
carbon dioxide than those in B.

Which would sell for the best price?
Why are these lettuces bigger?

Investigation 12.10   What is the effect of carbon dioxide on the rate of photosynthesis?

How could you change Experiment 12.8 to find out
the effects of carbon dioxide?
(**Hint**: Adding sodium hydrogen carbonate to water
increases the concentration of carbon dioxide.)

Remember, other factors like light intensity and
temperature must stay constant.

Check your plan with your teacher before you start.

Look at the graph:

Increasing carbon dioxide increases the rate of
photosynthesis up to a point X.
But what happens after this point X?

After point X **another** factor must be limiting
photosynthesis.
What do you think this other factor could be?

What would happen to the rate of photosynthesis if
the light intensity or the temperature was increased?

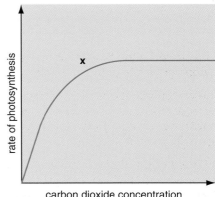

rate of photosynthesis

carbon dioxide concentration

▷ Leaves

What words would you use to describe a leaf?
Flat? Thin? Green?

The leaf is where photosynthesis takes place.
It is very well adapted for this job.

Leaves have:
- **a large surface area** – to absorb light rays.
- **a thin shape** –so gases can diffuse in and out easily.
- green **chlorophyll** – to absorb light.
- **Veins** – to support the leaf surface and to carry
  substances to and from all the cells in the leaf.

Experiment 12.11   Looking at leaves
Look closely at each surface of a leaf with a lens.

- Is the upper surface glossy? Why is this?

- Which surface is the darker green?
  Does most light get to this surface?

On the inside

To find out how a leaf works we need to look at a
thin slice under the microscope.

cuticle : waterproof layer that also
cuts down the water lost by
evaporation

upper epidermis : single
layer of cells with no
chloroplasts.Light goes
straight through

palisade layer : the
palisade cell contains
lots of chloroplasts.
Most photosynthesis
occurs here

spongy layer : more rounded cells with lots
of **air spaces** between them. Gas exchange
occurs here

lower epidermis : no thick cuticle. Has lots
of tiny holes called **stomata** (singular **stoma**)
These allow gases to diffuse in and out

vein : contains tubes called
xylem that bring water and
salts to the leaf and tubes
called **phloem** that take
dissolved food away

Experiment 12.12   Looking at a leaf section
Put a slide of a section of a leaf on the microscope.
Look for these structures under low power.
Now look at each type of tissue under high power.

▶ Stomata

These small holes on the underside of the
leaf let gases diffuse in and out.
(The singular of stomata is stoma.)

- Carbon dioxide diffuses in for photosynthesis.
- Oxygen made in photosynthesis diffuses out.
- Water vapour diffuses out.

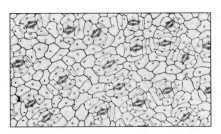

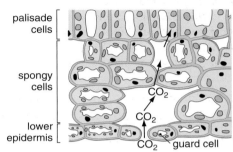

Carbon dioxide diffuses into the leaf for
photosynthesis

Experiment 12.13   Where are the stomata?

Try dropping a leaf into a beaker of boiling water.
From which surface do bubbles appear?
What is the air coming out of?

Why are most stomata on the underside of the leaf?
What might block them on the upper surface?
Would more water be lost by evaporation if they
were on the upper surface facing the sun or on the
shaded lower surface?

Opening and closing

Stomata can be opened and closed by **guard cells**.

Stomata usually open during the day.
Water passes into the guard cells by **osmosis**.
This makes them bend so the stoma opens.
Carbon dioxide diffuses into the leaf for photosynthesis.

The stomata close at night.
Water passes out of the guard cells by osmosis.
They straighten up so the stoma closes.

The stomata also close in hot dry weather.
Why do you think this is?
Would the plant stay upright if it lost a lot of water?

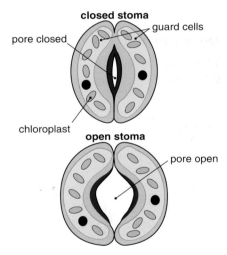

Experiment 12.14   Looking at stomata

Paint a small square (1 cm × 1 cm) on the underside
of a leaf with nail varnish.
The nail varnish makes an imprint of the leaf surface.
Wait for the varnish to dry completely then peel it off.
Put it on a slide with a drop of water and cover-slip.
Observe and draw 2 or 3 stomata at high power under
the microscope.
Repeat for the upper surface of the leaf.

▶ Gas exchange

All living things, including plants, carry out respiration.
What gas do they need for this?
What gas do they get rid of?

For respiration plants need to:
- take in oxygen, **and**
- give out carbon dioxide.

Respiration takes place **all the time**.

Can you think of when carbon dioxide and oxygen move in the opposite direction?

For photosynthesis plants need to:
- take in carbon dioxide, **and**
- give out oxygen.

Photosynthesis only takes place **in the light**.

These gases pass into and out of leaves through the stomata.

Photosynthesis

carbon dioxide + water ➞ sugar + oxygen

Respiration

sugar + oxygen ➞ carbon dioxide + water

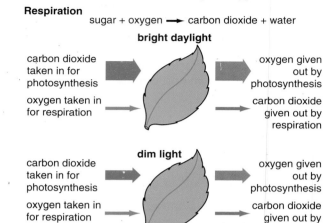

bright daylight

carbon dioxide taken in for photosynthesis → oxygen given out by photosynthesis

oxygen taken in for respiration → carbon dioxide given out by respiration

dim light

carbon dioxide taken in for photosynthesis → oxygen given out by photosynthesis

oxygen taken in for respiration → carbon dioxide given out by respiration

dark

oxygen taken in for respiration → carbon dioxide given out by respiration

---

Experiment 12.15   Photosynthesis and respiration

Set up 3 boiling-tubes as shown here:
Put 5 cm^3 of hydrogen carbonate indicator into each tube.
Put a leaf in tubes 1 and 2 so that each is supported by the wall of the tube.
The underneath of the leaf should face inwards.
Put leaf 1 in darkness by covering the tube with tin foil.
Leave the tubes near a light for 2 to 3 hours.

If carbon dioxide is added to the air, the hydrogen carbonate indicator will turn yellow.
If carbon dioxide is used up from the air, the hydrogen carbonate indicator will turn purple

Look at your results.
- In which tube was carbon dioxide released by the leaf?
- In which tube was carbon dioxide taken up by the leaf?
- What was the purpose of tube 3?

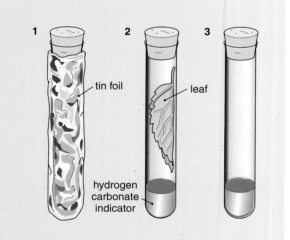

During daylight plants produce *more* oxygen by photosynthesis than they use up in respiration.
At night plants produce *only* carbon dioxide by respiration.

▶ Chlorophyll

If you grind a leaf up with some propanone,
you can extract the chlorophyll.
But is this a pure substance or a mixture of
different substances?

Experiment 12.16   Separating leaf colours

Grind up some leaves with 25 cm^3 propanone.

Filter the extract.

Put 5 cm^3 of the solvent in a boiling tube and
close it with a rubber bung.

Cut a strip of filter paper to fit the tube.

Put a spot of extract on the pencil mark X.
Let it dry then repeat the operation several
times.
Hang the paper strip in the boiling tube with
the bottom in the solvent.

Take the paper strip out before the solvent
reaches the top. Let it dry.

- How many different colours can you see?
  These will all be different leaf pigments.

⚠ solvents are highly flammable
wear eye protection

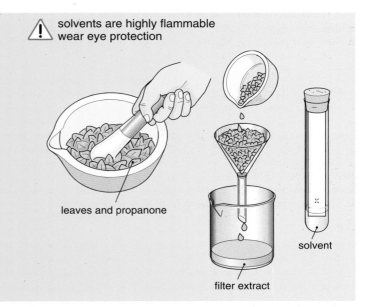

leaves and propanone

filter extract

solvent

But why does chlorophyll **look** green?

The diagram shows what light looks like
after it has passed through a prism:
The rainbow of colours is called a **spectrum** .

Now look what happens when the light then
passes through an extract of chlorophyll:

Which colours have been **absorbed** by
chlorophyll?
Which colours are not absorbed by
chlorophyll?

Chlorophyll absorbs most colours except green.
Leaves look green because they **reflect** and **transmit**
green light.

Chlorophyll strongly absorbs red and blue light.
This is the 'right sort' of light needed for photosynthesis.
Light intensity can limit the rate of photosynthesis.
But not having the right colours or **wavelengths** of
light can too.

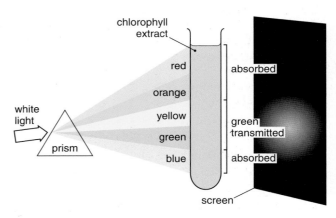

▶ Plant growth

Have you seen bottles of 'plant food' for sale?
What do you think these contain?

Plants need more than carbon dioxide and water
for healthy growth.
They also need **mineral salts** or **nutrients**.
These are usually found in the soil.
Nutrients are taken up in small amounts by the roots.

Can you remember why plants need nitrates?

They need the nitrogen to make proteins.
So nitrogen is one nutrient needed for growth.

Magnesium is used to make chlorophyll.
What would leaves look like if magnesium
was lacking in the soil?
Leaves without enough magnesium look yellow.
We say the plant is **deficient** in magnesium.

A shrub lacking magnesium

Experiment 12.17   *The effects of nutrients on growth*

You can use **water cultures** to find out why
plants need different nutrients.

Set up some test-tubes as shown here:

Each solution lacks a certain nutrient except No. 1
which has all of them.

Leave the apparatus in good light for 6 weeks.

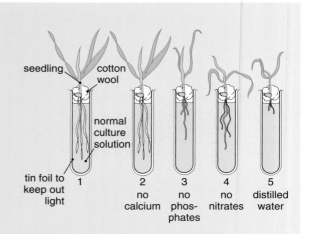

- What sort of things would you look for
  in the plants after 6 weeks?
  How about colour and size of leaves?
  How about length of stems and roots?

- How would you measure any changes?

- Why do you think the tubes were covered with tin foil?
  Does this stop other plants growing in the water?

Symptoms shown by plants deficient in nutrients include:

- Lack of nitrate – stunted growth and yellow older leaves.

- Lack of phosphate – poor root growth and purple younger leaves.

- Lack of potassium – yellow leaves with dead spots.

▶ Fertilisers

What happens if the soil does not contain enough nutrients?

The farmer or gardener adds more as **fertiliser**.
Fertilisers replace the missing nutrients.

The graph shows the yield of winter wheat with
different amounts of nitrogen fertiliser:
What is the yield with no nitrogen fertiliser?
What amount of fertiliser would you use?

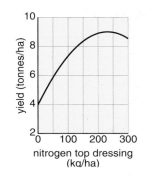

NPK fertilisers contain:

- Nitrogen (N) for growth of leaves and stems,

- Phosphorus (P) for healthy roots,

- Potassium (K) for healthy leaves and flowers.

Both phosphorus and potassium help the reactions in photosynthesis
and respiration to work.

The proportions of nitrogen, phosphorus and
potassium (N : P : K) are shown on the fertiliser bag.

This fertiliser is called 25 : 0 : 16.
What does this mean?

Natural or chemical?

Chemical or artificial fertilisers are used in
huge amounts.
They are easy to store and add to the land.
The farmer knows exactly how much of each
nutrient there is in the fertiliser.
The farmer has to be very careful about how
much fertiliser is used and when.
Rain can wash fertiliser into rivers and streams
where it causes water pollution. (This is covered
in Chapter 21.)

Natural fertilisers include farmyard manure
and composts.
Some farmers prefer these because they
add **humus** to the soil.
Humus improves the structure of the soil.
Natural fertiliser rots down and releases
nutrients more slowly.
The problem for the farmer is that the amount
of each nutrient in the fertiliser is not known.

Make a table of the advantages and disadvantages
of natural and chemical fertilisers.

▶ Biology at work : Hydroponics

Hydroponics is the growth of plants without soil.
Most of tomatoes, cucumbers and sweet peppers are
grown this way.

Peat culture

Have you seen tomatoes growing in gro-bags?
This is known as **peat culture**.
It is not used much by commercial growers.
Peat is acid and does not contain many nutrients.
So the peat has to be treated before it can be used.

It is very popular with gardeners.
But this has meant digging up peat bogs and damaging
the environment.

Cucumbers grown in artificial media

Nutrient film technique

Plants grown using this technique are supported in sterile sand
or rockwool.
A solution is circulated to the roots of each plant.
The solution has :
- oxygen bubbled through it – so the roots can respire
- the correct type and amounts of nutrients
- the best pH for growth.

It is easy to alter the amounts and types of mineral salts.
This will be different for different crops and for different
stages of development of the plants.

This technique has been trialed by the Desert Development
Centre in Egypt.

*Tomatoes grown by
nutrient film technique*

▷ Biology at work: Glasshouse production

Growers try to improve the yield of their crops.
They try to give them the best possible conditions
for photosynthesis to take place.

Conditions inside a glasshouse allow plants to:

- grow earlier in the year
- grow in places where they would not normally
  grow well.

How are these conditions provided?

- **Temperature**
  Sunlight heats up the inside of the glasshouse.
  The glass stops a lot of this heat from escaping.
  Electric or paraffin heaters can be used in
  cold weather.
  Ventilator flaps can be opened to cool the glasshouse
  if it gets too hot.

Ventilator flaps operate automatically

- **Light**
  The glass lets in sunlight.
  Artificial lighting can be used to grow plants
  when sunlight gets too low.
  Blinds can shade out very strong light.

- **Carbon dioxide**
  Growers can pump carbon dioxide into glasshouses
  to increase the rate of photosynthesis.
  Sometimes paraffin heaters are used.
  These increase both the temperature and carbon dioxide
  because when paraffin burns it releases carbon dioxide.

- **Water**
  Many glasshouses have automatic watering systems.
  When needed, sprinklers and humidifiers come on.

Water misting of cabbages

All these factors may be controlled by computer.
Sensors are used to detect each factor.
The feedback is processed by the computer.

Summary

- Green plants use sunlight to make food by photosynthesis.
  Chlorophyll inside chloroplasts, is used to absorb the light.
  Carbon dioxide and water are needed for photosynthesis.
  Sugars are produced in photosynthesis and can form other carbohydrates, amino acids, proteins and fats.
  Oxygen is released as a waste product during the process.

- Plants are important for food, medicines, habitats and controlling the amounts of carbon dioxide and oxygen in the air.

- The rate of photosynthesis can be limited by light intensity, carbon dioxide and temperature.

- Leaves are well adapted for absorbing light and gas exchange.

- Stomata control exchange of gases and water loss.

- Photosynthesis takes place in light but respiration occurs all the time.

- Red and blue is the type of light most used in photosynthesis.

- Mineral salts are important for healthy plant growth.

▶ Questions

1. Copy and complete:
   Green plants make their own food by . . . . .
   Green . . . . in the chloroplasts of the leaves traps the sun's . . . . . Raw materials for this process are carbon . . . . and . . . . . Sugars are made in the leaves and are soon changed to . . . . . The waste product of this process is the gas . . . . .

2. The graph shows the effect of increasing the amount of carbon dioxide on the rate of photosynthesis of a pond weed.

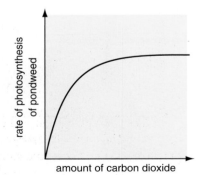

   a) What other conditions must be kept constant if this is to be a fair test?
   b) How do you think the amount of carbon dioxide was increased?
   c) Why did the graph increase to begin with?
   d) Why do you think the graph levels off?

3. Three geranium plants were kept in the dark for 24 hours.
   Each was then covered with a bell-jar A, B and C. The apparatus was left in the light for 5 hours as shown here:

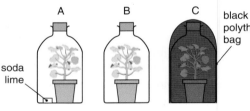

   a) Why were the 3 plants left in the dark before the start of the experiment?
   b) What was the soda lime for in bell-jar A?
   c) Why was black polythene put over bell-jar C?
   d) After 5 hours a leaf from each plant was tested for starch.
      What colour would each leaf go with iodine? Try to explain each of the results.

4. Lettuces can be grown in tunnels made with clear polythene.
   a) Give 2 reasons why clear polythene increases the yield of lettuces.
   b) Why do the tunnels not need to be moved to water the plants?
   c) Why is carbon dioxide added to the air in the tunnels?

5. The apparatus was used to collect the gas released by water plant:

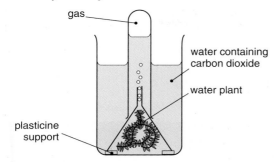

a) How could you test the gas for oxygen?
b) Why is the gas collected in the test-tube not pure oxygen?
c) Why was the water enriched with carbon dioxide?

A lamp was placed at different distances from the water plant.
The number of bubbles released per minute was recorded:

Distance from lamp (cm)	Number of bubbles per minute
100	6
60	10
40	18
30	24
20	25

d) Plot these results as a line-graph.
e) Try to explain any pattern that you find in the results.
f) Why was a piece of thick glass placed between the lamp and the plant?

6. To find out if photosynthesis has taken place in a leaf we can carry out a test.
Copy out the stages listed on the left. Match each one with the correct reason on the right.

Stage in test	**Reason**
wash the leaf in cold water	to test for starch
boil the leaf in ethanol	to soften it
cover the leaf with iodine	to remove the ethanol
dip the leaf in boiling water	to extract the chlorophyll

7. a) Name the parts of the leaf labelled A to G:

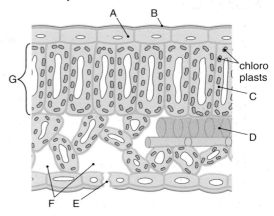

b) Match each label with one of these functions:
  i) Carries water and mineral salts to the leaf.
  ii) Prevents too much water loss from the upper surface.
  iii) Opens to allow gases to pass into and out of the leaf.
  iv) Most photosynthesis takes place here.
  v) Gases from here pass into the spongy cells.
  vi) Light is able to pass straight through this layer.
  vii) These cells contain most chloroplasts.

8. The rate of photosynthesis of a tree was recorded for 36 hours.

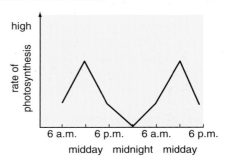

Use the graph to answer these questions.
a) When was the rate of photosynthesis highest?
b) When would most carbon dioxide be released into the air?
c) When would most oxygen be released into the air?

Further questions on page 248.

TRANSPORT and WATER RELATIONS

chapter 13

"General Sherman" redwood tree

A transport system

Most living things need a transport system.
Only very small organisms can carry things
around their body by diffusion.

What things do cells need to stay alive?
What do they need to get rid of?

Our transport system is the blood.
It brings food and oxygen to our cells.
It removes carbon dioxide and waste chemicals.

Plants have a transport system too.
They have lots of thin tubes inside them.
These carry liquids up and down the stem
and all around the plant.

Some tubes are called **xylem** (sigh-lem).
They carry water and mineral salts.
The roots take in the water and dissolved salts.
These pass up the stem in the xylem to the leaves.

Some tubes are called **phloem** (flow-em).
They carry dissolved food like sugars and amino acids
which are made in the leaves by photosynthesis.
The phloem carries the food to every part of the plant.

The phloem also carries **hormones** around the plant.
These hormones control cell division for growth of the
stem, roots and leaves.
Hormones also control the growth of flowers and fruits.

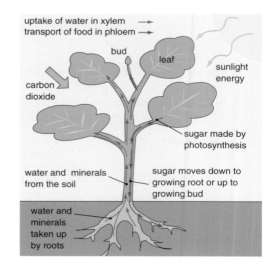

uptake of water in xylem →
transport of food in phloem →

bud — leaf

sunlight energy

carbon dioxide

sugar made by photosynthesis

water and minerals from the soil

sugar moves down to growing root or up to growing bud

water and minerals taken up by roots

Inside the root

To find the transport tissue of a root we
need to slice it open and look inside.
The diagram shows what a root tip looks
like under the microscope:

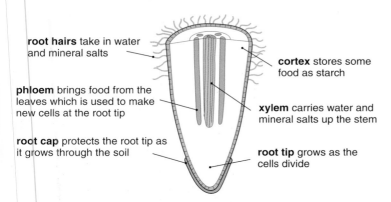

root hairs take in water
and mineral salts

cortex stores some
food as starch

phloem brings food from the
leaves which is used to make
new cells at the root tip

xylem carries water and
mineral salts up the stem

root cap protects the root tip as
it grows through the soil

root tip grows as the
cells divide

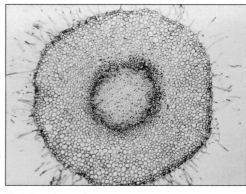

*Section through a young root.
Notice the many root hairs.*

Inside the stem

We can find out what is inside a stem by cutting
a thin slice and looking at it under a microscope:

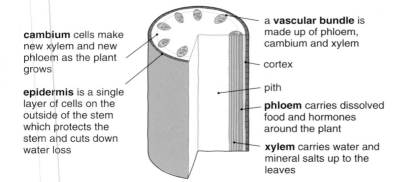

cambium cells make
new xylem and new
phloem as the plant
grows

a **vascular bundle** is
made up of phloem,
cambium and xylem

cortex

epidermis is a single
layer of cells on the
outside of the stem
which protects the
stem and cuts down
water loss

pith

phloem carries dissolved
food and hormones
around the plant

xylem carries water and
mineral salts up to the
leaves

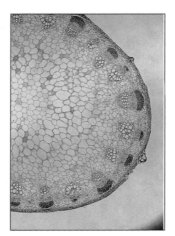

Section through a young stem

Experiment 13.1   Water transport in the xylem

Stand some celery in water containing a blue
dye for a few hours.
Carefully cut off a length of about 2 cm.
Look at the cut end. Can you see where the dye is?
The dye has been carried up the xylem tubes.

Carefully cut out a 2 cm length of xylem.
Put it onto a slide with a cover-slip.
Look at it under the microscope.

sharp scalpel

▷ Into the roots

The roots anchor the plant in the soil.
Another important role of the roots is
to take up water and mineral salts.

Just behind the root tip are microscopic hairs.
These are called **root hairs**.
Water passes into the root hairs by **osmosis**.
Do you remember what happens in osmosis ?

The water in the soil has a weak solution of
salts.
The cell sap in the root hair has a stronger
solution.
Water passes from the soil into the root hair by
osmosis.

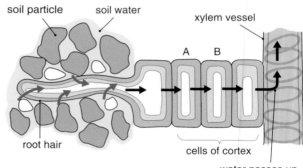

The water has diluted the cell sap
in the root hair cell.
The root hair cell now has a weaker cell sap
than cell A.
Water passes from the root hair cell into cell A
by osmosis.

The pathway of water across a root

The water has diluted the cell sap in cell A.
Cell A now has a weaker cell sap than cell B.
So water passes from cell A into cell B by
osmosis.

This continues across the whole of the root
cortex.

Water eventually reaches the xylem.

Water is carried up the xylem to the leaves.

Experiment 13.2   Looking at root hairs
Look closely at a section of a young root under
the microscope.

Look at the root hairs.

● What is their shape like ?
● How does their shape help them to take in water ?

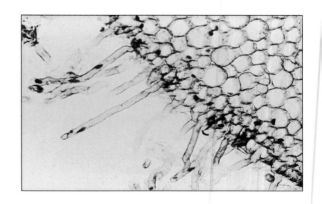

Root hairs are long and thin.
They have a large surface area through which
water and mineral salts can enter.

▷ Up to the leaves

Water is pulled up the xylem in the stem from the roots.

The water is used for photosynthesis and to stop the plant from wilting.
Water evaporates from the leaves into the air.
This is called **transpiration**.

As water is used up or lost from the leaves, more is sucked up from the xylem vessels.
It's a bit like sucking water up a straw.
So there is a continuous flow of water from the roots to the leaves.
This movement of water up the xylem is called the **transpiration stream**.

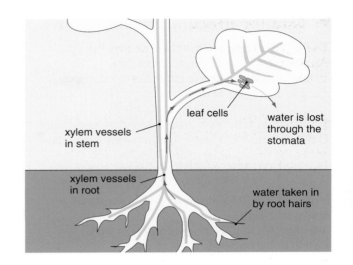

Experiment 13.3   To demonstrate transpiration

You can prove transpiration takes place by setting up the apparatus shown here:
Mark clearly the level of the water in each flask.
Weigh each flask.
Now leave the apparatus for 24 hours.

- Has the level dropped in flask A? Why has it?
- Is flask A now lighter? Why is this?

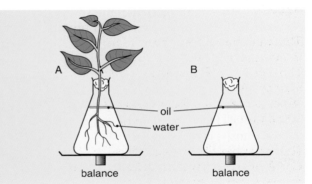

More about transpiration

- Water first evaporates from the spongy cells into the air spaces.
- The air spaces become full of water vapour.
- Water vapour diffuses through the stomata into the air.
- The water lost from the spongy cells is replaced by more water from the xylem.

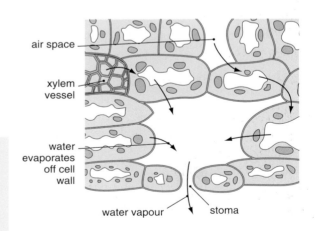

Experiment 13.4   Comparing water loss from each side of a leaf

Cobalt chloride paper is blue when dry and goes pink when it comes into contact with water.
Put a piece of cobalt chloride paper on each side of a leaf. Keep the paper in place with 2 slides and elastic bands.
See on which side the paper turns pink first.
- Will it be the side with most stomata?

▶ Factors affecting transpiration

More transpiration takes place during the day than at night.
This is because the stomata are open during the day and close at night.

The stomata may also close in very dry conditions.
This is because the water lost in transpiration is not being replaced by water from the soil.
The stomata close to reduce transpiration.

If the plant still does not get enough water it will start to **wilt**.
Its cells have lost so much water that they are no longer **turgid** or full of water.
Turgid cells are firm and give the plant support.
If the cells become **flaccid** then the plant becomes soft. The stem is no longer upright and the leaves droop.

Scanning electron micrograph of open stoma.

Experiment 13.5   Stomata and water loss

Set up 4 leaves as shown here:
Vaseline will block the stomata and slow down transpiration.

Look at the leaves after a few days.
• Which do you think has lost most water ?

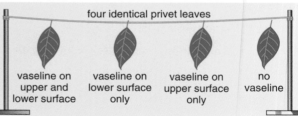

four identical privet leaves

| vaseline on upper and lower surface | vaseline on lower surface only | vaseline on upper surface only | no vaseline |

Other factors affecting transpiration are environmental. Look at the graphs:

• **Windy** conditions increase the rate of transpiration.

• **Humid** conditions decrease the rate of transpiration.
   The air contains a lot of water already.

• **Warm** conditions increase the rate of transpiration.
   The air can hold more water vapour.

• **Light** causes the stomata to open.
   This increases the rate of transpiration.

It's a bit like washing on a line.
What conditions dry the clothes quickest ?
What conditions dry the clothes more slowly ?

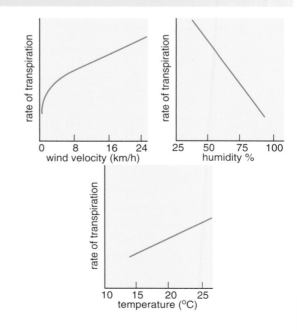

▷ Measuring transpiration

It is not easy to measure the rate of transpiration.
But you can use a **potometer** to measure the rate
of water **uptake**.
The amount of water lost is actually less than the
amount of water taken in by the roots.
This is because some of the water is used up in
photosynthesis.

Experiment 13.6   Measuring the rate of water uptake

Fill a capillary tube by submerging it in water.
Cut the end of a shoot under the water.
Attach it to the capillary tube with a piece
of rubber tubing.
Take the capillary tube out of the water.
Clamp the apparatus in the position shown.
See how far the water travels along the
tube in 5 minutes.

⚠ sharp cutting instruments

slanting cut

Now try it with a fan near the potometer
• Does the rate increase? Why is this?

Now try putting a polythene bag over the shoot.
This makes conditions humid.
• Does the rate decrease? Why is this?

• Would a black plastic bag make the rate
  decrease even more?
  Why do you think this is?

water evaporating

bubble moves along as water
moves up to the leaves

plastic tubing

Here is a more expensive potometer.
It works in the same way.
Vaseline is put on the rubber bung.
What do you think the reservoir is for?
How could you get the air bubble back
to the beginning of the scale?

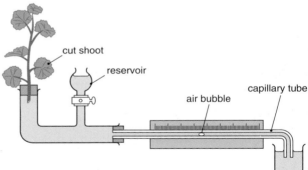

cut shoot

reservoir

capillary tube

air bubble

Investigation 13.7   Plan an investigation on the rate of transpiration

You could use weight loss and water intake as a
measure of the rate.
You could look at the effects of different variables on
different plants.
You could investigate how different numbers of stomata
affect the rate.

Check your plan with your teacher before you start.

▷ Mineral salts

The plant needs mineral salts.
For instance, nitrates are needed to make proteins.

There is only a weak solution of these salts in the water in the soil.
Often salts are taken up even though there are less in the soil than there are in the root.

These salts cannot enter the root by diffusion.
Why not?

The salts are taken up by **active transport**.
Active transport can collect salts against a concentration gradient.
This needs energy from respiration.

Again the root hairs give a large surface area for taking up mineral salts.
There are many air spaces in the soil.
Oxygen passes from this air into the root hair too.

Mineral salts are carried up to the leaves with water in the xylem vessels.

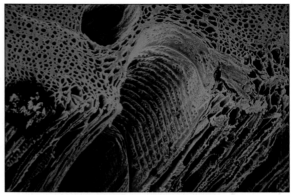

*Scanning electron micrograph of xylem vessels.
Note the thick bands that support the vessels*

▷ Transporting food

Food is made in the leaves by photosynthesis.
The soluble products are sugars, amino acids and fatty acids.
These are carried to all parts of the plant in solution in the phloem. This is often called **translocation**.

Xylem are dead tubes but phloem is living tissue.
Movement of substances in the phloem is thought to involve active transport. The plant cells have to use energy to move the dissolved substances along.

Where does the food end up?

- Sugars are changed to starch and stored in the root cortex and in seeds.

  Sugars also form cellulose for new cell walls at the growing root tip and shoot tip.

- Amino acids make proteins needed to make new cells.

- Fatty acids form fats that are stored in many seeds.

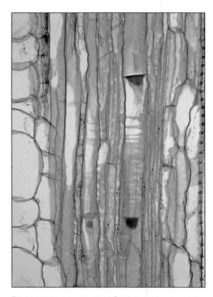

Photomicrograph of phloem vessels

Biology at work: Monocultures and crop rotations

Monocultures

A **monoculture** is growing the same crop on the same land, year after year.

The main benefit of monocultures is an economic one :

- Increased use of machinery and decreased labour costs means that continuous cropping of one crop brings greater economic returns per unit area of land.

- However, monocultures require the use of lots more fertilisers and pesticides to maintain high yields.

- The use of chemical fertilisers does not improve the structure of the soil, unlike organic fertilisers which rot down and provide the soil with humus as well as nutrients.

- The pH of the soil may need to be carefully regulated to meet the needs of the crop. First the soil pH is tested, and then lime is added if the soil is too acid or peat if it is too alkaline.

- Monocultures also provide large areas that can become infested with pests and diseases, which have to be controlled. **Aphids** can spread diseases such as **tobacco mosaic virus**. Aphids feed on the sap in the phloem tubes in crop stems. They use special mouthparts called **stylets** to penetrate the phloem. The viruses enter the phloem in the saliva of the insect and multiply. Aphids are the main **vectors** (transmitters) of viruses between plants.

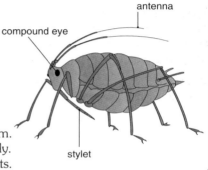

Crop rotations

The use of inorganic fertilisers and monocultures has led to the loss of the traditional crop rotations.

Crop rotation influences the amounts of nutrients that need to be added to grow different crops.
For example, winter wheat grown after another cereal needs far more nutrients than if it is grown after a root crop. This is because a root crop, like potato, takes up far less nutrients than a cereal crop.

Growing a planned sequence of crops has been practised for many years. The Norfolk four-year rotation uses a **ley**. This is a grass/ legume mix that can be grazed by livestock. **Legumes** (the pea family) increase the amount of nitrogen in the soil and so increase its fertility (see page 373).

Different crops need different methods of cultivation, which leads to an improvement in soil texture.
Also, growing different crops breaks the cycle of crop pests. So there is less chance of a crop pest or disease getting a grip than in the case of growing monocultures.

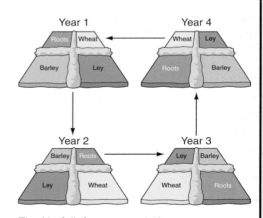

The Norfolk four-year rotation

Summary

- Plants have a transport system made up of tubes called xylem and phloem.
  Xylem carries water and mineral salts from the roots up the stem to the leaves.
  Phloem carries dissolved food from the leaves to all parts of the plant.
  The phloem also transports hormones around the plant.

- Water passes into the root hairs from the soil water by osmosis.

- Mineral salts are taken up by active transport.

- Leaves lose water to the air by transpiration. Transpiration stream allows water to travel from the roots up the stem to the leaves. Transpiration is controlled by the opening and closing of stomata.
  Environmental factors like wind, humidity and temperature can affect transpiration.

- The soft parts of a plant are supported by turgid cells.

▶ Questions

1. Look at the diagram of the root hair in the soil:

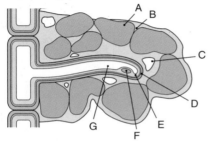

   a) Name the parts labelled A to G.
   b) Explain how water gets into the root hair from the soil.
   c) Give 2 other functions of a root hair.

2. The graph shows the rate of transpiration and the rate of water uptake in small pine tree:

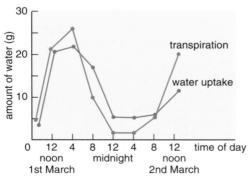

   a) Compare the rate of transpiration with the rate of water uptake
      i) during the day   ii) during the night
   b) State the date and the time when the rate of transpiration was highest.

3. Copy and complete:
   Water passes into a root . . . . by . . . . . Mineral . . . . are taken up by . . . . transport. A root hair has a . . . . surface . . . . for taking up water and mineral salts.
   Water is lost from the leaves by . . . . . This is controlled by the opening and closing of the . . . . . Dissolved . . . . and hormones are carried to all parts of the plant in the . . . . .

4. A potometer was used to measure water uptake by a leafy shoot.

Conditions	Time taken for the water to move 100 mm (minutes)
cool, moving air, in daylight	2
cool, still air, in daylight	6
warm, moving air, in daylight	1
warm, still air, in daylight	3
warm, still air, at night	60

   a) From the table, state 3 conditions which affect the rate of water movement through the plant.
   b) In cool, moving air, in daylight, work out the rate of water movement in mm per minute.
   c) Give 2 ways in which the air around the shoot would be affected if it was covered with a transparent plastic bag.
   d) Give two reasons why loss of water from the leaves is important to a plant.

Further questions on page 252.

chapter 14

Plant reproduction and growth

Reproduction in plants can be either sexual or asexual. Can you remember the difference?

In sexual reproduction male and female sex cells are made.
They join together at fertilisation.

In asexual reproduction there is always one parent.
All the offspring are identical to the parent.
No sex cells are made.

▶ Vegetative propagation

Many flowering plants can reproduce asexually.
A new plant grows out from part of the parent plant.
This is called **vegetative propagation**.

Pine seedlings growing from a fallen log

Strawberries have side branches called **runners**.
They grow over the soil and form buds.
Each bud grows into a new plant.

A potato is really a swollen underground stem called a **tuber**.
New shoots grow from the buds or 'eyes'.

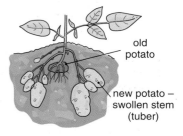

A **corm** *is a short underground stem.*
New corms form on the side of the old one.
They break off and become new plants.

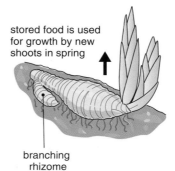

stored food is used for growth by new shoots in spring

Iris **rhizomes** *are underground stems that grow sideways in the soil.*
Their stored food gives the new plants a start in the spring.

branching rhizome

Corms, tubers and rhizomes are all **storage organs**.
They fill up with food, like starch, in the summer.
Over the winter they remain alive in the soil.
The next spring, the new plants use the stored food to grow until their new leaves develop.

233

▷ Artificial propagation

Plant growers use vegetative propagation to make many new plants quickly.

They can also make sure that the new plants have the same good features as the parent plant, such as disease-resistance or shape of flower. How is this possible?

Experiment 14.1   Taking a cutting

Find a non-flowering shoot of geranium.

Cut it just below the point where a leaf joins.

Remove the lower leaves.
Dip the cutting in rooting powder.

Put the cutting into compost to root.
This will take about 2 weeks.

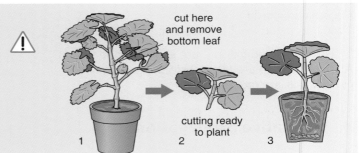

Grafting is used to reproduce roses and fruit trees.

You cut a twig from the plant you want to be increased.
You now join it to the stem of a rooted tree.
The cut surfaces are taped together.
The graft soon heals to give a new plant.

Grafting is useful if plants are difficult to grow from seed.

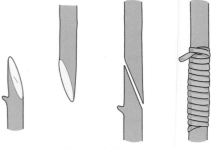

A simple grafting technique

Cloning

This involves growing cells of a plant in **tissue culture**.
Everything must be carried out in sterile conditions.
Some pieces of tissue are removed from the parent plant.
They are transferred to a culture tube containing nutrient agar.
The cells divide and form **explants**.
These are genetically indentical to the parent plant and to each other (**clones**).
These can eventually be grown in compost.

Tissue culture is a good way of producing many new plants all with the good features of the parent.

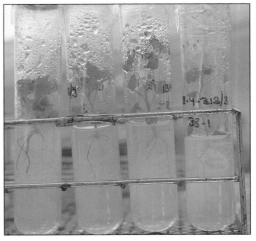

Explants growing in nutrients agar

▷ Flowers

People give flowers to friends and relatives.
But they don't just look and smell nice.
They are the plant's reproductive system.
They make seeds that grow into new plants.

Flowering plants carry out sexual
reproduction and make sex cells.
The male sex cells are **pollen grains**.
The female sex cells are **egg cells**.
A **seed** is made when a pollen grain
fertilises an egg cell.

Flower structure

Flower parts are often arranged in rings.
Let's start at the outside and work inwards:

- **Sepals** are a bit like small leaves.
  They protect the flower in the bud.

- **Petals** are often coloured and scented.
  Many have a **nectary** at the base.
  The nectary makes sugary **nectar**.
  Visiting insects land on the petals.

- **Stamens** are the male sex organs.
  Each one is made up of 2 parts:
  the **anther**, where the pollen is made, and
  the **filament**, a little stalk which holds
  the anther.
  In this flower there are 4 stamens.

- **Carpels** are the female sex organs.
  Each carpel is made up of a **stigma**,
  a **style** and an **ovary**.
  Inside the ovary is the **ovule**.
  The ovule contains the female **egg cell**.
  In this flower there is one carpel in
  the middle of the flower.

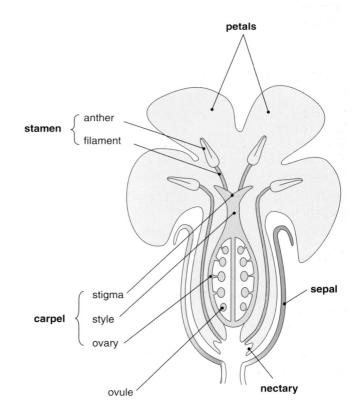

Different flowers

Flowers all have the same basic plan.
But there are many different types.
They have different shapes and
different numbers of petals,
stamens and carpels.

Look at these three different flowers.
How are the petals arranged?
How many stamens and carpels are
there in each one?
How are they arranged?

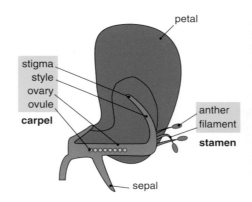

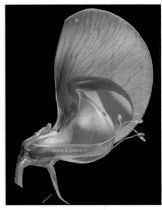

Sweet pea.

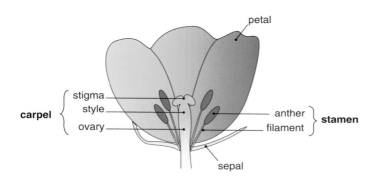

Tulip

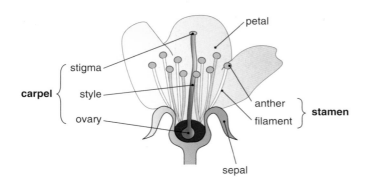

Apple

Experiment 14.2   Looking at a flower
Use a lens to look at a flower in detail.
Cut the flower in half like the ones in
the pictures above.
See if you can find all the parts labelled.

Pollen

Pollen grains are made inside the anthers.
The anthers split open when they are ripe.
Millions of pollen grains are released.
The pollen grains must get from the anthers
to the female sex organs.

The transfer of pollen from the anther of a
flower to the carpel is called **pollination**.

Once a pollen grain has reached the carpel
its job is to fertilise an egg cell.

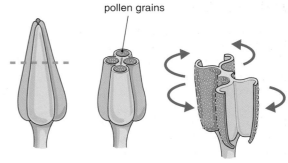

Anthers split open to release pollen grains

Experiment 14.3   Looking at pollen grains

Remove a stamen from a flower.

Use a mounted needle to remove some pollen
from the anther.

Put the pollen onto a slide with a drop of
water and cover-slip.

Look at the pollen grains under the microscope.

The carpel

The carpel is made up of the stigma, style and ovary.

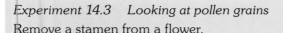

* Pollen grains land on the sticky **stigma** during
  pollination.
* The **style** joins the stigma to the ovary.
* The **ovary** surrounds and protects the **ovule**.
  Inside the ovule is the **egg cell**.

Are these flowers ?

Some flowers do not have colourful petals, scent
or nectar.
Flowers of grasses and cereals look very different.
They don't look like flowers at all.
They do not have sepals or petals.

But they do have :
* large anthers that hang outside the flower,
* large feathery stigmas that catch any pollen
  grains in the air,
* lots of very light pollen.

How do you think that pollination takes place in
grasses and cereals ?

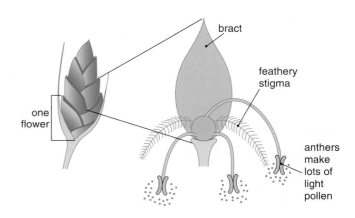

▷ Pollination

There are 2 main methods of pollination:
by insects and by the wind.

Carried by insects

Look at the picture showing **insect pollination**:

- In what ways do flowers attract insects?

- Why does the insect reach down into the first flower?

- How does the insect carry pollen to the second flower?

- Where does the insect leave the pollen in the second flower?

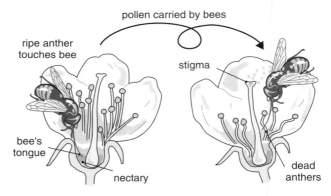

Blown by the wind

Look at the picture showing **wind pollination**:

- Why do the anthers hang outside the flower?

- Why are the stigmas so large and feathery?

- Why is so much pollen made?

- Why is the pollen so light?

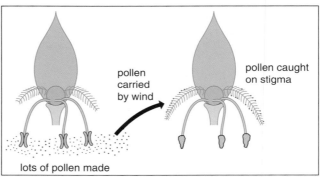

Insect-pollinated flowers have:	Wind-pollinated flowers have:
• colourful, scented petals and nectar to attract insects • anthers and stigmas inside the flower for insects to rub against • small amounts of sticky pollen are made which can easily stick to insect's bodies	• anthers hanging outside the flower to catch the wind • large, feathery stigmas which catch pollen grains in the air • lots of smooth, light pollen is made which can easily be blown by the wind

Sometimes the pollen from the anthers of one flower lands on the stigma of the same flower. This is called **self-pollination**.

Cross-pollination is where pollen from the anthers of one flower lands on the stigma of another flower of the same species. Cross-pollination results in more variation.

▷ Fertilisation

What happens in fertilisation?

A pollen nucleus must join with an egg nucleus
to make a seed.
How does this happen in a flowering plant?

Pollination is complete when the pollen grains land
on the female stigma.
The pollen nucleus must reach the egg cell.
But that's right down inside the ovary!

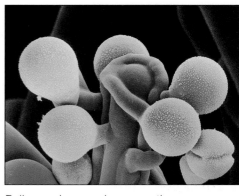

Pollen grains growing on a stigma

Going down

The pollen grains start to grow.
They each form a **pollen tube**.
The pollen tube grows down the style to the ovary.
It gets food from the tissues of the style.
As it grows, the pollen tube carries the
pollen nucleus with it.

The first pollen tube reaches the ovary.
It enters the ovule through the **micropyle**.
The pollen nucleus fuses with the egg cell nucleus.
This is fertilisation.

How is it that only **one** pollen nucleus gets to
fertilise the egg cell?

What do you think the fertilised egg
grows into?

The fertilised egg grows into the **embryo**.
The ovule forms the **seed** with the embryo inside it.
The ovary forms the **fruit** with the seeds inside it.

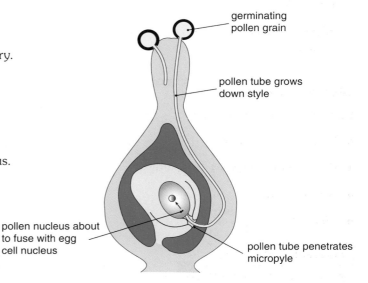

germinating
pollen grain

pollen tube grows
down style

pollen nucleus about
to fuse with egg
cell nucleus

pollen tube penetrates
micropyle

Experiment 14.4   Growing pollen grains

Put some 10% sucrose solution onto a cavity slide.

Shake some pollen grains onto the solution.

Place a cover-slip over the slide.

Leave the slide in a warm place for 30 minutes.

Then use your microscope to look for growing
pollen tubes every 10 minutes.

▷ Fruits and seeds

After fertilisation the petals fall off.
They have done their job.

The fertilised egg grows into the **embryo**.
This will eventually grow into the new plant.

Each ovule grows to form a **seed**.
Each seed is made up of :
- the embryo,
- a food store,
- a seed coat or **testa**.

The ovary forms the **fruit**.
The fruit's job is to spread the seeds.
This is called **dispersal**.

*Pea flower
after fertilisation*

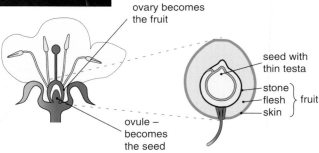

How a plum flower grows into a plum fruit

▷ Dispersal of fruits and seeds

Why do you think seeds are scattered ?
Would they grow well if they were all
crowded together ?
They would compete for space, water and light.
How do you think seeds are scattered ?

Dispersal by the wind

These fruits and seeds are dispersed by the wind :

*Dandelion and thistle seeds have
a parachute of fine hairs.
These are easily carried away by
the wind.*

*Sycamore, elm and ash fruits have wings.
These make them fall to the ground
slower
– so they are carried further by the wind.*

*Poppy fruits sway in the wind.
The seeds are shaken out through
holes
– like pepper out of a pepper-pot.*

Dispersed by animals

Brightly coloured fruits like honeysuckle and wild rose attract birds and other animals. When they eat the fruits the tough seed coat stops the seeds from being digested in the animal's gut.
The seeds pass out of the body in the faeces, usually miles away.

Some fruits like burdock have hooks that catch on animal fur or on our clothes. They can be carried a long distance before they drop off.

Hazelnuts and acorns are stored by squirrels. They may be dropped or forgotten about.

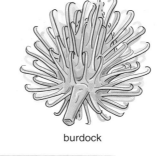

burdock

Self-dispersal

Some plants throw their seeds away.
The fruit wall dries and splits.
This happens so quickly that the seeds are thrown out quite a distance.

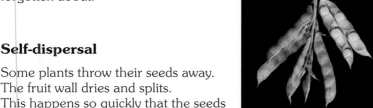

Lupin fruits split open to flick out their seeds

Investigation 14.5

Carry out an investigation to see how seeds fall.

You could make some model seeds that are identical. Release the seeds from a known height and time how long it takes them to reach the ground.

What variables could you change to make the seeds fall at different rates?
Why would a slow rate of fall be an advantage to a seed?

Check your plan with your teacher before you start.

Experiment 14.6   Looking at seeds

Try cutting open a broad bean seed or a French bean seed. ⚠

Can you find the parts in the picture?

Look for the embryo.
Can you find the new shoot and new root?

What food is stored in this seed?
What chemical tests could you use to find out?

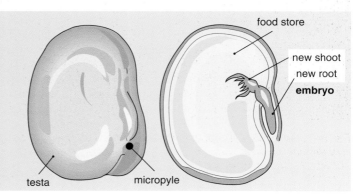

food store

new shoot
new root
embryo

testa

micropyle

▷ Germination

If a seed lands where conditions are good, it will start to grow.
Germination is when the embryo begins to grow.

The embryo grows a new root or **radicle** and
a new shoot or **plumule**.
Can you find them in the picture below?

The radicle and plumule need food for growth.
They get this food from the **food store**.
The embryo uses this until its own leaves
are able to make food by photosynthesis.
In a bean the stored food is in the **cotyledons**.

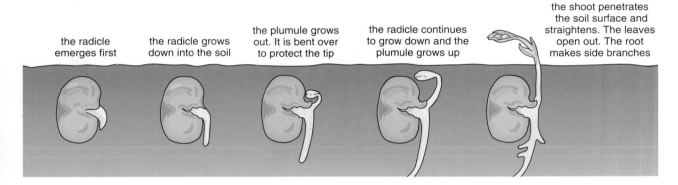

| the radicle emerges first | the radicle grows down into the soil | the plumule grows out. It is bent over to protect the tip | the radicle continues to grow down and the plumule grows up | the shoot penetrates the soil surface and straightens. The leaves open out. The root makes side branches |

Conditions for germination

Three conditions are needed for seeds to germinate:

- **Water** is needed before the seed can swell
  up and burst open.
  It is also needed for the food store to be
  made soluble to feed the embryo.

- **Oxygen** is needed for respiration.

- **Warmth** is needed for proper growth.
  Many seeds will not grow until the spring
  or summer.

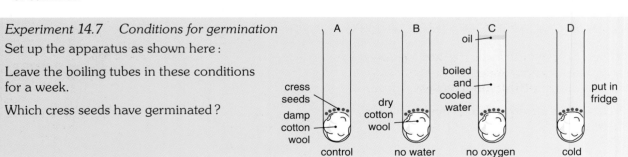

Experiment 14.7   Conditions for germination

Set up the apparatus as shown here:

Leave the boiling tubes in these conditions
for a week.

Which cress seeds have germinated?

cress seeds
damp cotton wool
control

dry cotton wool
no water

oil
boiled and cooled water
no oxygen

put in fridge
cold

▷ Growth in plants

In animals, cell division and growth takes place in all parts of the body.

In plants, cell division and growth takes place mainly at the root tips and the shoot tips.

Control of growth

If you cut off a shoot tip the shoot stops growing. But if you put the shoot tip back on it starts to grow again.

The shoot tip makes a hormone called **auxin**.
The auxin stimulates the shoot to grow.
The auxin causes the cells to elongate.

Plants respond to things like light, gravity and water.
Parts of the plant either grow towards them or away from them.
These slow growth responses are called **tropisms**.

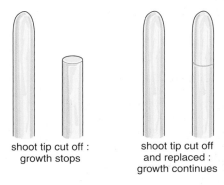

shoot tip cut off : growth stops

shoot tip cut off and replaced : growth continues

How light affects growth

Look at the photograph of the cress seedlings:

They have been put in a window for some time.
The shoots have grown towards the light.

How is this controlled?

- When a shoot only gets light from one side most auxin is found on the shaded side.

- The auxin makes the shoot grow more on the shaded side.

- The shoot bends towards the light.

This sort of response is called a **phototropism**. Because shoots grow *towards* the light we say that they are **positively phototropic**.

What is the advantage to the shoot of growing towards the light?

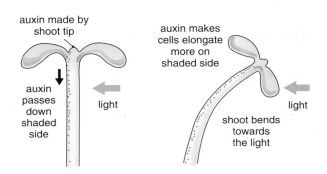

auxin made by shoot tip

auxin passes down shaded side

light

auxin makes cells elongate more on shaded side

shoot bends towards the light

light

How gravity affects growth

Why is it that which ever way a seed is planted,
the root always grows down and
the shoot always grows up?

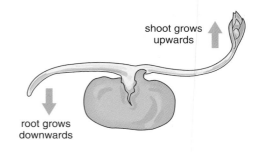

shoot grows
upwards

root grows
downwards

The stimulus in this case is gravity.

Shoots grow up, away from gravity.
Roots grow down, towards gravity.
Again auxin controls this growth.

If a plant is put on its side the auxin builds up
on the lower side of the shoot and root.

- In the shoot the auxin stimulates it to grow
  more on the lower side.

- This causes the shoot to bend upwards.

- In the root the auxin also builds up
  on the lower side.
  But auxin **slows down** growth in a root.

- So the upper side of the root grows quicker
  than the lower side.

- The root bends downwards.

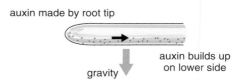

auxin made by root tip

gravity

auxin builds up
on lower side

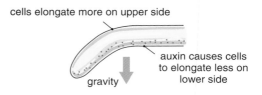

cells elongate more on upper side

auxin causes cells
to elongate less on
lower side

gravity

A growth response to gravity is called a **geotropism**.

Explain why we say that
- roots are **positively geotropic**, and
- shoots are **negatively geotropic**.

What is the advantage to the plant of its shoot growing
away from gravity and its root growing towards gravity?

Auxin also has other effects on plant growth.
As it passes back from the tip of a stem, auxin
prevents side-shoots forming.

What do you think would happen if the tip of the
stem was removed?
The auxin will no longer be made so the side-shoots
start to grow.

Why does hedge clipping produce a much bushier hedge?

▶ Biology at work : Plant hormones

Rooting powder contains synthetic auxins.
A cutting is dipped into the rooting powder.
The powder stimulates the cut shoot to grow roots.

Carnations and chrysanthemums are grown
in this way.

Synthetic auxins are also used as selective
weed-killers.
They kill the weed by making it grow too fast.
The auxins are sprayed on the leaves, so
broad-leaved weeds are affected.
Narrow-leaves grasses and cereals
are not affected.

Auxins control **ripening** by telling the ovary
to develop into a fruit.
They are normally made by the developing embryo.

Some growers spray synthetic auxins on unpollinated
flowers of tomato plants and pear trees.
Fruits form without fertilisation.
So these fruits have no pips !

Have you ever eaten seedless grapes or
seedless satsumas ?
These have been grown with the help of
synthetic plant hormones.

Plant hormones can also be used to regulate
the ripening of fruit during transport.

Ethene is made by many fruits.
It causes the fruit to ripen.
Bananas are picked when they are unripe and
transported in ships.
During storage ethene is used to make them ripen.
So when they arrive for sale they have changed
from green to yellow !

Summary

- Many plants reproduce asexually using storage organs. This is called vegetative propagation.

- Plant growers use artificial propagation to produce many new plants economically.

- Many plants have flowers as organs of reproduction.
  The male sex cells or pollen grains are made inside the anthers.
  The female sex cells or egg cells are made inside the carpel.

- Pollination is the transfer of pollen from the anthers to the stigma of a flower of the same species. Pollination can be carried out by insects or by the wind.

- The pollen nucleus joins with the egg nucleus during fertilisation.

- Fruits and seeds are dispersed by the wind, by animals or by self-dispersal.

- Seeds need water, oxygen and warmth to germinate.

- Plant growth and development is controlled by hormones.
  These hormones can be used commercially to produce seedless fruit, to act as a rooting powder and as selective weed-killers.

▷ Questions

1. Copy and complete:
   The male parts of a flower are called the . . . . .
   Each stamen is made up of an . . . . and a filament. The . . . . grains are made inside the . . . . . The female parts of a flower are called the . . . . . Each carpel is made up of a . . . . style and . . . . . During pollination, the pollen grains are transferred from the . . . . to the . . . . of a flower of the same . . . . . The pollen grain starts to grow down the . . . . forming a pollen . . . . .
   When the pollen tube reaches the ovary the pollen . . . . joins with the . . . . nucleus to form the . . . . egg. This is called a . . . . .

2. a) Name the parts A–D on the diagram of a section of a broad bean seed:

   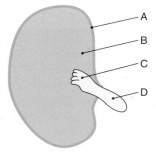

   b) What is the function of the parts A and B?
   c) What 3 conditions are needed for germination?

3. a) What is the difference between self-pollination and cross-pollination?
   b) Give 2 ways in which pollen from insect-pollinated flowers is different to the pollen from wind-pollinated flowers.
   c) Write down 3 other differences between insect-pollinated and wind-pollinated flowers.

4. a) Name the parts in the diagram of half a wallflower:

   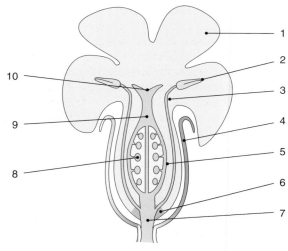

   b) Give the functions of parts 1, 2, 4 and 10.
   c) How do you think that this flower is pollinated? Give your reasons.

5. a) Explain briefly how fertilisation occurs in flowering plants.
   b) What happens to each of the following after fertilisation:
      i) the petals
      ii) the ovule
      iii) the ovary?

6. Some plants can be produced from stem cuttings. A part of the stem is cut from a plant. Some of its leaves are removed and the cut end is placed in suitable soil. Cells at the base of the stem divide and form roots.

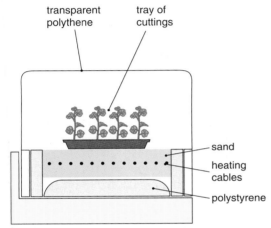

a) What type of reproduction takes place by this method of plant production?
b) Name the type of cell division taking place at the base of the stem cutting.
c) Taking stem cuttings is a useful way of reproducing blackcurrant bushes, all of which will be the same. Explain why the seeds from a blackcurrant bush would be less likely to produce plants that were all the same.
d) What type of substance would you add to the base of cuttings to encourage root growth?

7. Arrange the following events in the correct order:

A	Pollen formation takes place in the anther.
B	Pollen tube grows down into the ovary.
C	A pollen nucleus joins with an egg nucleus.
D	Anthers split open to release the pollen.
E	Insects transfer pollen from the anthers to the stigma.

8. In the last century, European vineyards were almost destroyed by an insect which kills vines by eating their roots. The American vine is resistant to the insect. All European vines are now grown from stem cuttings grafted onto the rooted stocks of the American vine.

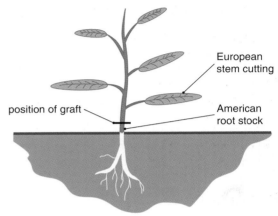

a) Explain why the grapes produced on this type of vine are considered to be European rather than American.
b) Recently, a European vine resistant to the insect has been developed by biotechnologists. Explain how large numbers of disease-resistant vines could be produced quickly from the one vine resistant to the disease.

9. The diagram shows a wind-pollinated flower:

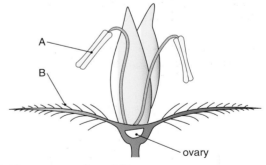

a) Name parts A and B.
b) Give 2 features of wind-pollinated flowers shown in the diagram.
c) Explain how this flower is cross-pollinated by the wind.

Further questions on page 253.

247

Further questions on Plants as organisms

▶ Feeding in plants

1. Leaves are organs of photosynthesis. They come in all shapes and sizes but all of them are adapted to absorb as much light as possible.
   a) Give **one** way in which leaves are adapted to absorb light. [1]
   b) The diagram shows a cross-section through a leaf.

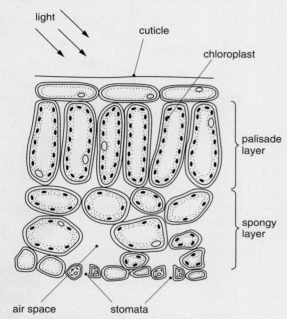

light

cuticle

chloroplast

palisade layer

spongy layer

air space   stomata

   Explain the following observations:
   i)   The cuticle is transparent. [1]
   ii) Most chloroplasts are found in the palisade layer. [1]
   iii) Air spaces are found mostly in the spongy layer. [1]
   c) What is the substance in chloroplasts which absorbs light? [1]
   d) Explain how each of the following affects the rate of photosynthesis in a potted plant.
   i)   Moving it nearer to the window. [1]
   ii) Moving it to a colder room. [1]
                                                    (OCR)

2. A student was asked to find if plants need light to make starch.
   She was given a potted plant which had been kept in a dark cupboard for 48 hours. She covered part of the leaf with aluminium foil as shown in the diagram which follows.

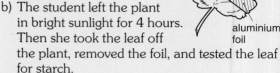

aluminium foil

   a) Why did she cover part of the leaf with aluminium foil? [1]
   b) The student left the plant in bright sunlight for 4 hours. Then she took the leaf off the plant, removed the foil, and tested the leaf for starch.
   i)   Name the solution which is used to test for starch. [1]
   ii) The diagram shows the leaf after the starch test. What colour would parts **X** and **Z** go after the test? [2]

X

Z

   c) Write a conclusion for the student's experiment. [1]   (AQA)

3. The graph shows the amount of sugar contained in the leaves of a group of plants in a glasshouse over a period of a week.

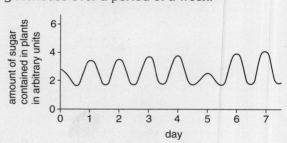

amount of sugar contained in plants in arbitrary units

day

   a) i)   Copy and complete the word equation to show how sugar is produced:

$$.... + ... \xrightarrow[\text{chlorophyll}]{\text{sunlight}} \text{sugar} + \text{oxygen} \quad [2]$$

   ii) Name the process shown by the equation. [1]
   b) i)   Explain the rise and fall in the sugar level each day. [2]
   ii) Suggest a reason for the overall increase in the amount of sugar present each day. [1]
   iii) Suggest a reason for the lower peak on day **5**. [1]
   c) Suggest **two** reasons why putting a gas fire in the glasshouse might increase the amount of sugar produced. [2]   (EDEX)

248

4. Plants convert light energy into chemical energy during photosynthesis. The graph shows the effect of light intensity on the rate of photosynthesis.

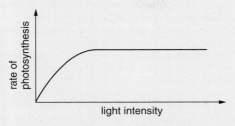

a) i) Explain the relationship between light intensity and the rate of photosynthesis. [2]

ii) Suggest one other variable that affects the rate of photosynthesis. [1]

iii) Sketch a curve to show how this variable would affect the rate of photosynthesis (put the variable on the horizontal axis and the rate of photosynthesis on the vertical axis). [1]

b) Glucose is made by photosynthesis. What can the plant use the glucose for? [1]
(EDEX)

5. The table below shows the results of an investigation to find the effect of carbon dioxide concentration on the rate of photosynthesis.

Concentration of carbon dioxide in air (%)	Rate of photosynthesis (arbitrary units)
0	0
0.2	35
0.4	70
0.6	105
0.8	115
1.0	120
1.2	120
1.4	120

a) Draw a line graph of these results on a sheet of graph paper. [2]

b) Use the graph to describe the effect of carbon dioxide concentration on the rate of photosynthesis. [2]

c) The rate of photosynthesis may be affected by factors other than carbon dioxide concentration. Give **two** of these factors. [2]

d) Some crops are grown in greenhouses. Give **two** advantages of growing crops in greenhouses. [2] (AQA)

6. a) Plants need mineral salts for healthy growth. Give the chemical names of two types of mineral salts. [2]

b) A farmer wants to increase his yield by sensible use of fertilisers. The graph shows how the mass of crop produced from a field depends on the quantity of nitrogen used.

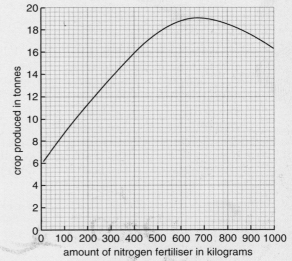

What is the maximum mass of crop that could be produced by using nitrogen fertilisers on the field? [1]

c) Many of the chemicals in fertilisers dissolve in water. When it rains, some of the fertiliser is washed out of the soil into rivers and streams.
What effect does the fertiliser in the river water have on the river plants:
i) Immediately or in the short term; [1]
ii) In the long-term? [1]

d) Some people prefer to eat "organically grown" food. This is food which has been grown without the use of synthetic fertilisers, pesticides or weedkillers.
Excluding cost, describe **two** advantages and **two** disadvantages of eating "organically grown" food. [4] (AQA)

Further questions on Plants as organisms

7. The diagram shows a plant leaf during photosynthesis.

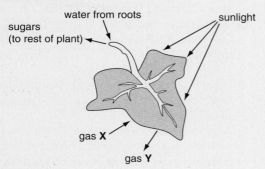

a) Name:
   i)   gas **X**
   ii) gas **Y**   [2]
b) Name the tissue which transports:
   i)   water into the leaves
   ii) sugars out of the leaves   [2]
c) Why is sunlight necessary for photosynthesis ?   [1]
d) Some of the sugars produced by photosynthesis are stored as starch in the roots. Explain, as fully as you can, why it is an advantage to the plant to store carbohydrate as starch rather than as sugar.   [3]   (AQA)

8. Maple leaves were analysed for their sugar and starch content over a 24 hour period. The data, together with the light intensity readings, are shown in the chart below.

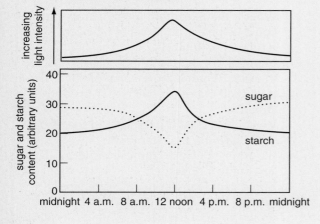

a) i)   State the relationship between light intensity and starch production.   [2]
   ii) Sugar and starch are products of photosynthesis. Suggest why the level of sugar in the leaf is highest at night.   [1]
   iii) Give the word equation for photosynthesis.   [2]

   reactants   **products**

   $$\dots + \dots \xrightarrow{\text{light}} \dots + \dots$$

   iv) I) By using the information in the chart, choose the time you would expect to find the highest concentration of oxygen in the air at the surface of the leaf. Copy the table and tick (✔) **one** box only.   [1]

Time	Tick
midnight	
4 a.m.	
8 a.m.	
12 noon	
4 p.m.	
8 p.m.	

   II) Explain your answer.   [2]
b) i)   Name the green substance present in the leaf.   [1]
   ii) Where in the cell is this substance found ?   [1]
   iii) What is the function of this substance in photosynthesis ?   [1]   (WJEC)

9. The diagram shows a section through a green leaf.

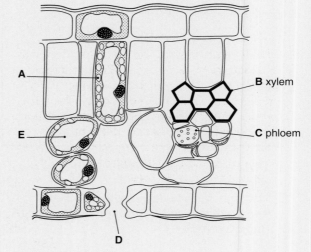

250

a) Copy the table and match **each letter** to the description of its function. [5]

Letter	Description of its function
	transports sugar
	absorbs light
	produces pressure inside cells
	carries water from the stem to the leaf
	allows water to leave by evaporation

b) The amount of carbon dioxide in the air around a crop of wheat was measured during two different days, **X** and **Y**. The results were plotted as the following graph.

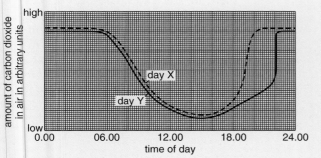

i) What process was responsible for the drop in carbon dioxide ? [1]
ii) Suggest why there is a difference between the graphs for **X** and **Y**. [1]
c) At what time did the wheat plants give out most oxygen ? [1]
d) Name **two** substances found in the soil which could help the growth of the wheat. [2] (WJEC)

10. The diagram shows an experiment which was set up to try to discover the effect of carbon dioxide concentration on the volume of a gas produced by Canadian pondweed. The gas is produced by the plant during photosynthesis. The pondweed was kept in different concentrations of sodium hydrogencarbonate solution. Sodium hydrogencarbonate adds carbon dioxide to the water.

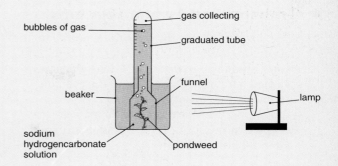

a) Name the gas collecting in the graduated tube. [1]
b) The results table shows the volume of gas collecting in the graduated tube at different concentrations of sodium hydrogencarbonate solution.

concentration of sodium hydrogencarbonate solution (%)	0	1.0	2.0	3.0	4.0	5.0
volume of gas collected (mm³/min)	3	12		42	48	48

i) Plot the results as a **line graph** and join the plots. [3]
ii) Use the graph to estimate the volume of gas produced at 2.0% sodium hydrogencarbonate solution. [1]
iii) What range of concentration of sodium hydrogencarbonate gives the fastest rate of photosynthesis ? [1]
iv) Explain the shape of the graph from 4.0% sodium hydrogencarbonate solution onwards. [1]
v) Suggest **one** reason why the pondweed produced gas (photosynthesised) at 0% sodium hydrogencarbonate. [1]
c) Suggest **two** external factors, not mentioned in the question, which must be kept the same for the experiment to proceed fairly. [2] (WJEC)

▷ Transport and water relations

11. The diagram shows the apparatus used in a laboratory investigation of water loss from and water uptake by a green plant. The roots were washed carefully before placing the plant in the measuring cylinder.
The apparatus containing the plant was weighed at the start of the investigation and again 24 hours later.

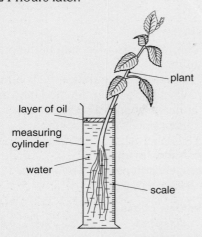

The scale on the measuring cylinder was used to read the volume of water before and after the 24-hour period.
The table shows the results obtained.

	Mass of apparatus containing plant/g	Volume of water in measuring cylinder/cm³
Start of investigation	220	100
24 hours later	210	88

a) Calculate the loss of mass due to water loss from the plant during the 24-hour period. Show your working. [1]
b) Calculate the mass of water which has been absorbed by the roots of the plant during the 24-hour period. Show how you arrive at your answer. [2]
c) With reference to the mechanisms by which water moves upwards in a green plant, explain why your answers to a) and b) above are quite similar. [4]
d) Explain why the amount of water absorbed by the roots is not exactly the same as the amount of water lost by the plant. [1]

e) Explain why a plant growing in natural conditions would be unlikely to lose the same mass of water on each of several days. [2]
f) A plant growing in a natural environment might, under certain conditions, lose far more water than it absorbs by the roots. Describe the effect this would have on the plant. [2] (OCR)

12. a) Plants lose water through their leaves.
  i) What name is given to the loss of water from the leaves? [1]
  ii) What name is given to the pores through which this water is lost? [1]
  iii) Explain why the movement of water through plants is important to them. [3]
b) The loss of water from a leafy shoot can be shown using a potometer. A potometer is shown in the diagram. As water is lost from the leaf the bubble slowly moves along the scale from left to right.

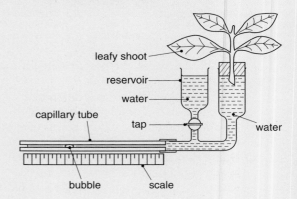

What will be the effect on the movement of the bubble of :
  i) increasing the temperature of the air around the leafy shoot; [1]
  ii) increasing the humidity of the air around the leafy shoot; [1]
  iii) opening the reservoir tap? [1]
c) Plants which live in dry, desert-like areas often have leaves which are modified to form sharp spines or prickles. State two ways that these modified leaves help the plant to survive in the desert. [2] (AQA)

13. The roots of a green plant act as a link between the plant and the water in the soil.
a) For which life process does the green plant need water as a raw material? [1]
b) The drawing shows a sectional view of a root hair on a root in some soil.

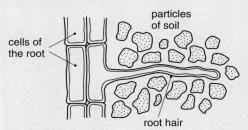

Describe, in detail, how the water passes from the soil into the root hair. [4]
c) Much of the water going into the root has to get to the leaves. Explain how water travels upwards through the stem to the leaves. [3] (AQA)

▶ Reproduction and growth

14. The diagram shows flowers from two plants of the same species.

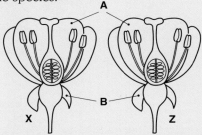

a) State the functions of the parts labelled **A** and **B**. [2]
b) Mrs Jones wants to cross plant **X** with plant **Z**. She collects pollen from plant **Z** using a paintbrush and transfers it to plant **X**.
   i) Name the part of plant **Z** from which she will get the pollen. [1]
   ii) Name the part of plant **X** that she should brush the pollen on to. [1]
c) Describe how a pollen grain develops after pollination has taken place. [2]
d) When Mrs Jones crossed a red flowered plant with a white flowered plant, all of the offspring inherited the red flower colour. What does ''inherited'' mean? [3]
(EDEX)

15. The table shows the height in mm, of two pea seedlings during the first 8 days after germination.

Days after germination	1	2	3	4	5	6	7	8
Seedling **P** height/mm	0	2.5	6.0	14.0	24.0	32.0	44.0	62.0
Seedling **Q** height/mm	0	1.5	4.0	10.0	16.0	20.0	36.0	58.0
Mean seedling height/mm	0	2.0	5.0	12.0				

a) What was the height of seedling **P** on day 3? [1]
b) On what day was seedling **Q** 20 mm in height? [1]
c) Work out the mean height of the seedlings **P** and **Q**, for each of the last four days. [4]
d) On a sheet of graph paper, plot mean height of pea seedlings against time. Join up the points you have plotted with straight lines. [4] (OCR)

16. The diagram shows three plant stems, **A**, **B** and **C**, at the start and end of an experiment.

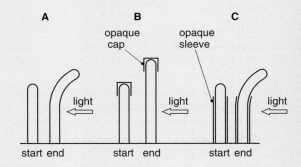

a) What does this experiment suggest about which region of a plant stem is sensitive to the stimulus of light? Give reasons for your answer. [3]
b) Explain what causes the plant stem to bend towards the light. [3]
c) Suggest how this response is beneficial to plants. [2] (OCR)

chapter 15

Look around at the other people in your class.
We are all similar.
We all have two arms, two legs, two eyes,
a nose, and so on.
We all belong to the same **species**.

If you take another look you'll see that there
are also many differences.
None of us are identical.
Some people are taller or heavier, others have
different colour hair, skin or eyes.
This is called **variation**.
Individuals of the same species still vary quite a lot.

Look at these rose bushes:
They show variation too.
They have different colours, different heights and
some have more flowers than others.

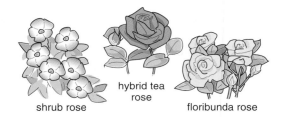

hybrid tea
rose

shrub rose   floribunda rose

Think back to some of the differences between people.
What would happen if you measured the heights
of all the pupils in your year group?
You would get a whole range of heights from small to tall.
Most pupils would be about average height.
This type of variation is called **continuous variation**
because there is a continuous range of heights from
small to tall.
Can you think of any other examples of continuous variation?

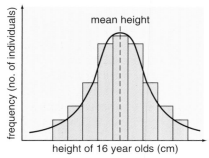

Some people have attached ear lobes.
Other people's ear lobes are free and not attached.
Some people can roll their tongues, other people can't.
These are both examples of **discontinuous variation**.
Here there is no range or inbetweens.
You can either do something or you can't.
You either have something or you haven't.

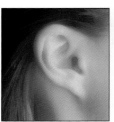
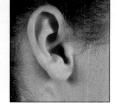

attached lobes   *free lobes*

▷ Inheritance versus environment

Imagine if some clones were taken from a carrot plant.
They would all be genetically the same.
Will they all be identical when they grow into adult
carrot plants?

It depends upon whether they have the same things
from the environment.
What happens if some do not get enough light, water
or nutrients?
They will not grow so well.

So individuals will show variation
because of two causes: **genetic** and **environmental**.

Why do you look like you do?

You get some characteristics from your parents.
You **inherit** them.

But other characteristics do not come from your
parents.
They are caused by the way you lead your life.
These are due to the effects of your **environment**.

Can you roll your tongue like the girl in the photograph?
It is not something that you can learn to do.
You have either inherited it or you haven't.

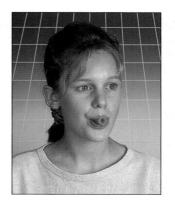

Look at this Olympic athlete:
She needs speed, agility and strength.
These are not just inherited.
They are improved by training, diet and the
right lifestyle.
These are environmental causes of variation.

Can you think of any other human characteristics
that are affected by the environment?

Which of these characteristics are inherited
and which are environmental?

blood group	neat writing	hair length	freckles
eye colour	an accent	shape of nose	scars
hair colour	body weight	skill at languages	

▷ The variety of life

There are millions of different plants and animals
in the world.
They may differ in their appearance, their behaviour
or where they live.

If we look carefully we can see similarities and differences.
Sparrows, wasps, robins and bees are all animals that fly.
But sparrows and robins belong together and so do
wasps and bees.

We can divide living things up into groups.
The members of these groups have similar features.

For instance, cats and dogs are mammals because
they both have fur.
But there are also many differences between them.
So we divide mammals up into smaller groups like
the cat family and the dog family.

Snakes and lizards are reptiles because they both have
scaly skin.
But there are many differences between them.
So we divide reptiles up into smaller groups like
the snake family and the lizard family.

A group of animals or plants that are very similar
may be in the same **species**.
A species is a group of individuals that can breed
together to produce fertile offspring.

For instance, all domestic dogs belong to the
same species.
They may all look different, but they can mate and
give birth to cross-breeds that are perfectly healthy.

There are 2 types of variation between living things.
There is :

- variation between *different species*

  and

- variation between *members of the same species*.

▷ Sorting things out

How could you find out the name of a plant or animal?

You could look through the pictures in a book until you found the right one.
But that would take a lot of time and effort.

Scientists use **keys** to identify living things.
A key has a number of questions.
You start at the beginning and answer "yes" or "no" to each question.
It soon takes you to the plant or animal you want.

Use this branching key to identify the animals below.

start here

has it got legs? → yes / no

has it got a shell? → yes / No

has it got 6 legs? → yes / no

snail   earthworm

spider

has it got 2 pairs of wings? → yes / no

wasp   housefly

Use the numbered key below to identify the same animals.
It is set out differently from the first key, but it works in the same way.
Start at the beginning and answer the question at each stage.

1	Has legs	Go to 2
	Has no legs	Go to 4
2	Has 6 legs	Go to 3
	Has 8 legs	Spider
3	Has 1 pair of wings	Housefly
	Has 2 pairs of wings	Wasp
4	Has a shell	Snail
	Has no shell	Earthworm

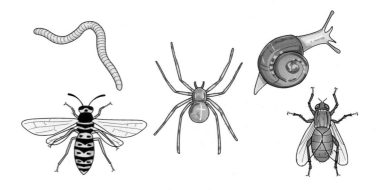

Scientists have tried to give every species a name of its own.
Similar living things have been put in the same group.
This is called **classification**.
The largest groups are called **kingdoms**.
There are 5 of these kingdoms.

▷ The animal kingdom

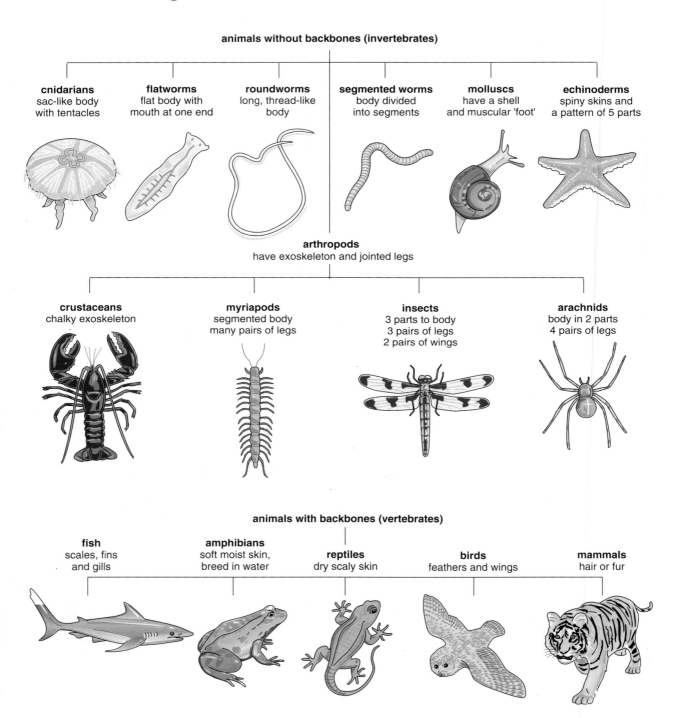

animals without backbones (invertebrates)

cnidarians
sac-like body
with tentacles

flatworms
flat body with
mouth at one end

roundworms
long, thread-like
body

segmented worms
body divided
into segments

molluscs
have a shell
and muscular 'foot'

echinoderms
spiny skins and
a pattern of 5 parts

arthropods
have exoskeleton and jointed legs

crustaceans
chalky exoskeleton

myriapods
segmented body
many pairs of legs

insects
3 parts to body
3 pairs of legs
2 pairs of wings

arachnids
body in 2 parts
4 pairs of legs

animals with backbones (vertebrates)

fish
scales, fins
and gills

amphibians
soft moist skin,
breed in water

reptiles
dry scaly skin

birds
feathers and wings

mammals
hair or fur

The plant kingdom

plants

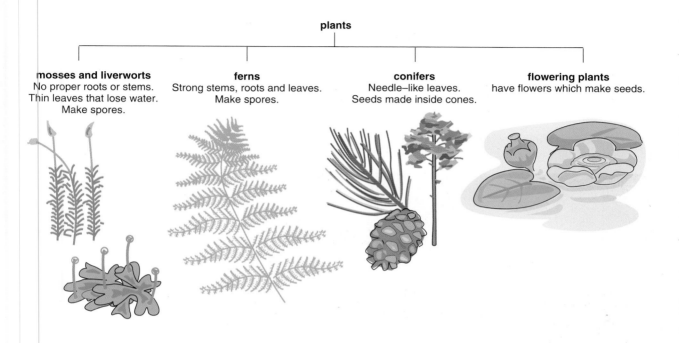

mosses and liverworts
No proper roots or stems.
Thin leaves that lose water.
Make spores.

ferns
Strong stems, roots and leaves.
Make spores.

conifers
Needle–like leaves.
Seeds made inside cones.

flowering plants
have flowers which make seeds.

The other three kingdoms

simple organisms

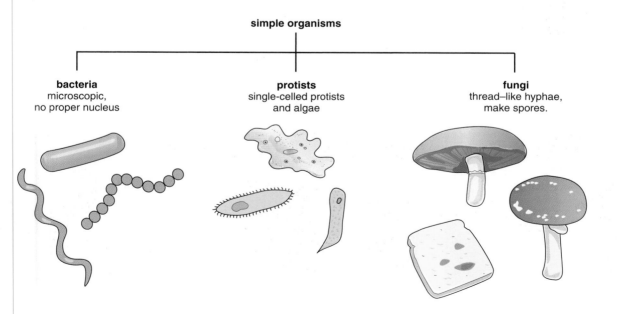

bacteria
microscopic,
no proper nucleus

protists
single-celled protists
and algae

fungi
thread–like hyphae,
make spores.

▷ Animals

Animals without backbones

We call animals that do not have a backbone **invertebrates**.
We can divide invertebrates into smaller groups:

1. Cnidarians ('nid-arians')

- Most of these live in the sea.
- They have a sac-like body with one opening.
- Tentacles with stinging cells surround the mouth.
- They paralyse their prey and push it into the mouth.

The sea anemone attaches to a rock using a sucker

Jellyfish swim by opening and closing like an umbrella

2. Worms

There are three major groups of worms:

Flatworms have a flattened body with a mouth at one end.
Some live in freshwater, but most are parasites of animals.

Roundworms have long, thread-like bodies.
Some live in the soil, but many are parasites inside plants and animals.

Segmented worms have long, tube-shaped bodies made up of segments.
The earthworm is found in the soil, but most segmented worms live in the sea.

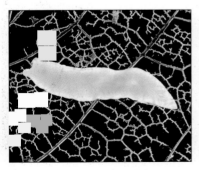

This flatworm glides through the water using tiny hairs or cilia

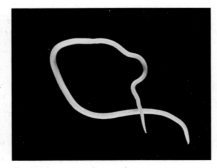

Roundworms do not have segments

Fertile soil contains large numbers of earthworms

3. Molluscs

This group includes snails, slugs and squids.
- Their bodies are soft but not segmented.
- Many of them have 1 or 2 shells to protect them.
- They have a muscular 'foot' to burrow or move around with.

Snails use their foot to move along on a trail of slime. They have rough tongues for shredding up plants.

Cockles and other 'bivalves' have 2 shells. They filter tiny plants and animals from the water.

4. Echinoderms

- These animals all live in the sea.
- They have tough, spiny skins.
- The body has a pattern of 5 parts.
- They move around on tube-feet.

The starfish has 5 arms. It can use them to pull the 2 shells of a mussel apart to feed on the soft insides.

Sea urchins have a pattern of 5 parts on their shells. They are protected by sharp spines and cling to rocks with their tube-feet.

5. Arthropods

These are the largest group of invertebrates.

- The word 'arthropod' means 'jointed leg'.
  All the animals in this group have jointed legs.
- Their bodies are also divided into segments.
- They are supported by a hard skeleton on the outside of the body
  called an **exoskeleton**. When they grow too big for their
  exoskeleton, they **moult** and grow a new one.
- On their heads are feelers or **antennae**.

The arthropods are made up of 4 smaller groups:

Crustaceans ('cru-stations')

- Nearly all of these live in water (woodlice are an exception).
- They breathe oxygen using their **gills**.
- They have more than 4 pairs of legs but less than 20 pairs.
- Many have a chalky exoskeleton. This protects them like a suit of armour.
- Crustaceans always have 2 pairs of antennae.

*Crabs have 5 pairs of legs.
They are protected by their
thick exoskeleton.*

*Shrimps do not have such a
thick exoskeleton. They have
long sensitive antennae.*

Myriapods

- These are the centipedes and the millipedes.
- They have long bodies made up of lots of segments.
  Do you think that centipedes really do have 100 legs?
  Do millipedes have 1000 legs?

*Centipedes have one pair of legs on each segment.
So the total number of legs depends upon how many
segments they have.
Centipedes are fast-moving carnivores.
They have powerful jaws and can paralyse their prey.*

*Millipedes have 2 pairs of legs on each body
segment.
They are slow-moving herbivores.
You can often find them feeding in a leaf litter.*

Insects

This is the largest group *within* the arthropods.
There are hundreds of thousands of different species.
They have been able to colonise most habitats in the world.

One reason why they are able to live on land so successfully is that their skin or **cuticle** is waterproof and stops them losing much water. Their bodies are divided into 3 parts : the head, the thorax and the abdomen.
On the thorax there are 3 pairs of legs and usually 2 pairs of wings.
They have one pair of antennae on the head and **compound eyes**.
They breathe through holes in the sides of the body called **spiracles**.
Insects often pass through different **larval** stages in their life as they grow.

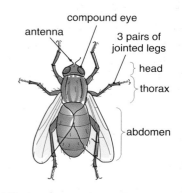

What makes an insect ?

Butterflies are useful because they pollinate flowers

Can you see the 3 parts of the body on this wasp ?

Arachnids

This is the spider group.
- They have bodies divided into 2 parts.
- They have 4 pairs of legs and no wings.
- They have no antennae but paralyse their prey with poison fangs.

Many spiders spin silken webs to catch their prey

Scorpions use a sting in the tail to paralyse their prey

263

Animals with backbones

We call animals that have a backbone **vertebrates**.
All vertebrates have an internal skeleton made of
either bone or cartilage.

There are 5 main groups of vertebrates:

1. Fish

- These live all the time in water.
- They are streamlined and have fins for swimming.
- They breathe oxygen from the water with their **gills**.
- Their skin is covered with scales.

*The scales of this fish point backwards for
streamlining*

Fish use fins to steer through the water

2. Amphibians

- These have smooth, moist skin.
- They breed in water.
  Sperm and eggs are released into the water so fertilisation is external.
- Fertilised eggs hatch into swimming tadpoles.
- On land, the adults breathe by using lungs.
  In water, they can breathe through their skin.

Amphibians have soft, moist skin

Tadpoles are larval stages. They breathe using gills.

More vertebrates

3. Reptiles

- These have dry, scaly skin to cut down water loss.
- They can live in dry regions, away from water.
- They have lungs to breathe air.
- Fertilisation takes place inside the female's body.
- They lay eggs with leathery shells.

Reptiles have dry, scaly skin

Does this fearsome predator remind you of a dinosaur? Dinosaurs were reptiles too.

4. Birds

- They have feathers and wings.
- Most of them are able to fly.
- They have no teeth but their beaks are adapted to deal with different types of food.
- They lay eggs which are protected by hard shells.

The beak and claws of the eagle are adapted for catching and tearing its prey

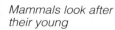

Sedge warblers feeding young in the nest

5. Mammals

- They have hair or fur.
- All mammals, even aquatic ones, use lungs for breathing.
- Fertilisation is internal and the young are born already well developed.
- Female mammals suckle their young on milk from **mammary glands**.
- Both birds and mammals are **warm blooded**. This means that they are able to regulate their body temperature. They can keep it constant even though the outside temperature changes.

Mammals look after their young

Aquatic mammals still use lungs to breathe air

265

▷ Plants

There are 2 kinds of plants:

plants which make spores like mosses, liverworts and ferns.
They make **spores** that grow into new plants.

plants which make seeds like conifers and flowering plants.
They make **seeds** that grow into new plants.

1. Plants which make spores

Mosses and liverworts

- They live in damp places.
- They have thin leaves that lose water easily.
- They do not have proper stems or roots.
- They make tiny spores instead of seeds.
  The spores are carried away by the wind.

In the summer mosses make spore capsules. The ripe capsules open and the spores are shaken out.

Liverworts grow flat on the ground.

Ferns

- They have strong stems, roots and leaves.
- Their leaves have a waxy layer to cut down water loss.
- They have tubes called **xylem** inside the plant.
  These transport water and support the plant.
- The spores are made on the underside of the leaves.

Each patch on the underside of the leaf contains lots of spores

Fern leaves grow out in a clump from a thick underground stem or rhizome

266

2. Plants which make seeds

Conifers

- Many are evergreen and keep their leaves all through the year.
- The leaves are like needles to cut down water loss.
- They have xylem for water transport and support.
- They do not have flowers. Instead they make male and female **cones**.

After fertilisation the seeds are made inside the female cones.

Coniferous plantations now cover many hill slopes

Flowering plants

- These have flowers containing reproductive organs.
- Pollen is carried from one plant to another by insects or by the wind.
- The flowers make seeds after fertilisation. These grow into new plants.
- Flowering plants are very successful at colonising the land. They are able to live in dry, hot places where there is little water.

Many flowering plants are pollinated by insects

Plants like the birch have their flowers pollinated by the wind

When the flowers of the horse chestnut have finished, the seeds are made inside fruits

267

▷ The other three kingdoms

1. Bacteria

- These are made up of one cell with no proper nucleus.
- They can only be seen by using a microscope.
- There are different cell shapes – rods, spheres and spirals.
- Bacteria are found everywhere – in the air, in the water and in the soil. They can also live in and on plants and animals.

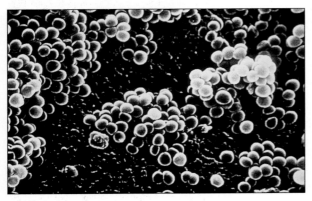

These sphere-shaped bacteria can cause a sore throat

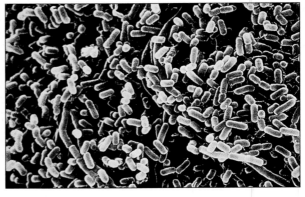

These rod-shaped bacteria are found inside the human intestine

2. Protists

- Some protists are made up of a single cell. (Others have many cells and are called **algae**.)
- They have a proper nucleus in the cell.
- They live in water or inside other organisms.
- They are not plants, animals, bacteria or fungi.
- Some have chlorophyll and can feed like plants.
- Others have to take food into their cells.

Single-celled protists

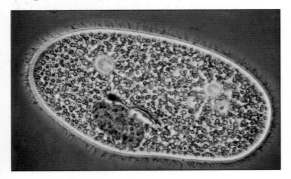

Paramecium is covered in tiny hairs called cilia. They enable it to swim through the water.

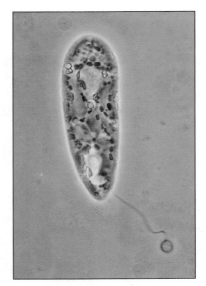

Euglena also moves around in water. But it has chlorophyll and feeds like a plant.

Algae

- These larger protists are often found in ponds or in the sea.
- They are like plants because they have chlorophyll and make their own food.
- Unlike plants they do not have leaves, stems or roots.

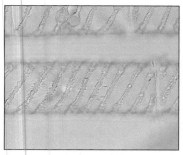

These beautiful filaments of Spirogyra form the green slime that you sometimes see floating on the surface of ponds

The bladder wrack is a brown seaweed common on the mid-shore.
It contains a brown pigment as well as chlorophyll.

This red seaweed is called Palmaria.
It is found on the lower shore.
A red pigment hides the chlorophyll.

3. Fungi

- These are the mushrooms, toadstools, moulds and yeasts.
- They are often made up of thin threads called **hyphae**.
- Some of them look like plants. They do not contain chlorophyll and so can not make their own food.
- They produce spores which grow into new fungi.
- Many fungi are **saprophytes**.
  They feed on dead and decaying material.
- Others live on or inside other organisms and are called **parasites**.

Bread mould spreads its hyphae over uncovered food and so spoils it.

Toadstools and mushrooms are the parts of the fungus that make the spores. These Fly Agaric fungi are poisonous.

Summary

- A species is a group of individuals that can breed together to produce fertile offspring.

- Variation occurs between different species and between members of the same species.

- Keys have a number of questions that enable you to identify living things.

- Living things can be classified into 5 kingdoms: bacteria, protists, fungi, plants and animals.

- Animals can be classified as vertebrates (have a backbone) or invertebrates (have no backbone).

- Plants can be classified as those that make spores and those that make seeds.

- Living things that are neither animals nor plants are classified as either bacteria, protists or fungi.

▷ Questions

1. Copy and complete:
   Animals with backbones are called . . . . . They can be divided into 5 groups: fish, ... , reptiles, ... , and mammals. Animals without backbones are called . . . . . One of the largest groups of invertebrates is the . . . . or jointed-legged animals. This group can be divided up into 4 smaller groups: crustaceans, ... , insects and . . . . . The plant kingdom can be divided up into 4 smaller groups: mosses and liverworts, ... , flowering plants and . . . . . The other 3 kingdoms are the . . . . , protists and . . . . .

2. The animal in the diagram lives inside the bladder of a frog:
   It is flat, has no segments, has only one opening to its gut and lacks a skeleton.

   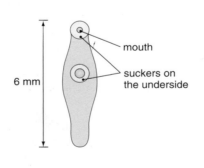

   Use your observations of the diagram to answer the following:
   a) Give 2 reasons why the animal is not a segmented worm.
   b) Give 2 reasons why the animal is not a mollusc.
   c) Suggest the group that the animal belongs to.
   d) What do you think the suckers are for?

3. Look at the 3 animals:

   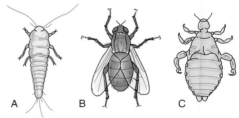

   a) Give 3 features which all 3 animals have and which you can see in the diagrams.
   b) To which group of animals do they belong?
   c) C lives on the skin of a mammal and feeds on its blood.
      i) Suggest one feature in diagram C which helps it to live on the skin.
      ii) How would this feature help?

4. When a scientist visited a desert island, she discovered some insects. She made some drawings and brought them back to the laboratory.
   Here are the sketches:

   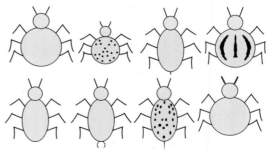

   a) Make up a name for each insect.
   b) Try making up a key to identify them.

5. Read the descriptions and decide which group each one refers to:
a) Lay eggs with a shell on land.
   Have wings and feathers but no teeth.
b) Body divided into 3 parts.
   Have 6 legs and usually 2 pairs of wings.
c) Have thin leaves and live in damp places.
   Reproduce using spores.
d) Have no segments. Have a muscular foot and some have a shell.
e) Do not have chlorophyll. Have a body made of thin threads called hyphae.
f) Are warm-blooded. Have hair and females make milk to feed their young.

6. Use the key to identify the seashore animals A, B, C, D, E and F.

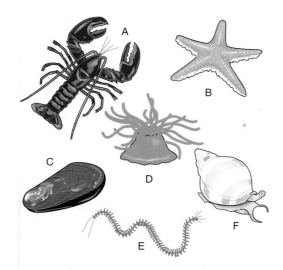

1	Divided into segments	Go to 2
	Not divided into segments	Go to 3
2	Has large claws	Lobster
	No large claws	Ragworm
3	Has a shell	Go to 4
	No shell	Go to 5
4	Shell has 2 pieces	Mussel
	Shell has 1 piece	Dog-whelk
5	Animal has 5 arms	Starfish
	Does not have 5 arms	Sea anemone

7. Decide, on the basis of their structure, which is the odd one out of the following:
a) Daffodil, jellyfish, bluebell, grass.
b) Camel, snake, eagle, tapeworm.
c) Snail, locust, spider, centipede.
d) Mould, toadstool, seaweed, mushroooom.
e) Frog, newt, toad, lizard.
f) Pine, sycamore, daisy, dandelion.
g) Carp, dolphin, stickleback, shark.

8. Use the key below to identify the leaves of these common trees:

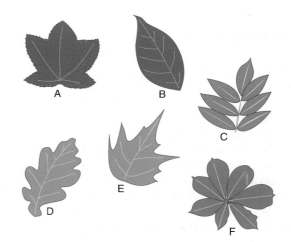

1	Leaves simple (not divided into leaflets)	Go to 2
	Leaves compound (divided into leaflets)	Go to 5
2	Leaves divided into 5 lobes	Sycamore
	Leaves not divided into 5 lobes	Go to 3
3	Edge of leaf smooth	Privet
	Edge of leaf not smooth	Go to 4
4	Edge of leaf toothed	Silver birch
	Edge of leaf with rounded lobes	Oak
5	Leaflets arranged like fingers of a hand	Horse chestnut
	Leaflets in pairs on leaf axis	Mountain ash

chapter 16

INHERITANCE

Why do we look like our parents?
Why do we have some of our mother's features
and some of our father's features?

Inheritance is the way in which parents pass
on their characteristics to their offspring.
The study of inheritance is known as **genetics**.

You should remember that parents pass on
their genes to their offspring.

Genes from the father are inside the sperm nucleus.
Genes from the mother are inside the egg nucleus.
At **fertilisation** the nucleus of the sperm
joins with the nucleus of the egg.
A new individual grows from the fertilised egg
or zygote.

So half of the genes come from the father and half
come from the mother.

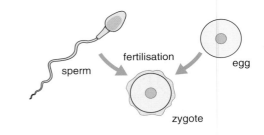

sperm   fertilisation   egg

zygote

▷ The material of inheritance

Inside nearly all cells there is a nucleus.
The nucleus contains thread-like **chromosomes**.
These chromosomes carry the **genes** that control
all your characteristics.

Look at the picture of human chromosomes:

If you were to count them, you would find 46.
They are different shapes and sizes.
You can separate them into identical pairs.
Can you see how many pairs there are?

Chromosomes occur in pairs.
But there are different numbers of chromosomes
for different species of animals and plants.
Humans have 23 pairs, cats have 19 pairs.
Fruit flies have only 4 pairs.

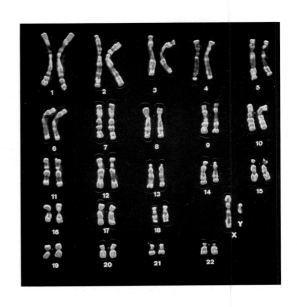

▷ What's a gene?

Each chromosome is made up of thousands of **genes**
arranged like beads on a necklace.
It is the genes that carry the genetic information that
affects how we grow and what we look like.
For instance there is a gene for eye colour,
and others for hair colour and for height.

If we could unravel a chromosome, it would
form an extremely long thread.
That thread is made up of a chemical called **DNA.**
DNA stands for **deoxyribonucleic acid.**
No wonder we call it DNA!

A single gene is made of a short length of DNA.
So the long thread that makes up a chromosome
contains hundreds of genes.

A DNA molecule is made up of thousands of units,
each called a **nucleotide.**
A single nucleotide is made up of three molecules :

- a phosphate
- a sugar
- a base

The sugar and phosphate molecules join up and
form the backbone of the DNA strand.
The bases are attached to the sugar molecules.

In fact if you look at the diagram, you will see that DNA
is made up of **two** strands of nucleotides.
It is rather like a ladder.
The sugars and phosphates make up the uprights
of the ladder and the bases make up the rungs.
And then the whole molecule is twisted into
a **double helix** – a bit like a spiral staircase.

Base pairing

So how is the DNA molecule kept together?
If you look at the diagram you can see that the bases
join together.
Each pair of bases is held together by hydrogen bonds.

There are four different bases in DNA : **thymine (T)**,
adenine (A), cytosine (C) and **guanine (G).**
The bases always pair up in the same way :

> **Adenine (A) pairs with thymine (T).**
> **Cytosine (C) pairs with guanine (G).**

Although the hydrogen bonds holding the two chains
of nucleotides together are weak, there are many of them.
So altogether they keep the 'double helix' in shape.

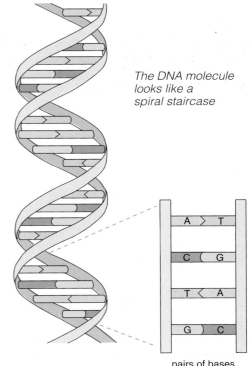

*The DNA molecule
looks like a
spiral staircase*

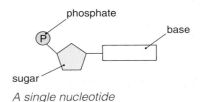

pairs of bases
form the steps
on the staircase

A single nucleotide

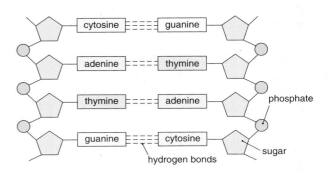

▷ The DNA detectives

In the 1950s, a great deal of work was being carried out by scientists eager to discover the nature of DNA.

The American biochemist **Erwin Chargaff** analysed samples of DNA from different organisms.
He always found that the amounts of adenine (A) were equal to the amounts of thymine (T), and that the amounts of cytosine (C) were equal to the amounts of guanine (G).

What conclusions can you draw from this evidence?

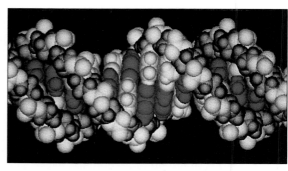

Computer graphic representation of a DNA molecule

It suggests that adenine (A) pairs up with thymine (T) and that cytosine (C) pairs up with guanine (G).

About the same time **Rosalind Franklin** and **Maurice Wilkins** were working at King's College, London.
They used a technique called **X-ray diffraction** to work out how the atoms inside the DNA molecule were arranged.
It involves firing a beam of X-rays into crystals of DNA.
The X-rays hit the atoms and are scattered on to a photographic plate.
When the photographic plate is developed, it can help to build up a picture of what the 3-D structure of DNA is like.

The double helix

The molecular structure of DNA was finally worked out by **James Watson** and **Francis Crick**, working in Cambridge in 1953.
Watson was an American biochemist working in Britain and Crick was an English physicist, turned biochemist.
They used Chargaff's results and the X-ray diffraction pictures produced by Franklin and Wilkins.

Watson and Crick with their DNA model

They pieced together cut-out models of the molecules involved.
It took hours of discussion and painstaking manipulation of the model.
Eventually they were able to build a 3-D model of the structure of DNA.
It turned out to be a beautiful 'double helix' structure.
Furthermore, each half of the molecule could separate from the other and make an exact copy of itself.
This meant that chromosomes and genes could also make exact copies of themselves when cells divide.

Watson and Crick were so excited at their discovery that they dashed out of the Cavendish Laboratory and ran down the street looking for people to tell!

In 1958, Rosalind Franklin died of cancer.
In 1962, Francis Crick, James Watson and Maurice Wilkins were awarded the Nobel Prize for their work on DNA structure.
No doubt Rosalind Franklin would also have shared the prize if she had lived longer.

Rosalind Franklin

▷ Making new DNA

When a cell divides the chromosomes split length ways
and each half enters the new cell.
Why do you think that this is important?

Each new cell must have the same chromosome number
as the parent cell.

If the chromosomes are able to make exact copies of
themselves then so must the genes and so must DNA.
Otherwise the new cells would not have all the correct
genetic information that they need.

Before a cell divides, the amount of DNA contained
inside its nucleus, doubles.
But how does this happen?

- Firstly the hydrogen bonds holding the bases together break.
- Then the DNA double helix unwinds to give two single strands.
- Each single strand attracts separate nucleotides present
  inside the nucleus.
- These nucleotides line up along each single DNA strand following
  the 'rule of base pairing'. So C lines up alongside G and A alongside T.
- The nucleotides join up and so two new DNA molecules are formed
  and each one is an identical copy of the parent cell's DNA.

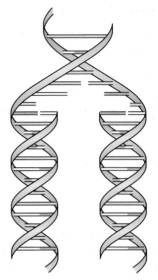

*A DNA molecule making two
identical copies*

Making proteins

To make a protein, lots of amino acids have to join together.
The type and sequence of the amino acids determines what
the protein will be like.
For instance, it could be an enzyme, a hormone or a protein in muscle.

DNA is only found inside the nucleus.
Proteins are known to be made in structures called **ribosomes**,
which are found in the cytoplasm of a cell.

So if DNA controls the making of a protein, how does the information
get from the nucleus to the ribosomes ?

The answer is another molecule called **ribonucleic acid (RNA)**.
This is formed in a similar way to the making of new DNA.
The **m-RNA** copies the base sequence on DNA and carries it out
of the nucleus, through a nuclear pore to the ribosomes.

Another type of RNA called **t-RNA** picks up amino acids and carries
them to the ribosomes.
The t-RNA slots into the m-RNA and gives up its amino acid.
The amino acids bond together forming a long chain – the protein.
The sequence of bases on DNA that codes for a protein is called
the **genetic code**.

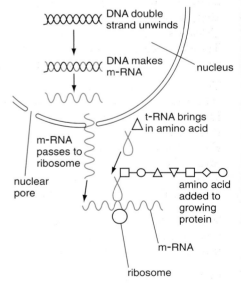

How DNA controls protein synthesis

▷ Mitosis

You should remember that new cells are made by
cell division.
Mitosis is a kind of cell division.
All cells are made by mitosis **except** the sex cells.
When a cell divides by mitosis it splits into 2 new
daughter cells.
These daughter cells are identical to the cell that
they came from and to each other.

When does mitosis happen?

● Mitosis occurs in **growth**.
  When living things grow they make new cells.
  Mitosis makes these new cells whether it is in
  the growth of a baby, the healing of a wound,
  the germination of a seedling, or replacing red blood cells.

● Mitosis also occurs in **asexual reproduction**.
  The cells in the parent plant or animal divide to
  make new cells which form the new individual.

Cells dividing by mitosis

Stages in mitosis

Before a cell can divide by mitosis it must make a
second set of chromosomes.
What would happen if the cell split into two before
it made a second set?
How many chromosomes would each daughter cell have?

In between cell divisions the chromosomes look like a
tangle of threads.
When a cell is about to divide the chromosomes
become clearly visible.

*Chromosomes are visible in
the cell on the right*

Let's look at what happens to **one** pair of chromosomes during mitosis:

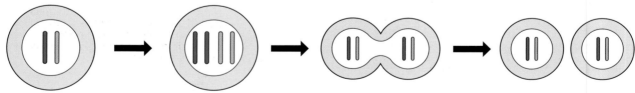

One of the 23 pairs
of chromosomes in
the nucleus just
before the cell is
about to divide.

Each chromosome
makes an identical
copy of itself. For a
moment there are
92 chromosomes in
the nucleus.

The cell starts to
divide into two.
One complete set
of chromosomes
goes into each of
the two new
daughter cells.

Two new daughter cells,
each identical to the cell
they came from.

▷ Meiosis

If a sperm cell and an egg cell both had
46 chromosomes like other body cells,
what would happen at fertilisation?
The fertilised egg would have 92 chromosomes –
twice as many as it should have!

Fortunately sex cells, like sperm and eggs, are
made by a different kind of cell division.
This cell division is called **meiosis**.

Meiosis halves the number of chromosomes.
So egg cells and sperm cells only have 23
chromosomes each.
The fertilised egg will have 46 chromosomes,
23 from the mother, in the egg, and 23 from
the father, in the sperm.

Where do you think meiosis occurs in a woman?
Where do you think meiosis occurs in a man?

Meiosis occurs in the sex organs.
The ovaries make eggs by meiosis.
The testes make sperm by meiosis.

Where do you think meiosis occurs in plants?

The anthers make pollen by meiosis.
The ovaries make egg cells by meiosis.

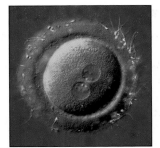

A fertilised human egg or zygote

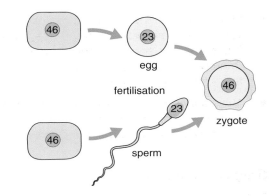

Let's look at what happens to **one** pair of chromosomes during meiosis:

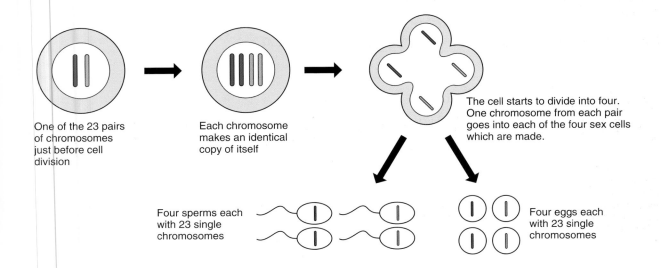

One of the 23 pairs
of chromosomes
just before cell
division

Each chromosome
makes an identical
copy of itself

The cell starts to divide into four.
One chromosome from each pair
goes into each of the four sex cells
which are made.

Four sperms each
with 23 single
chromosomes

Four eggs each
with 23 single
chromosomes

▷ A boy or a girl ?

Your chromosomes also determine which sex you are.

Can you remember how many chromosomes humans have ?

46 – these occur in 23 pairs.
22 are matching pairs.
But the last pair sometimes do not match.

Pair 23 are called the **sex chromosomes**.
It is these that determine whether you are
a boy or a girl.

If you are male, one of the sex chromosomes
is longer than the other.
You will have one long **X chromosome** and
one much shorter **Y chromosome**.

If you are female, your sex chromosomes look alike.
You will have two identical **X chromosomes**.

What happens to the chromosomes when eggs
and sperm are made ?

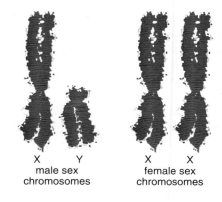

X   Y
male sex
chromosomes

X   X
female sex
chromosomes

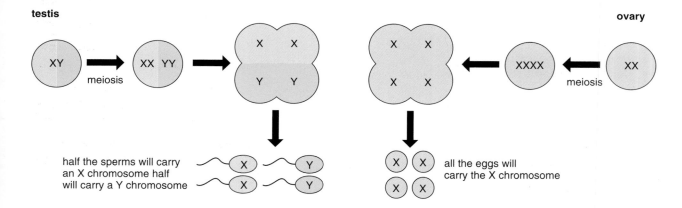

The diagram shows how sex is inherited :
All the eggs contain an X chromosome.
Half the sperms contain an X chromosome
and half a Y chromosome.
At fertilisation, the egg may join with either
an X sperm or a Y sperm.
Since there are equal numbers of X and Y sperms, the
child has an equal chance of being a boy or a girl.

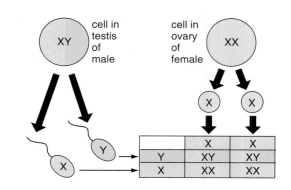

▷ Gregor Mendel

Gregor Mendel was an Austrian monk and teacher.
He was born in 1822, the son of a farmer.
At the monastery, Mendel kept a small garden plot
where he experimented growing pea plants.
He studied the way their characteristics were passed
on from one generation to the next, looking for patterns.

Mendel chose to study features that were easy to observe
such as plant height, flower colour and seed shape.
Pea plants were also easy to grow and Mendel was able to
either self-pollinate or cross-pollinate the flowers.

Mendel was painstaking in his methods: planning his work,
and meticulously collecting and recording his results.
He was also able to analyse the huge amount of data that
he built up and so come to sound scientific conclusions.

The amazing thing about Mendel's work is that he worked
out the underlying rules of inheritance before anything
had been discovered about DNA, genes or chromosomes.

Look at the diagram to see some of the characteristics that
Mendel studied.

What do you notice ?

The characteristics that he studied were either one thing
or another.
This suggests that they are controlled by a single gene.

Pairs of genes

You know that chromosomes occur in identical pairs.
So each chromosome in a pair must carry the same
genes along its length.

Let's take a characteristic like hair colour.
The gene that controls hair colour lies on a particular
chromosome.
But since chromosomes are in identical pairs – a partner
chromosome must also carry a gene for hair colour.

So for a particular characteristic there must be **two** genes.
One on each chromosome in a pair.
So you have two genes for hair colour, two genes for eye
colour, and so on.

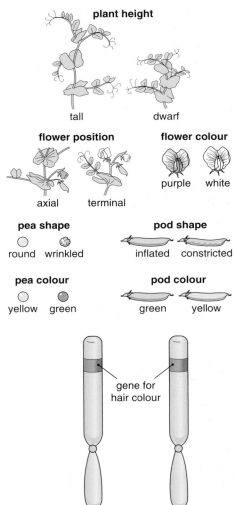

A pair of chromosomes

279

▷ More about genes

Do you remember how many genes there are for each characteristic?

You have **two** genes for each characteristic. The two genes are found opposite each other on neighbouring chromosomes.

Let's look at the genes for eye colour.

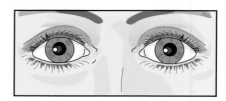

There are different forms of eye colour gene. There is an *eye colour gene that will give you blue eyes*, one that will give you brown eyes, one that will give you green eyes, and so on.

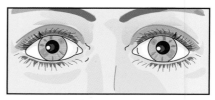

Different forms of the same gene are called **alleles**.

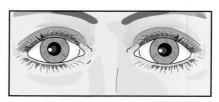

So instead of saying that you have two genes for eye colour you should really say that you have two alleles for eye colour.

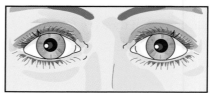

Let's say that **B** is the symbol for brown allele.
Let's say that **b** is the symbol for blue allele.

If you have two **B** alleles, you will have brown eyes.

Your **genotype** refers to the alleles that you have.
Your **phenotype** refers to your appearance.

So your genotype is **BB**
and your phenotype is brown.

We say that you are **homozygous** for eye colour because **both** of your alleles are the same.

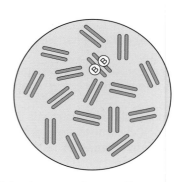

Both alleles for eye colour are the same : brown

▷ Dominant and recessive

If you have two **b** alleles, you will have blue eyes.

Your genotype is **bb**.
Your phenotype is blue.

You are **homozygous** for eye colour because both of your alleles are the same.

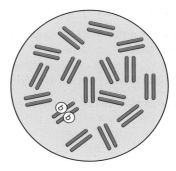

Both alleles for eye colour are the same : blue

What happens if you have one **B** allele and one **b** allele ?

Your genotype is **Bb**.

We say that you are **heterozygous** for eye colour because your two alleles are different.

But what is your phenotype ?
Will you have one brown eye and one blue eye ?

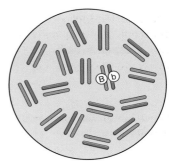

*These alleles for eye colour are different :
one brown and one blue.*

When there are two *different* alleles, one is stronger than the other.
The stronger allele masks the weaker one.
The brown allele is stronger than the blue allele and masks it.
So the person will have brown eyes.

We say that the brown allele is **dominant**.

We say that the blue allele is **recessive**.

Here are some examples of dominant and recessive characteristics :

Dominant	Recessive
freckles	no freckles
dark hair	light hair
tongue rollers	non-tongue rollers
free ear lobe	ear lobe joined
normal skin colour	albino

How do you inherit your eye colour?

You should remember that you have **pairs** of chromosomes.
One chromosome in each pair came from your **father** and one came from your *mother*.

This means that for each pair of alleles that you have, one came from your **father** and one came from your *mother*.

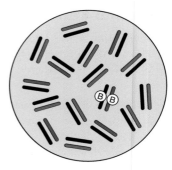

The black chromosomes come from the father and the red chromosomes come from the mother

What happens if a mother and a father are both heterozygous for brown eye?
What colour eyes will their children have?

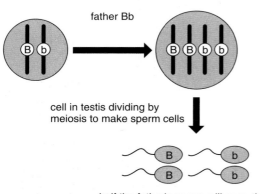

father Bb

cell in testis dividing by meiosis to make sperm cells

half the father's sperm will carry the B allele and half will carry the b allele

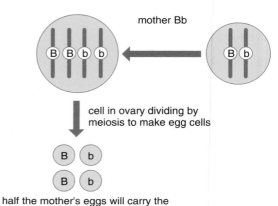

mother Bb

cell in ovary dividing by meiosis to make egg cells

half the mother's eggs will carry the B allele and half will carry the b allele

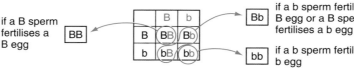

if a B sperm fertilises a B egg — BB

Bb — if a b sperm fertilises a B egg or a B sperm fertilises a b egg

bb — if a b sperm fertilises a b egg

So two heterozygous brown-eyes parents could have brown-eyed or blue-eyed children.
Which are they more likely to have?

What would happen if the mother was homozygous blue-eyed and the father was homozygous brown-eyed?

What would happen if the mother was homozygous blue-eyed and the father was heterozygous brown-eyed?

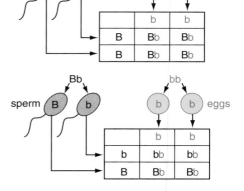

▷ Genes in action

Suppose that you went in for plant breeding.
You want to breed a plant with red flowers
with a plant with white flowers.
What do you do?

You take some pollen from the red flower and
put it onto the stigma of the white flower.
This is called carrying out a **cross**.
After the seeds develop you grow them into
new plants.
They all turn out to be red.
How can you explain this?

*Sweet pea flowers
show variation*

The picture gives an explanation:

There are 2 alleles for flower colour.
R codes for red and **r** codes for white.
The red flowers were homozygous red (**RR**).
The white flowers were homozygous white (**rr**).

The pollen grains contained only *one* allele **R**.
The eggs also contained just *one* allele **r**.
So after fertilisation all the offspring were **Rr**.
They are heterozygous red, because the red allele
was dominant.

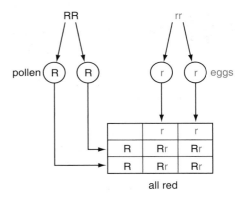

Taking it further

Suppose you breed the offspring of this first cross.
This time you cross a plant with red flowers (**Rr**)
with another with red flowers (**Rr**).
Both plants will be heterozygous.
The result is a mixture of red flowers and
white flowers.
How can you explain this?

This time each plant made pollen or eggs half of which
contained the red allele **R** and half the white allele **r**.
The alleles can now pair up in 4 different ways
at fertilisation:

1 × **RR** – gives red
2 × **Rr** – gives red
1 × **rr** – gives white.

So there will be 3 red flowers to 1 white flower.

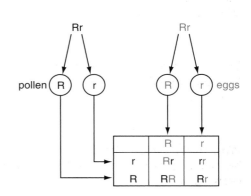

▷ More crosses

Does the same thing happen in animals?

Let's look at the inheritance of coat colour in mice.

There are grey mice and white mice.
We can show the grey allele as **G**.
We can show the white allele as **g**.

What happens if you cross a homozygous
grey mouse with a homozygous white mouse?
The picture shows you:
All the offspring are grey.
So the grey allele **G** is dominant to the white allele **g**.

Now cross two heterozygous grey mice (**Gg**):

There are 3 grey offspring to 1 white offspring.
The white offspring must have two recessive alleles –
it must be homozygous white (**gg**).
But the grey can be either homozygous grey (**GG**)
or heterozygous grey (**Gg**).

The ratio of the phenotypes is 3 grey : 1 white.
The ratio of the genotypes is 1**GG** : 2**Gg** : 1**gg**.

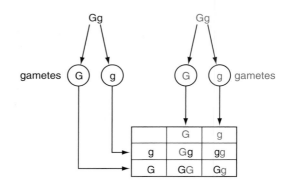

Test cross

But how can we tell if a grey mouse is homozygous (**GG**)
or heterozygous (**Gg**)?
Not just by looking at it.

How do we know if our red flowers are homozygous (**RR**)
or heterozygous (**Rr**)?

We have to carry out a **test cross**.
This means that we cross the unknown parent
with a homozygous recessive parent. That is with
a white mouse or a white flowered plant.

Again let's use the picture to explain:

If our red flower is homozygous (**RR**),
crossing it with a white flower (**rr**)
gives all red flowers (**Rr**).
If our red flower is heterozygous (**Rr**),
crossing it with a white flower (**rr**)
gives half red and half white.

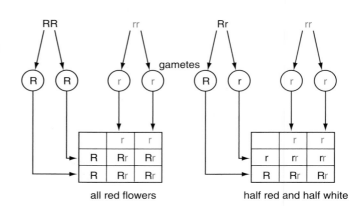

all red flowers   half red and half white

▷ Mutations

A **mutation** is a change in a gene or a chromosome.
It can cause a change in a characteristic.

Sometimes this change can be harmful, but sometimes
mutations can be neutral or even beneficial.

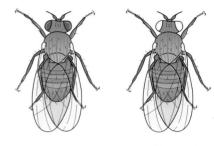

One of the first mutations studied was in the fruit-fly.
The normal eye colour is red.
But a **mutant** white eye form was discovered.
A gene controlling eye colour had suddenly changed.
This was due to a change in the structure of the DNA.
The gene no longer coded for the production of red
eye colour. It now coded for white eyes.

A similar example occurs in **albinos**.
A gene controls production of the skin pigment **melanin**.
This protects the skin from ultra-violet light.
It also gives you a suntan and freckles !

In albinos, the structure of a gene changes or **mutates**.
So it no longer codes for the production of melanin.
Albinos occur in other animals too.
Can you think how this hedgehog could be at a disadvantage ?

Gene mutations are usually recessive.
They can be hidden by a dominant allele.
As you will see on the next page, **cystic fibrosis**
is a disease caused by a gene mutation.

Down's syndrome is caused by a chromosome mutation.
A woman produces an egg with 24 chromosomes instead
of the normal 23.
If this egg is fertilised the baby will have 47 chromosomes
– one more than normal.
Down's syndrome affects about one baby in 650.

Down's children are very affectionate

Mutations can occur naturally.
But it is now known that radiation and some chemicals
can cause mutations.
Alpha and beta particles and X-rays and gamma rays
are the most damaging.
Atom bombs were dropped on Japan at the end of the
Second World War.
This exposed people to massive doses of radiation.
The result was an increase in the rate of mutations and
many babies were born with defects.

Hiroshima in March, 1946

Sickle cell anaemia

Sickle cell anaemia is an inherited disease
of the blood.

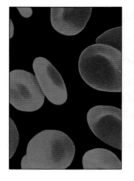

Look at these two photographs of red blood cells:

What differences can you see?

The blood on the right is from a person
suffering from sickle cell anaemia.
Can you see that the red cells are an odd shape?
They have formed an S-shape like a sickle.

These red cells have abnormal haemoglobin.
This makes it difficult for the red cells to
carry oxygen.
This inherited disease is common in West Africa.

Sickle cell anaemia is caused by a recessive allele.
The child inherits the allele from each parent and
is homozygous recessive.

The interesting thing is that the heterozygous
individual becomes resistant to **malaria**.
Malaria is a fatal disease caused when a microbe
gets into red cells.
The microbes don't affect sickle shaped blood cells
in the same way.
So being heterozygous or a **carrier** can be an
advantage in malarial regions.

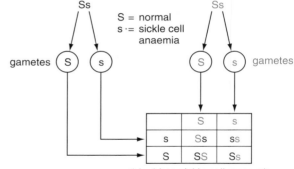

1 in 4 has sickle cell anaemia

Genetic counselling

The parents of a child with a genetic disease can get help
from a **genetic counsellor**.
They can work out the chances of the couple's next
child having the disease.
It is then up to the parents to decide if they are willing
to take the risk of having more children.
There may be a history of a genetic disease in a family.
The counsellor tries to find out as much as possible
out the family history.
ce can then be given about the risks of children being
ith the disease.

▷ Genetic engineering

Many inherited diseases are caused when the body can not make a particular protein.

For instance, people with haemophilia can not make the protein Factor 8.
Diabetics can not make the protein insulin.

Genetic engineering can be used to make large amounts of these proteins.

Genetic engineering means removing a gene from one living organism and putting it into another.

This is how it has been used to help diabetics:

- The human gene that codes for the production of insulin is identified.

- Special enzymes are used as 'chemical scissors'. These cut out the insulin-making gene from the rest of the DNA.

- A circular piece of DNA called a **plasmid** is removed from a bacterium.

- The human insulin-making gene is put into the plasmid.

- The plasmid is put into a bacterium.

- The bacterium makes insulin.

- The bacteria multiply very rapidly. All the bacteria produced will have the insulin gene. Lots of insulin will be made.

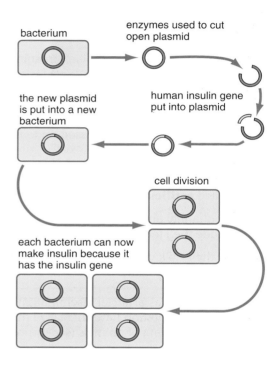

bacterium

enzymes used to cut open plasmid

human insulin gene put into plasmid

the new plasmid is put into a new bacterium

cell division

each bacterium can now make insulin because it has the insulin gene

Genetic engineering makes it possible to make insulin quickly and cheaply on a large scale.
The bacteria are grown inside huge industrial fermenters called **bioreactors**.
The microbes grow quickly under ideal conditions.
Each bacterium is an identical **genetic clone** with a copy of the insulin-making gene.
The insulin is extracted and purified.

Before genetic engineering, diabetics had to use insulin that had been extracted from sheep or pigs.
This often produced reactions since it was different from human insulin.
Genetic engineering has made it possible to produce large amounts of safer drugs much more quickly.

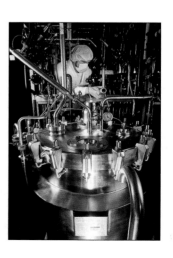

▷ Biology at work: Genetic fingerprinting

The DNA in your cells is as unique as your
fingerprints.
Unless you have an identical twin your 'genetic
fingerprint' is different from anyone else's.

Scientists take a sample of blood or hair and extract
DNA from it.
Sections of the DNA can be used to produce a pattern
rather like a bar-code.
Everyone's bar-code will be different.

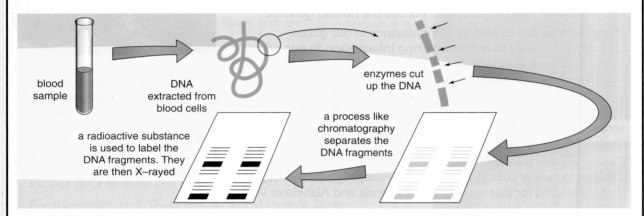

blood sample → DNA extracted from blood cells → enzymes cut up the DNA → a process like chromatography separates the DNA fragments → a radioactive substance is used to label the DNA fragments. They are then X-rayed

Genetic fingerprinting can be used to solve crimes.
The bar-code of a suspect may match up with
a sample taken from the scene of a crime.

Look at the genetic fingerprints in the picture:
Compare them with that of a sample taken from
the murder scene.
Are any of the suspects guilty?

Can you think of any other uses for genetic
fingerprinting?

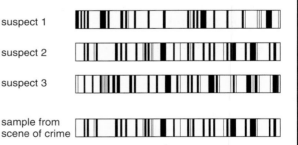

suspect 1

suspect 2

suspect 3

sample from scene of crime

One of the first times that this technique was used
was in the case of a Ghanaian family.
The mother said that her son had been born in Britain
and had emigrated to Ghana to be with his father.
When he wanted to return to Britain the authorities
claimed that he was not the woman's real son.

How do you think genetic fingerprinting was used to
solve this case?

▷ Biology at work: Genetically modified foods

Genetically modified (GM) foods are the result of the rapid developments that have taken place over recent years in genetic engineering.
Using specialised enzymes, it is now possible to cut out specific DNA sections and transfer them into plant cells.
These beneficial genes can give the plant advantages such as resistance to disease, increased yield or better taste.

Most people have probably already eaten genetically modified food products such as vegetarian cheese, tomato puree and soya. But in 1999 research into GM potatoes prompted debate and public concern about the safety of GM foods.

Greenpeace activists removing GM maize in Norfolk.

GM foods – the benefits

Scientists and the biotechnology companies have been quick to stress the safety of GM foods and their benefits:

- **Solving global hunger** – genetic modification could feed more people if crops are produced that are able to tolerate frost, drought and salty soils. Food production could be increased in marginal areas. Genes are not harmful to eat since we digest all the DNA in our food.
- **Environmentally friendly** – GM crops can be resistant to insects, weeds and diseases so there would be less use of pesticides. Also genes that improve nitrogen uptake would mean less need for chemical fertilisers and lessen the environmental threat they cause.
- **Consumer benefits** – GM foods have already been produced with an improved flavour and better keeping qualities. They are easier to produce and require fewer additives.

Packaged food which includes soy sauce made from GM soya beans

GM foods – the concerns

- **Environmental safety** – there are worries that new GM plants will become successful weeds. Pollen from GM crops resistant to weedkillers may be transferred to other plants by insects or the wind.
- **Food safety** – how would you like to eat food that contains foreign genes ? These new gene combinations may have effects that are so far unknown. They may result in harmful substances being produced. Has enough research been carried out on the chances of this happening ?
- **Changes in farming structure** – there may be an increase in the trends towards larger farms that are more capital intensive. This would disadvantage smaller, less economical farms.
- **Biodiversity** – increasingly fewer companies will control plant breeding, reducing the number of plant varieties and wild relatives.
- **Animal health** – at present there are no products of animal biotechnology in food shops. Any developments in animal production that affect animal welfare are increasingly likely to be resisted.

Assessing disease resistance in GM rice under glasshouse conditions

chapter 17

EVOLUTION

Evolution is about change.
Things tend to change with time.
Think about cars, bicycles or aircraft.
How have they changed over time?
They have gradually improved.

Some animals and plants from the past
do not exist today.
Why do you think this is?

Some of today's animals and plants did
not exist long ago.
Why do you think this is?

Many living things change to suit their environment.
They **adapt** to suit the conditions.
These **adaptations** help them to survive and to breed.
So the adaptations are passed on to the offspring.

Any plant or animal that occurs in large numbers in
a particular environment must be well adapted to
that environment.

To survive it has to **compete** with other individuals
in its species for things like food and space.
It also has to compete with other species around it.
Not all of the plants and animals will survive.
There is a **'survival of the fittest'**.
But this does not mean the healthiest.
It means the survival of those individuals that are
best adapted to their environment.

Evolution is the gradual change in the features or
characteristics of a species.
If a living thing has features that help it to survive,
then it will breed and pass on its genes to its offspring.
Living things that don't have useful features are less
likely to survive and to breed.

▷ Survival

Many plants and animals produce large numbers of offspring.
A cod lays over 3 million eggs.
Each poppy plant makes over 15 000 seeds.

The scientist Charles Darwin worked out that one pair of elephants could have 19 million descendents after 700 years — if they all survived !

So why is the world not over-run by elephants ?

Why don't poppies completely cover the Earth ?

The reason is that not all of the offspring survive.
Most of the cod's eggs do not grow to adult fish.
Many eggs and young are eaten.

Many poppy seeds may be eaten.
Others may not land in soil where they can grow into new plants.

Can you think of any other factors that prevent offspring surviving in each generation ?

What about :

- competition for food
- predators
- disease
- climate
- drought ?

Predation by hyenas

So which individuals do survive ?

There is some luck involved, but, in general, it is the best adapted individuals that survive to breed.
There is a 'survival of the fittest'.

The best adapted individuals will pass on their features to their offspring.
So the next generation will have a larger proportion of these better adapted individuals.

The sea eagle is a well adapted predator

▷ Charles Darwin

Most scientists used to think that all living things
had remained the same since the Earth was created.
But as they learned more about the different plants
and animals, some scientists started to question this.

Instead they suggested that species had changed and
that new species are being formed.
They thought that similar species descended from a
common ancestor by a process of gradual change.

This was the **theory of evolution**.
The first person to collect together evidence to
support the theory was Charles Darwin.

Darwin was a British naturalist.
In 1831, he set sail on the survey ship HMS *Beagle*.
He travelled around the world.
Darwin visited many different islands studying the wildlife.
He was impressed by the huge variety of plants and animals
that he found.
He brought back a large collection of plants, animals
and fossils.

HMS *Beagle*

In 1859, Darwin published his famous book, *The Origin of Species*.
In it he presented evidence to support his ideas.
He also described how evolution might have taken place.
He called it the **'theory of natural selection'**.

About the same time, Alfred Russel Wallace (another British naturalist)
also presented his ideas on evolution.
Darwin's and Wallace's theories were based upon the same ideas:

**organisms produce large
numbers of offspring**

**in any species there is
variation between individuals**

**there is a struggle
for existence**

**organisms with useful characteristics
are more likely to survive and pass
them on to the next generation**

The Galapagos finches

On his voyage in HMS *Beagle*, Darwin visited a group of islands off the coast of South America.
He was fascinated by the animals and plants of the Galapagos Islands.

Darwin studied 13 different varieties of finches.
He suggested that they must have descended from birds that had flown to the islands, or been blown there, from the mainland.

He noticed differences in the beaks of the finches.
They had different beaks for different diets.
Some had thick beaks to crush seeds.
Others had slender beaks to catch insects.
Could they have all evolved from the same ancestor?

Darwin suggested that seed-eating finches had reached the islands from the mainland,
but that there was not enough food for all the birds.
Finches with slightly different beaks were able to eat other types of food.
These finches survived to breed and passed on their adaptations to their offspring.

Darwin thought that the finches evolved into different varieties by **natural selection**.

Marine iguana from the Galapagos Islands

How has this woodpecker finch become adapted to feed on insects in bark?

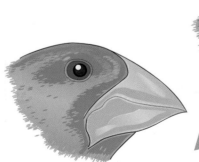

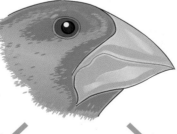

seed–eating finches
from mainland

many continued
to eat seeds

lots of competition for
food among seed–eating finches

many did not survive

population of seed–eating finches remained stable

a few had slightly different
beaks, they could eat insects

far less competition for
food among insect–eating finches

far more of these finches survived

population of insect–eating finches increased

▷ Selection in action

Natural selection results in adaptations to the environment being selected and passed on.
So with time, a population will become better adapted.

Insecticides are used to kill insect pests.
But a few individuals do not die.
They are able to break the insecticide down and make it harmless.
We say that they are **resistant**.

These insects will survive to breed.
So the numbers of resistant insects in the population will increase.

Resistance can spread quickly because insects reproduce rapidly.
Larger amounts of insecticide need to be used.
This is very expensive.
Eventually a different insecticide is tried.
But in time, the insects will develop resistance to this too.

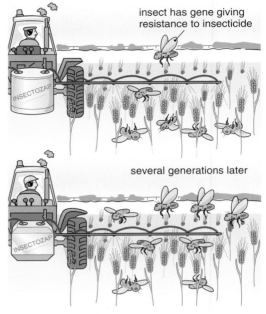

Resistant insects survive to breed and so their numbers increase

Super rats

Rats are also pests.
They eat stored food and carry disease.

Warfarin is a rat poison that was first used in the 1950s.
By now many rat populations are resistant to warfarin.
These 'super rats' are not killed even by large doses of warfarin.

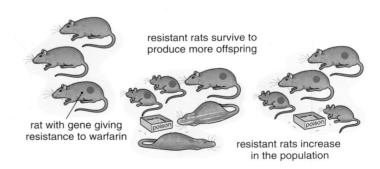

Resistant bacteria

Some bacteria develop resistance to antibiotics.
In a population of bacteria, there will be some individuals that have resistant genes.
These bacteria are not killed by the antibiotic.
Bacteria reproduce very quickly.
Soon most of the bacteria are resistant to the antibiotic.

▷ The peppered moth

Changes in the environment can bring about changes in a population by natural selection.

There are 2 types of peppered moth:

- a pale, speckled form, and
- a dark form.

The moths feed at night and rest on tree trunks during the day.
Their main predators are birds.

Before 1850 the dark variety of peppered moth was rare.
But by 1895 almost the whole population of moths in some cities was dark.
Why do you think the dark moth became so common in industrial areas?

Pollution from heavy industries killed the lichen that grows on the bark of trees.
Soot from factories also blackened the tree trunks.

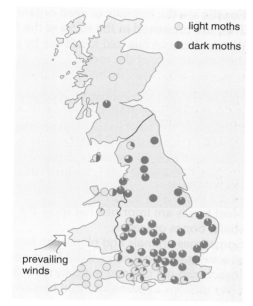

The proportions of dark and light peppered moths found in different areas of Britain today

Look at the photograph:

Which type of moth is best camouflaged on lichen-covered bark?

Which type of moth is best camouflaged on dark trees?

Against a lichen-covered tree, the light variety was difficult for birds to see.
So in clean areas, it survived to breed and its numbers increased.

Against dark trees, the dark form is better camouflaged.
So in industrial areas, it survived to breed and it became the most common form.

Look at the map above showing the proportions of light and dark moths in Britain today.

In which areas are the dark moths more common?

In which areas are the light moths more common?

Explain why this is in each case.

Two varieties of peppered moth

301

▷ Evolution of the horse

Fossil evidence has been pieced together to suggest how the modern horse has evolved. The ideas are shown here:

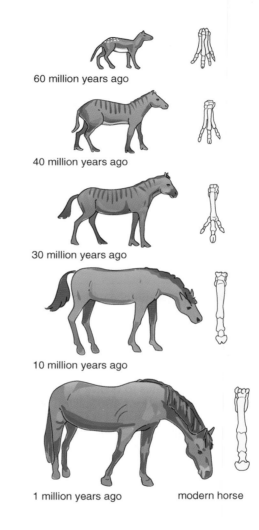

60 million years ago

40 million years ago

30 million years ago

10 million years ago

1 million years ago   modern horse

What changes can you see between each of the different stages?

Why has natural selection operated to produce the modern horse?
Could there have been a change in its environment?

Sixty million years ago a lot of the countryside was marshy.
There were small trees and bushes that offered cover so that animals could hide from predators.

But by one million years ago the environment had changed.
Grassland had replaced the trees and bushes.
There was no cover for animals to hide.
The faster an animal could run, the better its chance of escaping a predator — and surviving.
Animals with long necks might get a better view of any predators coming.

Flat feet with splayed-out digits make it less likely that an animal will sink in marshy ground.
But they are no good for fast running.

The modern horse has long legs and runs on one digit.
It can move fast over hard ground.
Would it have done so over marshy ground?

The ancestors of the modern horse were probably much smaller individuals that hid from predators.
With the change in the environment, natural selection favoured animals that were able to out-run their predators.

There was another reason why natural selection also favoured animals with longer necks.
These were better equipped to graze on the new grasslands.

▷ Extinction

Many species of animals and plants that once inhabited the Earth have died out or become **extinct**.
Nobody really knows why the dinosaurs became extinct, but probably their environment changed.
Natural selection operated against them.
Their dominant position was eventually taken over by the mammals.

If natural selection operates then the less well-adapted species will become extinct.
Perhaps they can't compete for food as well as other species can or they don't avoid predators so well.

Humans are responsible for the extinction of thousands of species. The giant otter, wood bison, Parma wallaby and Tasmanian wolf have been totally destroyed.

An increasing human population needs more food.
This has meant the destruction of natural habitats to give room to grow crops.

Other animals have been hunted to extinction.
Often these animals breed slowly and usually live a long time.
We are all aware of the plight of the whale.
Giant hardwood trees of the rainforests are suffering the same fate.
They are valuable — like the whale meat and oil.
They are being cut down faster than they can reproduce.

The dodo once lived on the island of Mauritius in the Indian Ocean where it had no natural predators. It was a large bird that could not run or fly. Humans hunted it for its meat.
Pigs, cats and monkeys, introduced to the island by humans ate its eggs and young.
Much of its natural forest habitat was also destroyed by settlers.
By the 1690s it was extinct.
The dodo was unable to survive the rapid changes to its environment caused by humans.

We must help future generations by conserving wildlife and by preserving the environment.

The Tasmanian wolf

▷ Biology at work: Reclaiming mining tips

Mining produces a lot of waste or spoil.
The spoil contains large amounts of toxic
metals like lead, copper and zinc.
What can be done with these spoil tips?

Apart from looking ugly, the tips are dangerous.
Some of the poison waste can drain into rivers
or get blown onto farmland.
What problems can this cause?

Coal mining produces waste or spoil

Attempts have been made to grass over the spoil tips.
But plants just would not grow on them.
Apart from the toxic metals, the tips are:

- low in plant nutrients

- very dry, because water quickly drains through

- very acid.

Scientists have found some types of grass that
are **tolerant** to large amounts of toxic metal.
These grasses must have evolved over time.
Some plants developed resistance to the metals.
They survived and reproduced.
So the numbers of tolerant plants increased.
This is another example of natural selection.

But just planting tolerant grasses is not enough.
Other work has to be done to reclaim the tips:

- Large amounts of fertilisers are added
  to correct the shortage of nutrients.

- Lime is added to neutralise the acid.

- With time humus forms and retains the water.
  In some areas sewage sludge was used.
  It was poured over tips to add nutrients and form humus.

*Grasses tolerant to mine spoil have been used for
recolonisation of tips*

Do you think that eventually normal plants
will be able to grow on the tips?
Trees planted on reclaimed tips have always died.
Why do you think this is?
Do you think that it would be safe for sheep to graze
on the grass of reclaimed tips?
Why not?

Summary

- Evolution is the change in a species that leads to the formation of a new species. It takes place over a long period of time.

- Organisms produce large numbers of offspring but few of them survive.

- Organisms that become well adapted to their environment have a better chance of survival. They survive to breed and pass on their adaptations to their offspring.

- There is a 'struggle for existence' leading to the 'survival of the fittest'.

- Charles Darwin and Alfred Russel Wallace put forward the theory of natural selection.

- Pesticide resistance and camouflage in moths are recent examples of natural selection.

- Fossils provide evidence that organisms have evolved.

▷ Questions

1. Copy and complete:
Organisms are able to produce large numbers of . . . . . Many of these die due to . . . . for food, predators, ... and climate. The best . . . . individuals are more likely to survive and pass on their . . . . to the next generation. Charles . . . . and Alfred . . . . suggested how evolution could take place through natural . . . . . . Fossils have provided . . . . to show that organisms have evolved.

2. In the 1940s some strains of bacteria became resistant to the antibiotic, penicillin.
The bacteria were able to survive, reproduce and so cause disease.
a) What was this an example of?
b) How would you fight the penicillin-resistant strains of bacteria?

3. Look at these 3 fossils:

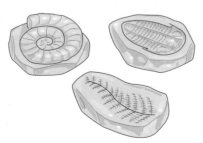

a) Which living things are they most like? Give the reasons for your choice.
b) Explain briefly how fossils can form.
c) Find out the names of 5 animals that are extinct.
Try to find out how they became extinct.

4. Snails are eaten by thrushes. Some snails have shells that are very striped, others are unstriped. Each September for several years a scientist counted all the snails he could find in an area of grassland. Here are his results:

Year	% covered by grass	Number of snails with ...	
		very striped shells	unstriped shells
1971	98	58	13
1972	25	24	22
1973	5	2	33
1974	97	34	10
1975	96		
1976		9	43
1977	98	68	13

a) State: i) a probable number of snails that you would have expected to find in 1975
ii) a probable percentage cover of grass in 1976.
b) i) All the snails were of the same species. During the seven years of study a single specimen was found with a completely black shell. What word would you use to describe this unusual form of the species?
ii) Choose the best answer. The term which best explains the results in the table is:
1 heredity
2 natural selection
3 conservation
4 artificial selection.

Further questions on page 325.

chapter 18

BIOTECHNOLOGY

Did you have yoghurt or toast for breakfast today ?
Is there a cheese roll in your sandwich box ?
How about smothering those chips in vinegar ?

If the answer to any of these questions is 'yes',
then you have just used a few of the products
of **biotechnology**.

Biotechnology is the way that we use living organisms,
in particular microbes, to produce useful substances.

Some of the products of traditional biotechnology ...

Although it sounds like something 'bang up-to-date',
many of the processes involved have been around
for centuries.
The use of yeast in brewing and bread-making, for example,
goes back thousands of years.

Nowadays fermentation (which is the basic process behind
brewing) can be carried out on an industrial scale. This allows
scientists to produce vast quantities of useful products.
For example, have you ever eaten **Quorn™** ?
This is a meat substitute produced from a fungus.
When did you last have an antibiotic like penicillin ?
This is also produced by large-scale fermentation.

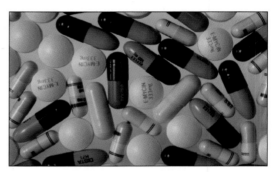

... and a more up-to-date example

It is not just the food and drug industries that use biotechnology.
The efficient treatment of sewage uses microbes to convert
organic waste into simpler substances.

In countries like Brazil with limited supplies of oil,
biotechnology is being used to make petrol substitutes
from materials like cane sugar.

Have you ever seen someone testing their blood sugar
with a hand-held electronic meter ?
This is yet another example of biotechnology in action
using something called a **biosensor**.

So, as you can see, there is hardly a person on the planet
whose life is not touched by biotechnology.

An electronic biosensor for testing blood glucose level

▷ Microbes and biotechnology

Many biotechnological processes use microbes
to make their products. This applies equally
to traditional processes like bread-making and
to more recent developments like antibiotic production.

So why are microbes so widely used ?
Here are just a few of the reasons :

- Microbes reproduce very quickly.
  This means that in a short space of time, scientists
  can grow a large quantity of the required organism.

- Unlike animals or plants, microbes can convert raw
  materials into the finished product very quickly,
  i.e. in hours rather than months or weeks.

- The use of microbes means that food production
  can be independent of the climate.

- Microbes grow very easily on a variety of cheap waste
  materials, possibly produced by other industrial processes.

- With the aid of genetic engineering, scientists can quickly
  alter microbes and so modify the product. Breeding new
  varieties of plants and animals can take a long time.

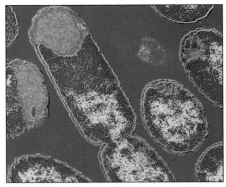

Microbes can reproduce very quickly

Growing microbe cultures

Before scientists can use microbes in industrial-scale fermenters,
they must grow cultures that are uncontaminated.
This means cultures that contain **only** the microbe they want.

You may have carried out simple experiments with microbes
in school.
Hopefully you will have followed safety precautions when
doing this work. These rules apply to biotechnologists too.

*Traditional food production is very
climate-dependent*

Some simple but important rules are :

- Any cuts should be covered with a clean, waterproof dressing.

- No eating or drinking during practical work with microbes.

- Washing hands before and after handling microbes.

- Taping the lids of Petri dishes securely.

- Never opening the lid of a sealed Petri dish.

Aseptic techniques for growing microbes

The word **aseptic** literally means 'excluding microbes'.
Using aseptic technique actually means following
certain procedures so that you only grow the microbes you want.

Step 1

- Before you start to work with microbes:
  - wash your hands and
  - swab the bench with disinfectant.

Step 2

- You will be given a sterile agar plate.
  Keep the lid on the Petri dish.
- Label the lid with your name.

Step 3

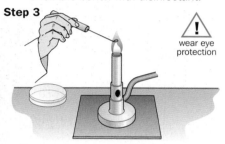

! wear eye
   protection

- Heat an inoculating loop in a Bunsen
  flame until it is red hot.

Step 4

- Unscrew the bottle and hold the opening
  of it in a flame for **2 seconds.**

Step 5

- Dip the sterile loop into the microbe
  sample and then replace the cap on
  the bottle.

Step 6

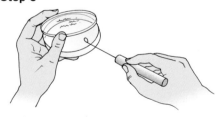

- Slightly lift the lid. Gently streak the
  loop over the surface of the agar.
  Replace the lid.

Step 7

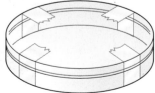

- Seal the Petri dish with Sellotape. Put the
  dish upside down in an incubator at 25 °C
  for 2–3 days.
  Never open a sealed Petri dish.

Step 8

- Swab the bench with disinfectant.
- Wash your hands.

▷ Biotechnology and food production

As we have already seen, the use of microbes
in food production goes back thousands of years.
But if we look at processes such as cheese, bread
and wine production, we can see how the
traditional methods have been improved with
the aid of modern technology.

Cheese-making

Cheese is produced by the action of bacteria on milk.

Nowadays, cheese makers use pasteurised milk.
Why do you think this is necessary?
Pasteurisation kills the bacteria naturally present in milk.
This means that the only bacteria present will be the ones
that are actually put there. These bacteria are known as
lactic acid bacteria (*Lactobacillus*).
They turn **lactose** (milk sugar) into lactic acid.

The low pH now present makes the milk **curdle**.
This means that the protein in the milk turns into
a semi-solid called **curd**. This process is aided
by the addition of an enzyme called **rennin**.

This enzyme was originally extracted from the stomachs
of calves. However, it can now be produced in greater
quantities by genetic engineering.

Salt is now added to the curd.
This not only enhances the flavour, but it also acts as a
preservative.

Depending on what type of cheese is being made,
other bacteria will now be added. These microbes
are known as **ripening bacteria** and they break down
the protein and fat in the cheese.

Blue cheeses, like stilton, gain their characteristic
appearance through the action of a fungus which is
added to the curd.

In order to speed up cheese production, manufacturers
can add bacterial enzymes rather than the bacteria
themselves.
Can you see why this would speed things up ?
It is the enzymes themselves that change the lactose
into lactic acid. If enzymes are added directly, there
is no delay while the bacteria make them.

*Cheese making is big business
nowadays*

*Curds that form the basis of Wensleydale
cheese*

*A fungus gives blue cheese its veiny
appearance*

Yoghurt manufacture

Yoghurts have become very popular over recent years. Yoghurt-making shares some similarities with cheese production.

Pasteurised milk is once again the starting point. Firstly the milk is thickened with skimmed milk powder often used as a thickening agent.

Unlike cheese-making which is best in cool conditions, yoghurt production needs a temperature of about 40 °C. This temperature has three advantages :

- It helps to thicken the milk protein.
- It reduces the oxygen level.
- It is the ideal temperature for growth of the bacteria.

Why do you think a low oxygen level is required ? Most of the bacteria used in cheese and yoghurt production prefer anaerobic conditions.

Once the milk is at the ideal temperature, the bacteria are added. In yoghurt manufacture the bacteria used are different to those used in cheese production. However they still do the same job, namely converting milk sugar into lactic acid. This usually takes place in large, stainless steel fermentation tanks.

As with cheese production curds are made, but in yoghurt they are much less solid.

The yoghurt is then cooled before it undergoes the final stage of production. This often involves mixing the yoghurt with fruit to create the many different flavours of yoghurt now available.

Some yoghurts are treated to remove all bacteria, whilst others contain 'live' cultures. These bacteria supplement the bacteria naturally found in the gut, and aid digestion.

Cheese and yoghurt manufacture are both examples of batch processes.

This type of process involves producing a set amount of product. The process then stops and all the equipment is cleaned and sterilised before starting all over again.

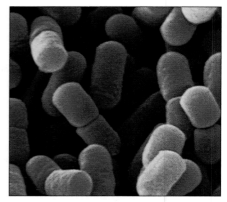

Lactic acid bacteria under the electron microscope

Adding the bacteria to the pasteurised milk

A yoghurt containing live bacteria

Wine-making and brewing

Wine and beer production is yet another example
of centuries-old biotechnology.
As with cheese and yoghurt, microbes are
the all-important living organisms.

This time, though, not bacteria but yeast
– a microscopic fungus – is used.

Look back at page 81, why is yeast used to make
alcohol ?
You will remember that when yeast respires without
oxygen it is carrying out **fermentation.**
Yeast uses sugars as its energy source and produces
alcohol, carbon dioxide and some energy.

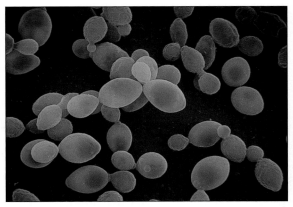
Yeast is a useful fungus

One of the main differences between wine and beer
production is the *source* of the sugars.

To make wine, ripe grapes are crushed to extract
their juice. This juice is rich in sugar and this is the
energy source for the yeast.

In beer production, barley grains are the source of
the sugar.
In a process called **malting**, these grains are allowed
to germinate for a few days. During this time, enzymes
break down the starch in the grains into a sugar called
maltose.
This sugar is contained in a brown liquid called **wort**.
Now in a process called **mashing**, yeast is added to the
wort and fermentation begins.
To give beer its characteristic bitter flavour, hops are
then added.

Treading grapes to extract the juice

The mashing process produces some useful by-products.
A foamy layer of carbon dioxide covers the fermenting
mixture.
This is often collected for use in other industrial processes.
Also some of the yeast can be removed.
It can then be used as a starter culture for another brew,
and also to make yeast spreads.

Brewing can be done at home with 'home-brew kits'.
But most beer is brewed on an industrial scale in huge
copper vats. These containers can produce thousands
of litres at a time. Brewers also use computer technology
to carefully monitor and adjust the conditions
in the vats.

*Checking the brewing process
in a large copper vat*

Baking

Baking is another example of using yeast to help produce a food.

Bread is made from **dough**. This contains flour, water, salt, sugar and yeast.
This mixture is kept at a warm temperature. The yeast starts to ferment the sugar and, as we have already seen, produces alcohol and carbon dioxide gas.
The bubbles of gas cause the dough to rise. The bread is then baked in a hot oven. This expands the bubbles of gas making the bread 'light' in texture. It also evaporates the alcohol, leaving behind the traditional taste of bread.

A commercial bakery

Soy sauce

If you have ever eaten a Chinese meal, you will know that soy sauce is an important ingredient.
What you probably don't know is that soy sauce is also produced with the aid of microbes.

The commercial production of this sauce involves not only yeast, but another fungus called **Aspergillus**. The third member of the microbe team are the lactic acid bacteria we met in cheese-making.

The basic ingredients are soya beans and wheat grains.
To a mixture of cooked beans and roasted grains is added a culture of *Aspergillus*. This fungus grows on the grains and turns starch into sugar.

The next step is to add yeast which ferments the mixture using the newly formed sugars.
This is followed by a long period of cold fermentation carried out by the lactic acid bacteria.

The mixture is now filtered to remove the raw sauce. This is then pasteurised to kill any bacteria present. Finally it is put into bottles which have been sterilised by steam cleaning.

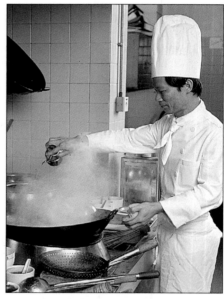

▷ Industrial fermentation

You may have carried out simple experiments on fermentation in school. If so, you probably used basic laboratory apparatus like that shown on page 81.

Clearly, this kind of apparatus is no good for producing large quantities of useful materials such as **penicillin.**
Industrial fermenters can, in fact, hold as much as 500 000 dm^3 of fermenting mixture.
Also the conditions within these huge tanks can be very carefully controlled.

We can use the example of penicillin production to show how these fermenters work.

A culture of the fungus ***Penicillium*** is added to the fermenter. It then thrives in the ideal conditions maintained inside.
These include :

- **Adding nutrients** such as sugar, ammonia and vitamins.

- **Maintaining a constant temperature** of about 30 °C.

- **Maintaining a constant pH** of about 6.5.

Once fermentation has started, it takes about 30 hours for penicillin production to start.

Why does it take so long?
The fungus has to complete its main growth phase, and use up most of the nutrients **before** it starts to release penicillin into the surrounding liquid.

After about six days, fermentation is complete. The mixture is drained out of the fermenter and then filtered. The penicillin is then extracted as a salt-like material.

This process is known as **batch cultivation**.
After the six days, the fermenter is emptied, cleaned and sterilised ready for the next batch.
Continuous cultivation allows production to take place in a fermenter for several weeks.

A large industrial fermenter

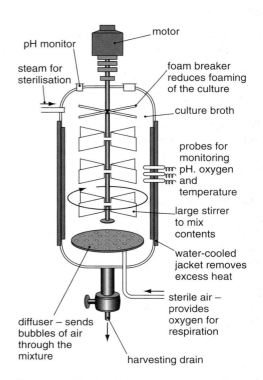

This type of industrial fermenter allows for continuous cultivation

▷ Sewage treatment

Raw sewage is made up of a number of unpleasant materials: not just faeces and urine, but industrial waste and run-off from roads and paths.

Not only is it unpleasant, but it is also a major health hazard.

As recently as the 19th century, raw sewage was a familiar sight in open drains in towns and cities.

Nowadays, thanks in part to biotechnology, raw sewage is broken down into harmless substances that can safely be put into rivers.

Sewage treatment is divided into three main categories.

- **Primary treatment** involves removing large solids, like paper and twigs, with filters called **screens**.
  Then grit and organic solids are removed by allowing them to settle out in large tanks.
  In biology, the word **organic** refers to material from living organisms.

- **Secondary treatment** uses biotechnology to deal with the sewage.
  Microbes, mainly bacteria, act on material suspended in the sewage.
  This treatment involves at least two stages.
  One involving **anaerobic** organisms and the other **aerobic** organisms.
  Most of the secondary treatment is in fact aerobic.

- **Tertiary treatment** again involves a period of settling.
  The liquid from the secondary process passes into large tanks.
  Here microbes and any remaining organic material settles out to form a **sludge**.
  This sludge may be used as a 'starter culture' for the next secondary treatment.
  Otherwise, it undergoes further treatment before disposal.
  This might involve dumping at sea or spreading on land as a soil conditioner.

A COURT FOR KING CHOLERA.

Untreated effluent flowing into a river

Aeration of sewage – an important part of secondary treatment

Activated sludge

The main part of secondary sewage treatment is known as the **activated sludge process**.

Developed in the 1920s, this process *actively* pumps air through the sewage.
This causes solid material to be deposited in a **sedimentation tank**.
This so-called **activated sludge** contains bacteria, fungi and single-celled organisms.
These organisms respire in the aerobic conditions and break down the waste into minerals, gases and water. For example, ammonia is converted into nitrates.

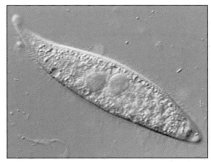

A single-celled organism found in activated sludge

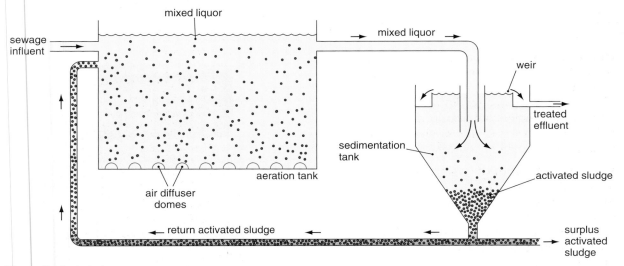

The activated sludge process

Secondary treatment can also involve **biological filters**.
These are beds of gravel which are covered by a film of microbes.
The liquid from the primary treatment is sprayed over these beds from large rotating arms.
As the liquid trickles down through the gravel, the microbes again break down the organic matter.

The sludge from the primary and secondary processes can be used to produce **methane**.
This is the result of digestion by anaerobic bacteria.
The methane can be used as a fuel to provide heat and generate electricity.

Biological filters

▷ Biology at work: Biofuels

Biofuels are literally fuels made from biological material, such as animal dung, sugar cane and plant waste. This material can be fermented to produce a variety of fuels such as methane gas, alcohol and biodiesel.

Have you ever seen gas flares burning on waste-disposal sites?
These flares are burning off a **biogas** that builds up underground where waste material is decaying. This biogas is mainly a gas called **methane**. Methane can be produced when cattle dung is digested by anaerobic bacteria. In parts of the developing world, such as Africa, small fermenters called **biodigesters** (or digesters) are used to make this gas. It can then be used to provide heat and power – just as in this country we use bottled gas in caravans.

The material left over, after digestion is completed, can make an excellent fertiliser for crops.

Have you ever thought how we would manage without petrol ?
Some countries that have no oil supplies of their own have developed a biofuel substitute.

Brazil, for example, uses fermenters to produce ethanol (alcohol). The raw material often used is sugar-cane juice which contains a lot of carbohydrate. Glucose from maize starch is another raw material. This is obtained by treating the starch with carbohydrase enzymes.

Alcohol is a good substitute for petrol, because it has a high energy content and when burned creates less pollution.

Have you noticed fields of bright yellow flowers in the countryside?.
This crop is **oil seed rape**. The oil that is obtained from it can be converted into a fuel called **biodiesel**. This fuel again has the big advantage over petrol-based fuels of being less polluting when burned.

As fossil fuels become more and more scarce, it is possible that biofuels will play an increasing role in world fuel supplies.

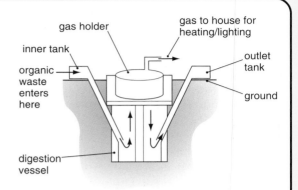

A simple biodigester

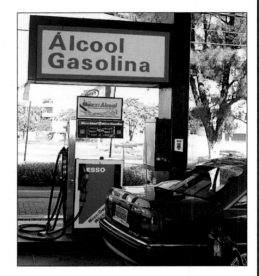

▷ Biology at work: Mycoprotein – a food for the future ?

We have already seen how fermentation of microbes can be used to produce many traditional food products. Also, how fermentation on an industrial scale allows the production of vast quantities of material.

Microbes are very good at producing protein.
In the 1960s, the food producers Rank Hovis McDougall (RHM) began a research programme that led to the production of **mycoprotein**.

'Never heard of it !'
Well, the chances are you have eaten it in the school canteen.

Mycoprotein is a high protein material produced by a fungus called ***Fusarium.***
This fungus was originally discovered in a field in the south of England.
RHM quickly realised how valuable it might be as a food material.
Some of its advantages are :

● It is fibrous and so can take on a meat like texture.

● It is high in protein.

● It doesn't have an unpleasant taste.

Just like penicillin, mycoprotein is made in huge fermenters.
This time, though, the technique is **continuous culture**.
This means that the nutrients are *continually* added and the product *continually* removed.

Mycoprotein makes an ideal meat substitute.
Since the mid-1980s it has been actively used in this way.
It is marketed under the name **Quorn**™.
You can find it in a variety of meat dishes, such as savoury pies and curries.

Is mycoprotein the food of the future ?
Could it help to relieve the threat of famine ?
Well, yes, in theory, if it can be produced cheaply and in sufficient quantities.
But at the moment its big attraction is as a healthy low-fat alternative to meat.

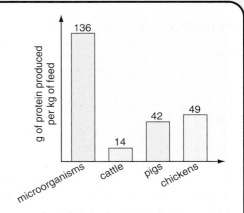

Fusarium *growing on a cereal*

Some food products derived from mycoprotein

Summary

- Biotechnology involves the use of living organisms to make useful products.

- In most cases the living organisms are microbes – mainly bacteria and fungi.

- Microbes can reproduce and convert raw materials into products very quickly.

- Working with microbes requires careful aseptic techniques. These avoid contamination and danger to health.

- Fermentation is the key reaction in many biotechnological processes.

- Industrial fermenters allow mass production under carefully controlled conditions.

- Many traditional foods, like bread and cheese, are products of biotechnology.

- Biotechnology is also responsible for products with great future potential, such as biofuels and mycoprotein.

- Efficient disposal of raw sewage and the availability of clean drinking water also depend on biotechnology.

▷ Questions

1. Copy and complete :
   Biotechnology uses . . . . organisms to make useful products. The most commonly used organisms are . . . . and . . . . . .
   Microbes have a number of advantages, such as their fast rate of . . . . . Many of the products of biotechnology depend upon microbes carrying out . . . . . This reaction plays an important part in making bread and . . . . . As well as traditional foods, biotechnology also produces . . . . .
   This material is a very good substitute for meat. Drugs such as . . . . are also produced by microbes in huge . . . . .

2. Explain the need for the following procedures :
   a) Petri dishes should be sterilised before use.
   b) Inoculating loops should be passed through a flame and then allowed to cool before use.
   c) The lid of a Petri dish should be sealed and not opened once microbes have grown.

3. Microbes are commonly used in biotechnology. Explain the advantage of each of these features of microbe growth :
   a) Microbes can reproduce quickly.
   b) Microbes can grow easily on waste material.
   c) Microbes are very efficient protein producers.

4. a) Give three examples of traditional foods made with the help of microbes.
   b) What are the main differences between the production of cheese and yoghurt ?

   c) Describe how fungi are used in the production of both blue cheese and soy sauce.

5. a) Which microbe is involved in brewing, baking and wine-making ?
   b) What is the source of the sugars that are fermented in :
   i) brewing and
   ii) wine-making ?
   c) How do bubbles of carbon dioxide gas help to make bread ?

6. This drawing shows a fermenter used to make penicillin.

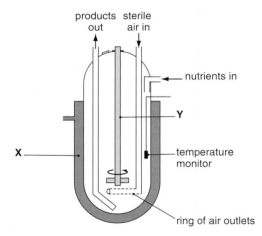

a) Name parts **X** and **Y**.
b) Name two nutrients that would need to be added.
c) Why is air bubbled through the fermenter ?
d) Why must this air be sterile ?

7. This graph shows the concentration of mould, glucose and the antibiotic streptomycin in a fermenter.

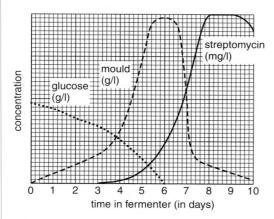

a) What happens to the glucose concentration during the manufacture of streptomycin ?

b) Explain why the glucose concentration changes in this way.

c) Why does the concentration of antibiotic reach a peak *after* the peak in the concentration of the mould ?

8. a) What is the name of the fungus from which mycoprotein is produced ?

b) Give two advantages of this fungus for food production.

c) How is mycoprotein manufacture in a fermenter different to that of penicillin ?

This table shows a comparison between mycoprotein and beef.

Nutrient	Mycoprotein (% dry mass)	Beef (% dry mass)
protein	40	60
fat	10	30
minerals	3	1
fibre	30	0

d) Use this information to explain why mycoprotein is a healthy alternative to meat.

9. An investigation was carried out to investigate how quickly milk curdled in different pHs. The enzyme rennin had been added to the milk as part of the cheese-making process. The results are shown in this table.

pH	2	3	4	5	6
Time taken to curdle milk (mins)	4	2	3	6	13

a) Plot a line graph of these results.

b) What is the best pH for the enzyme to curdle the milk ?

c) It was found that milk did not curdle at all at pH 9.
Suggest a reason why the enzyme does not curdle milk at this pH.

10. Yoghurt manufacture requires a temperature of around 40 °C.

a) Explain precisely why this is the best temperature to use.

b) What is meant by the term 'live culture' ?

c) Why is pasteurised milk often used in yoghurt manufacture?

11. Foods such as cheese, yoghurt, wine and bread are all made with the aid of microbes.

a) Explain why during their manufacture temperatures no higher than 40 °C are used.

b) Explain why the final part of bread manufacture is at over 200 °C.

12. a) Name three materials that make up the effluent that is treated at sewage works.

b) The first stage of treatment is a purely physical process. Briefly describe what happens.

c) What part do microbes play in the activated sludge process ?

d) After treatment to what uses can the sludge be put ?

Further questions on Variation, inheritance, evolution and biotechnology

▷ Inheritance

1. The diagram shows a partly completed section of a DNA molecule.

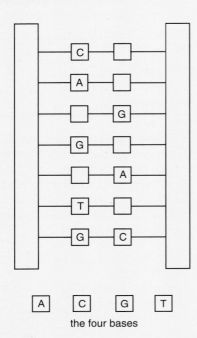

the four bases

a) Copy and complete the diagram by writing the letters of the missing bases in the boxes. [2]

b) Mutations can occur because of changes to DNA.
   i) Name **two** possible causes for an increase in the normal rate of mutation. [2]
   ii) Explain how a change in the DNA structure can cause a cell to form a different protein. [3] (EDEX)

2. a) i) Describe in outline the process of mitosis. [6]
   ii) State **two** ways in which meiosis differs from mitosis and explain the significance of each difference. [4]
   iii) State where meiosis takes place in males and in females. [2]

b) The effect of a mutation occurring during meiosis can have a serious effect on a future child.
   i) What is a mutation? [2]
   ii) Name **one** condition caused by a chromosome mutation occurring during meiosis. Explain how this type of mutation could have occurred and given rise to a child showing the condition. [6]
   (OCR)

3. The gene which controls the formation of haemoglobin exists in two forms. The normal form of gene (H) produces normal haemoglobin. The mutant form of the gene (h) produces 'sickle' haemoglobin. People who are homozygous for the mutant form of the gene suffer from a condition called sickle cell anaemia. When their haemoglobin gives up its oxygen, the red blood cells change to a sickle shape. These sickle shaped cells may stick together and block small blood vessels, often causing death.
   People who are heterozygous for the gene produce both normal and 'sickle' types of haemoglobin, but do not usually suffer from sickle cell anaemia.
   The family tree below shows the inheritance of haemoglobin type.

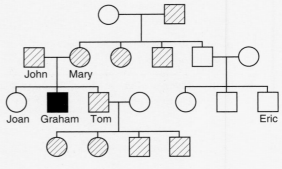

key
male female

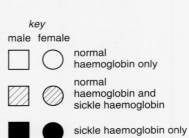

normal haemoglobin only

normal haemoglobin and sickle haemoglobin

sickle haemoglobin only

a) Look at the family tree and then copy and complete the genetic diagram below to show how the children of John and Mary inherit haemoglobin type.

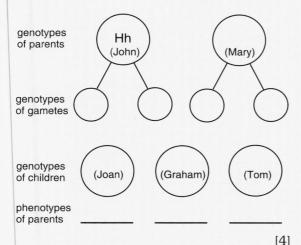

genotypes of parents — Hh (John), (Mary)

genotypes of gametes

genotypes of children — (Joan), (Graham), (Tom)

phenotypes of parents _____ _____ _____

[4]

b) The cousins, Joan and Eric, wish to marry but are worried their children may inherit sickle cell haemoglobin.
What advice would you give to them?
Explain the reason for your answer.

[2]
(AQA)

4. a) The diagram shows the chromosomes from a body cell of a male with Down's syndrome.

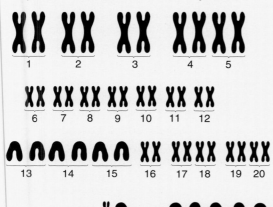

i) How do these chromosomes differ from those of a male who does not have Down's syndrome? [2]

ii) Down's syndrome occurs because of an irregularity that takes place during the development of an egg in the mother's ovary.
What is this irregularity? What must happen at fertilisation to produce a person with Down's syndrome? [2]

b) Huntington's chorea is a severe condition which causes mental deterioration and loss of muscular coordination. It is caused by the inheritance of a dominant allele. The effects of this allele do not normally appear until a person is at least over thirty years old.
The diagram shows a family pedigree for the inheritance of Huntington's chorea.

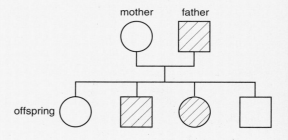

mother   father

offspring

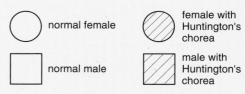

normal female   female with Huntington's chorea

normal male   male with Huntington's chorea

i) Draw a labelled genetic diagram to show the inheritance of the allele for Huntington's chorea in this family. Also show how it is possible for "normal" offspring to be born even though one parent was affected.
(Use **H** for the allele for Huntington's chorea; use **h** for the recessive allele)
[4]

ii) It is possible for an **HH** person to be unaware of the disease and pass it on to their children. Explain how this can happen. [1] (AQA)

Further questions on Variation, inheritance, evolution and biotechnology

5. The features of humans are either inherited or are caused by environmental influences.
    accidental loss of an arm   blood group
    eye colour   gender/sex   mass
    a) From the features listed choose:
        i) one which is controlled by environmental influences only. [1]
        ii) one which is controlled by inheritance only. [1]
        iii) one which is controlled by both environmental influence and inheritance. [1]
    b) Which part of the cell nucleus enables features to be passed from one generation to the next? [1]
    c) What is meant by the term **dominant allele**? [1]   (OCR)

6. A couple decide to have a child. The father and mother are both heterozygous for the gene for albinism.
    Copy and complete the diagram below to show the genotypes of the parents, their possible gametes, and the possible genotypes and phenotypes of their children.
    Use the symbol **A** for the normal allele and the symbol **a** for the albino allele.

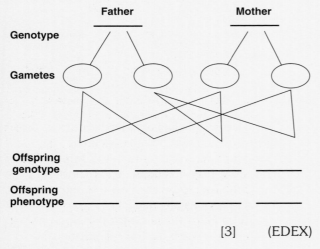

[3]   (EDEX)

7. The following diagram shows how scientists produced Dolly the sheep.
    a) i) Dolly was produced with the help of an unfertilised egg.
        Where did scientists get the DNA to put into this egg? [1]

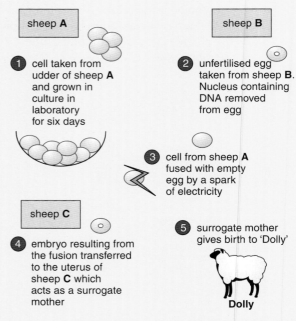

    ii) Suggest why it was important to remove the DNA from the unfertilised egg. [2]
    iii) Dolly is genetically identical to another sheep in the diagram. Which one? [1]
    b) Give **one** way in which this method is different from the normal method of sheep reproduction. [1]
    c) The production of Dolly was a significant advance in scientific work. The work may result in animal clones being produced in large numbers.
        Suggest why it is important that people are informed of new scientific advances. [2]
    d) Suggest one advantage of producing animal clones [1]   (NICCEA)

8. Read the following and answer the questions which follow:
    Cystic fibrosis is a genetic disease which affects the pancreas. The ducts of the pancreas become blocked. The disease also affects the mucus-producing glands of the bronchioles and these produce very large amounts of thick sticky mucus. This makes breathing difficult and reduces the ability of the respiratory system to remove microbes.
    The disease cannot be cured but some of the symptoms can be eased by the use of antibiotics, physiotherapy and careful control of the diet.

a) What is a genetic disease ? [1]
b) Explain why cystic fibrosis sufferers find breathing difficult. [1]
c) Suggest why antibiotics can help sufferers of cystic fibrosis. [1]
d) Tracy and Peter do not suffer from cystic fibrosis but one of their children, David, does suffer from it. Here is the family tree :

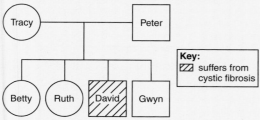

Use the following letters : **N** = normal (dominant) and **n** = cystic fibrosis (recessive)
What are the genotypes of :
  i)   Tracy [1]
  ii) Peter [1]
  iii) David [1]
  iv) What are the **two** possibilities of Gwyn's genotype ? [2]
e) Name any other genetic disease. [1] (WJEC)

▷ Evolution

9. In Britain there are two species of squirrels, red ones and grey ones. Adult grey squirrels are usually much heavier than adult red squirrels.
  a) i) **Genes** can cause this difference in weight. What are **genes**, and what do they do ? [2]
     ii) In one group of red squirrels many of the adults were much heavier than expected. Suggest and explain **one** reason for this, other than a genetic one. [2]
  b) Below is some more information about red and grey squirrels.

	Red squirrels	Grey squirrels
How long have they been in Britain	Thousands of years	Just over 100 years
Where are they found ?	In the evergreen forests of northern Britain	In most forests all over Britain
Size of the populations	Small, and getting smaller	Large, and getting larger
What do they eat ?	Pine cones	Most kinds of plant material
Maximum number of young born each year ?	8	12

Use the information in the table to explain **three** reasons why the population of red squirrels is getting less and the population of grey squirrels is increasing. [6] (AQA)

10. Galapagos is a group of islands in the Pacific Ocean. The islands are several hundred miles from the mainland of South America. Few animals have reached the islands. On one of the islands there are three types of finch.

  • One type feeds on soft seeds and some small insects.
  • Another type feeds on large seeds and large insects.
  • The third type feeds on small insects which it picks off leaves and twigs.

The drawings below show the heads of these three types of finch.

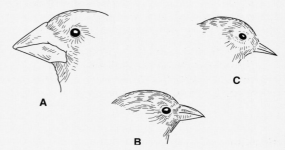

a) Which type of finch :
  i)   feeds on soft seeds and some small insects;
  ii) feeds on large seeds and large insects;
  iii) feeds on small insects which it picks off leaves and twigs ? [1]
b) Charles Darwin suggested that the three types of finch on the island had all evolved from one type of finch which had arrived from South America.
  i)   Name the process by which this evolution may have taken place. [1]
  ii) The finch that came from South America probably had a thick beak. Suggest how the thin beak could have evolved. [3] (AQA)

Further questions on Variation, inheritance, evolution and biotechnology

11. The diagram shows two types of peppered moth found on the trunks of trees in both city and countryside areas.

dark moth   light moth

Read the following passage about the peppered moth.

> The peppered moth is often used to provide evidence for evolution. Before the Industrial Revolution the moths found were light in colour. They were harder for birds to see on light coloured tree trunks. Fewer moths are eaten by birds if they are well hidden.
> During the Industrial Revolution, many trees in large cities became black with soot. In the daytime the moths rest on tree trunks. Dark coloured moths were better hidden on the trees than light coloured ones.
> Records showed that few light coloured moths survived in cities and few dark coloured moths survived in countryside areas. In 1956 the Clean Air Act gradually reduced the amount of smoke pollution. After 1956 the number of light coloured moths in city areas gradually increased.

a) Use this information to answer the following questions.
   i)   In which area were the greatest number of light coloured moths found after the Industrial Revolution? [1]
   ii) Describe and explain the effect of the Clean Air Act on the numbers of the two types of moth in city areas. [4]
   iii) Name the process of evolution described in the passage. [1]
b) Some students counted the number of moths they found resting on five trees in a city and five trees in a countryside area. The results are shown in the table below. Copy and complete the table by filling in the total number of moths counted and calculating the mean (average) number of moths found. [4]

Tree	City trees		Countryside trees	
	Dark moths	Light moths	Dark moths	Light moths
A	10	2	3	8
B	8	3	4	7
C	8	4	3	8
D	7	2	2	6
E	8	2	4	7
Total				
Mean				

c) Which group of trees showed the highest mean (average) number of moths? [1]
(OCR)

▷ Biotechnology

12. The drawing shows a commercial yoghurt-manufacturing process.

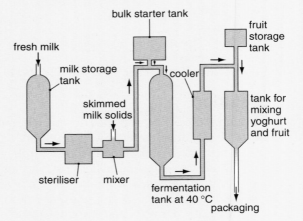

a) i) Suggest how the fresh milk is sterilised. [1]
   ii) Suggest why it is necessary to sterilise the fresh milk. [1]
b) The bulk starter tank contains a culture of bacteria. Describe the effect of these bacteria on the milk. [2]
c) Explain why the mixture in the fermentation tank is kept at 40 °C. [2]
d) In the cooler, the yoghurt is cooled to 4 °C. Suggest why this is done. [2] (AQA)

13. The diagram shows a biodigester used to manufacture penicillin.

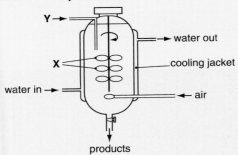

a) What is the function of **X** ? [1]
b) What is added to the biodigester through **Y** ? [1]
c) Explain why the cooling jacket is necessary ? [2]
d) Suggest why air is bubbled through the biodigester. [1] (NICCEA)

14. The table shows the change in pH of milk during the production of yoghurt.

Time (min)	0	20	40	60	80	100
pH	6.8	6.1	5.6	5.2	5.0	4.9

a) i) On a piece of graph paper, draw a line to show how the pH changes during 100 minutes.
Draw a curve of 'best fit'. [3]
   ii) What is the pH at 50 minutes ? [1]
b) Explain :
   i) the change in pH shown by the graph ; [3]
   ii) why milk is liquid but yoghurt is semi-solid. [1]
c) The milk used for yoghurt manufacture is usually at 30 °C. Why is this important for the process to take place most efficiently ? [2] (WJEC)

15. Biogas is a useful fuel. It can be made by microbes.
The diagram shows one design for a biogas generator.

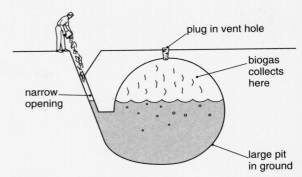

a) Suggest **two** sources of waste material which could be put into the biogas generator to produce biogas. [2]
b) What is the main gas in biogas ? [1]
c) Suggest advantages of having a narrow opening to the generator ? [3] (AQA)

16. Sewage is a water-borne mixture containing many substances, which must be broken down and removed before the water can be discharged into a river or the sea. The first stages of treatment remove large insoluble waste and grit, and then allow the crude sludge to settle out. The cloudy liquid at the top contains fine particles of organic matter in suspension and this is pumped into the activated sludge tanks. Micro-organisms are added which include aerobic bacteria and unicells :

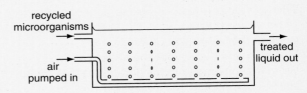

a) Give **two** functions of the air which is pumped in. [2]
b) The organic matter in the sewage is broken down.
Name **two** products which are formed. [2]
c) What use do the bacteria make of the organic matter ? [1]
d) Sometimes the raw sewage contains a high concentration of detergents.
Suggest a problem that this would cause in this process. [1] (AQA)

chapter 19

ADAPTATION & COMPETITION

Ecology is about how living things **interact**
with each other and with their environment.
Ecology is also sometimes called the study
of **ecosystems**.

The environment is made up of lots of different
ecosystems, such as a seashore, a wood or a river.
Each ecosystem is made up of 2 parts:
- a non-living part called the **habitat**, and
- a living part called the **community**.

The habitat is the place where the organisms live.
It has the conditions that they need to survive,
such as the right amount of light, oxygen or water
and a suitable temperature.

The community is all the plants and animals that
live in the habitat.

What is your habitat?
What conditions does it have to help you survive?

Look at the ecosystems shown here:
For each one think what the habitat is like.
Write down some animals and plants that might
live in each habitat.

Each community is made up of different **populations**
of animals and plants.
A population is a group of individuals of the same species.
For instance, a woodland community might have a population
of ground beetles, a population of bluebells and a
population of beech trees.
Each population in the community is **adapted**
to live in that particular habitat.

There is a great variety of different ecosystems.
They are found both on land and in water.
All ecosystems together make up the **biosphere**.

▷ Environmental factors

Each ecosystem has particular conditions
or **environmental factors**.
Animals and plants must be adapted to these
if they are to survive.

Water

Water is needed for all life to survive.
Organisms that live in dry places have
adaptations that cut down water loss.
In rivers and streams the animals and
plants have to withstand fast currents.
Seaweeds and seashore animals have to
cope with the battering of the waves.

*This lizard gets shade under rocks during
the hottest part of the day*

Temperature

Few living organisms can grow outside the
range of 0–40 °C.
But penguins can withstand temperatures
of −80 °C in the Antarctic.
And some bacteria have adapted to live in hot
springs at over 100 °C.

Light

Light is needed for photosynthesis.
Some plants are adapted to live in shade
while others thrive in full sunlight.
On the sea bed or in deep caves there is
no light at all.

Air

Few organisms can live without **oxygen.**
They need it for respiration.
Aquatic organisms take oxygen out of the water.
Plants also take in **carbon dioxide** for photosynthesis
and give out oxygen.
Animals use this oxygen for respiration and give
out carbon dioxide that the plants need for
photosynthesis.

▷ Biotic factors

These are factors caused by other **living organisms** present in the community.

Competition

Individual plants and animals may have to compete with each other for food, light, water and space. These terns are competing for nesting sites.

Predation

A **predator** is an animal that feeds by hunting and killing its prey.

The **prey** must escape from the predator if it is to survive.
This killer whale is attacking a sealion.

Disease

Some microbes cause diseases.
A **parasite** is an organism that lives in or on another organism called a **host**.
The parasite gets its food from the host.
The fish in the photograph has a fungal disease.

Grazers

These are animals that eat plants.
We sometimes call them herbivores.

Decomposers

These are microbes that break down dead and decaying material.
They are important in the cycling of nutrients.

Human activity can disrupt ecosystems

Effect of humans

Human activity affects the survival of other living organisms.
Industry, farming, forestry, transport and housing have all affected the survival of organisms by changing their habitats.

▷ Populations

A population is a group of individuals of the same species living in a particular habitat.

These are all populations:
- a shoal of herring in the sea
- dandelions in a lawn
- greenfly on a rosebush
- owls in a wood.

A population of snappers

Why do you think individuals live in populations?

There may be many reasons:
- the habitat provides food, shelter, light or other factors needed for survival
- the individuals come together to breed
- individuals may gain more protection in a group.

Can you think of any disadvantages of living in a population?

As the population grows, there may be overcrowding.
Individuals **compete** for food, space, light and other resources.
Some individuals will be better adapted to compete than others.
Those that are not so well adapted may not survive.

A population of wildebeest

Scientists study populations to find out how their numbers change:

- Mosquitoes carry malaria.
  Population studies of the mosquito help control the spread of the disease.

- Studying locust populations has led to reducing the damage that they do to crops.

- Monitoring the populations of threatened species, like the tiger, has helped in their conservation.

We try to control locust populations

▷ How populations grow

What happens if rabbits colonise a new area?

First a few individuals enter the new habitat.
There is enough food for them so they start
to breed.
There are no predators to keep their numbers
down.
At first they start to increase slowly.
But soon each generation doubles the size of the
previous one.
2 becomes 4 then 8, 16, 32, 64, 128, 256, 512,
and so on.
This maximum rate of growth is called
exponential growth.
It can only take place under ideal environmental
conditions.

Experiment 19.1   *Growth of a yeast population*

Put some yeast into sugar solution and keep it in
warm conditions.

Every half an hour look at a drop of the yeast under
the microscope and count the number of cells
in the field of view.

Some model results are shown in the graph:

● Explain what is happening to the yeast population
  at times X, Y and Z on the graph.

● Why did the yeast population stop growing?

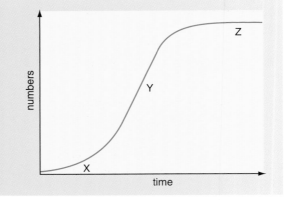

Why doesn't our yeast population go on increasing?

Here are some possible reasons:
● lack of food
● overcrowding
● build-up of poisonous waste made by the yeast.

Populations are able to grow very fast.
Animals can produce lots of eggs, and plants can
make lots of seeds.
So why isn't the Earth over-run with animals
and plants?

The answer is that not all of them survive.
Some things must be acting to **limit** the growth
of the population.

Huge numbers of red crabs on Christmas Island

▷ Checks on population increase

What sort of things could prevent a population increasing?

A number of factors can act as natural checks to stop the population becoming too large:

- **Food and water** are needed by all living things. If they become short then individuals compete for them. Some individuals will not survive so the population decreases.

- **Oxygen** shortage can limit numbers in a population that lives in water. Pollutants like sewage can lower oxygen levels in the water.

- **Toxic wastes** such as ammonia and urea are excreted by living organisms. These poisons can build up and limit population growth.

- **Overcrowding** can lead to unhygienic conditions, the spread of disease and stress.

- **Predators** have to kill their prey to feed. This limits the numbers in the prey population.

- **Disease** can spread quickly through large populations. It acts like predation to reduce numbers in the population.

- **Climate**, such as extreme heat or extreme cold, can reduce populations. Drought, floods and storms all affect population numbers.

- **Lack of shelter** can expose individuals to harsh climate or the risk of being killed by predators.

Human populations can be affected too

Evidence of Dutch elm disease

Sometimes populations do not level off. Instead they crash dramatically. The population may have run out of food or been affected by predators or disease. A crash in population numbers like this can happen very quickly. For instance, a whole swarm of greenfly can soon be eaten by money spiders.

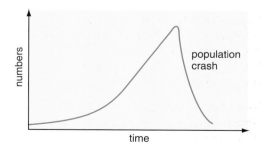

333

▷ Population size

What determines how big a population is?

The number of births adds to the population.
The number of deaths decreases it.

Many individuals can enter and leave a population.
You can probably think of lots of animals that can
do this. But plants can use seed dispersal to
join another population.

Movement into a population is called **immigration**.
Movement out of a population is **emigration**.

Estimating the size of a plant population

You may need to estimate the size of a population
for a scientific investigation.
You won't be able to count *all* the individuals in a
population so you need to take a **sample**.

This is easier to do if you are looking at plants.
You use a metal or a wooden frame called a **quadrat**.
Put the quadrat down on the vegetation.
Now count the number of a particular plant present
inside the quadrat.
Estimate how many quadrats you would need to cover
the habitat. Multiply this by the number of plants that
you found in the quadrat to get the total population.

To get a quick estimate of a particular
plant population you can use
percentage cover.
This is the amount of ground
covered by a particular plant
inside the quadrat.
We estimate this as a percentage.

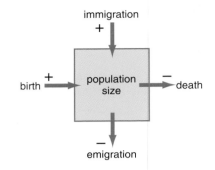

What is the percentage cover of each of these plants?

Using a quadrat

Investigation 19.2   What affects the size of a duckweed population?

Duckweed is a small, floating plant found in ponds.
It reproduces quickly to produce a large population.

Investigate what factors affect its growth.
You could try light, temperature, carbon dioxide or
nutrients.

Check your plan with your teacher before you start.

Estimating the size of animal populations

Sampling animals is more difficult.
They tend to move about.
Not many animals will stay in a quadrat!
Many animals only come out at night.
To get a sample we have to trap them – humanely.
We then use the **mark, release, recapture** method
to estimate the size of the population.

Using a harmless mark on a honey bee

This is how it works:

- collect a sample of animals (**M**)
- mark the captured animals – this should be a
  small harmless mark like a small paint dot
- release the marked animals into their habitat
- give them a day or two to mix back into the
  population
- collect a second sample (**S**)
- count the number of marked animals (**R**) in this
  second sample.

You can now use this equation to get an estimate
of the total population (**P**):

Do not be too ambitious in your choice of animal

Total population (**P**) = $\dfrac{\text{number in first catch } (M) \times \text{number in second catch } (S)}{\text{number of marked animals in second catch } (R)}$

$$P = \frac{M \times S}{R}$$

Here's a worked example:

Example

A pitfall trap like the one in the diagram was
used to catch 12 ground beetles.
Each was marked with a small dot of paint and released.
After 2 days a second catch gave 16 beetles.
Of these 4 were marked – they had been recaptured.

Number in first catch (**M**) = 12

Number in second catch (**S**) = 16

Number recaptured (**R**) = 4

Total population = $\dfrac{M \times S}{R} = \dfrac{12 \times 16}{4}$

$= 48$ ground beetles

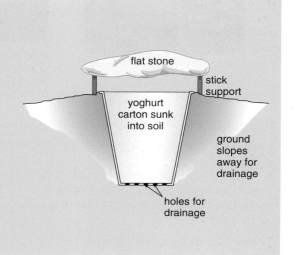

flat stone

stick
support

yoghurt
carton sunk
into soil

ground
slopes
away for
drainage

holes for
drainage

▷ Adaptations

Animals and plants must be adapted to
their habitats if they are to survive.

They may have special features that help them
survive, for instance, different birds have
different beaks that are adapted for a particular diet.
The behaviour of some animals is adapted to their habitat,
for instance, penguins huddle together to keep warm.

Look at some of the adaptations shown by
plants and animals on these 2 pages.
Think how each one aids survival.
Say whether the adaptations are
physical or behavioural, or both.

Cactus plants live in hot, dry places. Their leaves
are small spines and they can store water inside
their stems.
They have long roots to penetrate the soil.

Birds like these
swallows fly to
South Africa in
the winter

When the tide goes out,
this periwinkle shuts its
trap door tightly

This plantain weed grows on
paths. It grows very flat and has
strong deep roots.

The mayfly larva lives in fast-flowing
streams. It has a flattened,
streamlined body and clings to the
underside of rocks.

Investigation 19.3   What conditions do woodlice prefer?

Use choice chambers to investigate whether woodlice
prefer:
- dry or humid conditions (use damp cotton wool on one
  side and silica gel for the dry side)
- light or dark (use black polythene to cover one side).

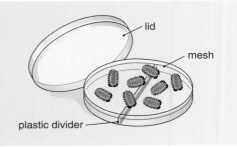

lid

mesh

plastic divider

▷ More adaptations

The adaptations on these 2 pages are inherited.
The better adapted individuals tend to survive.
They produce similar offspring with the same features.
This is how natural selection operates.

Penguins have a compact body shape. They are clumsy on land but fast, agile swimmers. They often huddle together when it is extremely cold.

This flounder can change its colour to fit its background

The feathery tufts of thistle seeds are blown by the wind

This dormouse spends most of the winter asleep

The fennec fox lives in desert conditions. It has a small body but extremely large ears. It lives in a burrow during the day and hunts at night. It has large eyes that help it see well in dim light.

Experiment 19.4   How do blowfly larvae respond to light?

Put a sheet of white paper flat on a bench.
Shine a lamp down on to it. Turn off the lamp.

Put 5 blowfly larvae on the paper.
Switch on the lamp and observe the behaviour of the blowfly larvae.

▷ Adaptations to extreme conditions

Desert conditions

Look at the photograph of the camel.
Some adaptations to desert conditions are shown below.
For each adaptation, say how it helps the camel to survive.

- It can drink 40 pints of water at one go.
  This takes 10 minutes.

- The stomach can store 500 pints of water for a short time.

- It loses little water : there is little urine and no sweating.

- No layer of fat under the skin.

- Fat is stored in the hump and can be respired to give 'metabolic water'.

- The body has a large surface area to volume ratio.

- It has large feet to spread the load.

- It has long legs (Hint : The hottest air is in the 1 metre above the desert sand).

- It can withstand an increase in normal body temperature of 9 °C.

Arctic conditions

Look at the photograph of the polar bear.
Some adaptations to arctic conditions are shown.
For each adaptation say how it helps the polar bear to survive.

- Compact shape. Body has a low surface area to volume ratio, so relatively little surface area for heat loss

- Small ears

- Thick layer of fat stored under the skin

- Very large feet covered with thick, rough skin and long, tough hair

- Thick, white fur

- Greasy fur which sheds water quickly after swimming

- Strong swimmer and a fast runner over the ice

- Female mates in summer, pregnancy does not occur until autumn

- Sharp teeth and long claws

▷ Competition

What does **competition** mean to you?
In a race, all the competitors try their
hardest to win.
In nature, plants and animals compete for
resources that are in short supply.

What do you think plants compete for?

If resources like light, space, water or
nutrients are scarce, plants compete for them.

What do you think animals compete for?

Many animals compete for a **territory**
(habitat).
If they are not successful they do not attract
a mate and can not breed.

Only those plants and animals that are able to
compete successfully will survive.
So competition restricts the size of a population.

There are 2 types of competition:

- competition between individuals of the **same**
  species
- competition between individuals of **different**
  species.

Boobies compete for nesting space

Competition within a species

What happens if you sow carrot seeds too close together?

The seedlings compete for space, light, water and nutrients.
Colonies of gulls compete for nesting sites.
There is often competition between members of
the same species.

Animals and plants tend to produce lots of offspring.
Often there are far more than can ever survive.
There will be competition between individual offspring
for scarce resources.
Only the best adapted will survive to breed.

Competition between individuals of the same species
means that only the 'best' genes are passed on to
the next generation.
As we saw in Chapter 17, there is a 'struggle
for existence' leading to the 'survival of the fittest'.

Red deer stags fight to mate with the females

339

Competition between different species

Have you ever seen a bird table in winter?
What happens when some crumbs are put on it?

Soon there are sparrows, blue tits, starlings and other birds all trying to get at the food.
The different garden birds are competing for a scarce resource – food.

Weeds are excellent competitors.
A weed is a plant growing where it is not wanted e.g. poppies in a field of barley.
Gardeners hate weeds because they are very hard to get rid of.
Weeds compete with other plants for light, water and space.

But how are they so successful?

If you look at the diagram of the dandelion it will give you some clues:

- They are able to reproduce quickly and produce a huge number of seeds.

- Their seeds germinate quickly in poor soil.

- They can grow very quickly and flower and set seed before other plants can.

- They can tolerate poor soil and harsh conditions.

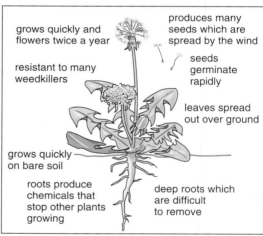

grows quickly and flowers twice a year

produces many seeds which are spread by the wind

resistant to many weedkillers

seeds germinate rapidly

leaves spread out over ground

grows quickly on bare soil

roots produce chemicals that stop other plants growing

deep roots which are difficult to remove

Competing with humans

Can you think of any animals and plants that compete with humans?
Weeds compete with the farmer's crops.
There are many animals that compete with us – we call them **pests**.
Locusts, cockroaches and rats are pests that compete with us for food.
Greenfly and whitefly are pests that do damage to our crops.
Screwworm fly is a serious pest of cattle, and mosquitoes spread malaria.

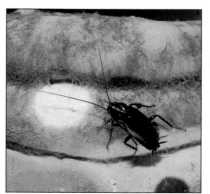

Cockroaches can spoil our food

▷ Predation

Predators kill other animals (their **prey**) for food.
Predators are usually bigger and fewer in number
than their prey. Why do you think this is?

Look at the wolf:
What things make it a good predator?

What other things make predators successful?

- Some hunt in a pack.
  They work together to catch the prey and
  share it.
- Attacking prey that is young, old, sick or injured.
  These prey are easier to overpower and kill.
  This also 'weeds out' the weaker individuals
  in the prey population.
- Catching large prey means that there is more
  food for the predator per kill.
- Not depending on one particular species of prey.
  If numbers go down, the predator can switch to
  another prey species.
- Migrating to areas where the prey is more
  plentiful.

Human predators

Humans still hunt and kill wild animals.
The best example is commercial fishing.
Improved fishing technology means more fish
are caught.
We hunt the fish using powerful fishing vessels,
sonar to detect shoals, and huge plastic nets.
Fishermen are so well equipped that they could
remove all of the fish from the sea.

Many species are now *overfished*.
Humans have been such successful predators that
future fish stocks are threatened.
International agreements have so far failed to
control the amount of fishing.

We should agree quotas on how many fish
can be caught.
We should avoid fishing during the breeding season
and use nets that catch only non-breeding adults,
leaving the small fish to survive and breed.

The size of fish stocks is being reduced to such an
extent that many are now on the verge of extinction.

Avoiding the predator

However well adapted the predator is,
some prey escape.

Look at the hare:
How is it adapted to escape predators?

What other things help prey to escape?

- Some try to run, swim or fly faster than
  the predator.

Predators find monarch
butterflies unpleasant
to eat

- Staying in large groups, like herds of antelope,
  helps survival.
  Many pairs of eyes can look out for predators.

- Some animals taste horrible!
  This makes them less attractive as a meal.
  Others like bees and wasps can sting
  the predator.

- Some prey has warning colours.
  This tells the predator to 'keep clear'.
  Hoverflies look like wasps and bees.
  But they have no sting and could be eaten.

- Camouflage helps to hide the prey.
  Many prey animals try to blend in with their
  surroundings.
  The trouble is many predators do too!

Can you find the katydid
insect in the picture?

- Some prey try shock tactics to startle a
  would-be predator.
  Can you see how this eyed hawkmoth can
  scare off a hungry bird?

Prey that escape are usually the best adapted.
They survive to pass on their genes to their
offspring.
Natural selection operates against weaker
less well-adapted individuals.

An eyed hawkmoth unfolds its wings

Predator–prey cycles

Predators try to kill their prey.
So obviously they have a big effect on
the size of the prey population.
But have you ever thought how the number
of prey affects the predator?

What would happen to a predator if the
animals it fed upon all died of disease?
Such drastic events do not happen often.
But if the prey becomes scarce, the predator
suffers too.

Look at the graph carefully:

① The prey has plenty of food.
It breeds and increases in number.

② The increase in prey numbers means that
there is more food for the predator.
So the predator breeds and increases
in number.

③ There are now lots of predators so more prey
will be eaten.
The number of prey goes down.

④ There are now less prey for the predator to
feed on.
Food will be scarce and many predators starve.

⑤ With fewer predators, more prey survive to
breed.
The prey numbers increase, and so the cycle
continues.

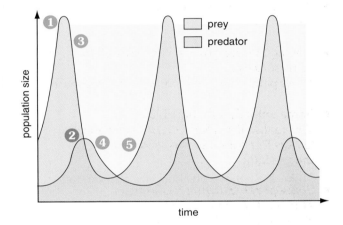

One of the best-known examples of the
predator–prey cycle is that of the lynx
and the snowshoe hare.
Both these animals were trapped for their fur.
The Hudson Bay Fur Company in Canada kept
records of the number of skins that trappers
brought in.
The graph shows the numbers between 1845
and 1935:

Can you see a pattern in the curves?

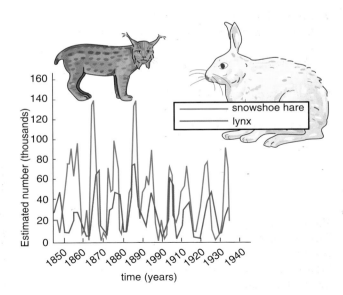

343

▷ Human populations

Human populations can change too.
At present the number of people on
the planet is growing at an alarming rate.

It has not always been so in the past.
For thousands of years there was only a
slow increase in the human population.
Lack of food, diseases, wars, and lack of
shelter meant that people did not live
very long.

Look at the graph:

What do you think has caused the huge
increases over the last 300 years?

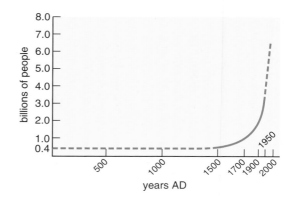

- Improved agriculture means that most
  people are better fed.

- Public health has improved.
  There are better water supplies and sanitation.

- Medical care has improved.
  People can be vaccinated against many diseases.

- Many disease-causing organisms can be
  controlled inside the body with drugs or
  outside the body by other chemicals.

What has been the effect of all these advances?

- Fewer children are dying from disease and
  lack of food.

- People are now living much longer.
  In Europe and North America the average life
  expectancy has risen to 68 years for men and
  73 years for women.
  In India life expectancy has been much lower.
  But improved health and living conditions has now
  lifted the average life expectancy there to 56 years.

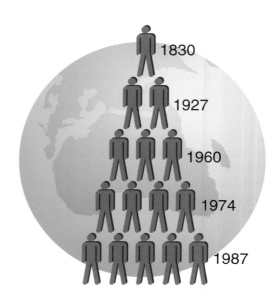

▷ Controlling human population growth

There are still controls on population increase.
Famines, floods, wars, plagues, earthquakes,
and other disasters, all take their toll.

But the overall trend is a rapid increase in
the world's population.
It is estimated that it could double in the
next 30 years.

There are wide variations between different
areas.

Look at the graph:

In Europe and North America the population is
virtually stable.
In other places the populations continue to grow.

The Earth has limited resources and limited space.
How can we reverse these trends?
The most obvious way is to reduce the birth rate.
But many groups of people have strongly held
religious or moral views on birth control and
family size. This means they may often have
large families.

The rate of increase is most influenced by the
proportion of child-bearing women in the population.

Look at these 2 population pyramids:

The base of the pyramid shows the percentage of
children below the age of 5 years.
The oldest people appear at the top.

Which country has:
● the greatest proportion of young people
● the greatest proportion of old people?
Why do you think this is?

What forecasts can you make about:
● the numbers of child-bearing women
  in each country in 10 years' time
● the birth rate in 10 years' time?

Increasing human population size
brings greater demands on resources and
problems for the environment.

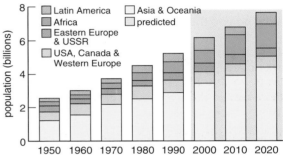

World population by regions, 1950–2020

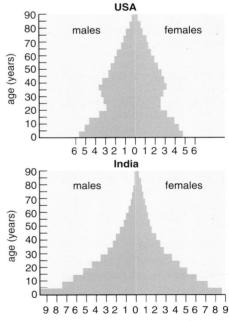

Percentage of the population in each age group.
$\left(\begin{array}{l}USA : 1\% = approx.\ 2\ million \\ India : 1\% = approx.\ 4\ million\end{array}\right)$

▷ The impact of human activity on the environment

The increase in the size of the human population is affecting
our environment all the time.
This impact on our environment comes from the economic factors
and the industrial requirements that go with a growing world population.

Deforestation

Forests help to keep the correct balance of carbon dioxide
and oxygen in our atmosphere.
They do this by taking in carbon dioxide and giving out oxygen
during photosynthesis.

Why do you think that this is important?

Forests also act as 'stores' of water, their leaves slow down the
rate of evaporation and the rate at which water reaches the soil.

So what are the reasons for deforestation ?
Why is there large-scale clearance of forests ?

- The world demand for timber as building materials.
- The demand for paper for newsprint, photocopiers, printers
  and office consumption.
- The clearing of land for farms, cattle ranches and plantations .
- Clearing for the construction of new roads and towns.
- To provide firewood and charcoal as fuels.

What are the consequences of deforestation?

- Destruction of forests increases the amount of carbon dioxide
  (a greenhouse gas – see page 372) in the atmosphere and so contributes
  to **global warming** and the chances of disastrous changes in climate.
- Dense vegetation prevents heavy rains from washing away the soil.
  With no roots to bind the soil together, **soil erosion** occurs,
  washing away nutrients and causing floods.
- Destruction of the rainforests means the **extinction** of thousands
  of species of plants and animals.

So what are the answers to stop the wholesale destruction of forests?

- **Reforestation –** involves the replanting of native trees.
  It is important that plantations do not replace native forests.
- **Sustainable management** of forests would involve removing
  trees but allowing natural replacement or planting of native species.
- **Recycling and energy conservation** would result in a reduced
  need to for 'new' sources of timber.

A paper recycling plant

Polluting the air and land

Humans are filling the air with many harmful gases.

- **Exhaust fumes** from cars contain lead, carbon monoxide
  (a gas poisonous in small amounts), nitrogen oxides and
  unburnt hydrocarbons.
  Motor exhaust fumes cause 60–90% of all air pollution in
  industrialised countries.
  Catalytic converters could be fitted to cars and new fuels
  could be used, for instance ethanol burns more cleanly
  than petrol.

- **Carbon dioxide** is given off when we burn fossil fuels
  like coal and oil.
  Deforestation is also causing a build-up of carbon dioxide
  in the atmosphere contributing to the **greenhouse effect**.
  (For details of the greenhouse effect and global warming
  see page 372.)

- **Sulphur dioxide** is also released when fossil fuels are burnt.
  Together with the nitrogen oxides from exhaust fumes, they
  cause **acid rain**.
  These gases can be carried over large distances by the winds
  before coming down as dry particles or dissolved in the rain.

  As lakes and rivers become acid, fish and small invertebrates die.
  The acid rain dissolves nutrients like potassium and calcium out
  of the soil, leaving the soil infertile.
  Toxic minerals, such as aluminium, are also washed out into
  the rivers and lakes killing fish and other wildlife.
  Acid rain also kills large number of trees – especially conifers –
  by damaging the roots and causing them to lose their leaves.

  The prevailing winds of Europe come from the south-west.
  Most of the acid gases are carried to Scandinavia, where
  they fall as acid rain in Sweden and southern Norway.
  In a similar way, Canada is paying the price for the acid gases
  released by industries in the United States.

The technology exists to combat acid rain:

- **Low sulphur fuels** could be used. Crushing coal and washing
  it with a solvent reduces its sulphur content.
- **Chemical plants** can be installed to remove the sulphur from
  emissions before they are released into the atmosphere.
- **Flue gas desulphurisation** removes the sulphur from
  power station chimneys by bombarding the waste gases
  with wet powdered limestone, neutralising the acid gases.
- **Catalytic converters** can be fitted to reduce
  the nitrogen oxides in the exhaust fumes of cars.

  These solutions are expensive, but are being gradually
  introduced to counter the expense of damage from acid rain.

Smog haze caused by air pollution in
Los Angeles

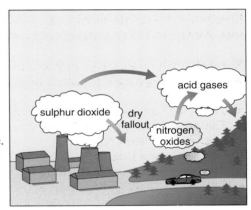

Acid rain damage to conifers

CFCs (chlorofluorocarbons)

CFCs are used in spray cans, refrigerators,
air-conditioning systems and in making plastic foam.
CFCs are also adding to the 'greenhouse effect'.
Along with carbon dioxide, methane and water vapour,
they are adding to the problems of global warming.

In addition, CFCs are causing the **ozone layer** to become thin.
This layer of ozone in the upper atmosphere protects
the Earth from harmful ultraviolet (UV) rays.
The first hole in the ozone layer appeared over the Antarctic
in 1985.
The size of the hole is increasing each year and a similar hole
is developing over the Arctic too.

Spray cans now use different propellants and are 'ozone-friendly'.
Chemists are working hard to find substitutes to use
in refrigerators and air-conditioning systems.

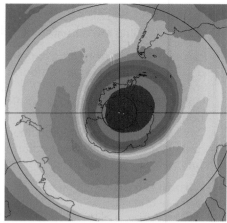

A map showing ozone concentration over the Antarctic. The ozone hole is at the centre

Radiation

Non-natural radiation comes from the testing and use of
nuclear weapons and leakages from nuclear reactors.

In 1986 there was an accident at the Chernobyl nuclear power
station. A huge cloud of radioactive material was released into
the atmosphere.
The winds blew the cloud across Europe.
Countries like Poland and Scandinavia were showered with
radioactive chemicals.

Some types of radiation are known to cause
cancers and deformed births.

A nuclear power station

Agricultural chemicals

The 'Green Revolution' between 1945 and 1975
brought about a doubling of world food production.
Agricultural chemicals had a lot to do with this success.

- **Fertilisers** made it possible to grow crops
  where the soil was previously too poor.
  Their use dramatically increases crop yields.
  But artificial fertilisers can cause pollution if they drain into
  rivers and streams (see page 374).

- **Pesticides** have been used to kill insects that eat crops,
  weeds that compete with crops, and fungi that cause disease.
  Without the use of pesticides, 45% of a crop could be lost.
  Pesticides have also saved millions of lives by killing the
  insects that spread malaria, typhus and yellow fever.
  But pesticides can be dangerous if they get into
  food chains (see pages 364–5).

Pollution of the rivers and seas

Pollutants, like fertilisers, drain from the land
into our rivers.
Domestic and industrial pollutants are often
discharged straight into rivers.
Sewage is our biggest single pollutant.
It can encourage the growth of algae and bacteria
which use up lots of oxygen.
Fish and small invertebrates die.

Our rivers empty toxic wastes into the sea :

- fertilisers and sewage encourage the growth
  of toxic algae
- pesticides are becoming concentrated in the
  tissues of shellfish
- radioactive chemicals are found in high
  concentrations around coastal nuclear power stations
- toxic metals, like mercury, copper and lead, are
  finding their way into the sea's food chains.

Oil spillages often hit the headlines.
The **Sea Empress** (1996), the **Braer** (1993),
Exxon Valdez (1989) and the **Amoco Cadiz** (1989)
released thousands of tonnes of crude oil into the sea.
But the worst oil pollution disaster occurred in
Kuwait (1990–91).
Iraqi forces destroyed oil wells, oil tankers
and installations by the coast. Hundreds of thousands
of tonnes of oil spilled into the Arabian Gulf.

We have become familiar with pictures of oil-covered
beaches.
Sea birds die when their feathers get clogged with oil.
They take in the oil when they try to clean themselves.
They soon die of exposure, drowning or starvation.
Seashore animals and plants become smothered by the oil.
Detergents are sprayed on the oil to try to disperse it.
But these are often toxic to marine life.

Kuwait oil wells set on fire

We have for too long thought of the sea as a vast
dumping ground.
The way we have polluted the seas in the past
is storing up problems for the future.

▷ Conservation

Conservation aims to keep ecosystems stable as environmental conditions change.

It is important that we conserve the environment for the benefit of future generations.

We have a duty of care to maintain the **biodiversity** (number of different plant and animal species) and protect endangered species.

As we have seen, habitats are being destroyed due to increased land-use for building, quarrying, dumping and agriculture. Human populations are creating greater demands upon food and energy and producing more waste.

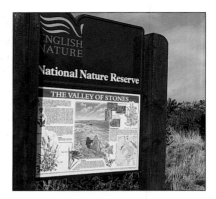

Endangered species

Many plants and animals have become extinct : the rock wallaby, wild ox, spectacled bear and Atlantic walrus are extinct or close to extinction. Deforestation has meant the extinction of thousands of rainforest plants that could have provided us with new medicines.

Their fate has been sealed owing to the destruction of their habitats and their over-exploitation for commercial use.

However, the American bison and the Saiga antelope in Russia have been brought back from the brink of extinction.

American bison

What are the facts ?

- We have already mentioned the need to conserve fish stocks. Many marine molluscs from the tropics, such as cowries, scallops, cone shells and clams are harvested for food or for their shells.

- Illegal ivory poaching resulted in a loss of half the elephants in Kenya and 90% in Uganda in the 1970s. As a result CITES, the Convention of International Trade in Endangered Species, imposed a world-wide ban on the ivory trade in 1989. This move led to a significant increase in the elephant population.

- The trade in furs and other animal skins seems senseless. There are plenty of imitation furs available, but the shooting and trapping has taken its toll on wild species. The demand comes mainly from the affluent countries in Europe and the USA.

- The trade in exotic birds takes 10 million birds from the wild each year. About half of these die even before they reach their destination.

The trade in exotic shells

Good news

In 1973, the World Wildlife Fund cooperated with the Indian government to set up 'Operation Tiger'. For many years, tiger numbers had been in decline owing to hunting, trapping and habitat destruction. The aim of the operation was not only to protect the tiger by legislation but also to conserve its whole environment.

Poaching to satisfy the Chinese market for traditional 'medicines' based upon tiger products still remains a threat to its survival.

Zoos and captive breeding programmes

Breeding animals in captivity, building up their numbers and eventually releasing them back into the wild has been increasingly common in many of the world's zoos.

The Arabian oryx (shown here) has been bred in captivity in Phoenix Zoo, Arizona, and herds released in areas where the species was previously extinct, such as Oman. Other species saved by captive breeding include the European bison and Pere David's deer.

Botanic gardens and seed banks

Botanic gardens are public gardens that keep collections of plants for conservation, research and education. We have seen the threat that deforestation, land development and agricultural expansion can bring to plant diversity.

There are now about 1600 botanic gardens worldwide, between them growing tens of thousands of plant species. Many of these are endangered species – by reintroducing them back into the wild we can conserve the natural vegetation.

Seed banks are cold stores of seeds that originally concentrated on commercial crops such as cereals and potatoes. They also conserve seed stocks of endangered or valuable species.

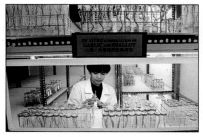

Seed bank at the Agricultural Research Centre, Taiwan

In southern England, the 80 million pound Millenium seed bank has been constructed. This building will store seeds from 10% of the world's estimated 250 000 wild flowering plants. This project stemmed from Britain's signing of the Convention on Biological Diversity in Rio, 1992.

Nearer home

In the UK, legislation protects wildlife in a number of ways :

- National Parks have been set up in England and Wales to protect large areas of outstanding natural scenery for the benefit of the public. For example : Snowdonia, Exmoor, the Broads and the Yorkshire Dales.
- National Nature Reserves (NNRs) are smaller and more numerous than the National Parks. They were set up to protect biodiversity in Britain and are so geared to conserving our native species.
- Sites of Special Scientific Interest (SSSIs) are areas that have been identified to conserve particularly rare and endangered species in Britain.

Other schemes in existence to protect our native wildlife include Heritage Coasts, the Farm Woodland Scheme, Set-aside, Tree Preservation Orders, Nitrate Sensitive Areas and the Royal Society for the Protection of Birds. Your teacher can provide you with websites for these organisations.

The ten National Parks and two equivalent areas (the Broads and New Forest) in England and Wales

351

▷ Biology at work : Biodegradation of oil and plastics

Biodegradation of oil

Oil pollution is usually dealt with in 2 ways :

- the oil is skimmed or pumped off the sea
- chemicals are used to break the oil down.

Eventually the oil sinks to the sea bed.
Here it can smother and kill marine animals
and plants. Chemicals in the oil are thought
to enter the food chains.

But oil is biodegradable – there are many
micro-organisms that can break it down.
The trouble is it usually takes a long time
for this to happen.

Chemical dispersants used to deal with oil pollution are often toxic to marine life

An improved technique has been used in the Gulf.
Oil-polluted areas are 'seeded' with special types
of microbes.
The complex hydrocarbons making up the
crude oil are split into simple, non-polluting
compounds.

Recovery time is about 2–3 years, but growth of
the oil-degrading bacteria may be limited by lack
of nutrients.
Bags of fertiliser (containing nitrates and phosphates)
can speed up bacterial growth and aid recovery.

But there is no quick answer to oil pollution.
The spills should be controlled at source.
The policy should be 'prevention is better than cure'.

Biodegradable plastics

Plastics used in packaging are a major pollutant.

British scientists have developed a type of plastic
called Biopol.
This can be broken down by microbes in the soil.
AstraZeneca is a leading UK chemical company.
Scientists there put bacteria into fermenters with
glucose and other nutrients.
The microbes make a chemical that can be turned
into Biopol.
When Biopol decomposes it produces carbon dioxide.

new → after 35 weeks

Biodegradable plastic bottles

Summary

- Ecosystems are made up of the habitat (non-living) and the community (plants and animals).

- A community is made up of different plant and animal populations.

- A population is a group of individuals belonging to the same species.

- In any ecosystem there are environmental and biotic factors to which organisms have to adapt.

- Structural and behavioural adaptations enable animals and plants to survive.

- Competition exists both within the members of a species and between different species.

- Populations are able to grow quickly but natural checks act against this increase. Births and immigration increase a population, deaths and emigration decrease it.

- Predator – prey cycles operate to control the numbers of each population.

- The natural checks on human populations have been removed resulting in huge increases.

- The impact of human activity on the environment is related to population size, economic factors and industrial requirements.

▷ **Questions**

1. Match these words with each of the following definitions :

    ecosystems   habitat   community
    population   niche   biosphere

    a) Organisms that interact within the same ecosystem.
    b) A group of individuals of the same species.
    c) The part of an ecosystem where plants and animals live.
    d) All the ecosystems belong to this.

2. Match the animals and plants in Column A below with their correct habitats in Column B :

Column A	Column B
lichen	wood
trout	path
hawthorn	rocky shore
groundsel	pond
squirrel	moorland
heather	river
frog	hedge
crab	wall

3. Duckweed was grown in a beaker of water. The number of plants counted each day is shown in the table :

Day	No. of plants
1	1
4	2
8	4
12	8
16	16
20	32
24	32
28	31
32	31

   a) Plot the results on a graph to show how the population size changes with time.
   b) Explain the shape of the curve.
   c) Suggest 2 factors that could have caused the population to become stable.

4. a) Name 4 factors that limit the growth of a population.
   b) For each of these factors explain the effect that it has on the population's growth.

5. Ten identical plots of land were cleared of weeds and then sowed with pea seeds.
After sowing, 9 of the plots were kept free of weeds for different lengths of time.
After 9 weeks, all the plants were harvested from each plot and weighed.
The results are shown in the graph:

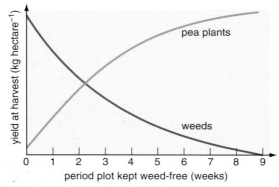

a) What conclusions can you draw about the competition between pea plants and weeds?
b) How could you estimate the total mass of weeds growing in a large field?
c) Design an experiment to test the prediction that pea plants growing at a high density produce fewer peas per plant than those growing at a low density.

6. The number of animals in a habitat were studied using the 'mark, release, recapture' technique. The results are shown in the table:

Animals	No. in 1st catch (*M*)	No. in 2nd catch (*S*)	No. of marked animals in 2nd catch (*R*)
millipedes	40	50	25
centipedes	50	60	20
beetles	16	15	6
woodlice	100	80	40
snails	20	15	10

a) Use the formula

$$P = \frac{M \times S}{R}$$

to work out the population of each animal.
b) Draw a bar-chart for each animal population.
c) Why should the animals not be marked with bright, permanent paint?

7. The graph was drawn from data collected from a lake over a period of 12 months.

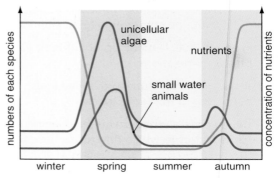

a) Name 2 environmental factors needed for algae to grow.
b) Explain why the number of algae increased from a winter low to a spring high.
c) Explain why the population of small water animals fell in late spring.
d) Explain why the concentration of nutrients fell in the spring but rose in autumn.

8. A population of rabbits lived on an island.
Predators such as weasels fed on the rabbits.
Some hunters came to the island and shot all the weasels.
The rabbit population increased. They began to compete for grass. Many rabbits starved.
Soon the rabbit population was about the same as it was before the weasels were shot.
a) What were the 4 populations involved?
b) Why do you think the hunters were wrong to shoot all the weasels?
c) What do you think will happen to the rabbit population in the future?

9. There are 4 main sources of pollution in the Mediterranean Sea.
These are:
● discarded packaging materials, especially plastics
● agriculture, especially fertilisers
● oil and chemical spills from ships
● sewage and waste from industry.
a) Which one of these sources is responsible for *all* the following types of pollution:
phosphates, nitrates, detergents, heavy metals?
b) Explain different methods that are used to try and clear up oil spills at sea.

Further Questions on page 376

ENERGY TRANSFER

chapter 20

We can put living organisms into groups based
on similar features.
But if we are looking at a community of living
things it is often more useful to group them
by looking at the way that they feed.

First of all we can divide up living things into
those that make their own food and those that don't.

Producers are able to make their own food from
simple substances like carbon dioxide and water.
Do you know of any producers?

Green plants use light as a source of energy to
make sugars from carbon dioxide and water.
Many bacteria are also producers.
Some use light as an energy source but most obtain
the energy they need from chemical reactions.

Producers ultimately produce the food for all
the other members of the community.

Light penetrating the tree canopy

All animals are **consumers**.
They cannot make their own food.
So they have to eat or consume it.

- **Primary consumers** are herbivores.
  They eat the producers – plants or bacteria.

- **Secondary consumers** are carnivores.
  They eat herbivores.

- **Tertiary consumers** are carnivores
  that eat secondary consumers.
  They are sometimes called top carnivores.

- **Decomposers** are microbes that feed on
  dead and decaying material.
  Most of these are bacteria and fungi.

*Which are the primary consumers and
secondary consumers in this photograph?*

Each feeding group belongs to a different **trophic level**.
('Trophic' comes from a Greek word and means 'to feed'.)

▷ Food chains

Food chains show us what eats what in a community.
They show the movement of food energy from one organism to the next.
Look at this food chain:

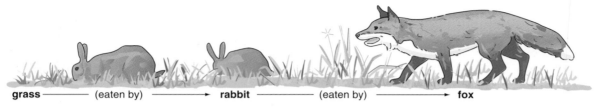

grass ——— (eaten by) ———→ rabbit ——— (eaten by) ———→ fox

The arrows show the direction in which the food energy is transferred
from one organism to the next.
This food chain tells us that the rabbit eats grass and the fox eats the rabbit.

Here is a food chain with 4 links:

oak leaves ——→ slug ——→ thrush ——→ sparrowhawk

Notice that the food chain always begins with a producer, often a green plant.
This can include parts of a plant, such as seeds, fruits or even dead leaves.
Here is a food chain where the primary consumer feeds on dead leaves.

dead leaves ——→ woodlouse ——→ blackbird

We can draw food chains from any community.
They may live on the land or in water.

Here is a food chain from the sea:

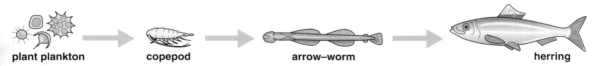

plant plankton ——→ copepod ——→ arrow–worm ——→ herring

If all the copepods died:
- What would happen to the number of arrow-worms
- What would happen to the numbers of plant plankton?

Here is a food chain from a lake. It has 5 links:

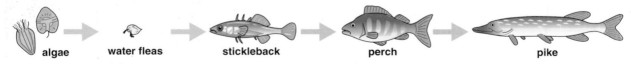

algae ——→ water fleas ——→ stickleback ——→ perch ——→ pike

What are the producers in this food chain?
What is the top carnivore?

▶ Food webs

In most communities animals will eat more than one thing.
Hedgehogs would get pretty fed up if they ate just snails!
They also eat beetles, earthworms and slugs.

A **food web** is made up of many
food chains.
It gives a more complete picture
of how animals feed.

Look at the woodland food web:

Can you find all the food chains?
Try writing them out.
There are 6 of them.

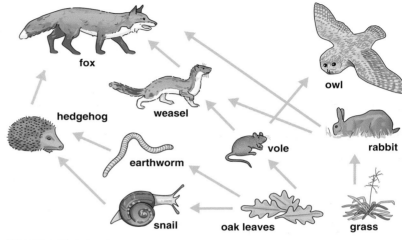

Woodland food web

Look at the seashore food web:
a) How many primary consumers are there?
b) How many secondary consumers are there?
c) Draw a food chain with 5 links from this food web.
d) Suppose all the starfish died from pollution.
   What would happen to the number of:
   i) mussels   ii) small algae?

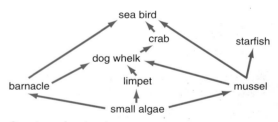

Seashore food web

The niche

If we look at a food web we can see how a particular
organism feeds.
This is part of its role or job in the community.
We call this its **niche**.
For instance, the winter moth feeds on the buds of
oak trees.
It provides food for many birds and parasites.
This is the *role* or *niche* of the winter moth.

If two organisms occupy the same niche, they will compete,
often until one of them becomes excluded from the community.
For instance, in Britain the North American grey squirrel
seems to be competing for the same niche as the native
red squirrel. They both want the same food and they both
want to live in the same nesting sites.

Competing for the same niche

357

▷ Pyramids of number

Food chains and food webs can show the
feeding relationships in a community.
But they do not tell us **how many** living
organisms are involved.
For instance, it takes many plants to feed
one herbivore and many herbivores to feed
one carnivore.

Look at the diagram:

Why are there far more leaves than caterpillars?
Why are there far fewer owls than shrews?

Look at the numbers in this food chain:

owl	1
shrews	10
caterpillars	100
oak leaves	600

We can show this information in a **pyramid of numbers**.
The area of each box shows us roughly how many living
things there are at each trophic level.
You start with the producers on the first level,
then the primary consumers on the second level,
the secondary consumers on the third, and so on.

- What happens to the **numbers** of individuals as you
  go up this pyramid?
- What happens to the **size** of each organism as you
  go up this pyramid?
- Why are the producers (like green plants) always on
  the first trophic level?

A problem with pyramids of number is that they do
not take into account the **size** of organisms at each
trophic level.
For instance, an oak tree and a grass plant each count
as one organism.
But one oak tree can support many more herbivores
than one grass plant can.
As a result some pyramids of number can have unusual
shapes.

Look at this pyramid of numbers:
The tertiary consumers are parasites.
Many of them feed on a single ladybird.
So this inverted pyramid looks top heavy.

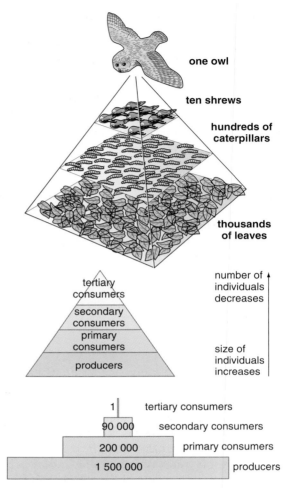

one owl

ten shrews

hundreds of
caterpillars

thousands
of leaves

number of
individuals
decreases

size of
individuals
increases

Pyramid of numbers for a grassland community in
0.1 hectare

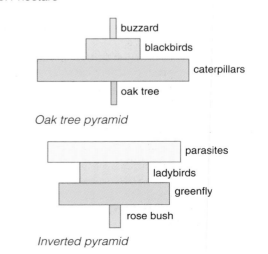

Oak tree pyramid

Inverted pyramid

▷ Pyramids of biomass

One way to overcome the problem of size is to measure **biomass** instead of numbers.

Biomass is the weight of living material.
So a biomass pyramid shows the actual weight or mass of living things at each trophic level.

To draw a biomass pyramid you first need to collect your data.
Take a sample of the organisms from each trophic level and weigh them.
Find the average mass for the sample.
Then multiply the mass by the estimated number present in the community.
Some scientists work out the dry mass because the water content can vary in living things.
But to do this you have to dry the organism in an oven which would kill it.

Biomass pyramids also have other drawbacks.

- The mass recorded is at one instant in time.
  So biomass pyramids do not take into account *how fast* an organism grows.
  For instance, grass grows at a fast rate, but because it is grazed its biomass at a particular time will be low.

Plant plankton grow quickly in the sea, but they only live for a few days.
So their biomass at a particular time is small.
But over say a year, their biomass is huge.
This biomass pyramid records only a few days' growth and so looks inverted :

- Biomass can vary with the seasons.
  For instance, the biomass of a beech tree is far greater in summer than it is in winter.
  Why do you think this is ?

In winter the tree will have lost the leaves, flowers and fruits that grow in the summer.

Biomass is the weight of living material

Biomass sampling on a rocky shore

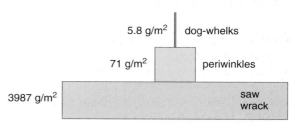

5.8 g/m² | dog-whelks

71 g/m² | periwinkles

3987 g/m² | saw wrack

Biomass pyramid for a rocky shore community

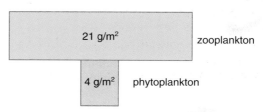

21 g/m² | zooplankton

4 g/m² | phytoplankton

Biomass pyramid for the English Channel

▷ Pyramids of energy

The best way to show what is happening in the feeding
relationships of a community is to use **energy pyramids**.

These show the amount of energy transferred
from one trophic level to the next.
This energy pyramid shows that 87 000 kJ/m²/yr
is passed to the tadpoles from the water plants.
The tadpoles pass on 14 000 kJ/m²/yr to the small
fish, and so on.

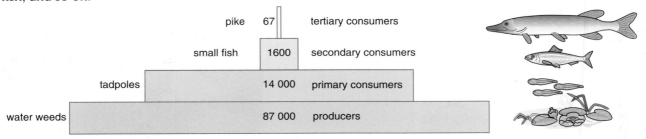

pike	67	tertiary consumers
small fish	1600	secondary consumers
tadpoles	14 000	primary consumers
water weeds	87 000	producers

A pyramid of energy for a pond (figures are in kJ/m²/year)

If the tadpoles got 87 000 kJ from the water plants
but only passed on 14 000 kJ to the small fish,
where did the other 73 000 kJ go to?
What have the tadpoles done with all that energy?
They will have used up a lot of it swimming around
and passed out some of it in waste.
In fact the only energy that they do pass on to the
small fish is that which they have used in growing.

Energy is always "lost" in this way as it is passed
from one trophic level to the next.
Of the 87 000 kJ of energy we started with only 67 kJ
will end up as part of the top carnivore, the pike!

Since only some of the energy is passed on an
energy pyramid is never inverted.
Its shape is not affected by the size of the organisms
or how many of them there are since it simply looks
at the amount of energy that is passed on.

Unlike pyramids of number or of biomass,
energy pyramids make it easy to compare the
efficiency of energy transfer from one trophic level
to the next in different communities.
If energy transfer is efficient then a lot of energy
will be passed on from one level to the next.

Although energy pyramids are better than pyramids
of number and pyramids of biomass it is difficult
to collect data for the energy at each trophic level.

*The larva of the great diving beetle also
feeds on tadpoles*

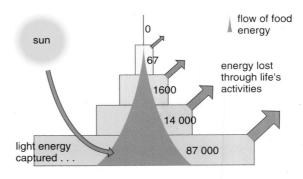

Pyramid of energy for the pond in kJ/m²/year

▷ Shortening the food chain

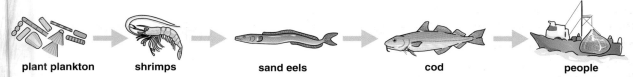

plant plankton   shrimps   sand eels   cod   people

Look at this pyramid of numbers:
It shows the estimated number of individuals that could
be supported on a 1000 tonnes of plant plankton in a year.
Humans are at the top of this pyramid.
How many cod would one human eat in a year?
It works out at about 1 cod a day.

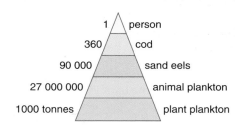

1	person
360	cod
90 000	sand eels
27 000 000	animal plankton
1000 tonnes	plant plankton

What if the food chain is shortened and people
ate sand eels instead of cod?
Thirty people could be supported in this way.
That's assuming each could get by on about
10 sand eels a day.

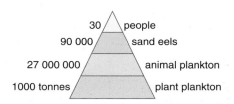

30	people
90 000	sand eels
27 000 000	animal plankton
1000 tonnes	plant plankton

What if the food chain is shortened again?
People now feed on animal plankton such as shrimps?
Could you get by on 100 shrimps a day?
If so this food chain could support 900 people in a year.

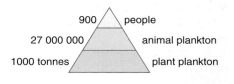

900	people
27 000 000	animal plankton
1000 tonnes	plant plankton

What if we remove the last animal in the food chain
and become vegetarian?
Feeding on 2 kg of plant plankton a day may not appeal to you.
But this could support 2000 people a year.

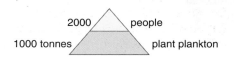

2000	people
1000 tonnes	plant plankton

What is the message from this exercise?
A vegetarian diet can support far more people.
If we cut down the number of links in the food
chain more individuals at the end of the food chain
can be fed.

This is because we are cutting down the 90%
'wastage' of energy that occurs between each
trophic level. The energy that is uneaten,
undigested or used in respiration at each level.

Why do you think that people in underdeveloped
countries tend to have vegetarian diets?

In the Western developed countries people have a
varied diet. It includes poultry, fish, lamb, beef and
pork. What does this tell you about the economies
of these countries?

The human population is increasing at an alarming
rate.
How do you think this will affect the future price of
meat?

The rising price of food is pushing us down the
food pyramid towards a vegetarian diet.

▷ Energy flow through producers

The energy in all ecosystems originally came from the Sun.
This energy can be transferred.
In photosynthesis green plants transfer sunlight energy into chemical energy in sugar.

Green plants (and some bacteria) are the only living organisms that are able to do this.
But photosynthesis is far less efficient than we think.

Most of the sunlight that falls on leaves is not absorbed and used.
- Some is reflected from the leaf's surface.
- Some passes straight through the leaf.
- Only part of the light is useful and can be absorbed by chlorophyll.

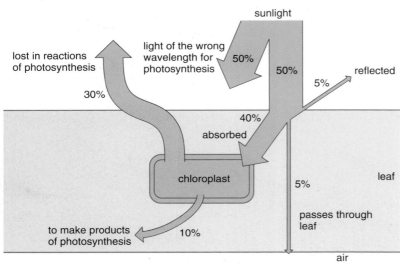

What happens to the light that falls onto a leaf?

The overall efficiency of energy transfer during photosynthesis is less than 10 %.
So only about 8 % of the sunlight energy reaching the plant is transferred into useful chemical energy.

This chemical energy is used by the plant for respiration and growth.

When the plant grows its biomass will increase.
This will provide food energy for herbivores.
It may be transferred between trophic levels from producers to primary consumers.

Some food energy may be transferred to decomposers.
This can happen when leaves are shed, fruits and seeds are dispersed and when the plant itself dies.
Decomposers eat the dead plant tissues to get energy.

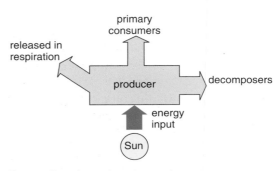

Energy flow through a green plant

Energy flow through consumers

Transfer of food energy from producers to primary consumers also involves 'wastage'. For every 100 g of plant material available only about 10 g ends up as part of a herbivore's body.

What are the reasons for this 90 % energy 'wastage' between trophic levels?

- Some food may not be eaten.
- Some food passes through the body of the herbivore without being digested.
- A lot of food is used in respiration.

Similar losses in food energy occur between other trophic levels.
Some carnivores are able to achieve a 20 % conversion efficiency.
So for every 100 g of herbivore that they eat 20 g ends up as part of their body.
This is because proteins are more efficiently digested than are carbohydrates and animals contain a lot more protein than plants.

Look at the diagram showing the energy intake and output of a cow:

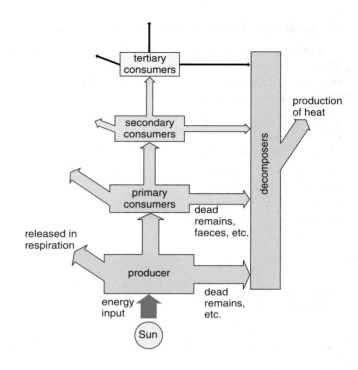

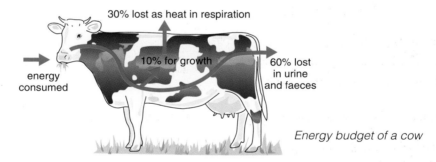

Energy budget of a cow

Of the energy in the grass the cow eats, over half if passed out of the body in faeces.
A lot of energy passes out as heat produced during respiration and in the urine.
What is left goes to increase the cow's biomass.

The cow's energy budget can be summarised as:

Energy intake	=	Energy transfer in respiration	+	Energy transfer into biomass	+	Energy in faeces	+	Energy in urine

▷ Pesticides in food chains

Pesticides are chemicals used to kill pests.
The main farm pests are insects, weeds and moulds.
Why do pests need to be controlled?
Without pesticides there would be a large decrease
in crop yield.

DDT is a very effective pesticide.
Only small amounts are needed to kill any insect.
DDT has saved millions of people from disease
and starvation.
It has been used to control the mosquitoes that
spread **malaria**.
It also helps reduce the numbers of insects that
eat food crops.

But DDT is dangerous and does not break down easily.
It stays in the environment for a long time.
It does not break down inside the body of an
animal either.
This means that it can pass along food chains.

Clear Lake in California was sprayed with DDT
to control midges.
Soon fish-eating birds like grebes began to die.
Their bodies had large amounts of DDT in them.

How do you think the pesticide got into the grebes?
What happens to the level of DDT as you go along
this food chain?
How do you explain this increase?

The DDT was first taken up by the plant plankton.
The animal plankton feed on many plant plankton.
So the level of DDT builds up in their bodies.
Each fish feeds on many animal plankton.
For each one it eats, a fish will get a dose of DDT.
Each grebe feeds on many fish.
For each one it eats, the grebe gets a dose of DDT.
So the DDT reaches a lethal level in the grebe first.
The pesticide has built up along the food chain.
This is sometimes called **bioaccumulation**.

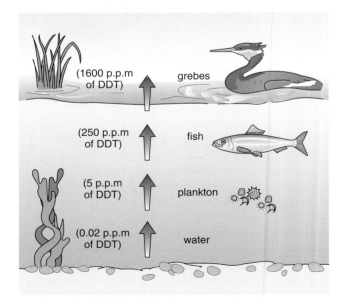

(1600 p.p.m of DDT) — grebes

(250 p.p.m of DDT) — fish

(5 p.p.m of DDT) — plankton

(0.02 p.p.m of DDT) — water

▷ Pesticides in Britain

In the late 1950s pesticides caused deaths to birds in Britain.
In the spring of each year large numbers of different bird species were found dead.
These included a lot of seed-eating birds like woodpigeons, pheasants and partridges.
Also predators like sparrowhawks, peregrine falcons and foxes.

High levels of a pesticide called dieldrin were found in the bodies.
Seeds were often dipped in dieldrin to protect them from pests.

Why do you think so many seed-eating birds died?
How did dieldrin become concentrated in the bodies of predators?

Birds of prey in particular were affected.
The dieldrin not only built up in their bodies it caused them to lay eggs with thinner shells.
Many eggs were crushed when the birds sat on them to incubate them.

Dieldrin was also used in sheep dips.
How could this have poisoned birds of prey like the golden eagle?

Pesticides like DDT and dieldrin are now banned from most industrialised countries.

What's the alternative?

In Holland lice are damaging trees.
Ladybirds are being set free into the Dutch countryside to kill the lice.
The ladybirds have been imported from California where they are specially bred.
This is an example of **biological control**.
Biological control is the use of predators, parasites and pathogens to control a pest species.
Many pests are alien species introduced into a country by accident.
The bicontrol agent can often be found in the pest's original country and can be imported to control the pest.
The big advantage of biological control is that it avoids the use of pesticides completely.

Sparrowhawk with a kill

Peregrine falcon at its nest

▷ Biology at work: Intensive food production

Modern farming has become more **intensive**.
Farmers try to produce as much food as possible by making
the best use of the available land, plants and animals.

Intensive poultry production

Animals need the right sort of food and a certain amount
of warmth to grow well.
Many animals are reared indoors so that:

Intensive turkey farming

- The amount and type of food can be controlled.
  High protein diets and additives make the animals
  grow as fast as possible.
- The temperature of their surroundings can be kept constant.
- The lack of exercise means that they put on weight quicker.
- Antibiotics control the spread of disease.

Many people do not like to see animals grown in these conditions.
They think that it is more humane for them to be outside.
More and more people think that the use of veal crates and
other types of animal pens should be banned.

Crop production

We have seen how crop growth can be increased by:

- Giving the best conditions for photosynthesis.
  Light, carbon dioxide and temperature can be controlled
  inside glasshouses.
- Using fertilisers to increase yields.
- Using chemicals to control insect pests, weeds and diseases.
- Breeding high yield crops.

Fish farming

Fish like salmon and trout can be kept in large cages.
Here their growing conditions can be carefully controlled by:

- Providing a high protein diet.
- Using chemicals to fight diseases and pests.
- Excluding predators and competitors.

There are worries that fish farming can cause pollution.
The concentration of fish in one place means wastes and
uneaten food can cause eutrophication problems (see page 374).

Summary

- Producers, including green plants and some bacteria, are able to make their own food.

- Producers provide food energy for primary consumers (herbivores).

- Primary consumers in turn provide food energy for secondary consumers (carnivores).

- Decomposers and detritivores feed upon dead and decaying material.

- These feeding relationships can be shown by food chains and food webs.

- The role that an animal or plant plays in its community is called its niche.

- Pyramids of number, biomass and energy can be used to show feeding relationships.

- A short food chain can support far more people than one with many links in the chain.

- Energy enters ecosystems as sunlight and leaves as heat.

- Only a fraction of the light falling on a leaf will be transferred to new plant biomass.

- There are 'wastages' of energy between different trophic levels.

▷ Questions

1. Copy and complete:
   Producers are able to make their own . . . . . Producers are fed upon by herbivores or . . . . consumers. These in turn provide food for . . . . consumers. Dead and . . . . material provides food for . . . . and detritivores. Feeding relationships can be shown in food . . . . and in food . . . . . Feeding relationships can also be shown in pyramids of . . . . , biomass and . . . . .

2. Look at the woodland food web:

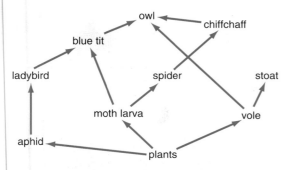

   a) Give one example from the food web, of each of these:
   i) a producer
   ii) a primary consumer
   iii) a secondary consumer.

   b) How many carnivores are there in the food web?
   c) Draw a food chain with 5 links in it.
   d) If all the spiders were killed by disease what would happen to the numbers of:
   i) moth larvae   ii) plants?

3. Look at this food web:

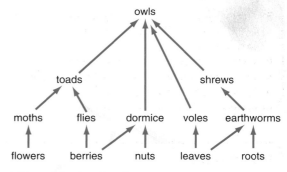

   a) From the food web name:
   i) two primary consumers
   ii) one secondary consumer.
   b) Construct, using the food web, two different food chains, each with 4 links.
   c) Why do most food chains begin with green plants?
   d) If all the owls were killed what would happen to the numbers of:
   i) dormice   ii) earthworms?

4. The numbers of plants and animals were counted at 3 different places in a pond. The results are shown in the table:

Place	Numbers counted			
	Small fish	Water flea	Duck	Small plants (Algae)
1	4	500	1	10 000
2	1	700	0	8000
3	3	680	1	7000
Totals				

a) Copy and complete the table.
b) Use the names in the table to draw a pyramid of numbers.
c) Explain why all the plants in the pond were found near the surface.
d) Plants are food for pond animals.
Give 2 other ways in which these animals depend upon plants.

5. The table shows information about 3 food chains:

Producer	Primary consumer
200 leaves	100 caterpillars
20 water weeds	200 insect larvae
5 cabbages	100 caterpillars
Secondary consumer	**Tertiary consumer**
5 thrushes	1 kestrel
5 small fish	1 otter
5 thrushes	500 fleas

a) Draw a pyramid of numbers for each food chain.
b) The average masses for the organisms in these food chains are:
leaf (5 g), caterpillar (4 g), thrush (70 g), kestrel (250 g), water weed (250 g), insect larva (10 g), small fish (300 g), otter (1 kg), cabbage (300 g), flea (0.04 g).
   i) Draw a biomass pyramid for each food chain using this data.
   ii) What differences can you see between each pyramid of number and each pyramid of biomass?

6. For every square metres of grass that it eats, a cow gets 3000 kJ of energy. It uses 100 kJ for growth, 1000 kJ are lost as heat and 1900 kJ are lost in faeces.
a) What percentage of the energy in one square metre of grass   i) is used for growth
   ii) passes through the gut and is not absorbed?
b) If beef has an energy value of 12 kJ per gram, how many square metres of grass are needed to produce 100 g of beef?

7. Look back at the diagram showing the energy budget of a cow on page 363.
a) How efficient is the cow at converting grass into biomass? Explain your answer.
b) What percentage of the energy intake is:
   i) present in the faeces and urine
   ii) used up in respiration?
c) Cows spend a lot of time grazing. In view of your other answers, why do you think this is?

8. In 1963, it was decided to kill mosquitoes by spraying a lake where they lived with a pesticide. The pesticide used is not poisonous to vertebrates unless it is in a concentration of 950 parts per million (p.p.m.). In 1964, large numbers of fish-eating birds were found dead in the lake. Study the table and the pyramid of numbers for the lake, then answer the questions:

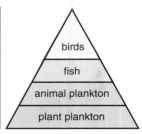

Organism	Concentration of pesticide (p.p.m.)
plant plankton	1
animal plankton	10
fish	100
fish-eating birds	1000

a) Name i) the producers
        ii) the primary consumers
b) Explain why fish survived in the lake in 1964 but not fish-eating birds.
c) Explain what you would expect to happen to the population of fish in the lake during 1965 if spraying continued.
d) Explain what you would expect to happen to the population of animal plankton as a result of c).
e) Name a heavy metal that can act as a poison.

Further questions on page 378.

chapter 21

NUTRIENT CYCLING

What happens to dead plants and animals?
They rot away or **decompose**.
Microbes are responsible for decomposition.
The **bacteria** and **fungi** (moulds) that make
dead things rot are called **decomposers**.
Decomposers also break down the waste
materials made by animals (faeces and urine).

Look at the diagram:

Plants need chemicals called **nutrients** for growth
These are usually found in the soil.
How do plants take up these nutrients?
How do these nutrients get into animals?
Name 2 ways in which nutrients get back into the soil.

Decomposers are the vital link in this story.
By decaying dead remains and waste, they
free the nutrients that were locked inside.
These nutrients can be used again by
other living things.

The nutrients that make up the bodies of living things
can be used again and again.
First they are released into the soil and are taken up by plants.
The nutrients are then passed on to animals when they eat
the plants.
We say that nutrients are **cycled**.

Most living matter (95%) is made up of just 6 elements:
carbon, hydrogen, oxygen, nitrogen, phosphorus and sulphur.
Living things must have a constant supply of these elements
if they are to make proteins, carbohydrates and fats.

These elements are found in the nutrients that living things
take in. For instance, carbon is found in carbon dioxide,
nitrogen is found in nitrates, and hydrogen is found in water.
If these nutrients were not cycled then living things would
not have the elements that they need.

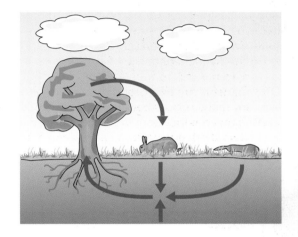

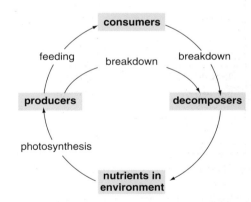

Cycling of nutrients in an ecosystem

▷ Decomposers and detritivores

Pieces of dead and decaying material are called **detritus**.
Small animals feed on this and help to break it down.
These animals are called **detritivores**.
Earthworms, fly maggots and woodlice are all detritivores.
They shred up a lot of the dead material into very small pieces.
This makes it easier for decomposers to break it down.
Without detritivores the process of decomposition would take much longer.

Some common detritivores

Decomposers are microscopic.
We only really notice them because they make things decay.
These bacteria and fungi are also responsible for rotting food.
So how do they decompose dead things?

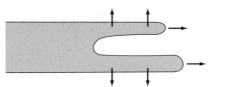

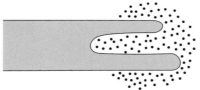

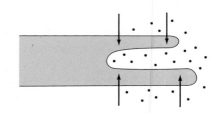

1. A fungus releases enzymes on to the dead remains

2. The enzymes digest the dead matter and make it soluble

3. The soluble products are taken up by the fungus

Fungi and bacteria use enzymes to digest their food.
These work in the same way as the enzymes in your gut.
The soluble products are taken up by the bacteria and fungi.

The decomposers absorb the food and use it for growth and for energy.
These bacteria and fungi may be eaten by other organisms and so the nutrients are passed on.

Decomposer food chain:

dead leaves ⟶ fungus ⟶ beetle ⟶ frog

Detritivore food chain:

dead animal ⟶ blowfly maggots ⟶ blackbird ⟶ sparrowhawk

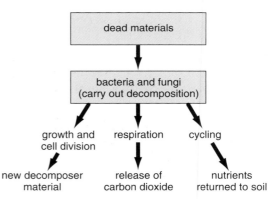

370

▷ The carbon cycle

All living things need carbon.
It is used to make carbohydrates,
proteins, fats, and other important
molecules. These molecules make up
living organisms.

The carbon comes from carbon dioxide in
the air. Plants use it in photosynthesis to
make food. Animals get the carbon by
eating plants.

How does carbon dioxide get back into
the air?

- Plants and animals use some of their
  food for respiration, releasing energy
  and carbon dioxide.

- Decomposers use dead plants and
  animals for food. They use some of
  the decaying material for respiration,
  releasing energy and carbon dioxide.

- Fossil fuels like oil, peat, coal, and gas
  contain carbon. When they are
  burned, carbon dioxide is released
  into the air.

These processes put carbon dioxide back
into the air as fast as plants remove it by
photosynthesis. So the amount of carbon
dioxide in the air should stay the same.

CO$_2$ is increasing

Changes in the amount of carbon dioxide in
our atmosphere are occurring.
The average concentration seems to be increasing.
Why do you think this is?

- More fossil fuels are being burnt than in the past.
  Power stations and factories use oil and coal as fuel.
  This releases large amounts of carbon dioxide into the
  atmosphere.

- Large areas of forest are being removed.
  In South America the trees are used for timber
  and the land is cleared for farming.
  As a result, there are fewer trees and less
  photosynthesis.
  So less carbon dioxide is being taken out of the air.

▷ Biology at work : Fertilisers

We have seen in Chapter 12 how using fertilisers
can increase the yield of crops.
The major elements in fertilisers are nitrogen (N),
phosphorus (P), and potassium (K).
Different fertilisers have different amounts of nitrates,
phosphates and potassium.
But before knowing which fertilisers to use the farmer
needs to know the nutrients already present in the soil.
Tests are carried out by the Agricultural Development
Advisory Service (ADAS).

The farmer then knows :

- the best type of fertiliser to use for his or her
  particular soil and crop.
- how much of the fertiliser to add.

Problems can occur if :

- the farmer uses too much fertiliser
- the fertiliser is added before a period of heavy rain.

The result of either of these is that fertiliser can cause
water pollution.

- Fertiliser can be washed through the soil into rivers
  and streams – this is called **leaching.**

- Once in the water it causes weeds and algae to grow.

- These plants eventually die and rot on the river bed.

- Decomposers like bacteria thrive with all the dead
  vegetation to eat.

- They multiply rapidly and use up a lot of oxygen.

- The river may become so low in oxygen that fish and
  freshwater invertebrates die.

lots of nutrients
make water
plants grow
quickly

nutrients
leach
from land

some plants don't
get enough light
and start to die

dead
plants
start to
decay

lots of microbes
feed on the dead
plants

O_2 O_2

microbes
respire

microbes multiply and use
up oxygen in respiration

shortage of oxygen
kills fish and other
animals

Adding nutrients to the environment is called **eutrophication**.

The nitrate time bomb

Nitrate fertilisers can become leached out of the soil.
They can trickle down into the bed-rock.
Some scientists believe that it is only a matter of time
before the nitrates enter our drinking water.
High nitrates in drinking water are known to cause
`blue baby syndrome'.
This stops the haemoglobin carrying enough oxygen.
The result can be respiratory failure.

Summary

- Decomposers are microbes that break down wastes and dead materials releasing nutrients. These nutrients are absorbed by plants and passed along food chains.

- Detritivores are small animals that help decomposition by feeding on detritus.

- Carbon is cycled through ecosystems by processes such as photosynthesis and respiration.

- Increase in carbon dioxide in the atmosphere contributes to the greenhouse effect and possible global warming.

- Different types of bacteria have different roles to play in the nitrogen cycle.

- Fertilisers are added to make up for shortage of nutrients in some soils.

- If nitrogen fertilisers are leached into rivers and streams they can cause pollution.

▷ Questions

1. Copy and complete:
   Bacteria and .... are able to rot down dead and .... materials. They are called ..... Detritivores are small .... that feed on decaying material called ..... The carbon dioxide concentration in the atmosphere is ..... This is because we are burning more .... fuels and clearing large areas of tropical ..... Carbon dioxide and .... vapour make up some of the .... gases.

2. a) What is the role of the following in nutrient cycles:
   i) decomposers   ii) green plants
   iii) detritivores?
   b) Explain why nutrients are used again and again in a community but energy is not.

3. The diagram shows part of the carbon cycle:

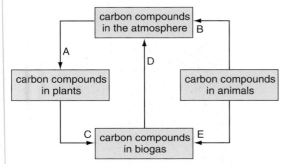

   Copy the diagram and replace the letters A to E with the correct label from this list:
      respiration   decay by bacteria
      photosynthesis   burning

4. a) Give 2 ways in which nitrogen can be added to the soil.
   b) How can nitrogen be taken out of the soil?
   c) Why do some farmers grow clover and then plough it into the soil before growing wheat?

5. The diagram shows some of the ways in which bacteria help the nitrogen cycle.

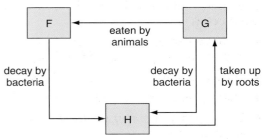

   Copy the diagram and replace letters F to H with the correct labels from this list:
   - nitrogen compounds in plants
   - nitrogen compounds in the soil
   - nitrogen compounds in animal wastes.

6. Rotting animal manure and straw can make a gas called methane.
   The decomposition takes place inside a closed tank called a **digester**.
   The gas can be piped away and used as a fuel. Design a digester to use straw and animal manure.
   - It will need to be air-tight.
   - Methane does not dissolve in water.
   - How will you get the gas to a cooker?
   Draw a sketch of your design and label it.

Further questions on page 380.

▷ Adaptation and competition

1.

Tree on its own   *Trees inside a wood*

The drawing above shows the shapes of trees grown on their own and inside a wood.
a) Write down **two** differences you can see between the tree grown on its own and those growing inside a wood. [2]
b) Trees inside the wood have to compete with each other for the things which they need to grow. List **three** things for which the trees compete. [3] (AQA)

2. Read the following information.

> Many animals and plants find it difficult to survive in hot deserts.
> - These deserts are very hot during the day, but very cold at night.
> - The ground is often sandy.
> - There is not much water.

> Camels can survive in these conditions. They have the following features.
> - They have humps in which body fat is stored.
> - They do not sweat very much.
> - They have large feet.
> - Their bodies are covered in fur.

Copy and complete the following table by explaining how each feature can help camels to survive in a desert.

Feature	How it helps survival
Has a fat store Does not sweat very much Has large feet Has fur	

[8]   (AQA)

3. The graph shows how a population of bacteria in a muddy puddle changed over a period of four days.

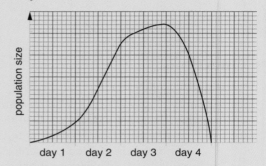

a) During which day, 1, 2, 3 or 4, is
   i) the population of the bacteria increasing most rapidly? [1]
   ii) the death rate becoming greater than the rate of reproduction? [1]
   iii) the rate of population growth beginning to be affected by limiting factors? [1]
b) State **three** factors which may limit the size of the population. [3]
c) i) What has happened to the bacteria by the end of day 4? [1]
   ii) Suggest a reason for this. [1] (OCR)

4. The graph shows the estimated number of herring present in the North Sea between 1952 and 1974.

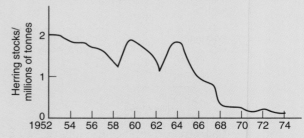

a) Suggest and explain the reason for the serious drop in herring stocks between 1964 and 1968. [2]

b) From 1976 to 1984 all herring fishing in the North Sea was banned. Suggest **one** ecological and **one** economic effect of banning herring fishing. [2]

c) Explain why fishing was banned for eight years even though herring grow to reproductive maturity in three to four years. [2]

d) Attempts have been made to protect cod and herring fisheries by allowing boats to catch a quota (limited amount) of each type of fish each year. Suggest why a quota system is only partly successful. [3] (OCR)

5. Polar bears live in areas close to the North Pole where it can be very cold. The diagram shows some of the blood vessels and the flow of blood through a polar bear's foot in cold conditions. The blood vessels are not drawn to the same scale

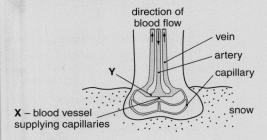

direction of blood flow
vein
artery
capillary
Y
X – blood vessel supplying capillaries
snow

a) Explain how the diameters of vessel **X** and **Y** help the polar bear to survive in cold conditions. [3]

b) Describe **one** way in which the blood flow through the foot would change in warmer conditions. [2]

c) It takes several months for younger polar bears to grow fur. During this time :
   they keep still ;
   they move only to feed off the mother's fat-rich milk ;
   they can be found huddling together.
   Choose **two** of these three points and explain how each helps a young polar bear to survive cold conditions. [1] (AQA)

6. A lynx is a type of wild cat which eats hares. The table shows the changes in the populations of these animals in an area of Canada between 1985 and 1995.
Use the information in the table to answer the following questions :

a) i) How many years did it take for the hare population to reach the size it was in 1985 ? [1]

   ii) In which year was the largest population of lynx ? [1]

Year	Number of lynxes (in thousands)	Number of hares (in thousands)
1985	72	130
1986	80	15
1987	40	85
1988	15	30
1989	7	20
1990	7	45
1991	11	55
1992	16	65
1993	25	60
1994	42	80
1995	55	130

b) When the hare population reached its peak in 1995 :
   i) What happened to the lynx population ? [1]
   ii) Suggest how this happened. [1]

c) Suggest **three** reasons for the large decrease in the number of hares from 1985 to 1986. [3]

d) In 1996 would you expect the lynx population to decrease, increase, or stay the same ? [1]

e) Since 1996 there has been a large increase in foxes which also feed on hares. Suggest :
   i) How this may affect the lynx population. [1]
   ii) Why it is affected in this way. [1] (WJEC)

▷ **Energy transfer**

7. The diagram shows part of a food web in a pond.

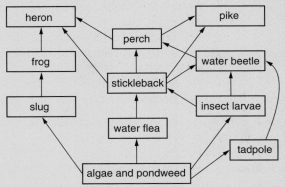

heron
pike
perch
frog
water beetle
stickleback
slug
insect larvae
water flea
tadpole
algae and pondweed

a) i) Name a carnivore shown in this food web. [1]
   ii) How many primary consumers are shown in this web ? [1]

377

Further questions on Living things and their environment

b) A local fishing club removes all of the pike from the pond. Explain what will happen to :
  i) the number of sticklebacks [1]
  ii) the number of frogs. [2]
c) The fishing club now stocks the pond with many carp. These are fish that eat a lot of plants. Explain the effect this is likely to have on the food web. [4] (EDEX)

8. Read the following account and answer the questions which follow.

> THE SCOTTISH MOORS
> The Scottish moors cover thousands of hectares of land. The main type of vegetation is heather and grass. These may grow to a height of 0.5 metre.
> The heather and grass provide food for grouse. The moors are also home to small mammals, called voles. These also feed on the heather and grass. The main predators on the moors are foxes which feed on both the grouse and the voles. During certain times of the year, the grouse are shot for food by grouse hunters. During the shoot, loud noises are made to frighten the grouse and make them fly. The hunters use guns to shoot them down.

a) Draw a food web for the organisms mentioned above, including humans. Your food web should make clear the direction of energy flow. [5]
b) Suggest what the heather and grass provide for the grouse, other than food. [1]
c) Gamekeepers try to reduce the number of foxes by shooting them.
  i) What would happen to the population of grouse if hunting and shooting foxes were banned? [1]
  ii) How would this change affect the vegetation on the moor? [1] (AQA)

9. A community in a woodland consists of oak trees, caterpillars, voles and owls. Many thousands of caterpillars feed on the leaves of a single oak tree. A single vole may eat a hundred caterpillars each day. An owl may eat three voles in one day.
a) The diagram shows four pyramids of numbers.

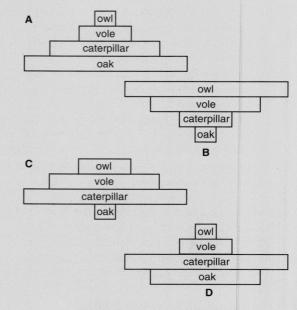

i)   Which **pyramid of numbers** is correct for this wooded community? [1]
ii) What is meant by the term **biomass**? [1]
iii) Draw a **pyramid of biomass** for the woodland community. [2]
iv) Explain how energy is lost to the surroundings between each level of your pyramid of biomass. [1]
b) In a town near to the woodland many additional houses and factories are built. Suggest and explain **one** effect this might have on the woodland community. [2] (OCR)

10. The diagram below shows the flow of energy through a food chain.

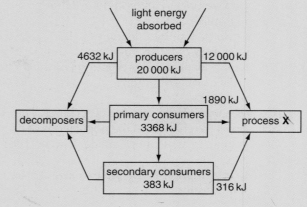

a) i) Name the process that occurs when energy is absorbed by the producers. [1]

ii) What energy change occurs in this process ? [1]

b) i) Name the process marked **X** in the diagram. [1]

ii) In what form is the energy released at **X** ? [1]

iii) What percentage of energy absorbed by the producers is then released by them in process **X** ? [1]   (WJEC)

11. The diagram shows the flow of energy through 1 m² of an ecosystem.

unit in each case is kJ per m² per year

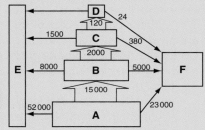

Key

A   producers

B   primary consumers

C   secondary consumers

D   tertiary consumers

E   heat transfer to environment

F   detritus feeders and decomposers

a) i) Name the process in which green plants transfer solar energy into chemical compounds.

ii) Name the process in living organisms which results in the transfer of heat to the environment. [1]

b) Tertiary consumers receive energy from secondary consumers.

i) Calculate the amount of heat energy which tertiary consumers transfer to the environment as a percentage of the energy received from secondary consumers. Show your working. [2]

ii) Primary consumers transfer a low percentage of their energy intake to the environment as heat. Tertiary consumers transfer a much higher percentage of their energy intake to the environment as heat. The tertiary consumers are mainly mammals and birds. The primary consumers are mainly insects and molluscs. Explain why mammals and birds lose a greater percentage of their energy intake to the environment as heat than do insects and molluscs. [2] (AQA)

12. a) Pollution caused by oil spills at sea can be a major environmental problem. Give **three** ways by which oil pollution of water can be treated. [3]

b) There is concern about increasing levels of nitrates in some water supplies.

i) Explain why the level of nitrates in water is increasing. [2]

ii) What effect does the increase in nitrate level have on plant growth ? [1]

iii) What effect does the increase in concentration of nitrates have on the level of dissolved oxygen in the river water ? [1]

c) Many farmers use various pesticides.

i) State **one** benefit to the farmer of using pesticides. [1]

ii) State **one** problem that can be caused in food webs by the use of pesticides. [1]   (AQA)

13. Under the following headings, compare the use of natural (organic) fertilisers with the use of artificial (inorganic) fertilisers.

a) Cost.

b) Way in which they are spread.

c) Length of effect in the soil.

d) Effect on soil structure.

e) Pollution risk. [10]   (OCR)

▷ **Nutrient cycling**

14. A paper factory pumps liquid effluent into a river. The effluent contains sugar. The diagram shows changes in water conditions for several kilometres downstream from the factory outflow.

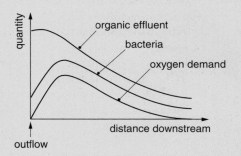

a) Explain why there is first an increase and then a decrease in the number of bacteria downstream from the outflow. [3]

Further questions on Living things and their environment

b) Oxygen demand is the amount of oxygen needed by organisms living in a river. State and explain how the oxygen demand changes as the number of bacteria in the river water increases. [2]

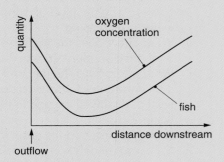

c) The diagram shows changes in oxygen concentration and number of fish downstream from the outflow. Explain why the curve of fish numbers is the same shape as that of oxygen concentration. [2]

d) The oxygen concentration in the river water increases with distance from the outflow. Suggest **two** ways in which this oxygen may enter the water. [2] (OCR)

15. Between 1880 and 1980 it has been estimated that about 40% of all tropical rainforest was destroyed; much of it was destroyed by burning.

a) Give **three** reasons why this large-scale deforestation has happened. [3]

b) Large-scale deforestation is affecting the levels of carbon dioxide in the air.
   i) What is happening to carbon dioxide levels? [1]
   ii) How does deforestation cause a change in the carbon dioxide levels? [2]
   iii) Explain some long-term effects that deforestation is likely to have on climate and soil fertility. [5]

c) Many types of habitat are being destroyed, with serious effects on the wildlife living there. What methods can scientists and governments use to protect this wildlife? [2] (EDEX)

16. This is a diagram of the carbon cycle.

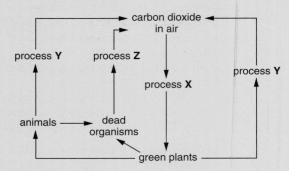

a) Name the processes **X** and **Y**. [2]

b) How does the carbon transferred from green plants become part of the body of an animal? [1]

c) Under the right conditions green plants can be changed to peat or coal.
   i) How does the carbon in coal become part of the carbon dioxide in the air? [1]
   ii) What environmental problem does this carbon dioxide cause? [1]
   iii) What is process **Z**? [1] (OCR)

17. In some countries farmers clear areas of forest by burning. The ash helps crops to grow well at first, but after a few years good crops cannot be grown. On mountain slopes the soil is easily washed away by heavy rain because there are no tree roots to hold it together.

a) How does the ash help the crops to grow well at first? [2]

b) Many farmers keep large numbers of cattle. Apart from producing carbon dioxide, explain how cattle make a particularly large contribution to the greenhouse effect? [2]

c) An area of forest was cut down. The concentration of nitrate in a stream in this area was measured before and after the forest was cut. The table shows the results.

Time	Concentration of nitrate in stream (mg per litre)
6 months before cutting	0.3
2 months before cutting	0.3
2 months after cutting	2.2
6 months after cutting	63.0

Suggest an explanation for the change in nitrate concentration. [2] (AQA)

18. Gardeners put leaves and weeds in a compost heap.
They leave this to rot into a peaty compost which is rich in plant nutrients, and can be used to improve soil fertility.

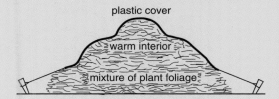

plastic cover

warm interior

mixture of plant foliage

Three gardeners living in different parts of Britain made compost heaps on the same day in Spring.
To speed the rotting process they covered them with plastic sheets and mixed them up each week using a fork.
The table gives some information about where the gardeners lived.

Gardener	Town	Average temperature /°C	Average annual rainfall /cm
A	London	13.2	61.0
B	Manchester	12.0	85.9
C	Edinburgh	11.0	69.9

a) i) Suggest which gardener's compost heap will be ready first. [1]
   ii) Explain your answer. [1]
b) How does mixing up the heap help speed up rotting? [1]
c) The gardener in Manchester forgot to replace the plastic sheet over his compost heap. Explain how this might affect the rotting. [1] (OCR)

19. The diagram shows the nitrogen cycle but some parts are missing.
a) Copy and complete the nitrogen cycle by writing the correct letter in each of the boxes provided. You may use each letter once, more than once, or not at all.
Choose the letters from the table below.
The first one has been done for you. [5]

Letter	A	B	C	D	E
Part of nitrogen cycle	Urine and faeces	Nitrogen fixation in root nodules e.g. of pea plants	Denitrifying bacteria	Death	Decay

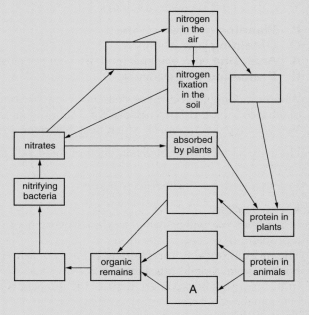

b) Suggest what might happen to a plant if it could not absorb nitrates. [1]
c) i) Why is it important that nitrogen is cycled? [2]
   ii) Carbon is also cycled.
      Name **two** processes which release carbon dioxide into the atmosphere. [2] (EDEX)

Doing your course work

GCSE exams have 20% of the marks awarded for course work. Often these marks will be awarded by your teacher while watching you do experiments or investigations in the laboratory.

Your marks will be awarded under 4 headings:

P   **Planning** to collect evidence
O   **Obtaining** your evidence
A   **Analysing** your evidence and drawing conclusions
E   **Evaluating** your evidence.

When marking you on these skills, your teacher has a checklist of what to look for. The checklist for 'Planning' is shown below. You will be given the mark which best describes your performance.

Here are some more details on each of the 4 skill areas:

'Practical skills are important'

P. Planning to collect evidence

- **Fair testing**
Sometimes you will be asked to plan an investigation to solve a problem or answer a question.
The most important thing here is to devise a *fair test*.
For example, look at Investigation 3.7 on page 37.
In this investigation you are comparing the action of biological and non-biological washing powder.
To make it a fair test, you should use the *same* stain, the *same* temperature, the *same* amount of powder, the *same* volume of water, the *same* wash time and the *same* amount of stirring.
This is called 'controlling the variables' so that only *one* variable changes (the type of washing powder).

- **Predicting**
Before starting your practical work, you should try to predict what you think will happen. To gain higher marks it is important to base your prediction on the science you know.
Say what you think will happen and then *explain why*.
Remember that you can use text-books and *other sources of information* to help you in your predicting and planning.

- **Selecting the most suitable apparatus**
It is important to use the most suitable equipment.
For example, to measure the volume of $100 \, cm^3$ of water, you should choose a measuring cylinder, not a beaker with a $100 \, cm^3$ mark on it. (Why?)
To measure a smaller volume of water you should choose a narrower measuring cylinder. (Why?)

Checklist for skill **P** PLANNING YOUR WORK	
Candidates:	Marks awarded
• plan a simple method to collect evidence	**2**
• plan to collect evidence that will answer your question • plan to use suitable equipment or other ways to get evidence	**4**
• use scientific knowledge to: – plan and present your method, – identify key factors to vary or control, – make a prediction if possible • decide on a suitable number and range of readings (or observations) to collect	**6**
• use detailed scientific knowledge to: – plan and present your strategy (the approach you have decided on) – aim for precise and reliable evidence – justify your prediction if you made one • use information from other sources, or from preliminary work in your plan	**8**

- **Deciding the number and range of your readings**

You need to consider **how many** measurements or observations to make in your experiments. Four is the minimum number of readings if you plan to show your results on a graph. Aim to collect at least 5 readings.

Your results must also cover a suitable **range** to answer the original question. For example, if you are looking at the effect of temperature on the rate of enzyme action, would you do tests at 20°C, 21°C, 22°C and 23°C? This is not a good range.

You also need to decide whether you need to repeat the tests and so get average readings.
This can improve the **reliability** of your results.

Reliability is good if someone following your method would be likely to get the same results as you

- **Safety**

The tests that you plan must be safe. You must consult your teacher to ensure that your plan is safe.

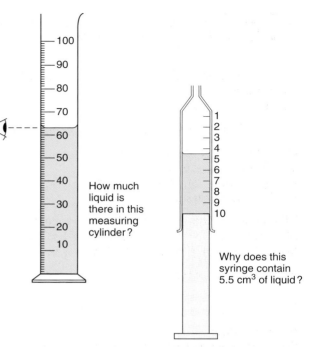

How much liquid is there in this measuring cylinder?

Why does this syringe contain 5.5 cm³ of liquid?

O. Obtaining your evidence

- **Making observations accurately**

Accuracy is important, as well as taking care in checking your readings.
Remember to correct for **zero-errors** (for example you should check that your balance reads zero before you start to use it).

When reading a scale, make sure you look at right-angles to it, so that you read the correct number.
When using a measuring cylinder, remember to read the **bottom** of the meniscus.

Consider whether using a **datalogger** will improve the quality of the evidence that you collect.

If one of your results seems unusual, make sure you repeat it. If it was an error, you do not have to include it when you consider your results at the end.

- **Recording your results**

Record your results in a table, labelling each column with the **quantity** you are measuring and its **unit**.

Here is a table for recording the effect of temperature on the rate of fermentation:

The first column shows the **independent variable** – this is what you change deliberately, step by step.
The second column shows the **dependent** variable – the size of this variable depends on the first one.
All other variables must be **controlled** (kept constant).

Checklist for skill **O** **OBTAINING YOUR EVIDENCE**	
Candidates :	Marks awarded
• use simple equipment safely to collect some results	2
• make adequate observations or measurements to answer your question • record the results	4
• make observations or measurements, – with sufficient readings, – which are accurate, and – repeat them if necessary • record the results clearly and accurately	6
• carry out your practical work – with precision and skill, – to obtain and record reliable evidence, – with a good number and range of readings	8

Fermentation by yeast

Temperature (°C)	Volume of carbon dioxide collected (cm³)
10	0.9
20	1.8
30	2.4
40	3.5

In some investigations you will need to split the second column into 3 or 4 to record repeated measurements. The last column will be your average reading

A. Analysing your evidence & drawing conclusions

• *Drawing graphs and bar-charts*

Having recorded your results, you will often need to draw a graph.

If the first column in your table (the independent variable) can have a continuous range of values, then use a line-graph. However if the first column can only have certain fixed values, then use a bar-chart.

If you draw a line-graph, do it in the steps shown here :

1) Choose simple scales.
   For example,
   1 large square = 1 centimetre (or 2 cm, 5 cm, 10 cm)
   Never choose an awkward scale like
   1 square = 3 cm or 7 cm

2) Plot the point and mark them neatly. Re-check each one.

3) If the points look as though they form a straight line, draw the best straight line through them with a ruler (and pencil).
   Check that it looks the best line.

4) If the points form a curve, draw a 'free-hand' curve of best fit.
   Never join the points 'dot-to-dot' with a ruler.

5) If a point is clearly off the line, you should always use your apparatus to repeat the measurement and check it.

• *Drawing a conclusion*

Every experiment has a 'conclusion'. This is a summary of what you found out (or sometimes what you didn't find !) Always look at your results or graph or chart to decide what you have discovered.
What reasonable or 'valid' deduction can be made from your results ? What pattern can you see ?

For example, from the photosynthesis investigation, shown in the graph you might conclude :
• As the distance between the lamp and the plant increases, the number of bubbles decreases..
• This is because a decrease in light intensity *reduces* the rate of photosynthesis

Then use your scientific knowledge to *explain* your conclusion.

Remember to refer back to your prediction, if you made one, and to *explain* why your results support it or not.

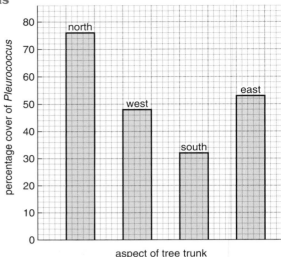

Example of a bar-chart showing the growth of the alga Pleurococcus on different sides of a tree trunk

Checklist for skill **A** ANALYSING YOUR EVIDENCE	
Candidates :	Marks awarded
• state simply what was found out	**2**
• show the results in simple diagrams, charts or graphs to help explain your evidence • spot any trends and patterns in the results	**4**
• draw and use diagrams, charts, graphs (with a line of best fit), or calculate answers from the results • draw a conclusion that fits with your evidence and explain it using your scientific knowledge	**6**
• use detailed scientific knowledge to explain a valid conclusion (drawn from analysing your evidence) • explain how well the results agree or disagree with any prediction made earlier	**8**

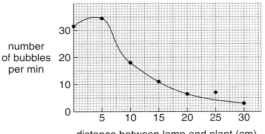

E. Evaluating your evidence

Having drawn your conclusions, you should now think about the *quality* of your investigation.
Ask yourself these questions to see if you could have improved your investigation:
- Were my results accurate?
- Did any seem strange compared to the others? These are 'anomalous' results.
- Should I have repeated some tests to get more reliable results? Could I improve the method?
- Did I get a suitable range of results?
- If there is a pattern in my results, is it only true for the range of values I used? Would the pattern continue beyond this range?
- Would it be useful to check my graph by taking readings *between* the values that I originally chose?
  For example, in the graph opposite, more points between 20 cm and 30 cm would confirm this shape of the curve.
- How could I develop my investigation to answer these questions, if given time?

Checklist for skill **E** **EVALUATING YOUR EVIDENCE**	
Candidates:	Marks awarded
• make a relevant comment about the method used or the results obtained	2
• comment on the accuracy of the results, pointing out any anomalous ones • comment on whether the method was a good one and suggest changes to improve it	4

• look at the evidence and:
   – comment on its reliability,
   – explain any anomalous results,
   – explain whether you have enough to support a firm conclusion
 • describe in detail further work that would give more evidence for the conclusion.
	6

Writing up your practical work

Aim to make your experimental write-ups as clear and concise as possible.
Try to accurately describe what you did (your method) without including unnnecessary details.
A good idea is to use a step-by-step approach to describe the different stages of your experiment or investigation.
For example, this is how you could write what you did when using pectinase enzyme to extract apple juice (see page 37):

The aim of an account like this is to give enough information so that another person could carry out your experiment in exactly the same way.

Diagrams are often useful in experimental write-ups.
They can show the 'set-up' of an experiment far better than a written description can.

1. I cut an apple in two halves, and chopped each half into small pieces.
2. I put the pieces into separate beakers labelled A and B.
3. I added 2 cm^3 of pectinase enzyme to the apple in beaker A, and 2 cm^3 of water to the apple in beaker B.
4. I placed both beakers in a water bath at 40°C.
5. I started the stop clock.
6. After 20 minutes, I filtered the juice from each of the apple pieces.

Use sub-headings to divide up your account:
Title – this should give the purpose of the experiment.
Prediction – this explains what you think will happen in an investigation.
Method – this describes 'what you did' and may include a list of the apparatus used and safety aspects.
Results – this is what you found and may include tables, graphs, calculations and written accounts.
Conclusion – this is an interpretation of your results and should refer back to your prediction if you made one.
Evaluation – this is an assessment of your experiment and how you could improve it if you did it again

Diagrams and drawings

Diagrams can be used to show what you have done in an experiment. A diagram of your experimental set-up can show the positions of different pieces of apparatus.

The photograh shows the apparatus used to investigate the effect of light intensity on the rate of photosynthesis. The diagram below shows clearly the important features of the set-up.

Such a diagram should be simple and two-dimensional.
A clear outline of the apparatus should be drawn. Try to avoid unnecessary detail.

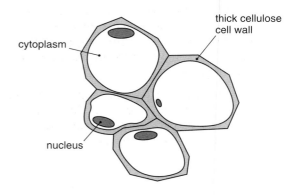

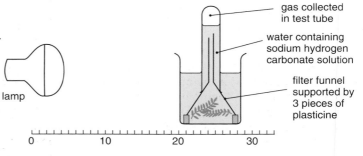

lamp

gas collected in test tube

water containing sodium hydrogen carbonate solution

filter funnel supported by 3 pieces of plasticine

Relevant diagrams can save a lot of writing and given an immediate visual impression of your experiment.

Drawings are used to show **biological** details. You need to be able to **observe** features of the specimen.
Try to make sure that your drawing shows the important details and is in proportion.

Here are some simple rules for drawings:
- Don't make your drawings too small – use a half A4 page of plain paper.
- Use a sharpened HB pencil and have an eraser handy.
- Use clear clean lines for your drawing.
- Avoid shading and the use of coloured pencils.
- Draw only what you can see in the specimen – it might not contain everything that's in a textbook drawing!
- Use relevant labels and clear label-lines arranged around the drawing.
- Don't try to draw too much – 2 or 3 cells well drawn is better than a dozen or so cells that lack detail and proportion.

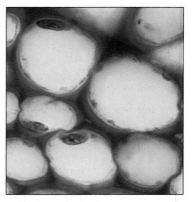

thick cellulose cell wall

cytoplasm

nucleus

Suggestions for a revision programme

1. Read the summary at the end of the chapter to gain some idea of the contents.
   Then read through the chapter looking at particular points in more detail, before reading the summary again.

2. Covering up the summary, check yourself against the fill-in-the-missing-word sentences at the end of the chapter.

   Remember to **re-read** the summary and to **review** each chapter after the correct revision intervals of 10 minutes, then 1 day, then 1 week (as explained on page 389). Continue in this way with all the other chapters in the book.

3. While reading through the summaries and chapters like this, it is useful to collect together all the statements in red and yellow boxes on a single sheet of paper. At this stage you will also find the checklists and revision quizzes from the Support Pack useful.

4. While you are going right through the book, do this for *every* chapter:
   a) Attempt the questions on the 'Further Questions' pages. These are all GCSE questions from previous years. Your teacher will be able to tell you which are the most important ones for your specification.
      You can check against your own particular specification on www.biologyforyou.co.uk.
   b) If there are multiple-choice questions in your examination, read the comments about them on page 391.

5. Read the section on 'Examination technique' on page 390, and check the dates of your exams. Have you enough time to complete your revision before then ?

6. Several weeks before the examination, ask your teacher for copies of the examination papers from previous years. These 'past papers' will help you to see :
   – the particular style and timing of your examination
   – the way the questions are asked, and the amount of detail needed
   – which topics and questions are asked most often and which suit you personally.

When doing these past papers, try to get used to doing the questions *in the specified time* – just like it will be in the examination.

It may be possible for your teacher to read out to you the reports of examiners who have marked these papers in previous years.

The Support Pack contains some extra past paper questions with guidance given on how to answer them. It also contains the answers at all the past paper 'Further questions' included in this book.

Revision techniques

Why should you revise?

You cannot expect to remember all the Biology that you have studied unless you revise. It is important to review all your course, so that you can answer the examination questions.

Where should you revise?

In a quiet room (perhaps a bedroom), with a table and a clock. The room should be comfortably warm and brightly lighted. A reading lamp on the table helps you to concentrate on your work and reduces eye-strain.

When should you revise?

Start your revision early each evening, before your brain gets tired.

How should you revise?

If you sit down to revise without thinking of a definite finishing time, you will find that your learning efficiency falls lower and lower and lower.

If you sit down to revise, saying to yourself that you will definitely stop work after 2 hours, then your learning efficiency falls at the beginning but **rises towards the end** as your brain realises it is coming to the end of the session (see the first graph).

We can use this U-shaped curve to help us work more efficiently by splitting a 2 hour session into 4 shorter sessions, each of about 25 minutes with a short, **planned** break between them.
The breaks **must** be planned beforehand so that the graph rises near the end of each short session.
The coloured area on the graph shows how much you gain:

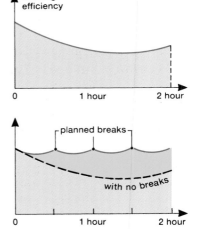

For example, if you start your revision at 6.00 p.m., you should look at your clock or watch and say to yourself, 'I will work until 6.25 p.m. and then stop – not earlier and not later.'
At 6.25 p.m. you should leave the table for a relaxation break of 10 minutes (or less), returning by 6.35 p.m. when you should say to yourself, 'I will work until 7.00 p.m. and then stop – not earlier and not later.'

Continuing in this way is more efficient **and** causes less strain on you.

You get through more work **and** you feel less tired.

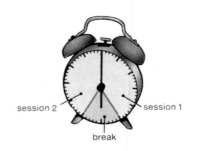

How often should you revise ?

The diagram shows a graph of the amount of information that your memory can recall at different times after you have finished a revision session :

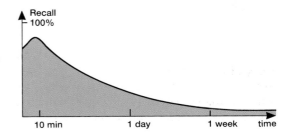

Surprisingly, the graph rises at the beginning. This is because your brain is still sorting out the information that you have been learning.
The graph soon falls rapidly so that after 1 day you may remember only about a quarter of what you had learned.

There are two ways of improving your recall and raising this graph.

● 1. If you briefly **revise the same work again after 10 minutes** (at the high point of the graph) then the graph falls much more slowly.
This fits in with your 10-minute break between revision sessions.
Using the example on the opposite page, when you return to your table at 6.35 p.m., the first thing you should do is **review**, briefly, the work you learned before 6.25 p.m.

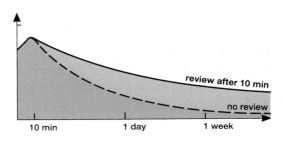

The graph can be lifted again by briefly reviewing the work **after 1 day** and then again **after 1 week**. That is, on Tuesday night you should look through the work you learned on Monday night and the work you learned on the previous Tuesday night, so that it is fixed quite firmly in your long-term memory.

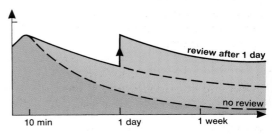

● 2. Another method of improving your memory is by taking care to try to **understand** all parts of your work. This makes all the graphs higher.
If you learn your work in a parrot-fashion (as you have to do with telephone numbers), all these graphs will be lower. On the occasions when you have to learn facts by heart, try to picture them as exaggerated, colourful images in your mind.

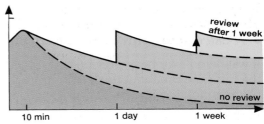

Remember: **the most important points about revision are that it must occur often and be repeated at the right intervals.**

	Mon	Tues	Wed	Thur	Fri
Biology	chap 3	chap 4	p25-9		
Chemistry	p 24-9	chap 5	p67		
Physics	p36-42				
History	chap 3				

Examination technique

In the weeks before the examinations:

Attempt as many 'past papers' as you can so that you get used to the style of the questions and the timing of them.

Note which topics occur most often and revise them thoroughly, using the techniques explained on previous pages.

Read through the statements in the red and yellow boxes and the chapter summaries.

Just before the examinations:

Collect together the equipment you will need:
- Two pens, in case one dries up.
- At least one sharpened pencil for drawing diagrams.
- A rubber and a ruler for diagrams.
  Diagrams usually look best if they are drawn in pencil and labelled in ink.
  Coloured pencils can be useful for making part of a diagram clearer, for instance, using red for oxygenated blood and blue for deoxygenated blood or colouring chloroplasts in green
- A watch for pacing yourself during the examination. The clock in the examination room may be difficult to see.
- **A calculator (with good batteries).**

It will help if you have previously collected all the information about the length and style of the examination papers (for **all** your subjects) as shown below:

Date, time and room	Subject, paper number and tier	Length (hours)	Types of question: – structured? – single word answers? – longer answers? – essays?	Sections?	Details of choice (if any)	Approximate time per page (minutes)
3rd June 9.30 Hall	Science (Double Award) Paper 1 (Biology) Foundation Tier	$1\frac{1}{2}$	Structured questions (with single-word answers and longer answers)	1	no choice	4–6 min.

In the examination room :

Read the front of the examination paper carefully.
It gives you important information.

Answering 'structured' questions :

- Read the information at the start of each question carefully. Make sure you understand what the question is about, and what you are expected to do.

- Pace yourself with a watch so you don't run out of time. If you have spare time at the end, use it wisely to check over your answers.

How much detail do you need to give ?

- The question gives you clues :
  - Give short answers to questions which start : '**State** . . .' or '**List** . . .' or '**Name** . . .'.
  - Give longer answers if you are asked to '**Explain** . . .' or '**Describe** . . .' or asked '**Why does** . . ?'.

- Look for the marks awarded for each part of the question. It is usually given in brackets, e.g. [2]. This tells you how many points the examiner is looking for in your answer.

- The number of lines of space is also a guide to how much you are expected to write.

- Always show the steps in your working out of calculations. This way, you can gain marks for the way you tackle the problem, even if your final answer is wrong.

- Try to write something for *every* part of each question.

- Don't explain something just because you know how to ! You only earn marks for explaining exactly what the question asks.

- Follow the instructions given in the question. If it asks for one answer, give only one answer. Sometimes you are given a list of alternatives to choose from. If you include more answers than asked for, any wrong answers will cancel out your right ones !

NATIONAL EXAMINING BOARD

Science : Biology
Foundation Tier
3rd June
9.30 a.m.

Time : 1 hour 30 minutes

Answer **all** the questions.

In calculations, show clearly how you work out your answer.

Calculators may be used.

Mark allocations are shown in the right-hand margin.

In what ways is your examination paper different from this one ?

If your exam includes 'multiple-choice' questions :

- Read the instructions very carefully.

- If there is a separate answer sheet, mark it exactly as you are instructed, and take care to mark your answer opposite the correct question number.

- Even if the answer looks obvious, you should look at all the alternatives before making a decision.

- If you do not know the correct answer and have to guess, then you can improve your chances by first eliminating as many wrong answers as possible.

- Ensure you give an answer to every question.

▷ Key skills

As you study Science or Biology, you will need
to use some general skills along the way.
These general learning skills are very important
whatever subjects you take or job you go on to do.

The Government has recognised just how important
the skills are by introducing a new qualification.
It is called the **Key Skills Qualification**.
There are six key skills :

- **Communication**
- **Application of number**
- **Information Technology (IT)**
- **Working with others**
- **Problem solving**
- **Improving your own learning**

Key skills are important in all jobs !

The first three of these key skills will be assessed by exams
and by evidence put together in a portfolio.
You can see what you have to do to get this qualification
in the criteria below.
You will probably be aiming for Level 2 at GCSE.
If you go for Level 2, you will cover the Level 1 criteria as well.

Communication

In this key skill you will be expected to :

- **Hold discussions.**
- **Give presentations.**
- **Read and summarise information.**
- **Write documents.**

You will do these as you go through your course and producing your
course work will help.
Look at the criteria below :

What you must do	Evidence
Contribute to a discussion	Make clear, relevant contributions : listen and respond to what others say ; help to move the discussion forward
Give a short talk, using an image	Speak clearly ; structure your talk ; use an image to make your main points clear
Read and summarise information from two extended documents (which include at least one image)	Select and read relevant material ; identify accurately main points and lines of reasoning ; summarise information to suit your purpose
Write two different types of document (one piece of writing should be an extended document and include at least one image)	Present information in an appropriate form ; use a structure and style of writing to suit your task ; make sure your text is legible and that spelling, punctuation and grammar are accurate, so that your meaning is clear

Application of number

In this key skill you will be expected to :

- **Obtain and interpret information.**
- **Carry out calculations.**
- **Interpret and present the results of calculations.**

What you must do	Evidence
Interpret information from two different sources (including material containing a graph)	Choose how to obtain the information, selecting appropriate methods to get the results you need ; obtain the relevant information
Carry out calculations to do with : • amount and sizes • scales and proportions • handling statistics • using formulae	Carry out your calculations, clearly showing your methods and level of accuracy ; check your methods and correct any errors, and make sure that your results make sense
Interpret the results of your calculations and present your findings. You must use at least one diagram, one chart (table) and one graph	Select the best ways to present your findings ; present your findings clearly and describe your methods ; explain how the results of your calculations answer your enquiry

Information Technology

In this key skill you will be expected to :

- **Use the internet and CD ROMs to collect information.**
- **Use IT to produce documents to best effect.**

What you must do	Evidence
Search for and select information for two different purposes	Identify the information you need and where to get it ; carry out effective searches ; select information that is relevant to your enquiry
Explore and develop information, and derive new information, and derive new information, for two different purposes	Enter and bring together information using formats, such as tables, that help development ; explore information (for example, by changing information in a spread sheet model) ; develop information and derive new information (for example by modelling a process on a computer)
Present combined information for two different purposes This work must include at least one example of text, one example of images and one example of numbers	Select and use appropriate layouts for presenting combined information in a consistent way (for example by use of margins, headings, borders, font size, etc.) ; develop the presentation to suit your purpose and types of information ; make sure your work is accurate, clear and saved appropriately

Careers

Have you thought what you want to do
when you leave school?
Biology can open the door to many careers.
It is often a good 'link subject' between
science and arts subjets.
So if you are looking to 'keep your options open'
at A-level, then Biology will fit in well with many
non-science subjects.
But hopefully you will want to learn more
about Biology because you enjoy it!
Here are some careers in which further study
in Biology will be an advantage, if not a
requirement:

agricultural biologist
animal technician
bacteriologist
biochemist
biotechnologist
botanist
brewer
Civil Service scientific officer
conservationist
dental technician
dentist
doctor
ecologist
environmental biologist
environmental health officer
farming and agriculture
farm manager
fish farming
food scientist
forensic scientist
forestry
freshwater biologist
geneticist
health scientist
horticulturalist
information scientist
journalist (science)
laboratory technician
lecturer in science
manager in industry
marine biologist
marketing

medical laboratory scientist
microbiologist
nurse
oceanographer
optician
pathologist
pharmacist
pharmacologist
physiologist
pollution controller
research biologist
soil scientist
sport scientist
teacher of science
veterinary surgeon/assistant
waste disposal scientist
water technologist
zoologist

An environmental scientist testing water

A pharmacist

a vet

an arctic ecologist

a biochemist

a farmer

a marine biologist

a botanist

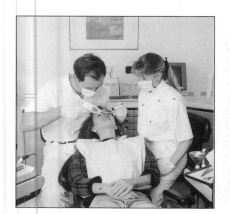

a dentist

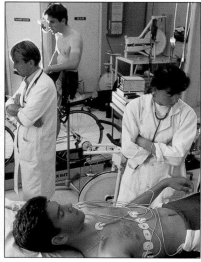

a sports scientist

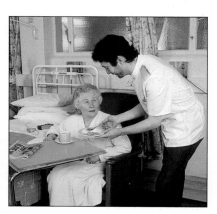

a nurse

Index

I

identical twins   168, 292
immunity   99, 179, 180
implantation   160, 162, 165
impulses   120, 123, 125, 144
in vitro fertilisation   167, 291
infections   174, 175, 176
influenza   173, 175, 181
inherited
    characteristics   255, 272,
        280–91, 337
    diseases   286–8, 289
injuries   151
insecticides   300
insects
    pests   300, 348, 364
    pollinating   235, 238, 263,
        267
    predators and prey   342, 365
    stings   365
    structure   139, 263
insemination, artificial   291
insulation of the body   47, 109
insulin   108, 114, 289
intestines   26, 34, 59, 60, 61, 268
invertebrates   88, 260, 262
iodine   32, 52, 206
iron   52, 98
irradiation   191

J

jellyfish   137, 260
Jenner, Edward   181
joints   138, 142–3, 144, 150, 151

K

keys to identify species   257
kidneys   47, 88, 107, 111–15
kilojoules   48, 49
kingdoms   257–9, 268–9
'kiss of life'   80
knees   142, 145, 151
Koch, Robert   171

L

lacteal   61
lactic acid   82
lactose   46
larvae   263, 264, 337
larynx   75
leaching   373, 374
leaves   16, 209, 214, 216–18, 227
legumes   231, 373
lenses   130, 131
levers   142
life processes   6
ligaments   131, 142, 151
light
    effect on plants   221, 228, 243
    energy   205, 355, 362
    intensity   211, 212, 217
    for photosynthesis   329
lightning   373
limbs   139, 140, 144
limiting factors   212
lipases   32, 38, 60

liquid skeletons   137
liquids   18, 19
Lister, Joseph   177
liver   46, 60, 107, 108, 111, 189
liverworts   266
lungs   74–7, 83, 93, 140, 187, 265
Luteinising Hormone (LH)   163
lymphocytes   97, 99, 180

M

malaria   65, 176, 183, 288, 331,
    348, 364
male reproductive system   157
mammals   139, 155, 265, 303, 305
mammary glands   265
man   159, 189, 277
mark, release, recapture   335
marrow (bone)   98, 99, 199, 140
measles   173, 179, 181
meat   145, 210, 361
medicines   182, 185, 210
medulla of the brain   125
meiosis   277
melanin   285
membranes   21–4, 26, 75, 161
Mendel, Gregor   279
menstruation   162, 163
metabolic rate   50, 132, 189
metals, toxic   306, 349
microbes
    decomposers   330, 352, 355,
        369
    causing disease   171
    protection from   178
    useful   171, 289, 309, 311–15,
        316–17, 318, 319
micropyles   239
microscopes   9
milk   52, 59, 190, 287, 290,
    311–12
mineral salts   218, 230
minerals   44, 51, 52
mining   306
mitochondria   9, 70
mitosis   276
molecules   18, 19, 27, 31, 57, 106
molluscs   261
monocultures   231
mosquitoes   65, 176, 183, 331,
    364
moths   301, 342, 357
motor neurone disease   122
motor neurones   119, 120, 122,
    123
moulds   182, 269, 364
moulting   138, 262
mouth   56, 58
movement   137, 138, 142, 143–5
    146–7, 148–9
mucus   58, 74, 159, 286
multiple sclerosis   120
mumps   181
muscle
    antagonistic pairs   144, 146
    cells   70, 122
    control   122, 143, 144, 145
    damaged   151
    during exercise   79, 82

of the eye   130, 131
fibres   143, 145, 151
heart   84, 91–2, 93, 94, 102,
    143
intercostal   76
for movement   137, 144, 145
voluntary, involuntary   143
mutations   285
mutualism   63
mycelium   172
myriapods   262

N

National Parks   351
natural fertilisers   219, 318, 375
natural selection   298–301, 304,
    305, 306, 337, 342
nectar   64, 235, 238
nephrons   112, 113
nerve impulses   120, 128
nerve cells (neurones)   119–20,
    122, 123, 125, 181
nerves   119, 120, 130, 131, 143,
    144
nervous system   118–125, 137,
    186, 188
niche of organisms   353, 357
nitrates   209, 218, 230, 269, 373–4
nitrifying bacteria   373
nitrogen   72, 209, 369
nitrogen cycle   373
nitrogen–fixing bacteria   373
nose   126, 127
nuclei of cells   9, 156, 159
nucleotide   297
nutrient film technique   220
nutrients   218, 219, 220, 369–70

O

obesity   50
oesophagus   59
oestrogen   158, 163, 166
oil spills   349, 352
oils in seeds   209
onion cells   11, 24, 206
optical fibres   66
organs
    animal   15, 155, 157, 158,
        277
    plant   16, 233, 235, 237
orgasm   159
osmosis   21–2, 24–5, 191, 215,
    226
ossicles of the ear   128, 129
oval window   128
ovaries
    animals   155, 277
    human   158–9, 162, 163, 164,
        165
    plants   235, 237, 239, 240,
        277
oviducts   158, 159, 160, 162, 165
ovulation   158, 162, 163
ovules   235, 237, 239, 240
oxygen
    in blood 77, 88, 89–90, 98, 101
    160

debt   82
to muscles   79, 82
and photosynthesis   209, 216
used in respiration   69, 72, 81
in soil   230
oxyhaemoglobin   98
ozone layer   348

P

pacemakers   94, 102
palisade cells and tissue   16
pancreas   60, 107, 108
paralysis   122, 181
parasites   182, 260, 269, 330, 331
partially permeable membranes 21,
    23, 24
Pasteur, Louis   171, 179, 190
pasteurisation   190
pathogens   182
pectinases   37
penicillin   182
penis   157, 158, 164
periodontal disease   56
periods   158, 162, 165, 166
peristalsis   59
permeable membranes   21, 23, 24
pesticides   320–1, 349, 364–5
pests   176, 300, 340, 364
petals   235, 236, 238, 240
pH   31, 34, 60, 107
phagocytes   97, 99
phenotypes   280, 281
phloem   224, 230
phosphorus   218, 219, 369, 374
photosynthesis   16, 205, 217, 362
phototropism   243
phytoplankton   356, 359
pills, contraceptive   164, 165
pituitary glands   132, 163, 166
placenta   160, 161
plankton   68, 356, 359, 361, 364
plant
    cells   8, 9, 11, 22, 23, 37, 209
    classification   266–8
    fat   47
    food stores   209
    growth   218–21
    organs   16
    responses   243
plaque   56
plasma   97, 98, 100, 101, 103
plasmid   179, 329
Plasmodium   65, 195
plasmolysis   24
platelets   97, 100
pleural membrane   75
plumules   242
poisonous waste   53, 174, 179,,
    306
poisons   26, 83, 99, 300, 333
    see also toxins
poliomyelitis   181
pollen   64, 235, 237, 238, 239, 277
pollination   237, 238–9, 263, 267
pollution
    of air   301, 306
    from oil and plastic   349, 352
    of water   219, 333, 374

Acknowledgements

I would like to thank John Jones, Robin Goldney and the Governors of Poynton County High School for arranging my secondment in order to write this book.

I am indebted to Nick Paul for all the help that he has given me during the re-write of *Biology for You*. I would particularly like to thank him for writing the Biotechnology chapter.

Thanks to Bob Wakefield and Margaret Bramwell for reviewing and improving the manuscript. I am particularly indebted to Bob for the many original ideas that he has selflessly given to the book and for his realism and sense of humour.

Thanks are also due to Nick Paul, Sue Adamson and Damian Allen for their interest and encouragement during the writing of the manuscript.

Particular thanks to Keith Johnson for his invaluable advice and his insight into the ways in which we learn and what makes a good textbook.

Thanks also to Simon Read, Adrian Wheaton, John Bailey, John Hepburn, Michael Cotter, Hilary Herrick and Janet Hawkins for their comments and suggestions.

The publishers gratefully acknowledge David Applin for his contribution as the copyright source of certain of the illustrations in this edition of *Biology for You*.

Acknowledgement is made to the following Examining Bodies for permission to reprint questions from their examination papers:

AQA   Assessment and Qualifications Alliance
OCR   Oxford, Cambridge and RSA Examinations
EDEX   Edexcel Foundation
WJEC   Welsh Joint Education Committee
NICCEA Northern Ireland Council for the Curriculum, Examinations and Assessment.
Website: www.biologyforyou.co.uk

Other books by Gareth Williams

Support Pack for Biology for You

Spotlight Science 7,8,9 with Keith Johnson and Sue Adamson

Science: On Target with Keith Johnson and Sue Adamson

Advanced Biology for You

Illustration acknowledgements

Action Plus: 133B, Richard Francis 134B, 290T   Adams Picture Library: 129T, 390R, 391TL   Adrian Meredith: 148T   Allsports: G Mortimore 82(3), D Cannon 118, C Mason 124B, 134T, D Rogers 151T, M Hewitt 255B, Simon Bruty 85   Ardea: 236T, J Mason 267TR, A P Paterson 283; J P Ferrero 332, J M Labat 336BL, S Meyers 342T   Biophoto Associates: 7B, 8, 9, 10, 13B, 23TL, 17R, 70B, 81B, 99, 108B, 120T, B, 122, 154BL, BR, 176, 183, 205, 206, 209B, 228BL, BR, 240BL, 261BR, 263TR, BR, 265TR, TL, 266TL, 268BL, BR, 269TL BR, BL, 276B, 319T, 336TR, 337TC, 340C, 342B, 370, 384B   Bruce Coleman: 296B, 302B, 355T, Kim Taylor 6T, 148B, 263TL, 301, E & P Bauer 6C, W Lankinen 109B, J Burton 7, 128, 241C, 256T, 262TR, 266TR, 285T, 337TL, BL, Dr F Sauer 137, 215, 236B, Dr E Pott 212B, J Fennel 240T, 255T, H Reinhard 240BR, 297TR, 299T, 340T, C Fredriksson 245C, D Hughes 262TL, P Hinchliffe 263BL, E Crichton 290B, G Ziesler 297C, 328T, D & M Plage 299B, H Lange 303B, E B Jurstrom 329T, G Dore 329B, J Van de Kain 330T, J Foott Productions 330CT, 341C, F Lanting 342CT, J & D Bartlett 355C   Bridgeman Art Library: Girandon 171TL, 298B   British Airways: 296TR   British Diabetic Association: 308B   Britstock IFA: Fred 51B   Bubbles Photolibrary: L J Thurston 44B, 129B, F Romboint 55, R Morton 102, S Price 126T, H Robinson 186B, D Dyland 285C   Collections: 186, A Steveking 168, 288, Roger Scruton 311M   Colorsport: 134M   Corbis: 65B, 177B, 186T   Corel (NT): 64B, 290M, 311T, 318B, 350CT, B, 351T   Diamar (NT): 231   Digital Vision (NT): 346T, 347, 316M   Ecoscene: Joel Creed 318T, Mike Whittle 337TR, John Farmar 350T, Alan Towse 350CB   Eye Ubiquitous: 296, 302, S Aidan 78, J Waterlow 86B, P Seheult 115   Frank Lane Picture Agency: Life Science Images 173, H Schrempp 262BR, D Hosking 267BR, H Clark 305T, R Hosking 336TL, Gerard Lacz 149, Ray Bird 309M   Gareth Williams: 334, 359   Garden Matters Photolibrary: 218, 245B   Gene Cox: 6B, 7T, 13T, 24, 88T, 101, 119B, 154BC, 225T, 226B, 266BR, 268TL, TR   Grant Heilman Photography: Runk/Schoenburger 207T   Holt Studios International: 190, Nigel Cattlin 209T, 211B, 214, 219T, B, 220T, B, 221T, B, 234T, B, 236C, 238B, 241B, 261TL, 262BL, 293B, P. Peacock 267TL, Ingan Spence 235   Health Education Council: 83   Hulton Getty: Chris Ware/Keystone 182   Hypoxico Inc: 85   Horticulture Reseach International: 213   Image State: 74T, 110T   Image Bank: Yellow Dog Productions 107, R Manani 108T, J Silverman 110BL, J Ward 119T, S Zarember 125, D W Hamilton 177B, P Frey 211T   Impact Photos: R Scruton 394L   J Allen Cash Photolibrary: 362   Magnum Photos Limited: ABBAS 349C   Martyn Chillmaid: 19T, B, 20, 22, 27, 30, 35, 45, 46, 47, 53, 54, 56, 69, 74, 79T, 81T, 97B, 106T, 114T, 124T, 175, 185, 187, 191, 192T, B, 210T, 225, 244, 245, 255C, 308T, 309B, 312B, 314B, 319B, 374, 384T   Mary Evans Picture Library: 181 (Engraving based on a sculpture by Monteverde (1 of 2), 279, Punch 1852 316T, 171C   Nick Cobbing: 293T   Natural Visions: Heather Angel 63, 70T, 88B, 138, 155TL, C, B, 224, 243, 260(5), 261TR, BL, 264TR, TL, BL, 265CL, CR, BL, BR, 266BL, 267BC, 269TC, TR, 330CB, 331T, C, 33B, 336BC, 340B, 341T, B Rogers (342CB, 347B, 360, 365B   Natural History Museum: Alan Warren 317T   Oxford Scientific Films: 25T, 233, 264BR, Steve Turner 62, G I Bernar 64T, 25T, 226T, John Forsdyke 312T, Peter O'Toole 312M, Manfred P Kage 313T, Philip Hart 317B, P Parks 156, Deni Brown 207B, London Scientific Films 225C, R Tyrell 296C, M Stonffer 297TL, D & M Plage 297B, B Lehnhansen 4B, 305C, T C Middleton 306B, C Monteith 329C, S Camazine 335, C Milkins 147, 336BR, V & M Gibson 338T, W Johnson 339T, M Hamblin 339B, M Leach 365T, R & J Kemp 365C, D Allen 366B, 233   P A News: 174, 181   Panos Pictures: J Hartley 345   Parke Davis & Company: 90   Photographers Library 391BL   Photri Inc: 84B   Popperfoto: Eric de Castro/Reuters 183B, Reuters 291, 285B, 333T   Rex Features: Nick Bailey 180, Jonathan Player 189   Robert Harding Picture Library: 256B, 331B, 338B   Science Photolibrary: 274, 95, NIBSC 184T, David Parker 184, Division of Computer Research and Technology/National Institute of Health 274T, A Barrington Brown 274M, Martin Bond 293M, A B Dowsett 171B, 309T, James Holmes/Cell Tech Ltd 37, 315, Dr G Murti 258, 98, J C Revy 29, Chemical Design 34, CNRI 66, 142TR, C, 272B, Professor P Motta/La Sapienza/Rome 89, Lunagrafix 94B, S Fraser (97T, 286), A Syred 100, J Mason 103T, B, M Clarke 114, J Hadfield 129C, DCR Salisbury 142TL, A Pasieka 142B, C Bjornberg 151B, Dr P Marazzi 172, J Watts 175T, T Bedder 177T, A Hart-Davis 179, C Raymond 182B, J King Holmes 212T, Dr J Burgess 228T, 239, 267BL, M Burnett 254R, V Vick 352T, P Plailly 391BC, St. Barts Hospital 391BR, P Yates 391CC   Sally and Richard Greenhill: 50, 51T   Still Pictures: 351B, Andre Maslennikov 316B, John Newby 337BR   Stockbyte (NT): 311B   Stone: 109T, 110BR, 150, 155, 272T, 277, 391TL, TC, B Thjomason 10T, B Thomas 32, 79B, T Henshaw 44T, B Bailey 70T, M McQueen 313B, M Rosenfield 289, 391CR, B Ayres 94T, T Vine 126B, J Wyland 127, N DeVore 130, S Cohen 166T, G Louce 166B, Scafer & Hill 210B, T Hunter 254L, S Walker 176T, H Grey 302C, D Reuse 303T, M Abrahams 306T, P Lamberti 328CB, B Marsden 330B, A Husme 341B, M Goldwater 344, P Tweedie 348CB, J Walker (349T 371T), D Paterson 366T, R Iwasaki 391TR, A Sacks 391CL   Telegraph Colour Library: 187B, VCL 83T, Bavaria-Bildagentur (126C, 188B), Japack PL 165, Planet Earth/M Mattock 305B, J P Lee 328CT, J Bracebirdle 328B, Airbourne Camera 348CT, L Rhodes 350T, M Keinitz 364, T Wiewandt 371B   Topham Picturepoint: Image Works (133T, 308M, 313C), Julio Etchart 173, Mark Antman 364B   TRIP: 314M   Zeneca Bio Products: 352B   Picture research by johnbailey@axonimages.com The diagram on p. 317 is adapted from *Biological Science Review*, March 2001.